digits™

Homework Helper

Grade 6 Volume 1

PEARSON

Boston, Massachusetts • Chandler, Arizona • Glenview, Illinois • Upper Saddle River, New Jersey

Acknowledgments for Illustrations:

Rory Hensley, David Jackson, Jim Mariano, Rich McMahon, Lorie Park, and Ted Smykal

ISBN-13: 978-0-13-327629-9
ISBN-10: 0-13-327629-5
1 2 3 4 5 6 7 8 9 10 V011 17 16 15 14 13

Contents

Unit A: Expressions and Equations

Authors and Advisors

Francis (Skip) Fennell
digits Author

Approaches to mathematics content and curriculum, educational policy, and support for intervention

Dr. Francis (Skip) Fennell is Professor of Education at McDaniel College, and a senior author with Pearson. He is a past president of the National Council of Teachers of Mathematics (NCTM) and a member of the writing team for the Curriculum Focal Points from the NCTM, which influenced the work of the Common Core Standards Initiative. Skip was also one of the writers of the Principles and Standards for School Mathematics.

Art Johnson
digits Author

Approaches to mathematical content and support for English Language Learners

Art Johnson is a Professor of Mathematics at Boston University who taught in public school for over 30 years. He is part of the author team for Pearson's high school mathematics series. Art is the author of numerous books, including Teaching Mathematics to Culturally and Linguistically Diverse Students published by Allyn & Bacon, Teaching Today's Mathematics in the Middle Grades published by Allyn & Bacon, and Guiding Children's Learning of Mathematics, K–6 published by Wadsworth.

Helene Sherman
digits Author

Teacher education and support for struggling students

Helene Sherman is Associate Dean for Undergraduate Education and Professor of Education in the College of Education at the University of Missouri in St. Louis, MO. Helene is the author of Teaching Learners Who Struggle with Mathematics, published by Merrill.

Stuart J. Murphy
digits Author

Visual learning and student engagement

Stuart J. Murphy is a visual learning specialist and the author of the MathStart series. He contributed to the development of the Visual Learning Bridge in enVisionMATH™ as well as many visual elements of the Prentice Hall Algebra 1, Geometry, and Algebra 2 high school program.

Janie Schielack
digits Author

Approaches to mathematical content, building problem solvers,and support for intervention

Janie Schielack is Professor of Mathematics and Associate Dean for Assessment and PreK–12 Education at Texas A&M University. She chaired the writing committee for the NCTM Curriculum Focal Points and was part of the nine-member NCTM feedback and advisory team that responded to and met with CCSSCO and NGA representatives during the development of various drafts of the Common Core State Standards.

Eric Milou
digits Author

Approaches to mathematical content and the use of technology in middle grades classrooms

Eric Milou is Professor in the Department of Mathematics at Rowan University in Glassboro, NJ. Eric teaches pre-service teachers and works with in-service teachers, and is primarily interested in balancing concept development with skill proficiency. He was part of the nine-member NCTM feedback/advisory team that responded to and met with Council of Chief State School Officers (CCSSCO) and National Governors Association (NGA) representatives during the development of various drafts of the Common Core State Standards. Eric is the author of Teaching Mathematics to Middle School Students, published by Allyn & Bacon.

William F. Tate
digits Author

Approaches to intervention, and use of efficacy and research

William Tate is the Edward Mallinckrodt Distinguished University Professor in Arts & Sciences at Washington University in St. Louis, MO. He is a past president of the American Educational Research Association. His research focuses on the social and psychological determinants of mathematics achievement and attainment as well as the political economy of schooling.

Randall I. Charles
digits Advisor

Dr. Randall I. Charles is Professor Emeritus in the Department of Mathematics at San Jose State University in San Jose, CA, and a senior author with Pearson. Randall served on the writing team for the Curriculum Focal Points from NCTM. The NCTM Curriculum Focal Points served as a key inspiration to the writers of the Common Core Standards in bringing focus, depth, and coherence to the curriculum.

> *Pearson tapped leaders in mathematics education to develop* **digits**. *This esteemed author team— from diverse areas of expertise including mathematical content, Understanding by Design, and Technology Engagement—came together to construct a highly interactive and personalized learning experience.*

Jim Cummins
digits Advisor

Supporting English Language Learners

Dr. Jim Cummins is Professor and Canada Research Chair in the Centre for Educational Research on Languages and Literacies at the University of Toronto. His research focuses on literacy development in multilingual school contexts as well as on the potential roles of technology in promoting language and literacy development.

Grant Wiggins
digits Consulting Author

Understanding by Design

Grant Wiggins is a cross-curricular Pearson consulting author specializing in curricular change. He is the author of Understanding by Design published by ASCD, and the President of Authentic Education in Hopewell, NJ. Over the past 20 years, he has worked on some of the most influential reform initiatives in the country, including Vermont's portfolio system and Ted Sizer's Coalition of Essential Schools.

Jacquie Moen
digits Advisor

Digital Technology

Jacquie Moen is a consultant specializing in how consumers interact with and use digital technologies. Jacquie worked for AOL for 10 years, and most recently was VP & General Manager for AOL's kids and teen online services, reaching over seven million kids every month. Jacquie has worked with a wide range of organizations to develop interactive content and strategies to reach families and children, including National Geographic, PBS, Pearson Education, National Wildlife Foundation, and the National Children's Museum.

Welcome to digits™

Using the Homework Helper

digits is designed to help you master mathematics skills and concepts in a way that's relevant to you. As the title *digits* suggests, this program takes a digital approach. *digits* is digital, but sometimes you may not be able to access digital resources. When that happens, you can use the Homework Helper because you can refer back to the daily lesson and see all your homework questions right in the book.

Your Homework Helper supports your work on *digits* in so many ways!

The lesson pages capture important elements of the digital lesson that you need to know in order to do your homework.

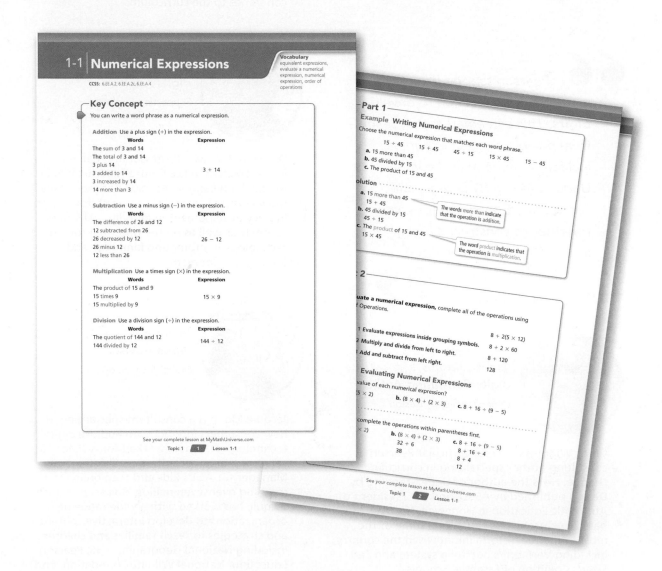

Every lesson in your Homework Helper also includes two pages of homework. The combination of homework exercises includes problems that focus on reasoning, multiple representations, mental math, writing, and error analysis. They vary in difficulty level from thinking about a plan to challenging. The problems come in different formats, like multiple choice, short answer, and open response, to help you prepare for tests.

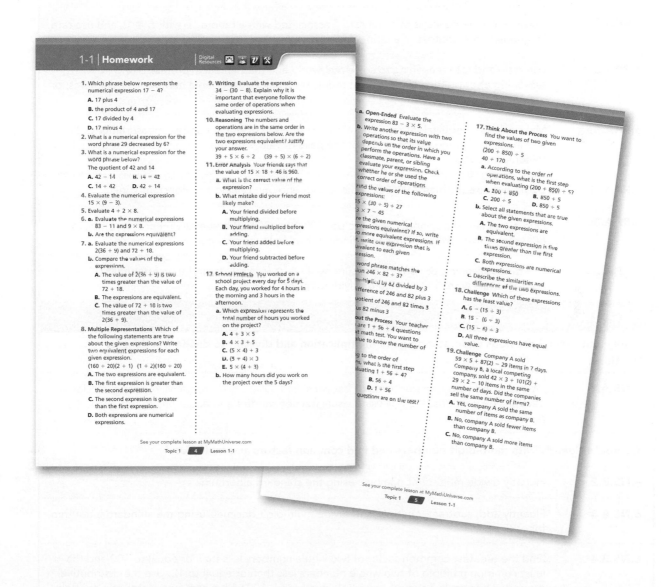

1-1 | Homework

Digital Resources

1. Which phrase below represents the numerical expression $17 - 4$?
   A. 17 plus 4
   B. the product of 4 and 17
   C. 17 divided by 4
   D. 17 minus 4

2. What is a numerical expression for the word phrase 29 decreased by 6?

3. What is a numerical expression for the word phrase below?
   The quotient of 42 and 14
   A. $42 - 14$ B. $14 - 42$
   C. $14 \div 42$ D. $42 \div 14$

4. Evaluate the numerical expression $15 \times (9 - 3)$.

5. Evaluate $4 + 2 \times 8$.

6. a. Evaluate the numerical expressions $83 - 11$ and 9×8.
   b. Are the expressions equivalent?

7. a. Evaluate the numerical expressions $2(36 + 9)$ and $72 + 18$.
   b. Compare the values of the expressions.
   A. The value of $2(36 + 9)$ is two times greater than the value of $72 + 18$.
   B. The expressions are equivalent.
   C. The value of $72 + 18$ is two times greater than the value of $2(36 + 9)$.

8. Multiple Representations Which of the following statements are true about the given expressions? Write two equivalent expressions for each given expression.
   $(160 \div 20)(2 + 1)$ $(1 + 2)(160 \div 20)$
   A. The two expressions are equivalent.
   B. The first expression is greater than the second expression.
   C. The second expression is greater than the first expression.
   D. Both expressions are numerical expressions.

9. Writing Evaluate the expression $34 - (30 - 8)$. Explain why it is important that everyone follow the same order of operations when evaluating expressions.

10. Reasoning The numbers and operations are in the same order in the two expressions below. Are the two expressions equivalent? Justify your answer.
    $39 + 5 \times 6 \div 2$ $(39 + 5) \times (6 \div 2)$

11. Error Analysis Your friend says that the value of $15 \times 18 + 46$ is 960.
    a. What is the correct value of the expression?
    b. What mistake did your friend most likely make?
       A. Your friend divided before multiplying.
       B. Your friend multiplied before adding.
       C. Your friend added before multiplying.
       D. Your friend subtracted before adding.

12. School Projects You worked on a school project every day for 5 days. Each day, you worked for 4 hours in the morning and 3 hours in the afternoon.
    a. Which expression represents the total number of hours you worked on the project?
       A. $4 + 3 \times 5$
       B. $4 \times 3 + 5$
       C. $(5 \times 4) + 3$
       D. $(5 + 4) \times 3$
       E. $5 \times (4 + 3)$
    b. How many hours did you work on the project over the 5 days?

See your complete lesson at MyMathUniverse.com

Topic 1   4   Lesson 1-1

a. Open-Ended Evaluate the expression $83 - 3 \times 5$.
b. Write another expression with two operations so that its value depends on the order in which you perform the operations. Have a classmate, parent, or sibling evaluate your expression. Check whether he or she used the correct order of operations

Find the values of the following expressions:
$15 \times (30 \div 5) + 27$
$3 \times 7 - 45$

Are the given numerical expressions equivalent? If so, write two more equivalent expressions. If not, write one expression that is equivalent to each given expression.

word phrase matches the ion $246 \times 82 \div 3$?
multiplied by 82 divided by 3
ifference of 246 and 82 plus 3
uotient of 246 and 82 times 3
us 82 minus 3

out the Process Your teacher are $1 + 56 \div 4$ questions t math test. You want to lue to know the number of

g to the order of s, what is the first step luating $1 + 56 \div 4$?
   B. $56 \div 4$
   D. $1 + 56$
questions are on the test?

17. Think About the Process You want to find the values of two given expressions.
    $(200 + 850) \div 5$
    $40 + 170$
    a. According to the order of operations, what is the first step when evaluating $(200 + 850) \div 5$?
       A. $200 + 850$ B. $850 \div 5$
       C. $200 \div 5$ D. $850 \div 5$
    b. Select all statements that are true about the given expressions.
       A. The two expressions are equivalent.
       B. The second expression is five times greater than the first expression.
       C. Both expressions are numerical expressions.
    c. Describe the similarities and differences of the two expressions.

18. Challenge Which of these expressions has the least value?
    A. $6 - (15 \div 3)$
    B. $15 - (6 \div 3)$
    C. $(15 - 6) \div 3$
    D. All three expressions have equal value.

19. Challenge Company A sold $59 \times 5 + 87(2) - 29$ items in 7 days. Company B, a local competing company, sold $42 \times 3 + 101(2) + 29 \times 2 - 10$ items in the same number of days. Did the companies sell the same number of items?
    A. Yes, company A sold the same number of items as company B.
    B. No, company A sold fewer items than company B.
    C. No, company A sold more items than company B.

See your complete lesson at MyMathUniverse.com

Topic 1   5   Lesson 1-1

Grade 6 | Common Core State Standards

Number	Standard for Mathematical Content
6.RP Ratios and Proportional Relationships	
Understand ratio concepts and use ratio reasoning to solve problems.	
6.RP.A.1	Understand the concept of a ratio and use ratio language to describe a ratio relationship between two quantities.
6.RP.A.2	Understand the concept of a unit rate $\frac{a}{b}$ associated with a ratio $a : b$ with $b \neq 0$, and use rate language in the context of a ratio relationship.
6.RP.A.3	Use ratio and rate reasoning to solve real-world and mathematical problems, e.g., by reasoning about tables of equivalent ratios, tape diagrams, double number line diagrams, or equations.
6.RP.A.3a	Make tables of equivalent ratios relating quantities with whole number measurements, find missing values in the tables, and plot the pairs of values on the coordinate plane. Use tables to compare ratios.
6.RP.A.3b	Solve unit rate problems including those involving unit pricing and constant speed.
6.RP.A.3c	Find a percent of a quantity as a rate per 100 (e.g., 30% of a quantity means $\frac{30}{100}$ times the quantity); solve problems involving finding the whole, given a part and the percent.
6.RP.A.3d	Use ratio reasoning to convert measurement units; manipulate and transform units appropriately when multiplying or dividing quantities.
6.NS The Number System	
Apply and extend previous understandings of multiplication and division to divide fractions by fractions.	
6.NS.A.1	Interpret and compute quotients of fractions, and solve word problems involving division of fractions by fractions, e.g., by using visual fraction models and equations to represent the problem.
Compute fluently with multi-digit numbers and find common factors and multiples.	
6.NS.B.2	Fluently divide multi-digit numbers using the standard algorithm.
6.NS.B.3	Fluently add, subtract, multiply, and divide multi-digit decimals using the standard algorithm for each operation.
6.NS.B.4	Find the greatest common factor of two whole numbers less than or equal to 100 and the least common multiple of two whole numbers less than or equal to 12. Use the distributive property to express a sum of two whole numbers 1–100 with a common factor as a multiple of a sum of two whole numbers with no common factor.

Number	Standard for Mathematical Content

6.NS The Number System (continued)

Apply and extend previous understandings of numbers to the system of rational numbers.

6.NS.C.5	Understand that positive and negative numbers are used together to describe quantities having opposite directions or values; use positive and negative numbers to represent quantities in real-world contexts, explaining the meaning of 0 in each situation.
6.NS.C.6	Understand a rational number as a point on the number line. Extend number line diagrams and coordinate axes familiar from previous grades to represent points on the line and in the plane with negative number coordinates.
6.NS.C.6a	Recognize opposite signs of numbers as indicating locations on opposite sides of 0 on the number line; recognize that the opposite of the opposite of a number is the number itself.
6.NS.C.6b	Understand signs of numbers in ordered pairs as indicating locations in quadrants of the coordinate plane; recognize that when two ordered pairs differ only by signs, the locations of the points are related by reflections across one or both axes.
6.NS.C.6c	Find and position integers and other rational numbers on a horizontal or vertical number line diagram; find and position pairs of integers and other rational numbers on a coordinate plane.
6.NS.C.7	Understand ordering and absolute value of rational numbers.
6.NS.C.7a	Interpret statements of inequality as statements about the relative position of two numbers on a number line diagram.
6.NS.C.7b	Write, interpret, and explain statements of order for rational numbers in real-world contexts.
6.NS.C.7c	Understand the absolute value of a rational number as its distance from 0 on the number line; interpret absolute value as magnitude for a positive or negative quantity in a real world situation.
6.NS.C.7d	Distinguish comparisons of absolute value from statements about order.
6.NS.C.8	Solve real-world and mathematical problems by graphing points in all four quadrants of the coordinate plane. Include use of coordinates and absolute value to find distances between points with the same first coordinate or the same second coordinate.

6.EE Expressions and Equations

Apply and extend previous understandings of arithmetic to algebraic expressions.

6.EE.A.1	Write and evaluate numerical expressions involving whole-number exponents.
6.EE.A.2	Write, read, and evaluate expressions in which letters stand for numbers.
6.EE.A.2a	Write expressions that record operations with numbers and with letters standing for numbers.

Number	Standard for Mathematical Content

6.EE Expressions and Equations *(continued)*

Apply and extend previous understandings of arithmetic to algebraic expressions.

6.EE.A.2b	Identify parts of an expression using mathematical terms (sum, term, product, factor, quotient, coefficient); view one or more parts of an expression as a single entity.
6.EE.A.2c	Evaluate expressions at specific values of their variables. Include expressions that arise from formulas used in real-world problems. Perform arithmetic operations, including those involving whole number exponents, in the conventional order when there are no parentheses to specify a particular order (Order of Operations).
6.EE.A.3	Apply the properties of operations to generate equivalent expressions.
6.EE.A.4	Identify when two expressions are equivalent (i.e., when the two expressions name the same number regardless of which value is substituted into them).

Reason about and solve one-variable equations and inequalities.

6.EE.B.5	Understand solving an equation or inequality as a process of answering a question: which values from a specified set, if any, make the equation or inequality true? Use substitution to determine whether a given number in a specified set makes an equation or inequality true.
6.EE.B.6	Use variables to represent numbers and write expressions when solving a real-world or mathematical problem; understand that a variable can represent an unknown number, or, depending on the purpose at hand, any number in a specified set.
6.EE.B.7	Solve real-world and mathematical problems by writing and solving equations of the form $x + p = q$ and $px = q$ for cases in which p, q, and x are all nonnegative rational numbers.
6.EE.B.8	Write an inequality of the form $x > c$ or $x < c$ to represent a constraint or condition in a real-world or mathematical problem. Recognize that inequalities of the form $x > c$ or $x < c$ have infinitely many solutions; represent solutions of such inequalities on number line diagrams.

Represent and analyze quantitative relationships between dependent and independent variables.

6.EE.C.9	Use variables to represent two quantities in a real-world problem that change in relationship to one another; write an equation to express one quantity, thought of as the dependent variable, in terms of the other quantity, thought of as the independent variable. Analyze the relationship between the dependent and independent variables using graphs and tables, and relate these to the equation.

6.G Geometry

Solve real-world and mathematical problems involving area, surface area, and volume.

6.G.A.1	Find the area of right triangles, other triangles, special quadrilaterals, and polygons by composing into rectangles or decomposing into triangles and other shapes; apply these techniques in the context of solving real-world and mathematical problems.
6.G.A.2	Find the volume of a right rectangular prism with fractional edge lengths by packing it with unit cubes of the appropriate unit fraction edge lengths, and show that the volume is the same as would be found by multiplying the edge lengths of the prism. Apply the formulas $V = lwh$ and $V = bh$ to find volumes of right rectangular prisms with fractional edge lengths in the context of solving real-world and mathematical problems.

Number	Standard for Mathematical Content

6.G Geometry (continued)

Solve real-world and mathematical problems involving area, surface area, and volume.

6.G.A.3	Draw polygons in the coordinate plane given coordinates for the vertices; use coordinates to find the length of a side joining points with the same first coordinate or the same second coordinate. Apply these techniques in the context of solving real-world and mathematical problems.
6.G.A.4	Represent three-dimensional figures using nets made up of rectangles and triangles, and use the nets to find the surface area of these figures. Apply these techniques in the context of solving real-world and mathematical problems.

6.SP Statistics and Probability

Develop understanding of statistical variability.

6.SP.A.1	Recognize a statistical question as one that anticipates variability in the data related to the question and accounts for it in the answers.
6.SP.A.2	Understand that a set of data collected to answer a statistical question has a distribution which can be described by its center, spread, and overall shape.
6.SP.A.3	Recognize that a measure of center for a numerical data set summarizes all of its values with a single number, while a measure of variation describes how its values vary with a single number.

Summarize and describe distributions.

6.SP.B.4	Display numerical data in plots on a number line, including dot plots, histograms, and box plots.
6.SP.B.5	Summarize numerical data sets in relation to their context, such as by:
6.SP.B.5a	Reporting the number of observations.
6.SP.B.5b	Describing the nature of the attribute under investigation, including how it was measured and its units of measurement.
6.SP.B.5c	Giving quantitative measures of center (median and/or mean) and variability (interquartile range and/or mean absolute deviation), as well as describing any overall pattern and any striking deviations from the overall pattern with reference to the context in which the data were gathered.
6.SP.B.5d	Summarize numerical data sets in relation to their context, such as by: Relating the choice of measures of center and variability to the shape of the data distribution and the context in which the data were gathered.

Numerical Expressions

Vocabulary
equivalent expressions,
evaluate a numerical
expression, numerical
expression, order of
operations

CCSS: 6.EE.A.2, 6.EE.A.2c, 6.EE.A.4

Key Concept

You can write a word phrase as a numerical expression.

Addition Use a plus sign (+) in the expression.

Words	Expression
The sum of 3 and 14	
The total of 3 and 14	
3 plus 14	
3 added to 14	$3 + 14$
3 increased by 14	
14 more than 3	

Subtraction Use a minus sign (−) in the expression.

Words	Expression
The difference of 26 and 12	
12 subtracted from 26	
26 decreased by 12	$26 - 12$
26 minus 12	
12 less than 26	

Multiplication Use a times sign (×) in the expression.

Words	Expression
The product of 15 and 9	
15 times 9	15×9
15 multiplied by 9	

Division Use a division sign (÷) in the expression.

Words	Expression
The quotient of 144 and 12	
144 divided by 12	$144 \div 12$

Part 1

Example Writing Numerical Expressions

Choose the numerical expression that matches each word phrase.

$$15 \div 45 \qquad 15 + 45 \qquad 45 \div 15 \qquad 15 \times 45 \qquad 15 - 45$$

a. 15 more than 45
b. 45 divided by 15
c. The product of 15 and 45

Solution

a. 15 more than 45

$15 + 45$

> The words more than indicate that the operation is addition.

b. 45 divided by 15

$45 \div 15$

c. The product of 15 and 45

15×45

> The word product indicates that the operation is multiplication.

Part 2

Intro

To **evaluate a numerical expression,** complete all of the operations using Order of Operations.

$$8 + 2(5 \times 12)$$

Step 1 Evaluate expressions inside grouping symbols.	$8 + 2 \times 60$
Step 2 Multiply and divide from left to right.	$8 + 120$
Step 3 Add and subtract from left right.	128

Example Evaluating Numerical Expressions

What is the value of each numerical expression?

a. $15 - (5 \times 2)$ **b.** $(8 \times 4) + (2 \times 3)$ **c.** $8 + 16 \div (9 - 5)$

Solution

Remember to complete the operations within parentheses first.

a. $15 - (5 \times 2)$
    $15 - 10$
    5

b. $(8 \times 4) + (2 \times 3)$
    $32 + 6$
    38

c. $8 + 16 \div (9 - 5)$
    $8 + 16 \div 4$
    $8 + 4$
    12

Part 3

Intro

Two numerical expressions are **equivalent** if, when you evaluate them, they equal the same value.

Example Comparing Numerical Expressions

Which of the following statements are true about the given expressions? Identify the true statements.

$$4 \times (1200 \div 20) \qquad\qquad 1200 \div 20$$

I. The two expressions are equivalent.

II. The first expression is four times as large as the second expression.

III. Both expressions are numerical expressions.

Solution

I. False.

$4 \times (1200 \div 20)$
$4(60)$
240

> The two expressions are not equivalent.

$1200 \div 20$
60

II. True.

$4 \times (1200 \div 20)$
$4(60)$

> The first expression is four times larger than the second.

$1200 \div 20$
60

III. True. Both expressions contain only numbers and operations.

The true statements are II and III.

1. Which phrase below represents the numerical expression $17 - 4$?

   A. 17 plus 4

   B. the product of 4 and 17

   C. 17 divided by 4

   D. 17 minus 4

2. What is a numerical expression for the word phrase 29 decreased by 6?

3. What is a numerical expression for the word phrase below?

   The quotient of 42 and 14

   A. $42 - 14$ **B.** $14 - 42$

   C. $14 \div 42$ **D.** $42 \div 14$

4. Evaluate the numerical expression $15 \times (9 - 3)$.

5. Evaluate $4 + 2 \times 8$.

6. **a.** Evaluate the numerical expressions $83 - 11$ and 9×8.

   b. Are the expressions equivalent?

7. **a.** Evaluate the numerical expressions $2(36 + 9)$ and $72 + 18$.

   b. Compare the values of the expressions.

      A. The value of $2(36 + 9)$ is two times greater than the value of $72 + 18$.

      B. The expressions are equivalent.

      C. The value of $72 + 18$ is two times greater than the value of $2(36 + 9)$.

8. **Multiple Representations** Which of the following statements are true about the given expressions? Write two equivalent expressions for each given expression.

   $(160 \div 20)(2 + 1)$ $(1 + 2)(160 \div 20)$

   A. The two expressions are equivalent.

   B. The first expression is greater than the second expression.

   C. The second expression is greater than the first expression.

   D. Both expressions are numerical expressions.

9. **Writing** Evaluate the expression $34 - (30 - 8)$. Explain why it is important that everyone follow the same order of operations when evaluating expressions.

10. **Reasoning** The numbers and operations are in the same order in the two expressions below. Are the two expressions equivalent? Justify your answer.

    $39 + 5 \times 6 \div 2$ $(39 + 5) \times (6 \div 2)$

11. **Error Analysis** Your friends says that the value of $15 \times 18 + 46$ is 960.

    a. What is the correct value of the expression?

    b. What mistake did your friend most likely make?

       A. Your friend divided before multiplying.

       B. Your friend multiplied before adding.

       C. Your friend added before multiplying.

       D. Your friend subtracted before adding.

12. **School Projects** You worked on a school project every day for 5 days. Each day, you worked for 4 hours in the morning and 3 hours in the afternoon.

    a. Which expression represents the total number of hours you worked on the project?

       A. $4 + 3 \times 5$

       B. $4 \times 3 + 5$

       C. $(5 \times 4) + 3$

       D. $(5 + 4) \times 3$

       E. $5 \times (4 + 3)$

    b. How many hours did you work on the project over the 5 days?

See your complete lesson at MyMathUniverse.com

13. a. Open-Ended Evaluate the expression $83 - 3 \times 5$.

   b. Write another expression with two operations so that its value depends on the order in which you perform the operations. Have a classmate, parent, or sibling evaluate your expression. Check whether he or she used the correct order of operations.

14. a. Find the values of the following expressions:

   $15 \times (30 \div 5) + 27$

   $23 \times 7 - 45$

   b. Are the given numerical expressions equivalent? If so, write two more equivalent expressions. If not, write one expression that is equivalent to each given expression.

15. Which word phrase matches the expression $246 \times 82 \div 3$?

   A. 246 multiplied by 82 divided by 3

   B. the difference of 246 and 82 plus 3

   C. the quotient of 246 and 82 times 3

   D. 246 plus 82 minus 3

16. Think About the Process Your teacher says there are $1 + 56 \div 4$ questions on the next math test. You want to find this value to know the number of questions.

   a. According to the order of operations, what is the first step when evaluating $1 + 56 \div 4$?

   A. $1 + 4$ **B.** $56 \div 4$

   C. $1 \div 4$ **D.** $1 + 56$

   b. How many questions are on the test?

17. Think About the Process You want to find the values of two given expressions.

   $(200 + 850) \div 5$

   $40 + 170$

   a. According to the order of operations, what is the first step when evaluating $(200 + 850) \div 5$?

   A. $200 + 850$ **B.** $850 + 5$

   C. $200 \div 5$ **D.** $850 \div 5$

   b. Select all statements that are true about the given expressions.

   A. The two expressions are equivalent.

   B. The second expression is five times greater than the first expression.

   C. Both expressions are numerical expressions.

   c. Describe the similarities and differences of the two expressions.

18. Challenge Which of these expressions has the least value?

   A. $6 - (15 \div 3)$

   B. $15 - (6 \div 3)$

   C. $(15 - 6) \div 3$

   D. All three expressions have equal value.

19. Challenge Company A sold $59 \times 5 + 87(2) - 29$ items in 7 days. Company B, a local competing company, sold $42 \times 3 + 101(2) + 29 \times 2 - 10$ items in the same number of days. Did the companies sell the same number of items?

   A. Yes, company A sold the same number of items as company B.

   B. No, company A sold fewer items than company B.

   C. No, company A sold more items than company B.

CCSS: 6.EE.A.2a, 6.EE.A.2b, 6.EE.B.6, Also 6.EE.A.2

Key Concept

Algebraic Expressions

A variable expression, or algebraic expression, consists of numbers, variables, and operation symbols.

A **variable** is a letter that represents an unknown value.

A **term** is a number, a variable, or the product of a number and one or more variables.

A **constant** is a term that contains only numbers.

A **coefficient** is the number part of a term with variables.

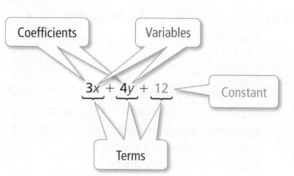

Part 1

Example Identifying Algebraic and Numerical Expressions

Classify each expression as either a numerical expression or an algebraic expression.

a. $120m$ **b.** $40(30)$ **c.** $75ab$

d. $51 \div 17$ **e.** $12(35 - 16)$ **f.** $5(d + 1)$

h. $x + 6y + 20$ **i.** $3x - 4y + 2z$ **j.** $14 \cdot 15$

Solution

Numerical expressions consist of only numbers and operation symbols. So the numerical expressions are:

b. $40(30)$ **d.** $51 \div 71$ **e.** $12(35 - 16)$

j. $14 \cdot 15$

Algebraic expressions consist of numbers, variables, and operation symbols. So the algebraic expressions are:

a. $120m$ **f.** $5(d + 1)$ **h.** $x + 6y + 20$

c. $75ab$ **i.** $3x - 4y + 2z$

Part 2

Intro

A quantity is something you can measure.
A variable quantity is a quantity that varies, or changes.

Example Identifying Variable Quantities

You have a prepaid cell phone. As you talk on the phone, the number of minutes you have left decreases. When you get below a certain number of minutes, you have to buy more.

Use the words shown at right to replace the blanks, and then identify which quantities are variable quantities.

  a. the number of ■ available on the phone
  b. the ■ per minute to buy more minutes
  c. the amount of ■ you spend buying minutes
  d. the ■ of minutes you use per call

Solution

  a. The number of minutes available on the phone decreases as you talk, so the number of minutes available varies.
  b. The cost per minute to buy more minutes doesn't change, so the cost does not vary.
  c. The amount of money you spend buying minutes depends on the number of minutes you buy, so the amount you spend varies.
  d. The number of minutes you use per call depends on how long you talk, so the number of minutes you use varies.

The only quantity that does not vary is the cost per minute. All of the other quantities vary based on how long you talk.

Part 3

Example Identifying Vocabulary Terms for Operations

Match each part of the expression $5(4x + 3) - (42y \div 6y)$ to the vocabulary term that describes it.

$5(4x + 3) - (42y \div 6y)$

5 and $(4x + 3)$

$(42y \div 6y)$

$(4x + 3)$

$5(4x + 3)$

Vocabulary Term	Part of the Expression
Product	
Sum	
Factors	
Quotient	
Difference	

Solution

Vocabulary Term	Part of the Expression
Product	$5(4x + 3)$
Sum	$(4x + 3)$
Factors	5 and $(4x + 3)$
Quotient	$(42y \div 6y)$
Difference	$5(4x + 3) - (42y \div 6y)$

1. Classify the expression $d + 7$ as either a numerical expression or an algebraic expression.

2. Classify this expression as either a numerical expression or an algebraic expression.

   $11 \cdot 12 - 5$

3. Which of these expressions are algebraic expressions? Select all that apply.

   A. $11x - 40y$ **B.** $8(15x)$

   C. $140 \div 35$ **D.** $70x - 55$

   E. $17 + 27 \cdot 16$

4. Justin is at the amusement park for 7 hours. The number of rides he goes on depends on how long the line is for each ride. Is the number of rides he gets to go on a variable quantity?

5. An office manager is renting a local hall for an upcoming event. The hall costs $175. The food costs $15 per person. The office manager is not sure how many people will attend. Which quantity is not a variable quantity— the cost per person for food, the number of people who will attend, or the total cost of the food?

6. Of the 26 households in a neighborhood, 16 have at least one dog. There are 19 dogs in the neighborhood. The owners walk their dogs at least three times a day. The number of times an owner walks his dog changes from day to day. Which of the quantities listed below are not variable quantities? Select all that apply.

   A. the number of households in the neighborhood

   B. the number of households in the neighborhood with at least one dog

   C. the number of times an owner walks his dog in one day

   D. the number of dogs in the neighborhood

7. Identify the factors in the expression $6(x + 5)$.

8. Describe the expression $(4x \div 2) - 9y$ using an appropriate term or phrase.

   A. quotient of two terms

   B. sum of two terms

   C. difference of two terms

   D. product of two terms

9. **Writing** Tyson works at a bakery. He works 8 hours each day. The amount of money he makes depends on how much he sells. He makes an extra $0.25 for each special that he sells. Select all the variable quantities in the list below.

   A. the number of hours he works each day

   B. the amount of money he makes each day

   C. the amount of money he makes per special sold

   D. the total amount of money he makes from selling specials

10. **Reasoning** Is the statement below true or false? Explain your answer. The expression $(14x + 7y) + 5x + 9(33y + 11)$ is the sum of three terms.

11. **Manufacturing** A manufacturing company has 20 machines. It runs all the machines from 8 A.M. until noon. From noon until 2 P.M., it runs only 8 machines. Then from 2 P.M. until close, it runs 11 machines. Decide which of the quantities below are variable quantities. Select all that apply.

    A. the number of machines the company has

    B. the number of machines running at any one time during the day

    C. the number of machines running from noon until 2 P.M.

See your complete lesson at MyMathUniverse.com

12. Which parts shown here can you correctly describe as the product of two terms within the expression $8(2x + 3) - (35 \div 7) + 15(6z)$? Select all that apply.

A. $(2x + 3) - (35y \div 7)$

B. $15(6z)$

C. $(35y \div 7)$

D. $8(2x + 3)$

13. It costs a company $3 to make an item. The company also pays $65 per day for its warehouse. The expression for the total cost to make x items in one day is $3x + 65$. Is this expression a numerical expression or an algebraic expression?

A. It is neither a numerical expression nor an algebraic expression because it contains both a number and a variable.

B. It is a numerical expression because it contains a number.

C. It is a numerical expression because it contains at least one number without a variable.

D. It is an algebraic expression because it contains a variable.

14. Think About the Process

a. Which of the expressions listed below are algebraic expressions? Select all that apply.

A. $70x + 3y + 118$

B. $(19 - 7) + 4(36 \div 18)$

C. $32 + 25(6b)$

D. $a + bc$

E. $45ab$

F. $250(230)$

b. What makes the algebraic expressions different from those that are not algebraic?

15. The cost to rent a car at a local car rental company is $20 per day for a mid-size car and $39 per day for a large car. An additional cost of renting the car is the cost of fuel. One option is to purchase a tank of gas at the time of rental for a set fee. Another option is that you can stop and refuel the tank yourself. Which quantities below are not variable quantities? Select all that apply.

A. the cost to refuel the tank yourself

B. the cost to purchase a tank of gas at the time of rental

C. the cost to rent a mid-size car for two days

D. the cost to rent a car for a day

16. Think About the Process How can you use parentheses to change the expression $12 \times 6y \div 2$ so that it is a quotient of two terms?

A. Place the parentheses around $y \div 2$.

B. Place the parentheses around $6y \div 2$.

C. Place the parentheses around $6y$.

D. Place the parentheses around $12 \times 6y$.

17. Challenge The food expense each week for a family is $31(7)$. The electricity expense each month is $15(n - 5)$. The expenses for their cars are $3y - 13z + 83$, $13d + 51$, and $3,264 \div 12$. The water expense each month is 70×23. The cable and internet expenses each year are $300 + 4x$ and $4x$. Which of these expenses are algebraic expressions? Select all that apply.

A. $70 - 23$ **B.** $3,264 \div 12$

C. $15(n - 5)$ **D.** $3y - 13z + 83$

E. $13d + 51$ **F.** $300 + 4x$

G. $31(7)$ **H.** $4x$

18. Challenge The expression $25x + 10(9zy) + (70x \div 5) + 23v$ represents some of the costs for a company. Describe this expression using an appropriate term or phrase.

Writing Algebraic Expressions

CCSS: 6.EE.A.2, 6.EE.B.6, Also 6.EE.A.2a

Part 1

Intro

You have described a real world situations using words or symbols. You can also write algebraic expressions to represent real world situations that have an unknown value.

Example Writing Algebraic Expressions from Words

Use the following operations and algebraic expressions to complete the table.

subtraction   addition $n + 20$ $n - 20$ $20 \div n$

Word Phrase	Operation	Algebraic Expression
a number plus 20		
20 times a number	multiplication	20n
the difference of a number and 20		
20 divided by a number	division	

Solution

Word Phrase	Operation	Algebraic Expression
a number plus 20	addition	$n + 20$
20 times a number	multiplication	20n
the difference of a number and 20	subtraction	$n - 20$
20 divided by a number	division	$20 \div n$

Part 2

Intro

When writing algebraic expressions, you can choose any letter to represent an unknown quantity.

Example Representing Real-World Situations Using Algebraic Expressions with One Operation

A state park has 3 lakes. In the spring, each lake was stocked with the same number of fish. What algebraic expression represents the total number of fish in the lakes?

Solution ·

Let f represents the number of fish in one lake. Then write the expression.

$3 \times f$, or $3f$ ← 3 lakes, each with f fish

The expression $3f$, where f is the number of fish in one lake, represents the number of fish in all lakes.

Part 3

Intro

The Know-Need-Plan graphic organizer is a tool that can help you in making sense of problems.

Suppose a store that personalizes T-shirts charges $15 for a shirt plus $2 for each letter. What algebraic expression can be used to represent the total cost of a shirt with n letters?

Know
• The cost of a T-shirt: $15
• The cost for one letter: $2

Need
An algebraic expression to represent the total cost of a T-shirt with n letters.

Plan
• Define what the variable represents.
• Write an algebraic expression.

Example Using Graphic Organizers to Write Algebraic Expressions

A national park charges $25 per bus and $12 per person for an organized tour group. What algebraic expression can be used to represent the total cost for a one-day tour with one bus and n people?

continued on next page >

Part 3

Solution ·

Know
- The admission fee per bus: $25
- The admission fee per person: $12

↓

Need

An algebraic expression to represent the total admission cost for the group

↓

Plan
- Define what the variable represents.
- Write an algebraic expression.

Define what the variable represents. Let n = number of people.

Write an algebraic expression.

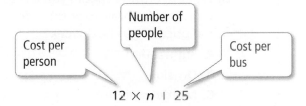

$$12 \times n \;|\; 25$$

The expression $12n + 25$ represents the total admission cost for the tour group.

1. Let *x* be a number. Translate the expression *x* ÷ 3 into an English phrase.

   A. the sum of the number and 3

   B. the quotient of the number and 3

   C. the product of the number and 3

   D. the difference of the number and 3

2. Let *k* be a number. Write a word phrase that represents the expression $9k - 2k$.

   A. The difference of nine times a number and two times the number

   B. The sum of nine times a number and two times the number

   C. The quotient of nine times a number and two times the number

   D. The product of nine times a number and two times the number

3. Write an algebraic expression for "43 more than *t*."

4. The length of a rectangle is six times the width. If the width is represented by *y*, then write an algebraic expression that describes the length.

5. Write an algebraic expression for "the height, *h*, increased by 6 inches."

6. Lindsey has 50 coins in her change purse that are either dimes or quarters. If *y* represents the number of quarters she has, write an algebraic expression in terms of *y* that describes the number of dimes.

7. A team is ordering sweatshirts and sweatpants for its players. Each sweatshirt costs $35 and each pair of sweatpants costs $17. Write an algebraic expression to represent the total cost if *x* players want sweatshirts and *y* players want sweatpants.

8. Penny pays $14 a month for her book club membership. With the membership, each book costs $5. Write an algebraic expression for her total bill for one month if she buys *b* books that month.

9. **Writing** Cassie and Connor are selling peaches. Yesterday, Cassie sold 31 peaches. Connor sold *p* fewer peaches than Cassie.

   a. Suppose Connor sold 50 peaches today. Explain how to write an expression for the number of peaches Cassie sold today if Connor still sold *p* fewer peaches than Cassie.

   b. Write an algebraic expression that represents the number of peaches Connor sold yesterday.

10. **Think About the Process** The price of gasoline changes from week to week. At one station last week, the price was six cents less than the price this week. Next week, the price at that station is expected to be three cents greater than the price this week. Let *g* represent the price of gas in cents this week.

    a. What operation should you use to write an algebraic expression for the price of gas next week?

    A. Subtraction

    B. Division

    C. Multiplication

    D. Addition

    b. Use this operation to write an algebraic expression for the price of gas next week.

11. **Reasoning** Manuel makes $8 per hour. He has worked 7 hours so far this week.

    a. How much has he made so far this week?

    b. Write an algebraic expression that describes how much he makes for *t* hours of work.

    c. Explain why it would be helpful for Manuel to write an algebraic expression for the amount he makes for working *t* hours.

12. Error Analysis Isabelle and Jackson's teacher asked them to write an algebraic expression for "the quotient of 54 and m." Isabelle's answer was $54 \div m$. Jackson's answer was $54 - m$.

a. Which student was correct?

b. What was the incorrect student's error?

A. The student used the incorrect operations and the incorrect order of the terms.

B. The student used the incorrect order of the terms.

C. The student used the incorrect operation.

13. Think About the Process A flower shop charges $29 for a bouquet. It costs an additional $9 to include the vase. Last month, the shop sold b bouquets and v of the bouquets included the vase.

a. What does the variable b represent?

A. The price of each vase

B. The number of customers

C. The price of each bouquet

D. The number of bouquets sold last month that included the vase

E. The number of bouquets sold last month

b. What does the variable v represent?

A. The price of each bouquet

B. The number of bouquets sold last month

C. The number of bouquets sold last month that included the vase

D. The price of each vase

E. The number of customers

c. Write an algebraic expression for the shop's total sales from bouquets and vases last month.

14. Event Planning It costs $200 to rent a room at an event center. The event center charges an additional $13 per person for food. Write an algebraic expression for the total cost of an event for n people.

15. Multiple Representations Select the two different word phrases for the algebraic expression $h + 6$.

A. h times 6

B. the sum of h and 6

C. 6 more than h

D. the product of h and 6

16. Write an algebraic expression for "84 more than the product of 167 and b."

17. For an order of T-shirts, a sports store manager makes a table showing the costs of 1, 4, and 9 T-shirts. Let s represent the number of T-shirts. Look for a pattern in the table. **(Figure 1)** Use it to write an algebraic expression for the cost of s T-shirts.

18. Challenge A salesperson sold 3 cars for a total value of 43,800 dollars. Her co-worker sold 7 cars for a total the value of d dollars.

a. Write an algebraic expression that represents the combined value of the cars sold by the salesperson and her co-worker.

b. Suppose the salesperson and each of n co-workers sold 3 cars a piece at a price of k dollars per car. What algebraic expression would represent the combined value of these sales?

19. Challenge A group of friends is planning a boating trip. It costs $2,500 to rent the boat. Lunch costs $13 per adult and $8 per child. Write an algebraic expression for the total cost for a group of b adults and c children.

(Figure 1)

T-shirts Costs			
Number of T-shirts	1	4	9
Cost	$3	$12	$27

Evaluating Algebraic Expressions

Vocabulary
evaluate an algebraic expression

CCSS: 6.EE.A.2, 6.EE.A.2c

Key Concept

Algebraic expressions have at least one variable. To evaluate an algebraic expression, replace each variable with a given value. Then evaluate the expression using order of operations.

Evaluate $2x - 5$ for $x = 3$ and for $x = 5$.

$x = 3$	$x = 5$
$2x - 5$	$2x - 5$
$2(3) - 5$	$2(5) - 5$
$6 - 5$	$10 - 5$
1	5

Part 1

Example Evaluating Expressions with One Variable

Evaluate each expression for the given value of the variable.

$$13 - m \qquad 35 + 2m \qquad 6m$$

a. $m = 5$
b. $m = 7$

Solution

a. To evaluate the expression, replace m with 5.

$13 - m$	$35 + 2m$	$6m$
$13 - 5$	$35 + 2(5)$	$6(5)$
8	$35 + 10$	30
	45	

b. To evaluate the expression, replace m with 7.

$13 - m$	$35 + 2m$	$6m$
$13 - 7$	$35 + 2(7)$	$6(7)$
6	$35 + 14$	42
	49	

Part 2

Example Evaluating Expressions with Two Variables

Evaluate each expression for $x = 5$ and $y = 8$.

$$3x + 2y \qquad 12xy + 20 \qquad 4(x + y) - 10$$

Solution ·

To evaluate the expression, replace x with 5, y with 8.

$3x + 2y$	$12xy \div 20$	$4(x + y) - 10$
$3(5) + 2(8)$	$12(5)(8) \div 20$	$4(5 + 8) - 10$
$15 + 16$	$60(8) \div 20$	$4(13) - 10$
31	$480 \div 20$	$52 - 10$
	24	42

Part 3

Example Evaluating Expressions in Real-World Situations

You can choose between two part-time jobs. You can earn $20 per lawn mowing lawns or you can earn $7 per hour washing cars. Which part-time job will help you earn more money?

    a. Write an algebraic expression to represent the money you earn for each job.

    b. How can you use the algebraic expressions you wrote in part A to compare the earnings of the two jobs?

    c. Suppose you could mow 2 lawns per week. In which job would you earn more money?

Solution ·

    a. Write an expression to represent each job.

    Mowing Lawns: The amount you earn mowing lawns is a variable quantity. It depends on the number of lawns you mow.

    Let m represent the number of lawns you mow.

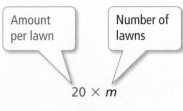

Amount per lawn   Number of lawns

$$20 \times m$$

$$20m$$

continued on next page >

Washing Cars: The amount you earn washing cars is also a variable quantity. It depends on the number of hours you work.

Let *n* represent the number of hours you wash cars.

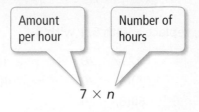

$$7 \times n$$

$$7n$$

b. You can evaluate the algebraic expressions for various numbers of lawns mowed and hours to compare the jobs.

Mowing Lawns: Evaluate 20*m* for 1 lawn, 2 lawns, 3 lawns, 5 lawns, 10 lawns, and 15 lawns.

m	1	2	3	5	10	15
20*m*	20	40	60	100	200	300

Washing Cars: Evaluate 7*n* for 1 hour, 2 hours, 3 hours, 5 hours, 10 hours, and 15 hours.

n	1	2	3	5	10	15
7*n*	7	14	21	35	70	105

continued on next page >

Solution continued

   c. Use the tables to compare the two jobs.

m	1	2	3	5	10	15
20m	20	40	60	100	200	300

If you mow 2 lawns per week, you will earn $40 per week.

n	1	2	3	5	10	15
7n	7	14	21	35	70	105

To earn that much money washing cars, you will have to work more than 5 hours per week.

So if you work 5 hours or less per week washing cars, then mowing lawns will be the higher paying job.

However, if you work more than 5 hours per week washing cars, then washing cars will be the higher paying job.

1. Evaluate $18 \div y$ for $y = 2$.
2. Evaluate $4z \div 7$ for $z = 35$.
3. Evaluate $4b + c$ for $b = 8$ and $c = 6$.
4. Evaluate $(3y - 6) \div x$ for $x = 3$ and $y = 6$.
5. You are part of a group of 8 students working on an art project. You bring 67 paper clips and your friend brings 13 to share evenly with the group. To find how many paper clips each student can use, evaluate the expression $(b + c) \div 8$ for $b = 67$ and $c = 13$.
6. **a.** Evaluate $11n$ for $n = 18$.

   b. Write a new expression that uses the same variable, n. Evaluate the new expression for $n = 18$.
7. Bruce is taking a taxi to the airport. The taxi charges an initial fee of $4 and then $2 per mile.

   a. Write an algebraic expression for the cost of a taxi ride of m miles.

   b. How much would a 9-mile taxi ride cost Bruce?
8. You are buying balloons for a party. A small balloon costs $2. A large balloon costs $5.

   a. Write an algebraic expression for the cost of x small balloons and y large balloons.

   b. Find the total cost for 15 small balloons and 6 large balloons.
9. **Writing** Evaluate $10p \div q + 4(r - 7)$ for $p = 9$, $q = 5$, and $r = 14$. Choose different values for one variable at a time. Explain the differences you see in the values of the expression.
10. **Reasoning** Ann has two job offers. Job A pays $12 per hour. Job B pays $8 per hour. Assume she works n hours per week.

    a. Write an expression for the number of dollars she would earn at each job.

    Job A ■

    Job B ■

    b. She would work 14 hours each week at job A. She would work 17 hours each week at job B. At which job would she earn more money?

    c. For what possible reasons would Ann choose job A? Job B?
11. **Error Analysis** Ben's teacher asks Ben to evaluate the expression $m - n \div 4$ for $m = 44$ and $n = 36$. Ben incorrectly states that when $m = 44$ and $n = 36$, then $m - n \div 4 = 25$.

    a. Find the correct value of the expression when $m = 44$ and $n = 36$.

    b. What error did Ben likely make?

    A. He substituted the value of n for m and the value of m for n.

    B. He used the incorrect order of operations.

    C. He added when he should have subtracted.

    D. He multiplied when he should have divided.
12. **Class Trip** A class is going on a trip to a museum. It costs $790 to rent a bus. Each ticket to the museum costs $11.

    a. Write an algebraic expression that represents the cost of the trip for n people.

    b. Evaluate this expression for 37 people.
13. **Mental Math** Evaluate $80 - c$ for $c = 50$.
14. **Think About the Process**

    a. What should you do first in order to evaluate $9 + 7t$ for $t = 6$?

    A. Multiply 7 and t.

    B. Replace t with 6.

    C. Divide 7 by t.

    D. Find $9 + 7$.

    b. Evaluate $9 + 7t$ for $t = 6$.

See your complete lesson at MyMathUniverse.com

15. Suppose you are given the algebraic expression $m + 45 \div 9$. Which of the following values should you use for m so that the value of the expression is 154?

A. 149   **B.** 8

C. 1,341   **D.** 40

16. a. Evaluate expressions $xy \div 2$ and $12x - y$ for $x = 10$ and $y = 20$.

    b. Which expression gives the greater value when evaluated for $x = 10$ and $y = 20$?

      A. $xy \div 2$ **B.** $12x - y$

      C. Their values are equal.

17. Think About the Process Your school sells 380 hats and 250 T-shirts for a fundraiser.

    a. If your school sells the hats at x dollars, write an expression for the number of dollars raised by the hat sales.

    b. If your school sells the T-shirts at y dollars, write an expression for the number of dollars raised by the T-shirt sales.

    c. How would you write an expression to find the total number of dollars raised by both the hat and T-shirt sales?

      A. Add the two expressions and divide by 2.

      B. Add the two expressions and multiply by 2.

      C. Add the two expressions.

      D. Multiply the two expressions.

    d. If a hat sells for $6 and a T-shirt sells for $7, how much money would the school raise?

18. a. Challenge Evaluate $4x + 28z + 9x - 8z$ for $x = 4$ and $z = 5$.

    b. You may have substituted for x twice and substituted for z twice when you were evaluating. Do you see a faster way to evaluate? If yes, explain.

19. Challenge You and a friend charge $24 to rake a yard. You get half the money. You also earn $9 an hour babysitting. Suppose you and your friend rake y yards and you babysit for n hours.

    a. Write an expression for how much money you would earn.

    b. How much money would you earn by raking 5 yards and babysitting for 5 hours?

CCSS: 6.EE.A.1, 6.EE.A.2c

Key Concept

Using exponents is an effective way of writing expressions that involve repeated multiplication of a factor.

Base The base is the repeated factor.

Base

$$8 \cdot 8 \cdot 8 \cdot 8 = 8^4$$

4 factors of 8

Exponent The exponent is the number of times the base is used as a factor.

Exponent

$$8 \cdot 8 \cdot 8 \cdot 8 = 8^4$$

4 factors of 8

Power A power is a number expressed using an exponent.

$$8 \cdot 8 \cdot 8 \cdot 8 = 8^4$$

Power
8 to the fourth power

Reading Powers

x^2 is read x to the second power or x squared.

x^3 is read x to the third power or x cubed.

x^4 is read x to the fourth power.

Exponents and the Order of Operations

$$20 + 3(9 - 7)^3$$

1. Evaluate expressions inside grouping symbols. $20 + 3(2)^3$
2. Evaluate powers. $20 + 3(8)$
3. Multiply and divide from left to right. $20 + 24$
4. Add and subtract from left to right. 44

Part 1

Example **Evaluating Numerical Expressions with Exponents**

Fill in each box to make a true statement. Then find the value of the expression.

a. $4 \times 4 \times 4 = 4^{\blacksquare} = \blacksquare$

b. $\blacksquare \times \blacksquare \times \blacksquare \times \blacksquare \times \blacksquare = 2^5 = \blacksquare$

c. $21 - 3^2 = 21 - \blacksquare = \blacksquare$

Solution ·

a. $\underline{4 \times 4 \times 4} = 4^3 = 64$

3 factors of 4

b. $2 \times 2 \times 2 \times 2 \times 2 = 2^5 = 32$

c. $21 - 3^2 = 21 - 9 = 12$

Part 2

Example **Evaluating Algebraic Expressions with Exponents**

What is the value of each expression for $a - 5$, $b = 12$, and $c = 9$?

a. $2a + 8$ **b.** $2c$ **c.** $5b$

d. $12a$ **e.** $b^2 - 63$ **f.** c^2

Solution ·

To evaluate the expression, replace a with 5 and b with 12, and c with 9.

a. $2a + 8$
$2(5) + 8$
$10 + 8$
18

b. $2c$
$2(9)$
18

c. $5b$
$5(12)$
60

d. $12a$
$12(5)$
60

e. $b^2 - 63$
$(12)^2 - 63$
$144 - 63$
81

f. c^2
$(9)^2$
81

Part 3

Intro

Suppose you want to find the area of one wall of a room.

If the room is x feet wide and x feet high, the area of the wall would be x feet $\cdot$ x feet, or x square feet.

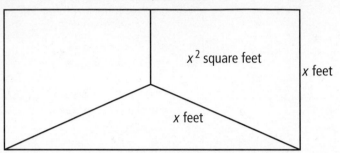

x^2 square feet

x feet

x feet

Example Solving Problems Using Exponents

Suppose you want to paint a room that has 4 walls. Each wall is a square wall with side length 10 feet. One gallon of paint will cover about 400 square feet. Will one gallon of paint be enough to give the room 2 coats of paint?

Solution ·

Know
- The dimensions of one wall
- The area one gallon of paint will cover

Need
- The area of one wall
- The total area to be painted

Plan
- Write an algebraic expression to describe the area of one wall.
- Find the total area of all 4 walls.
- Figure out how much of the total area 1 gallon of paint will cover.

Part 3

Solution continued

First, find the area of one wall.

$$10^2 = 100 \text{ square feet}$$

The wall side length is 10 feet

Then find the total area to be covered. Remember that you want to paint 4 walls.

Area of 4 walls = 4(100)
= 400 square feet

Remember that you want to give the walls 2 coats of paint.

Area to be painted = 2(400)
= 800 square feet

Finally, compare the total area to be painted with the area that 1 gallon of paint will cover.

$$400 \div 800 = \frac{1}{2}$$

1 gallon of paint will cover 400 square feet.

So one gallon of paint will not be enough to give the room two coats of paint. You will need two gallons of paint.

1. a. Rewrite the expression $3 \times 3 \times 3$ using an exponent.

  b. Find the value of the expression.

2. Think About the Process You are to write the expression below using an exponent.

$$9 \cdot 9 \cdot 9 \cdot 9$$

  a. Identify the base.

  b. Identify the exponent.

  c. Write the expression $9 \cdot 9 \cdot 9 \cdot 9$ using an exponent.

  d. Find the value of the expression.

3. a. Write the expression 2^3 using repeated multiplication.

  b. Find the value of the expression 2^3.

4. What is the value of $b^3 a$ if $b = 2$ and $a = 6$?

5. What is the value of $2p^2 + q^2$ for $p = 4$ and $q = 7$?

6. The area of a square is s^2, where s is the side length. Find the area of a square with side length 3 units.

7. The pilot of a hot-air balloon drops an object overboard at a height of 3,000 feet. The expression $16t^2$ represents the distance in feet that the object falls in t seconds, until the object hits the ground. Find the distance the object falls in 6 seconds.

8. Writing The area of a square is s^2, where s is the side length. Suppose you have three squares. One square has side length 8 feet. Another square has side length 5 feet. The third square has side length 3 feet. Is the sum of the areas of the two smaller squares equal to the area of the large square? Explain your answer.

9. Reasoning Is the statement $8 \cdot 8 \cdot 8 \cdot 8 \cdot 8 \cdot z \cdot z = (8z)^2$ true or false? Explain your reasoning. Also, support your answer with an example.

10. Error Analysis A teacher asks his students to give the meaning of $(2t)^3$. One of the students incorrectly says $(2t)^3$ means $2 \cdot t \cdot t \cdot t$.

  a. Express repeated multiplication for $(2t)^3$ using multiplication signs.

  b. What is the student's error?

   A. The student forgot a factor of t.

   B. The student multiplied by t instead of 3.

   C. The student did not include 2 in the base.

   D. The student incorrectly used t as the base, but the base is 2.

  c. Evaluate the expression $(2t)^3$ for $t = 2$.

11. Population The expression $n \cdot 2^3$ gives the population (in thousands) of an animal after 3 years, where n is the starting population in thousands. Find the population after 3 years if the starting population is 5,000.

12. Estimation Estimate the area of a square with side length 91 feet. Note that the area of a square is s^2, where s is the side length.

   A. 180 square feet

   B. 810 square feet

   C. 360 square feet

   D. 8,100 square feet

13. a. Mental Math What is the value of $s^2 - t^2$ for $s = 20$ and $t = 5$?

  b. Describe an easy way to mentally subtract the lesser square from the greater square.

14. Evaluate the expression $2st^2 - s^2$ below for $s = 2$ and $t = 8$.

15. Evaluate the expression below for $x = 4$ and $y = 6$.

$$x^2 + 3(x + y)$$

16. a. Challenge Which of the following is the correct meaning of $27x(yz)^5$?

    A. $27x(yz)^5 = 27x \cdot yz \cdot 5$

    B. $27x(yz)^5 = 27x \cdot yz \cdot yz \cdot yz \cdot yz \cdot yz$

    C. $27x(yz)^5 = 27xy \cdot z \cdot z \cdot z \cdot z \cdot z$

    D. $27x(yz)^5 = 27xyz \cdot 27xyz \cdot 27xyz \cdot 27xyz \cdot 27xyz$

    b. Evaluate the expression $27x(yz)^5$ for $x = 4$, $y = 2$, and $z = 1$.

17. Think About the Process A company needs to rent a storage space. It is looking at two differently sized spaces. Both spaces are cube-shaped. The smaller space has side length 6 feet. The larger space has side length 8 feet. You want to find the difference, in cubic feet, of the two spaces. Note that the volume of a cube is s^3, where s is the side length.

    a. What is the first step in finding the difference, in cubic feet, of the two spaces?

        A. Calculate the total area of the walls of the larger space.

        B. Evaluate the expression for the area of the wall of the larger space.

        C. Subtract the side lengths of the spaces.

        D. Evaluate the expression for the volume of the larger space.

    b. The larger space has _____ more cubic feet than the smaller space.

18. Challenge Suppose you want to tile a floor. The floor is a square with side length 12 feet. You want the tiles to be squares with side length 2 feet.

    a. How many tiles do you need to cover the entire floor? Note that the area of a square is s^2, where s is the side length.

    b. Find three other tile sizes that will cover the floor exactly with a whole number of tiles.

CCSS: 6.EE.A.2, 6.EE.A.2a

Part 1

▶ Intro

A bar diagram can be used to represent algebraic expressions. To make a bar diagram, draw a bar and divide it into two pieces. Then label the pieces.

Addition Model Write an algebraic expression for the word phrase *a number plus 32*.

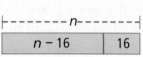

Expression
$n + 32$

Subtraction Model Write an algebraic expression for the word phrase *16 subtracted from a number*.

Expression
$n - 16$

▶ Example Representing Real-World Situations with Addition Expressions

A library had *x* number of biographies and bought 13 new biographies. What algebraic expression can be used to represent the total number of biographies the library has now?

Solution ·

Draw a bar to model the parts being added. Substitute the values into the bar diagram. Then find the sum of the parts.

biographies library had	new biographies

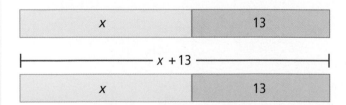

The expression that represents the number of biographies the library has now is $x + 13$.

Part 2

Intro

Just as with addition and subtraction expressions, you can model multiplication or division expressions with a bar diagram.

Multiplication Model Suppose each page of a photo album is designed to hold 4 photographs and an album can have p number of pages.

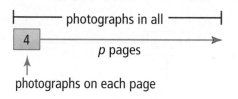

The expression representing the total number of photographs the album can hold is $4p$.

Division Model Suppose a company that manufactures the photo albums is packaging them for shipment. Each shipping box holds 12 albums.

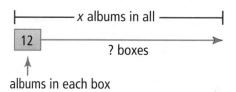

The expression representing the number of boxes needed to ship x number of photo albums is $x \div 12$.

Example Representing Real-World Situations with Division Expressions

A factory robot is used to pack 16 bottles of orange juice into each box. If the factory manufactures b bottles of orange juice per day, what expression can be used to represent how many boxes the robot packs per day?

Solution

You know that the robot packs 16 bottles of orange juice into each box and that the factory manufactures b bottles to pack.

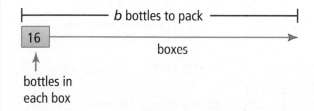

Use the bar diagram to write a division expression to represent the number of equally packed boxes. The model shows that the number of boxes is the quotient of b bottles in total and 16 bottles per box.

$$b \div 16$$

The expression representing the number of boxes the robot packs per day is $b \div 16$, or $\frac{b}{16}$.

1. Suppose a bookstore sells *b* copies of a book. The price of the book is $8.

   a. Which bar diagram models the total cost of the *b* books?

   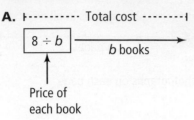

   A. |--------- Total cost --------|

   $8 \div b$ *b* books

   Price of
   each book

   B. |------- Total cost --------|

   8   *b* books

   Price of
   each book

   C. |-------- Total cost --------|

   b   8 books

   Price of
   each book

   D. |-------- Total cost --------|

   8   12*b* books

   Price of
   each book

   b. Write an algebraic expression for the total cost.

2. Isabella and Juan each have 18 books. Isabella gives Juan *b* books.

   a. Which bar diagram models the number of books Isabella has now?

   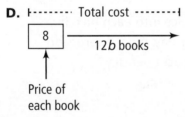

   A. |---------- 18 ----------|

   | *b* | $18 \div b$ |

   B. |---------- *b* ----------|

   | 18 | $b - 18$ |

   C. |---------- 18 ----------|

   | *b* | $18 - b$ |

   D. |---------- *b* ----------|

   | 18 | $b + 18$ |

   b. Which bar diagram models the number of books Juan has now?

   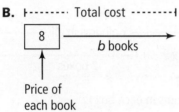

   A. |-------- $b \times 18$ --------|

   | *b* | 18 |

   B. |---------- 18 ----------|

   | *b* | $18 - b$ |

   C. |-------- $b + 18$ --------|

   | *b* | 18 |

   D. |---------- *b* ----------|

   | 18 | $b + 18$ |

3. Some friends are going to an amusement park together. The park charges $33 for each ticket. The total cost for the group is *c*.

   a. Choose the diagram that represents the total cost for the group.

   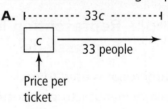

   A. |---------- 33*c* ----------|

   c   33 people

   Price per
   ticket

   B. |---------- *c* ----------|

   $33 $c \div 33$ people

   Price per
   ticket

   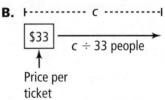

   C. |-------- $c + 33$ --------|

   $33   *c* people

   Price per
   ticket

   D. |---------- 33*c* ----------|

   $33   *c* people

   Price per
   ticket

   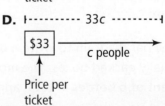

   b. Write an algebraic expression for the number of friends going to the park.

4. You go to the grocery store with $27. You spend m dollars at the store.

    a. Draw a bar diagram that models the number of dollars you have left.

    A. $\vdash\!\text{-----------}\ 27\ \text{-----------}\!\dashv$

m	$m + 27$

    B. $\vdash\!\text{--------}\ 27 - m\ \text{--------}\!\dashv$

27	m

    C. $\vdash\!\text{-----------}\ m\ \text{-----------}\!\dashv$

27	$m - 27$

    D. $\vdash\!\text{-----------}\ 27\ \text{-----------}\!\dashv$

m	$27 - m$

    b. Write an algebraic expression for the number of dollars you have left.

5. Think About the Process Suppose you walked 3 dogs this morning. You made $18 for walking these dogs. You walked 4 more dogs this afternoon and made d dollars. The bar diagram below represents the number of dollars you made. Describe what each part of the diagram represents.

$\vdash\!\text{-----------}\ 18 + d\ \text{-----------}\!\dashv$

18	d

    a. What does the part of the diagram labeled "18" represent?

      A. the total number of dollars you made

      B. the number of dollars you made walking dogs this morning

      C. the number of dollars you made walking dogs this afternoon

      D. the number of dogs you walked this afternoon

      E. the number of dogs you walked today

      F. the number of dogs you walked this morning

    b. What does the part of the diagram labeled "d" represent?

    c. What does the part of the diagram labeled "$18 + d$" represent?

6. Think About the Process A farmer is planting vegetables. Suppose one plot of land can have r rows of plants. Each row can have 13 plants. The bar diagram represents the total number of plants the farmer can grow in this plot.

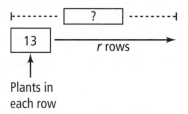

Plants in each row

What algebraic expression describes the missing label?

    A. $13 \div r$ **B.** $13r$

    C. $13 - r$ **D.** $13 + r$

7. Challenge According to fire codes, a large restaurant is allowed to have at most p people in it at any one time.

    a. Suppose 438 people are in the restaurant now. If 438 is less than p, draw a bar diagram to model how many more people can enter the restaurant.

    b. Use this model to write an algebraic expression that represents how many more people can enter the restaurant.

8. Challenge Scott bought 9 notebooks. His total cost was c. Each notebook was the same price.

    a. Draw a bar diagram to represent the price of each notebook.

    b. Write an algebraic expression for the price of each notebook.

    c. What would the bar diagram look like if Scott bought n notebooks?

See your complete lesson at MyMathUniverse.com

The Identity and Zero Properties

CCSS: 6.EE.A.2c, 6.EE.A.3, 6.EE.A.4

Vocabulary
Identity Property of Addition,
Identity Property of Multiplication,
Zero Property of Multiplication

Key Concept

Identity Property of Addition Adding 0 does not change the value of a number.

Arithmetic Example: $7 + 0 = 7$ and $0 + 7 = 7$
Algebraic Example: $a + 0 = a$ and $0 + a = a$ for any number a

Identity Property of Multiplication Multiplying by 1 does not change the value of a number.

Arithmetic Example: $9 \cdot 1 = 9$ and $1 \cdot 9 = 9$
Algebraic Example: $a \cdot 1 = a$ and $1 \cdot a = a$ for any number a

Zero Property of Multiplication Multiplying by 0 results in a product of 0.

Arithmetic Example: $8 \cdot 0 = 0$ and $0 \cdot 8 = 0$
Algebraic Example: $a \cdot 0 = 0$ and $0 \cdot a = 0$ for any number a

Part 1

Example Identifying Properties Shown By Numerical and Algebraic Statements

Determine which property each statement represents.

$0 \cdot x = 0$	$a \cdot 1 = a$	$0 + 1 = 1$
$1 \cdot a = a$	$1{,}000 \cdot 0 = 0$	$z + 0 = z$
$1 \cdot 99 = 99$	$x \cdot 0 = 0$	One plus zero is one

a. Identity Property of Addition
b. Identity Property of Multiplication
c. Zero Property of Multiplication

Solution

a. The Identity Property of Addition states that adding 0 does not change the value of a number.

$0 + 1 = 1$
$z + 0 = z$
One plus zero is one

Part 1

Solution continued

    b. The Identity Property of Multiplication states that multiplying by 1 does not change the value of a number.

$$1 \cdot 99 = 99$$
$$a \cdot 1 = a$$
$$1 \cdot a = a$$

    c. The Zero Property of Multiplication states that multiplying by 0 results in a product of 0.

$$1{,}000 \cdot 0 = 0$$
$$0 \cdot x = 0$$
$$x \cdot 0 = 0$$

Part 2

Example Using the Identity Property of Multiplication

At a carnival, you earn 1 point for each balloon you pop with a dart. You pop b balloons.

Write two equivalent algebraic expressions that show how many points you earned.

Solution ···

You get 1 point per balloon. You pop b balloons.

Multiply the number of points per balloon by the number of balloons.

$$1 \cdot b$$

Multiply the number of balloons by the number of points per balloon.

$$b \cdot 1$$

Both expressions equal b points.

Part 3

Example Using Properties to Simplify Expressions

Hockey teams earn 3 points for a win, 0 points for a loss, and 1 point for a tie. Use the expression below to find the total number of points Team A has earned. Name the properties you use to simplify the expression.

Hockey Records

Team	W	L	T
A	6	2	4
B	7	5	0

$$\left(3 \cdot W\right) + \left(0 \cdot L\right) + \left(1 \cdot T\right)$$

Solution

Write the algebraic expression.	$(3 \cdot W) + (0 \cdot L) + (1 \cdot T)$
Substitute the values from the Team A row.	$(3 \cdot 6) + (0 \cdot 2) + (1 \cdot 4)$
Multiply.	$18 + (0 \cdot 2) + (1 \cdot 4)$
Use the Zero Property of Multiplication to multiply.	$18 + 0 + (1 \cdot 4)$
Use the Identity Property of Multiplication to multiply.	$18 + 0 + 4$
Use the Identity Property of Addition to add.	$18 + 4$
Add.	22

1. Why are the expressions 0 and 8 · 0 equivalent?

2. Which statement below represents the Zero Property of Multiplication?

   A. 5 · 1 = 5   **B.** 1 · 5 = 0

   C. 0 + 5 = 5   **D.** 0 · 5 = 0

3. Use the Identity Property of Multiplication to write an expression equivalent to 90 · 1.

4. Use the Identity Property of Multiplication to write an expression equivalent to 1 · (2 + w).

5. Use the Zero Property of Multiplication to write an expression equivalent to 0 · 11.

6. Use the Zero Property of Multiplication to write an expression equivalent to 0 · (w + 6).

7. Evaluate the expression 2(4 · 1).

8. Evaluate the expression (0 · 4) + (7 + 0) + (8 · 1).

9. **a.** Which property explains why the expressions 15 · 0 and 0 are equivalent?

   A. the Identity Property of Multiplication

   B. the Identity Property of Addition

   C. the Zero Property of Multiplication

   b. Writing Discuss whether there is a Zero Property of Addition, what it would say, and how it compares to the Zero Property of Multiplication.

   c. Describe how the Identity Properties of Addition and Multiplication are alike and how they are different.

10. **a.** Which of the following is an example of the Zero Property of Multiplication?

   A. 0 · h = 0   **B.** h · 1 = h

   C. 0 · h = h   **D.** h · 1 = 0

   b. Write two more examples (one numerical and one algebraic) of this property.

11. **Error Analysis** Your friend incorrectly claims that the expression 26 + 0 is equivalent to 0 by the Identity Property of Addition.

   a. Use the Identity Property of Addition to write an equivalent expression.

   b. What error did your friend likely make?

   A. Your friend confused the Identity Property of Addition and the Zero Property of Multiplication.

   B. Your friend did not follow the order of operations.

   C. Your friend confused the Identity Property of Addition and the Identity Property of Multiplication.

12. **Reasoning** Write two expressions equivalent to 0 · (9 + 8) using the Zero Property of Multiplication. Explain your reasoning.

13. **Craft Sales** Your neighbor knits hats and scarves. He sells the hats and scarves at craft fairs. The hats sell for $8 each. He sells the scarves for $6 each. The expression 8h + 6s gives the number of dollars he makes selling h hats and s scarves. How many dollars does he make if he sells 1 hat and 3 scarves at a craft fair?

14. Use the Identity Property of Multiplication twice to write an expression equivalent to 1 · [1 · (c − d)].

15. A cash drawer contains ten-, five-, and one-dollar bills. An expression for the value in dollars of T tens, V fives, and N ones is 10T + 5V + 1N. Find the value in dollars of the bills in the drawer for T = 2, V = 0, and N = 4.

16. Think About the Process

a. How does the Identity Property of Multiplication help you evaluate the expression $(4 \cdot 1) + (1 \cdot 7)$?

   A. The property lets you remove the parentheses from the expression.

   B. The property lets you add without evaluating the expressions in parentheses.

   C. The property lets you evaluate the expressions in parentheses.

b. What is the value of the expression $(4 \cdot 1) + (1 \cdot 7)$?

17. Think About the Process Which properties help you evaluate the expression $(9 \cdot 0) + (1 \cdot 6)$?

a. Which property helps you evaluate the expression $(9 \cdot 0)$?

   A. The Identity Property of Multiplication

   B. The Zero Property of Multiplication

   C. The Identity Property of Addition

b. Which property helps you evaluate the expression $(1 \cdot 6)$?

   A. The Zero Property of Multiplication

   B. The Identity Property of Addition

   C. The Identity Property of Multiplication

c. Which property helps you evaluate the expression after you evaluate the expressions in parentheses?

   A. The Identity Property of Multiplication

   B. The Identity Property of Addition

   C. The Zero Property of Multiplication

d. Evaluate $(9 \cdot 0) + (1 \cdot 6)$.

18. Challenge You and your friend are studying for a test. Your friend gives you the expression $(9 + 0) + 8 + (7 + 0) + 2$. Evaluate the expression.

19. Challenge A beanbag target has three openings. The openings are red (worth 5 points), blue (worth 3 points), and yellow (worth 2 points). The expression $5R + 3B + 2Y + 0M$ gives the score for tossing R bags through red, B bags through blue, Y bags through yellow, and M bags that miss all three openings. In a game, each player tosses 10 beanbags. The results are shown.

Game Results				
Player	R	B	Y	M
Pat	4	2	1	3
Sam	1	4	3	2
Bob	3	1	2	4

a. Which player has the greatest score?

b. What is that score?

The Commutative Properties

Vocabulary
Commutative
Property of
Addition,
Commutative
Property of
Multiplication

CCSS: 6.EE.A.3, 6.EE.A.4

Key Concept

Commutative Property of Addition Changing the order of addends does not change the sum.

Arithmetic Example: $10 + 7 = 7 + 10$

Algebraic Example: $a + b = b + a$ for any numbers a and b

Commutative Property of Multiplication Changing the order of factors does not change the product.

Arithmetic Example: $7 \cdot 10 = 10 \cdot 7$

Algebraic Example: $a \cdot b = b \cdot a$ for any numbers a and b

Part 1

Intro

This diagram models the expression $25 + 56$.

25 + 56	
25	56

To find an equivalent expression, change the order of the addends.

56 + 25	
56	25

$25 + 56$ and $56 + 25$ are equivalent expressions.

Changing the order of the addends does not change the sum.

Example Using the Commutative Property of Addition

In the first ten months of the year, there were 555 earthquakes in the United States of magnitude 4.0 or greater. The remaining two months of the year are projected to have e earthquakes.

Draw diagrams and write two equivalent expressions to show the total number of earthquakes projected in the twelve-month period.

Part 1

Example continued

Solution ·

Step 1 Draw a diagram to show what you know. Write an expression that represents the total number of earthquakes.

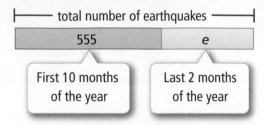

The total number of earthquakes is 555 + e.

Step 2 Use the Commutative Property of Addition to draw a related diagram, and then write an equivalent expression.

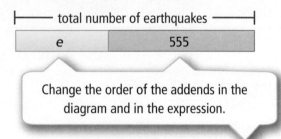

The total number of earthquakes is e + 555.

555 + e and e + 555 are equivalent expressions.

Part 2

Intro

This rectangle models the expression 3 · 4.

3 · 4 is 12 squares.

continued on next page >

Part 2

To find an equivalent expression for 3 · 4, change the order of the factors.

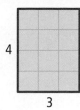

4 · 3 is 12 squares.

The rectangles have the same number of squares.

3 · 4 and 4 · 3 are equivalent expressions.

Example Using the Commutative Property of Multiplication

Each archaeologist *a* of an excavation team is responsible for 4 sections of the dig site.

Write two equivalent expressions that show the total number of sections under excavation.

Solution

Draw a diagram to show what you know.

Write an algebraic expression showing that each archaeologist is responsible for 4 sections.   *a* • 4

Use the Commutative Property of Multiplication to write an equivalent expression.   4 • *a*

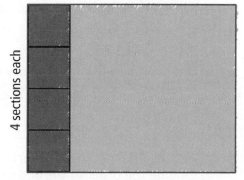

a · 4 and 4 · *a* are equivalent expressions.

Part 3

> ### Example Using Commutative Properties to Write Equivalent Expressions

Match each expression to an equivalent expression.

$14 \cdot x + x$ ba $14 + 15 + 6$ $75 + s$ $1b - 1a$
$a - b$ $b + a$ $4 \cdot s \cdot 25$ $4 \cdot 3 \cdot 25$ $x + 14 + x$

a. $14 + 6 + 15$ **b.** $4 \cdot 25 \cdot 3$ **c.** $b - a$
d. $4 \cdot 25 \cdot s$ **e.** $a \cdot b$ **f.** $x + x + 14$

Solution

a. Use the Commutative Property of Addition to write an equivalent expression. Change the order of the addends.

$14 + 6 + 15$
$14 + 15 + 6$

b. Use the Commutative Property of Multiplication to write an equivalent expression. Change the order of the factors.

$4 \cdot 25 \cdot 3$
$4 \cdot 3 \cdot 25$

c. Simplify the expression.

$b - a$
$1b - 1a$ ← $1b$ is the same as b.
        $1a$ is the same as a.

d. Use the Commutative Property of Multiplication to write an equivalent expression. Change the order of the factors.

$4 \cdot 25 \cdot s$
$4 \cdot s \cdot 25$

e. Use the Commutative Property of Multiplication to write an equivalent expression.

$a \cdot b$ ← $a \cdot b$ is the same as ab.
ba

f. Use the Commutative Property of Addition to write an equivalent expression. Change the order of the addends.

$x + x + 14$
$x + 14 + x$

1. Use the Commutative Property to rewrite the expression $x + 14$.

2. In the first 6 hours it is open, a bakery sells 19 cakes. The baker expects to sell c more cakes before the end of the day. Select two expressions below that model the number of cakes sold that day.

    A. $19 + c$ B. $c + 6$

    C. $c \cdot 19$ D. $19 \cdot c$

    E. $6 + c$ F. $c + 19$

3. Each of the 9 runners on a track team runs y laps. Select two expressions below that model the number of laps the team runs.

    A. $y + 9$ B. $9 \cdot y$

    C. $9 - y$ D. $y \cdot 9$

4. Use the Commutative Property of Multiplication to write an expression equivalent to $x \cdot 2$.

5. Which expression below is equivalent to $22 + 28$ by the Commutative Property of Addition?

    A. $32 + 18$

    B. $28 + 22$

    C. $25 + 25$

    D. $10 + 10 + 10 + 10 + 10$

6. Which of these expressions is equivalent to $2 \cdot 9 \cdot y$ by the Commutative Property of Multiplication? Select all that apply.

    A. $2 \cdot 9 \cdot y$ B. $2 \cdot y \cdot 9$

    C. $9 \cdot 2 \cdot y$ D. $2 \cdot 9 + y$

7. a. Which expression is equivalent to $70 + 50$ by the Commutative Property of Addition?

    A. $(70 + 50) + 0$

    B. $50 + 70$

    C. $(70 + 50) \cdot 1$

    D. $50 \cdot 70$

    b. What is the value of each of these equivalent expressions?

8. a. Which of these expressions are equivalent to $25 \cdot 13 \cdot 18$ by the Commutative Property of Multiplication? Select all that apply.

    A. $13 \cdot 25 \cdot 18$ B. $25 \cdot 18 \cdot 13$

    C. $325 \cdot 18$ D. $13 \cdot 450$

    b. What is the value of each of the equivalent expressions?

9. a. **Writing** Use the Commutative Property of Addition to write an expression equivalent to $q + 2$.

    b. Explain how you could use the Commutative Property to help you work with the expression $18 + q + 2$.

10. **Reasoning** Four friends decide to combine their marbles. One friend writes the expression $5 + 29 + 35 + 1$ to find the total number of marbles.

    a. Use the Commutative Property of Addition to write two more expressions for the total number of marbles.

    b. Another friend claims that the expression $5 + 35 + 29 + 1$ is easier to evaluate. How many marbles do the four friends have all together?

    c. Explain why the second expression is easier to evaluate than the first.

11. **Camping Trip** Yesterday, 5 friends planned their camping trip. They spent $27 per person to buy food for the trip.

    a. Select two expressions below that model the total amount of money they spent on food.

    A. $27 + 5$ B. $27 \cdot 5$

    C. $5 + 27$ D. $5 \cdot 27$

    b. How much did they spend on food for the camping trip?

12. The table shows the amounts of annual snowfall (in inches) for five cities. One expression for the total snowfall for the five cities is $78 + 54 + 23 + 53 + 80$.

Annual Snowfall for Five Cities

City	Amount (inches)
A	78
B	54
C	23
D	53
E	80

a. Which expressions below are equivalent to $78 + 54 + 23 + 53 + 80$ by a Commutative Property? Select all that apply.

    A. $78 + 54 + 53 + 23 + 80$

    B. $78 + 54 + 23 + 80 + 53$

    C. $54 + 78 + 23 + 53 + 80$

    D. $78 + 23 + 54 + 53 + 80$

b. Find the total annual snowfall for the five cities.

13. At a factory, each robot can assemble 49 items per hour. The expression $49 \cdot r \cdot 24$ represents the number of items that r robots assemble in one day.

a. Which expressions below are equivalent to $49 \cdot r \cdot 24$ by a Commutative Property? Select all that apply.

    A. $(49 \cdot r) \cdot 24$ **B.** $49 \cdot (r \cdot 24)$

    C. $r \cdot 49 \cdot 24$ **D.** $49 \cdot 24 \cdot r$

b. How many items could 18 robots produce in one day?

c. Explain why the expression $49 \cdot r \cdot 24$ represents the number of items that r robots assemble in one day.

14. Think About the Process A group of friends decides to share their comic books. Each person has 8 comic books to start with. If the number of friends is p, the total number of comic books is $8 \cdot p$.

a. What does the Commutative Property of Multiplication allow you to do with $8 \cdot p$?

    A. Write an equivalent expression by changing the order of the factors.

    B. Write an equivalent expression by adding 0 to the expression.

    C. Write an equivalent expression by writing the expression in parentheses.

    D. Write an equivalent expression by changing the operation in the expression.

b. Which expression below is equivalent to $8 \cdot p$ by the Commutative Property of Multiplication?

    A. $p + 8$ **B.** $8 \cdot d$

    C. $p \cdot 8$ **D.** $d \cdot 8$

c. If there are 5 friends in the group, how many comic books do they have in total?

15. Think About the Process You want to use the Commutative Property of Addition to find an expression equivalent to $112 + 288$.

a. How can you tell if another expression is the result of using the Commutative Property of Addition?

    A. The numbers have switched places from where they were in the original expression.

    B. The numbers are in the same places as in the original expression.

    C. The value of the expression is different from the value of original expression.

    D. The operation changes from addition to multiplication.

b. Which expression below is equivalent to $112 + 288$ by the Commutative Property of Addition?

    A. $304 + 96$ **B.** $96 + 304$

    C. $288 + 112$ **D.** $124 + 276$

c. Find the value of this equivalent expression.

CCSS: 6.EE.A.3, 6.EE.A.4

Vocabulary
Associative Property of Addition, Associative Property of Multiplication

Key Concept

Associative Property of Addition Changing the grouping of addends does not change the sum.

Arithmetic Example: $(2 + 5) + 3 = 2 + (5 + 3)$
Algebra Example: $(a + b) + c = a + (b + c)$ for any numbers a, b, and c

Associative Property of Multiplication Changing the grouping of factors does not change the product.

Arithmetic Example: $(4 \cdot 2) \cdot 3 = 4 \cdot (2 \cdot 3)$
Algebra Example: $(a \cdot b) \cdot c = a \cdot (b \cdot c)$ for any numbers a, b, and c

Part 1

Intro

The Associative Property of Addition says that you can change the grouping of addends in an expression without changing the value.

$$(13 + 4) + 6 = 13 + (4 + 6)$$

Grouping the 4 and 6 is smart because their sum is 10, which is easy to add to other numbers.

Example Using the Associative Property of Addition

A pilot's schedule for the month of May is 63 hours in-flight, 75 hours at work but not flying, and 25 hours on-call.

Use the Associative Property of Addition to write two equivalent expressions. Show the total number of hours the pilot spent in-flight, at work but not flying, or on-call.

Part 1

Example continued

Solution ·

One possible expression for the total number of hours is:

$$(63 + 75) + 25$$

Hours in-flight

Hours at work, but not flying

Hours on-call

Using the Associative Property of Addition, you can find an equivalent expression.

$$63 + (75 + 25)$$

Changing the grouping of addends does not change the sum.

Part 2

Example Using the Associative Property of Multiplication

An airline ships 3,000 lb of salmon each day. How many pounds of salmon are shipped in *w* weeks? Use the Associative Property of Multiplication to write two equivalent expressions.

Solution ·

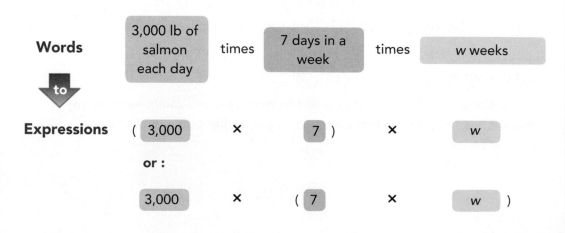

	3,000 lb of salmon each day	times	7 days in a week	times	w weeks
Words					

Expressions   (3,000   ×   7)   ×   w

or :

3,000   ×   (7   ×   w)

Example Using Properties to Write Equivalent Expressions

Use the given property to match each expression to an equivalent expression.

$(50 + 50) + 27$	$a + (a + 50)$	$(50 + 50) + a$	27
ab	$50 + 27$	$50 + 27 + a$	$50 + a$
$50(a + 27)$	$(a + 50) + a$	$(50 + 27) + a$	$0 + 27$

a. Associative Property of Addition: $50 + (50 + 27)$
b. Associative Property of Addition: $(a + a) + 50$
c. Associative Property of Addition: $50 + (50 + a)$
d. Identity Property of Addition: $27 + 0$
e. Identity Property of Addition: $ab + 0$
f. Identity Property of Addition: $50 + (27 + 0)$
g. Commutative Property of Addition: $50 + a + 27$
h. Commutative Property of Addition: $a + 50$
i. Commutative Property of Addition: $50(27 + a)$

Solution ·

Using the Associative Property of Addition:

a. $50 + (50 + 27) = (50 + 50) + 27$
b. $(a + a) + 50 = a + (a + 50)$ ⟶ Regrouping the addends does not change the value.
c. $50 + (50 + a) = (50 + 50) + a$

Using the Identity Property of Addition:

d. $27 + 0 = 27$ ⟶ Adding 0 does not change the value of the number.
e. $ab + 0 = ab$
f. $50 + (27 + 0) = 50 + 27$

Using the Commutative Property of Addition:

g. $50 + a + 27 = 50 + 27 + a$
h. $a + 50 = 50 + a$
i. $50(27 + a) = 50(a + 27)$ ⟶ Changing the order of the addends does not change the value.

1. Which expression is equivalent to $(h + 9) + 5$ by the Associative Property of Addition?

   A. $(h + 5) + 9$ **B.** $h + 9 + 5$

   C. $h + (9 + 5)$ **D.** $5 + (h + 9)$

2. Use the Associative Property of Multiplication to write an expression equivalent to $(2 \cdot 4) \cdot 6$.

3. Use the Associative Property of Addition to write an expression equivalent to $z + (q + d)$.

4. a. Which expression is equivalent to $(47 + z) + 0$ by the Associative Property of Addition?

   A. $(0 + 47) + z$ **B.** $47 + z + 0$

   C. $47 + (z + 0)$ **D.** $0 + (47 + z)$

  b. Which expression is equivalent to $(47 + z) + 0$ by the Identity Property of Addition?

   A. $47 + 0$ **B.** $47 + (z + 0)$

   C. $47 + z$ **D.** $z + 0$

5. Select two expressions that are equivalent by the Associative Property of Addition.

   A. $14 + (6 + 9)$ **B.** $9 + (6 + 14)$

   C. $(14 + 9) + 6$ **D.** $14 + (9 + 6)$

6. Game Show In the first three rounds of a game show, a team answers 4 questions correctly, 2 questions correctly, and 8 questions correctly.

  a. Use the Associative Property of Addition to write two equivalent expressions that show how many questions the team answers correctly.

  b. How many questions does the team answer correctly?

7. Error Analysis A class must use the Associative Property of Addition to write an expression equivalent to $38 + (18 + 14)$. One student incorrectly comes up with the expression $38 + (14 + 18)$.

  a. Use the Associative Property of Addition to write an expression equivalent to $38 + (18 + 14)$.

  b. What was the student's error?

8. Which expression is equivalent to $25 \cdot (41 \cdot r)$ by the Associative Property of Multiplication?

   A. $(25 \cdot 41) \cdot r$

   B. $r \cdot 25 \cdot 41$

   C. $r \cdot (25 \cdot 41)$

   D. $(25 \cdot r) \cdot 41$

9. a. Reasoning Which expression is equivalent to $0 \cdot (85 \cdot 58)$ by the Associative Property of Multiplication?

   A. $(58 \cdot 0) \cdot 85$ **B.** $0 \cdot (58 \cdot 85)$

   C. $0 \cdot 85 \cdot 58$ **D.** $(0 \cdot 85) \cdot 58$

  b. Which expression is equivalent to $0 \cdot (85 \cdot 58)$ by the Zero Property of Multiplication?

   A. $(58 \cdot 0) \cdot 85$ **B.** 0

   C. $(0 \cdot 85) \cdot 58$ **D.** $58 \cdot 85$

10. a. Multiple Representations Which expression is equivalent to $(49 + 55) + 43$ by the Associative Property of Addition?

   A. $49 + (55 + 43)$

   B. $49 + (43 + 55)$

   C. $49 + 55 + 43$

   D. $(55 + 49) + 43$

  b. Which expression is equivalent to $(49 + 55) + 43$ by the Commutative Property of Addition?

   A. $49 \cdot (55 \cdot 43)$

   B. $49 + (43 \cdot 55)$

   C. $49 \cdot 55 \cdot 43$

   D. $(55 + 49) + 43$

11. a. Use the Associative Property of Multiplication to write an expression equivalent to $4 \cdot (25 \cdot 16)$.

  b. Find the value of the expression $4 \cdot (25 \cdot 16)$.

  c. Explain how it is easier to use the new expression to find the value.

See your complete lesson at MyMathUniverse.com

12. Juan is planning to paint a room. He spends $33 on brushes, $80 on paint, and $20 on a drop cloth.

a. Use the Associative Property of Addition to write two equivalent expressions that show the total cost.

b. How can using the Associative Property of Addition make it easier to find the total cost?

    A. Grouping 33 and 20 makes finding the total easier because they are the least numbers in the expression.

    B. Grouping 80 and 20 makes finding the total easier because their sum is 100.

    C. Grouping 33 and 80 makes finding the total easier because they are the greatest numbers in the expression.

c. Find the total cost.

13. In a warehouse, there is a stack of 67 pallets. Each pallet holds 25 bags of gravel. A bag of gravel weighs 40 pounds.

a. Use the Associative Property of Multiplication to write two equivalent expressions that show the total weight of the gravel. Choose the correct answer below.

    A. $(67 \cdot 25) \cdot 40$ and $(67 \cdot 40) \cdot 25$

    B. $(67 \cdot 25) \cdot 40$ and $67 \cdot (40 \cdot 25)$

    C. $(67 \cdot 25) \cdot 40$ and $67 \cdot (25 \cdot 40)$

    D. $(67 \cdot 25) \cdot 40$ and $67 \cdot 25 \cdot 40$

b. Find the total weight of the gravel, in pounds.

14. Think About the Process On a 25-day road trip, a family drives at a constant speed of 51 miles per hour for 4 hours each day.

a. Which expression shows the number of miles the family drives?

    A. $(51 \cdot 4) \cdot 25$

    B. $(51 + 4) + 25$

    C. $(51 \cdot 4) + 25$

    D. $(51 + 4) \cdot 25$

b. How can you use the Associative Property of Multiplication to make it easier to find the number of miles the family drives?

    A. Regroup the factors to make the calculations easier. Group together two factors that have a product of 10 or 100.

    B. Regroup the factors to make the calculations easier. Group together two factors that have a sum of 10 or 100.

    C. Arrange the factors in a different order.

    D. Regroup the factors to use the Zero Property of Multiplication.

15. Think About the Process

a. What is the difference between the Associative Property of Multiplication and the Commutative Property of Multiplication?

    A. You can use the Associative Property of Multiplication to regroup the factors in an expression. You can use the Commutative Property of Multiplication to reorder the factors in an expression.

    B. You can use the Commutative Property of Multiplication to regroup the factors in an expression. You can use the Associative Property of Multiplication to reorder the factors in an expression.

    C. You can use the Associative Property of Multiplication with more than 2 factors. You cannot use the Commutative Property of Multiplication with more than 2 factors.

b. Which two expressions are equivalent by the Associative Property of Multiplication?

    A. $(56 \cdot 4) \cdot 25$ **B.** $56 \cdot (25 \cdot 4)$

    C. $(4 \cdot 56) \cdot 25$ **D.** $4 \cdot (56 \cdot 25)$

c. Which two expressions are equivalent by the Commutative Property of Multiplication?

    A. $56 \cdot (25 \cdot 4)$ **B.** $(56 \cdot 4) \cdot 25$

    C. $(4 \cdot 56) \cdot 25$ **D.** $4 \cdot (56 \cdot 25)$

CCSS: 6.NS.B.4

Vocabulary
common factor, composite number, factors, greatest common factor, prime factorization, prime number

Key Concept

What you know about factors can help you understand greatest common factors.

Factor A factor is a number that divides another number without a remainder.

The factors of 12 are: 1, 2, 3, 4, 6, 12
The factors of 42 are: 1, 2, 3, 6, 7, 14, 21, 42

Common Factor A common factor is a factor that two or more numbers share.

Factors of 12: 1, 2, 3, 4, 6, 12
Factors of 42: 1, 2, 3, 6, 7, 14, 21, 42

Common factors of 12 and 42: 1, 2, 3, 6

Greatest Common Factor The **greatest common factor** of two or more whole numbers is the greatest number that is a factor of all of the numbers. You can refer to the greatest common factor as the GCF.

Factors of 12: 1, 2, 3, 4, 6, 12
Factors of 42: 1, 2, 3, 6, 7, 14, 21, 42

Greatest common factor of 12 and 42: 6

Part 1

Example Finding Greatest Common Factors

What is the greatest common factor of 36 and 54?

Solution ·

Step 1 Write the factors of 36 and then write the factors of 54.

Factors of 36:

$$
\left.\begin{array}{l}
1 \cdot 36 = 36 \\
2 \cdot 18 = 36 \\
3 \cdot 12 = 36 \\
4 \cdot 9 \ = 36 \\
6 \cdot 6 \ = 36
\end{array}\right\}
$$

Ways to multiply 2 numbers together to equal 36

Arrange the factors from least to greatest: 1, 2, 3, 4, 6, 9, 12, 18, 36

Factors of 54:

$$
\left.\begin{array}{l}
1 \cdot 54 - 54 \\
2 \cdot 27 = 54 \\
3 \cdot 18 = 54 \\
6 \cdot 9 \ - 54
\end{array}\right\}
$$

Ways to multiply 2 numbers together to equal 54

Arrange the factors from least to greatest: 1, 2, 3, 6, 9, 18, 27, 54

Step 2 Find the common factors of 36 and 54.

1, 2, 3, 4, 6, 9, 12, 18, 36

1, 2, 3, 6, 9, 18, 27, 54

Step 3 Find the greatest common factor of 36 and 54.

1, 2, 3, 4, 6, 9, 12, 18, 36

1, 2, 3, 6, 9, 18, 27, 54

GCF

The greatest common factor of 36 and 54 is 18.

Part 2

Intro

Prime Number A prime number is a whole number greater than 1 with exactly two factors, 1 and the number itself.

The only factors of 2 are 1 and 2, so 2 is a prime number.
The only factors of 17 are 1 and 17, so 17 is a prime number.

1	**2**	**3**	4	**5**	6	**7**	8	9	10
11	12	**13**	14	15	16	**17**	18	**19**	20
21	22	**23**	24	25	26	27	28	**29**	30
31	32	33	34	35	36	**37**	38	39	40
41	42	**43**	44	45	46	**47**	48	49	50
51	52	**53**	54	55	56	57	58	**59**	60
61	62	63	64	65	66	**67**	68	69	70
71	72	**73**	74	75	76	77	78	**79**	80
81	82	**83**	84	85	86	87	88	**89**	90
91	92	**93**	94	95	96	**97**	98	99	100

Composite Number A composite number is a whole number greater than 1 with more than two factors.

9 is a composite number. It has 3 factors.

24 is a composite number. It has 8 factors.

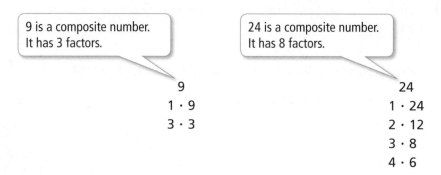

```
      9              24
    1 · 9          1 · 24
    3 · 3          2 · 12
                   3 · 8
                   4 · 6
```

Many other numbers are composite. For example, all even numbers greater than 2 are composite.

Prime Factorization The expression of a composite number as a product of prime factors. You can use a prime factorization tree to find the prime factorization of a number.

For example:
1. Write any 2 factors of 30.
2. If 1 of the numbers is prime, circle it.
3. Now draw 2 new branches with factors.
4. Circle any numbers that are prime.
5. Continue in this way until all of the branches end in a circled number.

The prime factorization of 30 is 2 · 3 · 5.

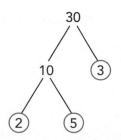

Part 2

Example Finding Prime Factorizations of Numbers

Find the prime factorization of 72. Use a factor tree.

Solution

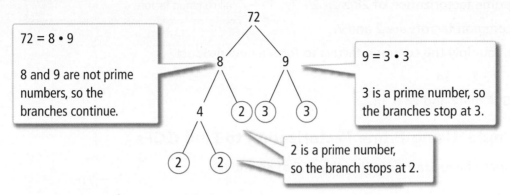

$72 = 8 \cdot 9$

8 and 9 are not prime numbers, so the branches continue.

$9 = 3 \cdot 3$

3 is a prime number, so the branches stop at 3.

2 is a prime number, so the branch stops at 2.

The prime factorization of 72 is the product of all of the prime numbers shown in the completed factor tree. The prime numbers are circled.

The prime factorization of 72 is $2 \cdot 2 \cdot 2 \cdot 3 \cdot 3$.

Check

$$2 \cdot 2 \cdot 2 \cdot 3 \cdot 3 = 72$$

The factors are all prime numbers.

The product of the factors is 72.

Part 3

Intro

You can use prime factorization to find the GCF of two or more numbers.

The prime factorization of 42 is ②· 3 · ⑦.

The prime factorization of 28 is ②· 2 · ⑦.

> To find the GCF of 42 and 28, identify all common factors.

The common factors are 2 and 7.

Then, multiply the common factors to form a new product.

$$2 \cdot 7 = 14$$

The GCF of 42 and 28 is 14.

Example Using Prime Factorization to Find GCFs

Use prime factorization to find the GCF of 84 and 63.

Solution

Step 1 Make a factor tree for each number.

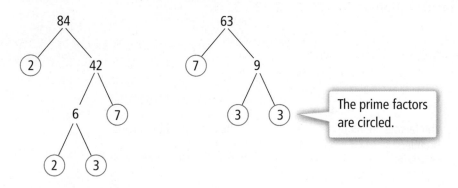

> The prime factors are circled.

Step 2 Write the prime factorization of each number and circle their common factors.

> 84 only has one 3 in its prime factorization.

$$84 = 2 \cdot 2 \cdot ③ \cdot ⑦$$

> 3 is circled only once in the prime factorization of 63.

$$63 = 3 \cdot ③ \cdot ⑦$$

Step 3 Multiply the common factors to form a new product.

$$3 \cdot 7 = 21$$

The GCF of 84 and 63 is 21.

1. Find the greatest common factor (GCF) of 20 and 45.

2. **a.** What are the factors of 8? Select all that apply.

   A. 4   **B.** 26
   C. 2   **D.** 1
   E. 8

   b. What are the factors of 26? Select all that apply.

   A. 2   **B.** 4
   C. 26   **D.** 1
   E. 13

   c. What is the GCF of 8 and 26?

3. **a.** Find the greatest common factor (GCF) of 50 and 12.

   Factors of 50:   1, 2, 5, 10, 25, 50
   Factors of 12:   1, 2, 3, 4, 6, 12

   A. 2   **B.** 12
   C. 1   **D.** 5

   b. For two numbers M and N, with $M < N$, can M be the GCF? Can N be the GCF? If yes, give an example. If no, explain.

4. **a.** Complete the factor tree.

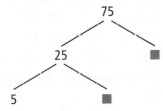

   b. What is the prime factorization of 75?

   A. $3 \cdot 5$ **B.** $3 \cdot 5 \cdot 5 \cdot 75$
   C. $3 \cdot 3 \cdot 5$ **D.** $3 \cdot 5 \cdot 5$

5. Complete the factor tree.

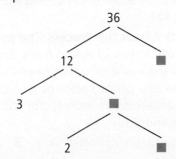

What is the prime factorization of 36?

   A. $2 \cdot 2 \cdot 3 \cdot 3$ **B.** $3 \cdot 3 \cdot 4$
   C. $2 \cdot 3 \cdot 12$ **D.** $3 \cdot 12$

6. **a.** Use a factor tree to find the prime factorization of 56. Draw your tree below.

   b. What is the prime factorization of 56?

   A. $2 \cdot 2 \cdot 2 \cdot 7$
   B. $2 \cdot 2 \cdot 7 \cdot 7$
   C. $2 \cdot 2 \cdot 2 \cdot 7 \cdot 56$
   D. $2 \cdot 7$

7. Use prime factorization to find the greatest common factor (GCF) of 78 and 27.

8. Use prime factorization to find the greatest common factor (GCF) of 54 and 90.

9. **String Lengths** You have two pieces of string. One is 27 cm long. The other is 45 cm long. You want to cut each piece of string into smaller pieces of equal length. Each length is to be a whole number of centimeters.

   a. What lengths are possible for pieces cut from the 27-cm piece of string? Select all that apply.

   A. 7 cm   **B.** 9 cm
   C. 2 cm   **D.** 5 cm
   E. 27 cm   **F.** 45 cm
   G. 3 cm   **H.** 1 cm

   b. What lengths are possible for pieces cut from the 45-cm piece of string? Select all that apply.

   A. 7 cm   **B.** 15 cm
   C. 27 cm   **D.** 5 cm
   E. 1 cm   **F.** 45 cm
   G. 9 cm   **H.** 3 cm

   c. What is the greatest common length?

10. **a.** Use a factor tree to find the prime factorization of 36.

   b. **Writing** Explain how you can use a factor tree to find the composite factors of 36.

11. Reasoning You are using a factor tree to write the prime factorization of 32. The factor tree below shows one pair of factors you can use.

a. Complete the factor tree.

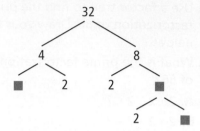

b. Find the prime factorization of 32.

  A. 1 · 32

  B. 2 · 2 · 2 · 4

  C. 2 · 4

  D. 2 · 2 · 2 · 2 · 2

c. Find another pair of factors you could use to begin the factor tree for 32. Compare the prime factorizations from both factor trees. What do you notice?

12. Think About the Process Two factors of 60 are 1 and 30.

a. Can you use 1 and 30 to start a factor tree for 60?

  A. No, because 1 is not a factor of 30.

  B. Yes, because 1 and 30 are the only factors of 60.

  C. No, because the product of 1 and 30 is not 60.

  D. Yes, because the product of 1 and 30 is 60.

b. Make a factor tree to find the prime factorization of 60. Choose the factors below.

  A. 2 · 30   **B.** 2 · 2 · 3 · 5

  C. 2 · 2 · 3 · 30 **D.** 2 · 2 · 3

13. Estimation You want to make bouquets of balloons. You choose 55 white and 20 red balloons. Every bouquet will have the same number of each color.

a. What is the greatest possible number of bouquets you can make using all the balloons?

b. Estimate how much you will earn if you sell each bouquet for $4.96.

14. a. Error Analysis Use the prime factorization of 56 and 84 to find the GCF.

b. Your friend says that the greatest common factor (GCF) of 56 and 84 is 14. Explain your friend's error.

15. Two groups of friends go to a movie. Each ticket costs the same amount. One group spends $26. The other group spends $91.

a. Select all possible ticket prices for the group that spends $26.

  A. $91   **B.** $26

  C. $1   **D.** $2

  E. $7   **F.** $13

b. Select all possible ticket prices for the group that spends $91.

  A. $26   **B.** $2

  C. $1   **D.** $7

  E. $91   **F.** $13

c. At most how much does each ticket cost?

d. At most how much does the group of 3 friends spend?

16. The prime factorization for a number N is 2 · 3 · 3 · 5. What is the greatest common factor (GCF) of this number and 42?

17. Think About the Process The prime factorizations of A and B are shown. Find the value of n that needs to be listed as a prime factor of B so that the greatest common factor (GCF) of A and B is 9.

Prime factorization of A: 3 · 3 · 3

Prime factorization of B: 2 · 2 · 3 · n

Vocabulary
Distributive Property

CCSS: 6.NS.B.4, 6.EE.A.3, Also 6.EE.A.4

Key Concept

Multiplying a number by a sum gives the same result as multiplying that number by each term in the sum and then adding the corresponding products.

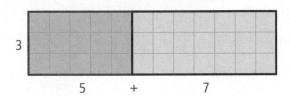

3(5 + 7)
3(12)
36

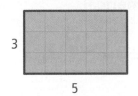

3(5) + 3(7)
15 + 21
36

Arithmetic Example: 3(5 + 7) = 3(5) + 3(7)

Algebra Example: $a(b + c) = ab + ac$ for any numbers, a, b, c

Multiplying a number by a difference gives the same result as multiplying that number by each term in the difference and then subtracting the corresponding products.

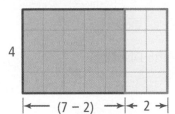   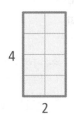

4(7 − 2)
4(5)
20

4(7) − 4(2)
28 − 8
20

Arithmetic Example: 4(7 − 2) = 4(7) − 4(2)

Algebra Example: $a(b − c) = ab − ac$ for any numbers a, b, c

Intro

You can use common factors to write equivalent expressions.

You can use the GCF of 50 and 15 to write an expression equivalent to 50 − 15. The GCF of 50 and 15 is 5.

Rewrite each number as the product of the GCF and another factor.

$$50 = 5(10) \qquad 15 = 5(3)$$

So, 50 − 15 is equivalent to 5(10) − 5(3).

Use the Distributive Property to write 5(10) − 5(3) as 5(10 − 3).

Example Using the Distributive Property for Numerical Expressions

Determine whether the two statements are equivalent by the Distributive Property.

a. 24 + 64 and 8(3 + 8)
b. 10 + 30 and 10(1) + 10(3)
c. 5(9) + 4(9) and 4(9) + 5(9)
d. 6(7 + 4) and 6(4 + 7)
e. 8(7) − 8(5) and 8(7 − 5)
f. 96 − 72 and 12(8 − 6)
g. 2(56) − 2(45) and 56(2) − 45(2)
h. 74 + 26 and 2(37 + 13)

Solution

a. Start with expression 24 + 64 and see if you can use the Distributive Property to write it as 8(3 + 8).

Step 1 Find the GCF and 24 and 64.

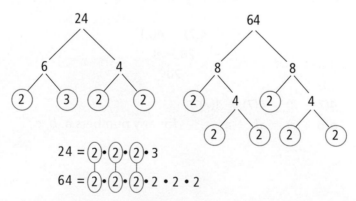

$$24 = 2 \cdot 2 \cdot 2 \cdot 3$$
$$64 = 2 \cdot 2 \cdot 2 \cdot 2 \cdot 2 \cdot 2$$

The GCF of 24 and 64 is 2 · 2 · 2, or 8.

continued on next page >

Part 1

Solution continued

Step 2 Rewrite 24 and 64 as the product of the GCF and another factor.

$$24 = 8(3) \qquad 64 = 8(8)$$

Step 3 Use the Distributive Property to find an expression equivalent to $24 + 64$.

$$24 + 64$$

Substitute the values found in Step 2. $\qquad 8(3) + 8(8)$

Use the Distributive Property. $\qquad 8(3 + 8)$

$8(3 + 8)$ is equivalent to $24 + 64$.

Similarly, the following expressions are equivalent by the Distributive Property:

b. $10 + 30$ and $10(1) + 10(3)$
e. $8(7) - 8(5)$ and $8(7 - 5)$
f. $96 - 72$ and $12(8 - 6)$
h. $74 + 26$ and $2(37 + 13)$

The following show equivalent expressions, but they are equivalent because of the Commutative Property.

c. $5(9) + 4(9)$ and $4(9) + 5(9)$
d. $6(7 + 4)$ and $6(4 + 7)$
g. $2(56) - 2(45)$ and $56(2) - 45(2)$

Part 2

Intro

You can also use the Distributive Property to find equivalent *algebraic* expressions.

Example Using the Distributive Property for Algebraic Expressions

Use the Distributive Property to match each expression to an equivalent expression.

$9(3y - 2)$	$18x + 27y$	$x(5 + 5 + 5)$	$5(2x + 5y)$
$20x - 4y$	$20x + 4y$	$4x + 20$	$x + 5$

a. $4(x + 5)$ $\qquad$ **b.** $27y - 18$ $\qquad$ **c.** $9(2x + 3y)$
d. $4(5x - y)$ $\qquad$ **e.** $5x + 5x + 5x$ $\qquad$ **f.** $10x + 25y$

continued on next page >

Part 2

Example continued

Solution ·

Method 1 Use the Distributive Property to rewrite $4(x + 5)$.

Distribute the 4 to each term inside the parentheses.	$4(x + 5)$ $4(x) + 4(5)$
Multiply.	$4x + 20$

An expression equivalent to $4(x + 5)$ is $4x + 20$.

Method 2 Use the GCF of $27y$ and 18 to write an expression equivalent to $27y - 18$.

The GCF of $27y$ and 18 is 9. Rewrite each number as the product of the GCF and another factor.

$$27y = 9(3y) \qquad\qquad 18 = 9(2)$$

So $27y - 18$ is equivalent to $9(3y) - 9(2)$.

Use the Distributive Property to write $9(3y) - 9(2)$ as $9(3y - 2)$.

You can use Method 1 and Method 2 to find the remaining equivalent expressions.

c. $9(2x + 3y)$ and $18x + 27y$ **d.** $4(5x - y)$ and $20x - 4y$

e. $5x + 5x + 5x$ and $x(5 + 5 + 5)$ **f.** $10x + 25y$ and $5(2x + 5y)$

Part 3

Example **Writing Equivalent Expressions Using the Distributive Property**

A family makes a budget for a camping trip to Spring Lake. Their budget per day is a $16 park fee and $45 for groceries.

Write two equivalent expressions that show the cost for camping and groceries for d days.

continued on next page >

Solution

Method 1 The park fee is $16 per day. So the expression $16d$ represents the park fee for d days.

Groceries cost $45 per day. The expression $45d$ represents the cost of groceries for d days.

The sum $16d + 45d$ represents the total cost for d days.

Method 2 Each day, the family will spend $16 for the park fee and $45 for groceries. The sum $16 + 45$ represents the cost each day.

If the family camps for d days, $d(16 + 45)$ represents the total cost for d days.

The equivalent expressions $16d + 45d$ and $d(16 + 45)$ each represent the total cost for d days of camping.

1. Select two expressions that are equivalent by the Distributive Property.

   A. $7(4 - 2)$

   B. $7(4) - 2$

   C. $(7 - 4)(7 - 2)$

   D. $7(4) - 7(2)$

2. Which expression is equivalent to $9(8 + 6)$ by the Distributive Property?

   A. $9(8) + 6$

   B. $9(14)$

   C. $(9 + 8)(9 + 6)$

   D. $9(8) + 9(6)$

3. Select two expressions that are equivalent by the Distributive Property.

   A. $3(7n + 2)$ **B.** $21n + 6$

   C. $21n + 2$ **D.** $3n + 3$

4. Which two expressions are equivalent by the Distributive Property?

   A. $(15 + 35) \div 5$

   B. $5(3) + 5(7)$

   C. $5(3 + 7)$

   D. $5(35 + 15)$

   E. $5(15 - 5) + 5(35 - 5)$

5. Which expression is equivalent to $5y + 2y$ by the Distributive Property?

   A. $52y$ **B.** $y(5 + 2)$

   C. $7y^2$ **D.** $(5 + 2) + (y + y)$

6. Use the Distributive Property to write an expression that is equivalent to $2(y + z)$.

7. Your friend does 25 push-ups and 60 sit-ups each night. For n nights, the expression $n(25 + 60)$ represents the total number of push-ups and sit-ups. Use the Distributive Property to write an equivalent expression that also shows the total number of push-ups and sit-ups for n nights.

8. You and a friend go shopping at a store where each item costs w dollars. You buy 7 items. Your friend buys 6 items. Use the Distributive Property to write equivalent expressions for the cost of your combined purchases.

9. **a. Writing** Use the Distributive Property to write an expression equivalent to $3(p^2 + 4y + 10)$.

   b. Tell how you would explain to another student what it means to distribute the 3 to each term inside the parentheses.

10. **a. Reasoning** Use the Distributive Property to write an expression equivalent to $4(u + 12)$.

    b. Write the algebraic expression $4(u + 12)$ in words.

    c. Write the equivalent expression in words. Describe the similarities and the differences in the two statements.

11. **a. Open-Ended** Which expression is equivalent to $30y + 24y$ by the Distributive Property?

    A. $3(10y + 8y)$

    B. $54 + y$

    C. $y(30 + 24y)$

    D. $30(y + 24)$

    b. Use the Distributive Property and different common factors to write two more expressions equivalent to $30y + 24y$.

12. **Shopping** The spring sale at a local store advertises one price for all items in a particular department. You buy 4 T-shirts and d pairs of shorts for 10 dollars each. An expression for the total cost of your purchases is $10(4 + d)$. Use the Distributive Property to write an expression equivalent to $10(4 + d)$.

13. Use the Distributive Property to write an expression equivalent to $7(q^2 + 5m + 10)$.

14. Error Analysis A sports team with 14 members is planning an end-of-season awards banquet. It costs $5 for each meal. To find the total cost of the meals, the team uses the expression $5(g + 14)$, where g is the number of guests attending the banquet. One team member incorrectly claims that the expression is equivalent to $5g + 14$.

a. Use the Distributive Property to write an expression equivalent to $5(g + 14)$.

b. What was the likely error?

A. The team member added the 5 to 14.

B. The team member added the 5 to each term in the parentheses.

C. The team member did not distribute the 5 to each term in the parentheses.

D. The team member multiplied the terms in the parentheses.

15. A family is going on vacation for 4 days. A rental car costs $66 per day and a hotel room costs v dollars per day. The total cost of the car and hotel room is the number of days multiplied by the sum of the daily cost of the rental car and the daily cost of the hotel room.

a. Which expression represents the total cost of the car and hotel room?

A. $v(4 + 66)$

B. $66(4 + v)$

C. $4(66 + v)$

D. $4 + (66 + v)$

b. Which expression below is equivalent to the expression for the total cost by the Distributive Property?

A. $264 + v$ **B.** $264 + 4v$

C. $4(v + 66)$ **D.** $66 + 4v$

16. Think About the Process

a. What is the first step to use the Distributive Property to write an expression equivalent to $6(14) - 6(4)$ in the form $a(b - c)$?

A. Find the value of the expression.

B. Multiply each term before subtracting.

C. Find a common factor in each term of the expression.

D. Change the order of the factors.

b. Which expression is equivalent to $6(14) - 6(4)$ by the Distributive Property?

A. $14(6) - 4(6)$ **B.** $6(4) - 6(14)$

C. $84 - 24$ **D.** $14(6 - 4)$

E. $4(14 - 6)$ **F.** $6(14 - 4)$

17. Think About the Process The Drama Club sold tickets to the school play. Adult tickets were $12 each. Student tickets were $6 each.

a. Write expressions for the cost of 41 adult tickets and the cost of 83 student tickets.

b. Write an expression that represents the total ticket sales. Choose the correct answer below.

A. $83(6 + 12)$

B. $41(12) + 83(6)$

C. $41(12 + 6)$

D. $41(6) + 83(12)$

c. Can you use the Distributive Property to write an equivalent expression for total ticket sales?

A. Yes, the terms of the expression $41(12) + 83(6)$ have a common factor, 12.

B. No, the terms of the expression $41(12) + 83(6)$ have different factorizations.

C. No, the terms of the expression $41(12) + 83(6)$ do not have any common factors.

D. Yes, the terms of the expression $41(12) + 83(6)$ have a common factor, 6.

Vocabulary
least common multiple, common multiple, multiple

CCSS: 6.NS.B.4

Key Concept

Multiple A **multiple** of a number is the product of the number and a whole number greater than zero.

To list the multiples of 2, find
$2 \cdot 1 = 2$
$2 \cdot 2 = 4$
$2 \cdot 3 = 6$
… etc.
Multiples of 2: 2, 4, 6, 8, 10, 12, 14, 16, 18, 20, …

To list the multiples of 5, find
$5 \cdot 1 = 5$
$5 \cdot 2 = 10$
$5 \cdot 3 = 15$
… etc.
Multiples of 5: 5, 10, 15, 20, 25, 30, …

Common Multiple A **common multiple** is a multiple that two or more numbers share.

The numbers 2 and 5 have many common multiples.

The first two are 10 and 20:

Multiples of 2: 2, 4, 6, 8, (10,) 12, 14, 16, 18, (20,) …

Multiples of 5: 5, (10,) 15, (20,) 25, 30, …

Least Common Multiple The **least common multiple (LCM)** of two or more numbers is the least multiple shared by all of the numbers.

The least common multiple of 2 and 5 is 10:

Multiples of 2: 2, 4, 6, 8, (10,) 12, 14, 16, 18, 20, …

Multiples of 5: 5, (10,) 15, 20, 25, 30, …

Part 1

Example Finding Least Common Multiples

List the first five multiples of 3 and 4. Then find the least common multiple.

Solution ....

Find the multiples of 3 by multiplying 3 times 1, 3 times 2, and so on.

Find the multiples of 4 by multiplying 4 times 1, 4 times 2, and so on.

3×1 3×2

Multiples of 3: 3, 6, 9, ⑫, 15, …

Multiples of 4: 4, 8, ⑫, 16, 20, …

4×1 4×2

The first multiple to appear in both lists is 12. The least common multiple of 3 and 4 is 12.

Part 2

Intro

You can use prime factorization to find the least common multiple of two or more numbers.

Prime factorization of 6: $2 \cdot 3$ Prime factorization of 9: $3 \cdot 3$

$= 2^1 \cdot 3^1$ $= 3^1 \cdot 3^1$

$= 3^2$

> Use what you know about exponents to rewrite the prime factorizations.

Use the greatest power of each factor to make a new product.

The greatest power of 2 is 2^1, or simply 2.   The greatest power of 3 is 3^2.

The LCM is $2 \cdot 3^2$, or 18. The least common multiple of 6 and 9 is 18.

Example Using Prime Factorization to Find LCMs

Use prime factorization to find the LCM of 8 and 12.

continued on next page >

Part 2

Example continued

Solution ·

Step 1 Find the prime factorizations of 8 and 12.

Prime factorization of 8 : 2 · 2 · 2, or (2³)

Prime factorization of 12 : 2 · 2 · 3, or 2² · (3)

Step 2 Circle the greatest power of each factor.

Step 3 Use the circled factors to write a new product.

LCM: 2³ · 3, or 24

The least common multiple of 8 and 12 is 24.

Part 3

Example Using LCMs to Solve Problems

A movie theater is celebrating its 10th anniversary by giving popcorn to every 10th movie-goer today. The owner's daughter is turning 14 today, so the theater is also giving a pretzel to every 14th movie-goer.

Find which movie-goer is the first to win both prizes.

Solution ·

The first movie-goer to win both prizes is the person whose position in the line is the LCM of 10 and 14.

Method 1 Find the LCM by listing multiples.

Multiples of 10: 10, 20, 30, 40, 50, 60, (70), …
Multiples of 14: 14, 28, 42, 56, (70), …

The least common multiple of 10 and 14 is 70.

Method 2 Use prime factorization to find the LCM.

Step 1 Find the prime factorizations of 10 and 14.

Prime factorization of 10: (2) · (5)

Prime factorization of 14: 2 · (7)

Step 2 Circle the greatest power of each factor.

Step 3 Use the circled factors to write a new product.

LCM: 2 · 5 · 7, or 70.

Both methods find that the least common multiple of 10 and 14 is 70. So the 70th person in line is the first to win both popcorn and a pretzel.

1. a. Find the first five multiples of 10.

$10 \cdot 1 = \blacksquare$

$10 \cdot 2 = \blacksquare$

$10 \cdot 3 = \blacksquare$

$10 \cdot 4 = \blacksquare$

$10 \cdot 5 = \blacksquare$

b. Find the first five multiples of 8.

$8 \cdot 1 = \blacksquare$

$8 \cdot 2 = \blacksquare$

$8 \cdot 3 = \blacksquare$

$8 \cdot 4 = \blacksquare$

$8 \cdot 5 = \blacksquare$

c. The LCM of 10 and 8 is $\blacksquare$.

2. a. Find the prime factorizations of 10 and 14.

b. Use the prime factorizations to find the least common multiple (LCM) of 10 and 14.

3. Find the least common multiple (LCM) of 4 and 26.

4. Last summer, Karl went to the beach every 5 days. Antonia went to the beach every 7 days. How often did they see each other at the beach?

5. The two discs in the figure rotate at different speeds. The smaller disc rotates once every 10 minutes. The larger disc takes 15 minutes to rotate. If they both start rotating at the same time, how long until the two arrows align again?

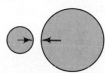

6. Write the first ten multiples of 6 and 21. Find the least common multiple (LCM) of 6 and 21.

Find the first ten multiples of 6.

6	6	6	6	6
×1	×2	×3	×4	×5
6	12	■	24	■

6	6	6	6	6
×6	×7	×8	×9	×10
36	■	48	■	60

Find the first ten multiples of 21.

21	21	21	21	21
×1	×2	×3	×4	×5
21	■	63	■	105

21	21	21	21	21
×6	×7	×8	×9	×10
■	147	■	189	210

The LCM of 6 and 21 is $\blacksquare$.

7. Estimation

a. What is the least possible value for the LCM of any two numbers?

A. the sum of the two numbers

B. the lesser of the two numbers

C. the product of the two numbers

D. the greater of the two numbers

b. What is the greatest possible value of the LCM of any two numbers?

A. the sum of the two numbers

B. the product of the two numbers

C. the lesser of the two numbers

D. the greater of the two numbers

c. Find the LCM of 10 and 15.

8. a. Writing Make factor trees for 125 and 50.

Factor 125:

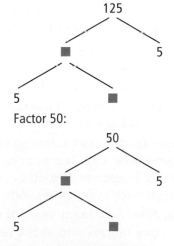

Factor 50:

b. The LCM of 125 and 50 is $\blacksquare$.

c. Explain how you used the factor trees to find the LCM.

9. **Winning Numbers** A group of people are waiting in line for a theater premier. Every 10th person in line will receive a free theater ticket. Every 15th person will receive a gift card for $40.

   a. Which person is the first to win both prizes?

   b. If there are 200 people in line, how many people will receive both prizes?

10. Use the prime factorizations to find the least common multiple (LCM) of the two numbers A and B.

    Prime factorization of $A = 2 \cdot 3 \cdot 3$
    Prime factorization of $B = 3 \cdot 3 \cdot 3$

    a. The LCM of A and B is ■.

    b. What are A and B?

11. **Think About the Process** Write the prime factorizations of 15 and 105. Use these factorizations to find the least common multiple (LCM).

    a. The prime factorization of 15 is ■.
    The prime factorization of 105 is ■.
    The LCM of 15 and 105 is ■.

    b. What do you notice about the factors of the LCM and the original factorizations?

       A. The factors of the LCM and the factors of 105 are the same.

       B. The factors of the LCM, 15, and 105 are all different.

       C. The factors of the LCM and the factors of 15 are the same.

       D. The factors of the LCM, 15, and 105 are all the same.

12. Two faucets start dripping at the same time. One faucet drips once every 6 seconds. The other faucet drips once every 14 seconds.

    a. After how many seconds do the two faucets drip at the same time?

    b. In 8 minutes (480 seconds), how many times do the faucets drip at the same time?

13. Two machines package items for shipping. One makes packages of 19 items. The other makes packages of 11 items. Suppose both machines start making a new package at the same time. It takes one second for each machine to pack one item. How many items does each machine pack before they again start making new packages at the same time?

14. **Think About the Process** To celebrate its grand opening, a store is giving a $10 gift certificate to every 55th customer. To celebrate the owner's birthday, the store is also giving a $50 gift certificate to every 91st customer.

    a. Which customer is the first to get two gift certificates?

    b. What do you notice about the factors of 55 and 91?

       A. The numbers 55 and 91 have the same factors.

       B. The number 91 is a multiple of the number 55.

       C. The numbers 55 and 91 have no common factors.

       D. The numbers 55 and 91 have only one common factor.

15. **Challenge** Two volunteer groups plant trees. Group A plants the trees in clusters of 3. Group B plants the trees in clusters of 10. Both groups plant the same number of trees. What is the least number of clusters that Group B plants?

CCSS: 6.NS.B.4, 6.EE.A.3

Part 1

Intro

The Think/Write graphic organizer is a tool that can help you make sense of problems.

It can be used to help simplify the expression $(7 \cdot 4) \cdot 5$.

Think

To simplify the expression $(7 \cdot 4) \cdot 5$, you have to multiply $28 \cdot 5$. Use the Associative Property to write an equivalent expression that is easier to compute.

Now you can quickly compute $7 \cdot 20$ in your head. Multiply $7 \cdot 2$ and add a zero to the end.

Write

$7 \cdot (4 \cdot 5)$

$7 \cdot 20 = 140$

The expression $(7 \cdot 4) \cdot 5$ can be simplified to 140.

Example Adding Costs Using the Associative Property of Addition

You are shopping for a camping trip to Spring Lake. You plan to buy a $55 sleeping bag, a $25 backpack, a $45 stove, and a $75 tent. Is the $240 you have in cash enough for the four items in your cart?

$55 $25 $45 $75

continued on next page >

Part 1

Example continued

Solution ·

Think	**Write**
The items in the shopping cart are a $55 sleeping bag, a $25 backpack, a $45 stove, and a $75 tent. Add the prices to find the total cost.	$55 + $25 + $45 + $75
Notice that $25 + $75 is $100. Use the Commutative Property to rearrange the numbers.	$55 + $45 + $25 + $75
Now, use the Associative Property to group the first pair of numbers and the second pair of numbers.	($55 + $45) + ($25 + $75)
Those sums are easier to do in your head!	$100 + $100 = $200
Do you have enough cash?	$200 is less than $240, so you have enough cash.

Part 2

Example Using GCFs to Solve Problems

The dimensions of a rectangular community garden are shown. The gardeners plan to divide the garden into equal-sized square plots. What is the greatest possible length of each square plot?

98 ft.

56 ft.

Solution ·

The garden has dimensions 98 ft by 56 ft. The garden must be divided into equal-sized square plots. So the greatest possible side length of each square plot is the GCF of 98 and 56.

continued on next page >

Part 2

Solution continued

Step 1 Make a factor tree for each number.

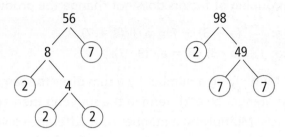

Step 2 Write the prime factorization of each number and circle their common factors.

$$56 = ②\cdot 2 \cdot 2 \cdot ⑦$$

$$98 = ②\cdot⑦\cdot 7$$

Step 3 Multiply the common factors to form a new product.

$$2 \cdot 7 = 14$$

The GCF of 98 and 56 is 14. So the greatest possible side length of each square plot is 14 ft.

Key Concept

Identity Property of Addition Adding 0 does not change the value of a number.

For any number a: $a + 0 = a$

Identity Property of Multiplication Multiplying by 1 does not change the value of a number.

For any number a: $a \cdot 1 = a$

Zero Property of Multiplication Multiplying a number by 0 results in a product of 0.

For any number a: $a \cdot 0 = 0$

Commutative Property Changing the order of addends does not change the sum. Changing the order of factors does not change the product.

For any number a: $a + 3 = 3 + a$
For any number a: $a \cdot 3 = 3 \cdot a$

continued on next page >

Key Concept

continued

Associative Property Changing the grouping of addends does not change the sum. Changing the grouping of factors does not change the product.

For any number a: $(a + 3) + 7 = a + (3 + 7)$
For any number a: $(a \cdot 3) \cdot 7 = a \cdot (3 \cdot 7)$

Distributive Property Multiplying a number by a sum gives the same result as multiplying that number by each term in the sum and then adding the corresponding products. Multiplying a number by a difference gives the same result as multiplying that number by each term in the difference and then subtracting the corresponding products.

For any number a: $3(a + 7) = 3a + 21$
For any number a: $3(a - 7) = 3a - 21$

Part 3

Example Identifying Errors in Applications of the Distributive Property

Describe and correct the error in reasoning.

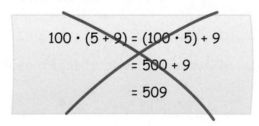

$$100 \cdot (5 + 9) = (100 \cdot 5) + 9$$
$$= 500 + 9$$
$$= 509$$

Solution

The Distributive Property is applied incorrectly in the first step.

To correctly distribute the 100 over addition, multiply both numbers inside the parentheses by 100.

Use the Distributive Property.	$100 \cdot (5 + 9) = (100 \cdot 5) + (100 \cdot 9)$
Multiply the expressions in parentheses.	$= 500 + 900$
Simplify.	$= 1400$

1. Each month, Ms. Chen spends $64 for dog food. She also spends $36 for cat food and $45 for bird seed. An expression for the total cost of pet food is 64 + (36 + 45). How much does Ms. Chen spend each month on pet food? (Hint: Use a property of operations to write an equivalent expression that is easier to evaluate.)

2. Midas has 18 silver coins and 12 gold coins. He wants to stack each kind of coin so that all the stacks have the same number of coins. What is the greatest possible number of coins that he can place in each stack?

3. **a.** Identify the property of operations you could use to write an expression equivalent to (0 · 3) + 5.

   b. Use that property to evaluate the expression (0 · 3) + 5.

4. An auditorium has 2 levels with 7 sections in each level. Each section has 5 rows with 9 seats in each row. To find the total number of seats in the auditorium, use the expression (2 · 7) · (5 · 9).

   a. Using properties of operations, which expression is easiest to evaluate?

   A. (9 · 5) · (7 · 2)

   B. (2 · 7) · (9 · 5)

   C. (2 · 5) · (7 · 9)

   D. (2 · 9) · (5 · 7)

   b. How many seats does the auditorium have?

5. In a calculating contest, one contestant sees the expression 4 · 5 · 0 · 16 · 40 · 22 and immediately evaluates it correctly. What is the value of the expression?

6. At a paint store, a customer buys 2 cans of red paint and 8 cans of green paint. Both colors cost $4 per can. An expression for the total cost is (4 · 2) + (4 · 8). What is the total cost? (Hint: Use a property of operations to write an equivalent expression that is easier to evaluate.)

7. Students in an art class cut colored paper into equal-sized squares. The paper measures 15 cm by 75 cm and they do not want to waste any of it. What is the greatest possible side length for each square piece?

8. **a.** Identify the properties of operations you could use to write an expression equivalent to 4 · 313 · 25.

   b. Use those properties to evaluate the expression.

9. A class must use properties of operations to write an expression equivalent to 100(7 + 3). One student incorrectly writes that the expression is equivalent to 100 · 7 + 3.

   a. Which property of operations could you use to write an expression equivalent to 100(7 + 3)?

   A. Associative Property of Multiplication

   B. Identity Property of Multiplication

   C. Distributive Property

   b. Which expression is equivalent to 100(7 + 3)?

   A. 7 · 100 + 7 · 3

   B. 100 · 7 + 100 · 3

   C. 100 + 7 · 3

   D. (7) (100 + 3)

   c. What was the student's error?

   A. The student added the 100 to each term in the parentheses.

   B. The student did not multiply both numbers inside the parentheses by 100.

   C. The student multiplied the terms in the parentheses.

   D. The student added the terms in the parentheses.

See your complete lesson at MyMathUniverse.com

10. The dimensions of a rectangular community garden are 63 ft by 45 ft. The gardeners plan to divide the garden into equal-sized square plots.

   a. What is the greatest possible side length of each square plot?

   b. How many square plots will there be with this side length?

   c. What will be the total area of the square plots?

   d. Explain how you can use the total area to check your work.

11. **Think About the Process** There are 18 boys and 60 girls working on a community service project. They work in groups where each group has the same number of boys and the same number of girls.

   a. What is the first step to finding the greatest number of groups possible?

     A. Divide 60 by 18.

     B. Subtract 18 from 60.

     C. Multiply 18 times 60.

     D. Find the factors of 18 and 60.

   b. What is the greatest number of groups possible?

12. **Think About the Process**

   a. How does the Distributive Property help you find an expression equivalent to $11(7 + 0)$?

     A. The property allows you to change the order of the addends in the expression.

     B. The property allows you to remove the parentheses from the expression.

     C. The property allows you to add the terms in parentheses.

   b. Which other property of operations could you use to find an equivalent expression?

     A. The Identity Property of Addition

     B. The Associative Property of Addition

     C. The Identity Property of Multiplication

     D. The Associative Property of Multiplication

   c. Evaluate the expression. Explain which property of operations you used and why.

13. **Challenge** You put 45 green marbles and 27 yellow marbles into bags. Each bag has the same number of green marbles and the same number of yellow marbles.

   a. What is the greatest possible number of bags you can make using all the marbles?

   b. How many green marbles are in each bag? How many yellow marbles?

   c. What is the least possible number of bags you can make using all the marbles? What other numbers of bags are possible so all the bags have the same number of green marbles and the same number of yellow marbles?

14. a. **Challenge** Identify the properties of operations you could use to write an expression equivalent to $10(m + g + p) + (6 \cdot 1) \cdot 3$.

   b. Which expression is equivalent to $10(m + g + p) + (6 \cdot 1) \cdot 3$?

     A. $m + g + p + 18$

     B. $10m + 10g + 10p + 18$

     C. $10m + 10g + 10p + 6$

     D. $10m + g + p + 18$

Expressions to Equations

Vocabulary
equation, false
equation, open
sentence, solution
of an equation,
true equation

CCSS: 6.EE.A.2, 6.EE.B.5

Part 1

Intro

An **equation** is a mathematical sentence that includes an equal sign to compare two expressions.

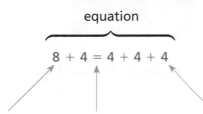

equation

$$8 + 4 = 4 + 4 + 4$$

This expression has the same value as this expression.

Example Distinguishing Between Expressions and Equations

Which are expressions? Which are equations? Classify each.

$56 + 8$	$27 = 3(9)$	$1000 \div 100p$	$11 \cdot 2 = 22$	$3 = 2z$
$27 - 17 = 5x$	$13a - 1$	$4(20) = 5(16)$	$750 \div 50x = 100$	$32z$

Solution

Expressions	**Equations**
$13a - 1$	$750 \div 50x = 100$
$32z$	$4(20) = 5(16)$
$56 + 8$	$3 = 2z$
$1000 \div 100p$	$27 = 3(9)$
	$11 \cdot 2 = 22$
	$27 - 17 = 5x$

An expression does not include an equal sign.

An equation includes an equal sign to show equal values.

Intro

One five-dollar bill is *equivalent* to five one-dollar bills.

Five one-dollar bills are *not* equivalent to five quarters.

Twelve eggs are *equivalent* to one dozen eggs.

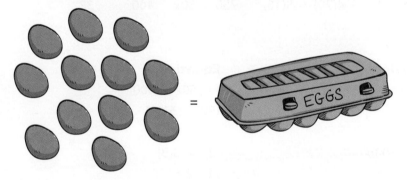

continued on next page >

Part 2

Intro continued

One dozen eggs is *not* equivalent to one egg.

Equivalent expressions always have the same value.

equivalent	**not equivalent**
2(12) and 20 + 4	2(12) and 2 + 12
5*w* and 2*w* + 3*w*	5*w* and 5 + *w*

Example Writing Equivalent Expressions

Write pairs of equivalent expressions.

$$3 \cdot 10 \qquad 5(3w) \qquad 25w - 15w \qquad 2(15)$$
$$20 - 10 \qquad 10w \qquad 15w$$

Solution ···

30×10 and 2(15) both simplify to 30, so 3×10 and 2(15) are equal.

30×10 ······························· 2(15)

Simplify. 30 ······························· **Simplify.** 30

5(3*w*) simplifies to 15*w*, so 5(3*w*) and 15*w* are equivalent.

$$5(3w)$$

Use the Associative Property. $(5 \times 3)w$

Simplify. $15w$

25*w* − 15*w* simplifies to 10*w*, so 25*w* − 15*w* and 10*w* are equivalent.

$$25w - 15w$$

Use the Distributive Property. $w(25 - 15)$

Simplify. $w(10)$

Use the Commutative Property. $10w$

Key Concept

There are different types of equations.

A **true equation** has equivalent expressions on each side of the equals sign.

A **false equation** has expressions that are *not* equivalent on each side of the equals sign.

An **open sentence** is an equation that includes one or more variables.

A **solution of an equation** is a value of the variable that makes the equation true.

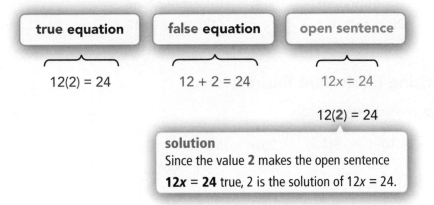

true equation	false equation	open sentence
$12(2) = 24$	$12 + 2 = 24$	$12x = 24$

$$12(\mathbf{2}) = 24$$

solution
Since the value **2** makes the open sentence **12x = 24** true, 2 is the solution of $12x = 24$.

Part 3

Example Checking Solutions of Equations

The path to the lake has been rigged with paintballs! If you step on the wrong flagstone, a paintball covers you in yellow paint. So far, three people in your group have yellow on their clothes. Can you find the correct path?

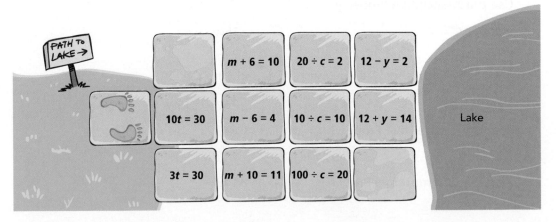

PATH TO LAKE →

		$m + 6 = 10$	$20 \div c = 2$	$12 - y = 2$	
$10t = 30$	$m - 6 = 4$	$10 \div c = 10$	$12 + y = 14$	Lake
$3t = 30$	$m + 10 = 11$	$100 \div c = 20$		

The equations with a solution of 10 mark the correct path. Which flagstones are safe?

continued on next page >

Part 3

Example continued

Solution

Check to see if 10 makes each equation true.

$m + 6 = 10$

$10 + 6 \overset{?}{=} 10$

$16 \neq 10$ ✗

$20 \div c = 2$

$20 \div 10 \overset{?}{=} 2$

$2 = 2$ ✓

$12 - y = 2$

$12 - 10 \overset{?}{=} 2$

$2 = 2$ ✓

$10t = 30$

$10(10) \overset{?}{=} 30$

$100 \neq 30$ ✗

$m - 6 = 4$

$10 - 6 \overset{?}{=} 4$

$4 = 4$ ✓

$10 \div c = 10$

$10 \div 10 \overset{?}{=} 10$

$1 \neq 10$ ✗

$12 + y = 14$

$12 + 10 \overset{?}{=} 14$

$22 \neq 14$ ✗

$3t = 30$

$3(10) \overset{?}{=} 30$

$30 = 30$ ✓

$m + 10 = 11$

$10 + 10 \overset{?}{=} 11$

$20 \neq 11$ ✗

$100 \div c = 20$

$100 \div 10 \overset{?}{=} 20$

$10 \neq 20$ ✗

You can safely step on the flagstones that have true equations.

1. Identify $g - h = 8$ as an expression or an equation.

2. Is $5x + 2(x - 4) = 6$ an expression or an equation?

3. Is $81 - 9 = 72$ true, false, or an open sentence?

4. Which expression is equivalent to $11c - 4c$?

 A. $5c + 2c$ **B.** $3c + 7c$

5. Use the distributive property to rewrite the expression $3(x + 8)$ without parentheses.

6. Circle the number that is a solution of $19 - q = 12$.

 8, 7, 4, 6, or 2

7. Which number is a solution to $x + 29 = 1 + 5x$?

 A. 8   **B.** 9

 C. 3   **D.** 7

 E. 6

8. Which equations have 6 as a solution? Select all that apply.

 A. $8b = 48$ **B.** $11 - b = 6$

 C. $b + 3 = 9$ **D.** $54 \div b = 9$

9. **Open-Ended** Think about the last time you went to your favorite store.

 a. Describe the items you bought, the cost of each, and how much you spent in all.

 b. Write an *expression* to represent your purchases.

 c. Write an *equation* using this expression and how much you spent in all.

 d. What is the difference between the expression and the equation you wrote?

  A. The equation includes and equals sign. The expression does not.

  B. The equation uses different variables than the expression.

  C. The expression uses more operations than the equation.

  D. The expression has more terms than the equation.

10. **Think About the Process** There are many expressions equivalent to $8(d + 7) - 6d$. Complete the following steps using the properties shown to find a particular equivalent expression. What is this equivalent expression?

 $8(d + 7) - 6d$
 $= \blacksquare$ Distributive Property
 $= \blacksquare$ Commutative Property of Addition
 $= \blacksquare$ Distributive Property
 $= \blacksquare$ Definition of Subtraction

11. **Reasoning** Name the properties of operations used in each step to show that the expressions $6 + 5(x + 9)$ and $5x + 51$ are equivalent.

 $6 + 5(x + 9)$ $\blacksquare$
 $= 6 + (5x + 45)$ $\blacksquare$
 $= 6 + (45 + 5x)$ $\blacksquare$
 $= (6 + 45) + 5x$ $\blacksquare$
 $= 51 + 5x$ Definition of Addition
 $= 5x + 51$ $\blacksquare$

12. **Error Analysis** A student was asked to use the Distributive Property to find an expression equivalent to $8(w - 4)$. The student got the expression $4w$. These expressions are not equivalent.

 a. What is the correct equivalent expression?

 b. Which sentence best describes what the student did wrong?

  A. The student did not apply the Distributive Property correctly.

  B. The student applied the Associative Property instead of the Distributive Property.

  C. The student added to simplify the expression. The student should have subtracted.

  D. The student subtracted to simplify the expression. The student should have added.

13. Writing Your teacher solved the equation $4x + 1 = 22 + x$. Unfortunately, due to messy handwriting, you are not sure if the solution is 2, 7, or 8.

   a. Describe how you can find the solution without solving the equation again.

   b. Use this to find the solution.

14. Entertainment A group of 4 friends is planning a fun day trip. To raft down a river costs $6 per person plus $5 for transportation of the raft. An amusement park costs $14 per person. A hot air balloon ride costs $30 per person, but they have a $40 group discount coupon.

Activity	Cost ($)
Raft Trip	$6n + 5 = 29$
Amusement Park	$14n = 29$
Balloon Ride	$30n - 40 = 29$

The table shows equations for the total cost of each activity for n people. Which activity should they choose if they want to spend exactly $29?

15. Is $15x + 10 = 13$ true, false, or an open sentence?

16. Select the number that is a solution to $4x + 7 = 43 - 2x$.

   3, 2, 8, 6, or 5

17. Think About the Process Write three different equations that have 1 as a solution. Use x as the variable. Use substitution to show that your equations are true when x is 1. What is the simplest possible equation that has 1 as a solution?

18. Challenge A rectangular lot has a fence around it. The longer side of the lot is 7 feet more than 4 times the length of the shorter side. Let the shorter side be w feet. Aimee and Jorge write expressions for the total amount of fencing. Aimee says there are $2(4w + 7) + 2w$ feet of fencing. Jorge says there are $2[(4w + 7) + w]$ feet. The correct amount of fencing is $10w + 14$. Are Aimee's and Jorge's expressions correct?

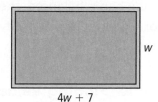

$$4w + 7$$

   A. Both expressions are correct.

   B. Only Aimee's expression is correct.

   C. Neither expression is correct.

   D. Only Jorge's expression is correct.

19. Challenge Which equations have 7 as a solution? Select all that apply.

   A. $56 \div v = 15 - v$

   B. $6v = 70 - 4v$

   C. $6v + 7 = 98 - 7v$

   D. $9v - 7 = 2v + 40$

Balancing Equations

CCSS: 6.EE.A.2

Part 1

Intro

Suppose you change one expression in a true equation. To keep the equation true you have to balance the other expression.

A pan balance can help you see the relationship between two quantities. When the pan is balanced, the quantities on each side are equal. If the pans are not balanced, the quantity on one side is not equal to the quantity on the other side.

Example Finding Values to Make Equations True

What must you do to the equation to make it true?
$8 + 7 + 12 = 15 + \blacksquare$

Solution ·

Model the known parts of the equation $8 + 7 + 12 = 15 + \blacksquare$.

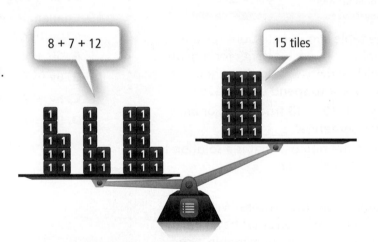

8 + 7 + 12

15 tiles

Combine the 1–tiles representing $8 + 7$ on the left side to match the 15 1–tiles on the right side.

8 + 7 = 15

continued on next page >

Part 1

Solution continued

Balance the equation by adding 12 to the right side.

Add 12 to the right side.

Check ·

$8 + 7 + 12 \stackrel{?}{=} 15 + 12$

$27 = 27$ ✔

Part 2

Example Modeling Equations Using Scales

This scale was balanced with x on one side and 5 on the other side. Somebody changed the right side of the scale and now the scale is unbalanced.

What must you do to the left side to get the scale to be balanced?

continued on next page >

Part 2

Example continued

Solution

The scale balanced when there was 1 *x* on the left side and 5 1–tiles on the right side.

Since 5 times as many 1's were placed on the right side of the scale, you need 5 times as many *x*'s on the left side of the scale to restore the balance.

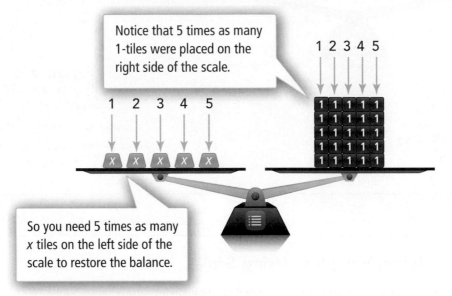

Notice that 5 times as many 1-tiles were placed on the right side of the scale.

1 2 3 4 5

1 2 3 4 5

So you need 5 times as many *x* tiles on the left side of the scale to restore the balance.

Part 3

Intro

Equivalent equations are equations that have exactly the same solutions.

Suppose you change both expressions in an equation.

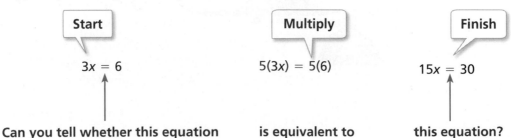

Start	Multiply	Finish
$3x = 6$	$5(3x) = 5(6)$	$15x = 30$

Can you tell whether this equation   **is equivalent to**   **this equation?**

Part 3

Example Checking Solutions to See If Equations are Equivalent

The solution of $n + 20 = 80$ is $n = 60$.

Is $n + 20 = 80$ equivalent to $n + 20 - 18 = 80 - 18$?

Explain.

Solution

Equivalent equations have the same solution.

You know that the solution of $n + 20 = 80$ is $n = 60$.

So check the solution $n = 60$ in $n + 20 - 18 = 80 - 18$.

$$n + 20 - 18 = 80 - 18$$

Substitute 60 for _n_. $\quad 60 + 20 - 18 \overset{?}{=} 80 - 18$

Simplify. $\quad\quad\quad\quad\quad\quad 62 = 62 \checkmark$

Since $n + 20 = 80$ and $n + 20 - 18 = 80 - 18$ have the same solution, the equations are equivalent.

1. a. Find the number to add that makes the scale balance.

12

9 + 3 + 17

b. Complete the equation
9 + 3 + 17 = 12 + ■.

2. a. Find the number to add that makes the scale balance.

5

2 + 5

b. Complete the equation
2 + 5 = 5 + ■.

3. This scale balanced with *x* on one side and 4 blocks on the other side. Your friend changed the scale, but had to leave before restoring the balance.

a. Find the number to multiply by on the left that makes the scale balance.

b. Complete the equation ■ · *x* = 20.

4. This scale balanced with 12 on the left side and 6*b* on the right side. Your teacher changed the scale, but did not have time to restore the balance.

2*b*

12

a. Find the number to divide by on the left that makes the scale balance.

b. Complete the equation
12 ÷ ■ = 2*b*.

5. This scale balanced when
n + 30 = 70. Suppose the left side becomes *n* + 13.

n + 13

70

a. How can you change the right side so that *n* + 13 = ■ is equivalent to *n* + 30 = 70?

A. Multiply the right side by ■.

B. Add ■ to the right side.

C. Divide the right side by ■.

D. Subtract ■ from the right side.

b. Complete the equation *n* + 13 = ■.

6. This scale balanced when
13 + *t* = 25. Suppose the left side becomes 20 + *t*.

25

20 + *t*

a. How can you change the right side so that 20 + *t* = ■ is equivalent to 13 + *t* + 25?

A. Multiply the right side by ■.

B. Add ■ to the right side.

C. Divide the right side by ■.

D. Subtract ■ from the right side.

b. Complete the equation 20 + *t* = ■.

7. Complete the following equation to make it true. 4(9 + ■) = 36 + 28

8. Error Analysis In math class, you are checking your friend's work. This is how he balanced an equation.

Unbalanced equation:
$16 \div 8 = 16 \div 8 - 1$
Balanced equation:
$16 \div 8 + 1 = 16 \div 8 - 1$

a. Find the correct balanced equation.

A. $16 \div 8 + 1 = 16 \div 8 + 1$

B. $16 \div 8 - 1 = 16 \div 8 + 1$

C. $16 \div 8 - 1 = 16 \div 8 - 1$

b. What error did your friend make?

A. He added 1 to the left side.

B. He subtracted 1 from the left side.

C. He subtracted 1 from the right side.

D. He added 1 to the right side.

9. Reasoning A scale presenting the equation $x = 9$ balances with x on one side and 9 on the other side. A second scale representing the equation $y = 18$ balances with y on one side and 18 on the other side. What must be true about x and y? Explain your reasoning.

A. $x = y$ **B.** $2x = y$

C. $x = 2y$ **D.** $9x = y$

E. $x = 9y$

10. a. Multiple Representation Draw scales to show that if $4x = 8$, then $x = 2$.

b. What operation must be used to show this?

A. Division

B. Multiplication

C. Addition

D. Subtraction

11. In math class, your equation-balancing team is given a starting equation. The team captain changes the equation, as shown. What do you have to change on the right side of the equation to balance it after the team captain's change?

Starting equation: $4x = 12$

Team captain's change: $8x = 12$

Fill in the blank to balance the equation. $8x = \blacksquare$

12. Rodney and Maria are making beaded bracelets. They use the equation $6b + 9p = 51$ to keep track of the number of beads. Let $6b$ be the number of blue beads. Let $9p$ be the number of pink beads. They decide to make matching necklaces using 3 times the number of beads. Complete the equation $\blacksquare b + \blacksquare p = 153$ to make it equivalent to the starting equation.

13. A math teacher writes the equation $25 \div 5 - 2 + 3 = 5 \blacksquare \blacksquare \blacksquare \blacksquare$ for a test. Which equation suggests a correct way to complete the right side of the equation to make the equation true?

A. $25 \div 5 - 2 + 3 = 5 \div 2 - 3$

B. $25 \div 5 - 2 + 3 = 5 \cdot 2 - 3$

C. $25 \div 5 - 2 + 3 = 5 - 2 + 3$

14. Think About the Process You start with the equation $12b = 24$. What step should you take to find the quantity that equals $4b$?

A. Divide 24 by b.

B. Divide 24 by 3.

C. Multiply 24 by b.

D. Multiply 24 by 3.

15. Think About the Process You start with the equation $4z = 12$. Your friend changes the equation as follows.

$$4z + 6 = 12$$

What should you do to the right side to make the equation equivalent to the starting equation?

A. Subtract 6 from 12.

B. Add $4z$ to 12.

C. Add 6 to 12.

D. Subtract $4z$ from 12.

Solving Addition and Subtraction Equations

CCSS: 6.EE.B.7

Vocabulary
inverse
operations

Part 1

Intro

When you solve an equation, your goal is to get the variable alone on one side of the equal sign.

The scale is balanced. You can represent what is shown on the balance scale with the equation $x + 3 = 6$.

$$x + 3 = 6$$

Notice what happens when you take away the same amount (three 1-blocks) from each side. Remove the three 1-blocks from the left side of the pan balance. The scale is now unbalanced.

$$x + 3 = 6$$

Intro continued

Now remove three 1-blocks from the right side. The scale is now balanced again. In the equation, you can represent removing the three 1-blocks from each side of the scale by subtracting 3 from each side.

$$x + 3 - 3 = 6 - 3$$

So the solution to the equation is $x = 3$.

$$x = 3$$

Example Solving Addition Equations

How many comic books do you need to add to the 17 comic books you already own to have a total of 30 comic books?

Solve the equation $17 + x = 30$, which models this situation.

Solution ·

Let x represent the number of comic books that should be added to 17 comic books to get 30 books.

You can use a model to find the value of x.

continued on next page >

Solution continued

The scale is balanced with *x* and 17 on one side and 30 on the other.

$$x + 17 = 30$$

To get *x* alone on the left side of the scale, remove seventeen 1-tiles from the left side. This represents subtracting 17 from the left side of the equation.

$$x + 17 = 30$$
$$x + 17 - 17 = 30$$

Now the scale is unbalanced and the equation is no longer true.

$$x + 17 = 30$$
$$x \stackrel{?}{=} 30$$

To balance the scale, remove an equal number of blocks from the right side as from the left side. Subtract 17 from the right side of the equation.

$$x + 17 = 30$$
$$x \stackrel{?}{=} 30 - 17$$

There are 13 blocks on the right side of the scale.
So the value of *x* is 13.

$$x + 17 = 30$$
$$x = 13$$

To have a total of 30 comic books, you need 13 more comic books.

Key Concept

Inverse operations are operations that undo each other.

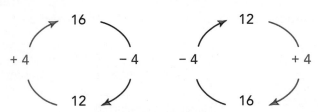

Subtraction undoes addition.   **Addition undoes subtraction.**

Addition and subtraction are inverse operations.

Part 2

Example   Identifying Inverse Operations for Addition and Subtraction

Each equation shows an operation. For each equation, identify the inverse operation of the operation shown as either addition or subtraction.

$$98 = n + 17 \qquad 17 = m + 6 \qquad 16 - m = 10$$

$$250 = p - 16 \qquad h + 7 = 21 \qquad d - 3 = 267$$

$$22 = 110 - a \qquad 39 = r - 12 \qquad 100 + y = 125$$

Solution ·

Inverse operations undo each other. Addition undoes subtraction, and subtraction undoes addition.

Addition	Subtraction
$16 - m = 10$	$h + 7 = 21$
$250 = p - 16$	$100 + y = 125$
$39 = r - 12$	$17 = m + 6$
$d - 3 = 267$	$98 = n + 17$
$22 = 110 - a$	

> Subtraction is the operation shown here, so addition is its inverse operation.

> Addition is the operation shown here, so subtraction is its inverse operation.

Example Using Inverse Operations to Solve Equations

Write a simpler equation equivalent to $y - 24 = 57$ to solve the original equation.

Solution ·

Use inverse operations.

> Addition undoes subtraction.

$$y - 24 = 57$$
$$y - 24 + 24 = 57 + 24$$
$$y + 0 = 81$$
$$y = 81$$

> To get the variable by itself, add 24 to each side.

A simpler, equivalent equation is $y = 81$.

Check ·

Substitute the value $y = 81$ into the original equation and simplify.

$$y - 24 = 57$$

> Substitute

$$81 - 24 \stackrel{?}{=} 57$$
$$57 = 57 ✔$$

1. Use the balance scale to solve the equation $x + 7 = 11$.

2. Use a balance scale to solve the following equation for the value of b.

$17 + b = 35$

3. Your friend lost all of her tennis balls, so she bought 12 new ones. Later, she found x tennis balls under the sofa. Now she has a total of 19 tennis balls. The equation $12 + x = 19$ models the situation. Use the balance scale to solve $12 + x = 19$. How many tennis balls did she find under the sofa?

4. The equation $x + 8 = 9$ shows an operation. What is the inverse of that operation?

  A. The inverse operation is addition.

  B. The inverse operation is subtraction.

5. Complete the sentence.

Subtracting 24 is the inverse of ■.

6. a. Write a simpler, equivalent equation to solve $w - 12 = 17$.

  b. What is the solution of $w - 12 = 17$?

7. Write a simpler, equivalent equation to solve $x - 24 = 40$.

8. You have a deck of t trading cards. You give 21 cards to a friend and have 9 left for yourself. How many cards were in the original deck? Write a simpler, equivalent equation to solve $t - 21 = 9$ and find the number of cards in the deck.

9. a. Writing Explain how using a balance scale can help you solve the equation $15 + y = 28$.

  b. What is the solution?

10. Think About the Process You and your friend have 32 pretzels to share. Your friend has 22 of them. If x is the number of pretzels that you have, the equation $x + 22 = 32$ models the situation. Use the balance scale to solve the equation. What should you do first?

  A. Remove 22 from the left side of the scale.

  B. Add 22 to the left side of the scale.

  C. Add x to the left side of the scale.

  D. Remove x from the left side of the scale.

11. Think About the Process A volunteer made M muffins for a bake sale. After selling 28 muffins, 21 muffins remained. The equation $M - 28 = 21$ models the situation. What is the first step in writing a simpler, equivalent equation to solve $M - 28 = 21$?

  A. Add M to each side of the equation.

  B. Subtract M from each side of the equation.

  C. Add 28 to each side of the equation.

  D. Subtract 28 from each side of the equation.

12. Mental Math There are a total of 80 students at a pep rally. If 50 of the students are girls, how many of the students are boys? The equation $b + 50 = 80$ models the situation. Use mental math and the balance scale to solve the equation $b + 50 = 80$.

See your complete lesson at MyMathUniverse.com

13. a. Reasoning The equation $p - 23 = 49$ shows an operation. Identify the inverse of that operation.

   A. The inverse operation is addition.

   B. The inverse operation is subtraction.

  b. Is it possible to solve the equation using subtraction? Explain your reasoning.

14. Error Analysis Pam and Jim are working on math homework. Their teacher gave them the following problem. Use an inverse operation to help solve the equation $x + 22 = 27$. As the first step in solving, Pam writes $x + 22 + 22 = 27 + 22$. Jim writes $x + 22 - 22 = 27 - 22$. Who is incorrect, and why?

  A. Jim is incorrect because he subtracted 22 from each side instead of adding.

  B. Pam is incorrect because she subtracted 22 from each side instead of adding.

  C. Jim is incorrect because he added 22 to each side instead of subtracting.

  D. Pam is incorrect because she added 22 to each side instead of subtracting.

15. Horse Count This year, a rancher counted 225 horses on the range. This count is 22 less than last year. How many horses did the rancher count last year? Let h be the number of horses counted last year. Write a simpler, equivalent equation to solve $h - 22 = 225$ and find the number of horses counted last year.

16. Use a balance scale to solve the equation $29 = 14 + x + 11$.

17. a. Write a simpler, equivalent equation to solve $17 + 28 = z - 30$.

  b. What is the solution?

18. Challenge In a bag of mixed nuts, there are 35 almonds, 34 hazelnuts, 32 walnuts, and p pistachios. The bag has a total of 134 nuts. How many pistachios are in the bag? Use a balance scale to solve the equation $35 + 34 + 32 + p = 134$ to find the number of pistachios.

19. Challenge Danielle had s dollars in her savings account. She used some of that money to go shopping. She spent $22 for a shirt and $24 for a video game. Her savings account balance is now $123. What was the original account balance? Write a simpler, equivalent equation to solve $s - 22 - 24 = 123$ and find the original account balance.

Solving Multiplication and Division Equations

CCSS: 6.EE.B.7

Part 1

Intro

Models can help you visualize and solve some equations.

$$3x = 27$$

A bar diagram uses bars of different lengths.

A balance scale compares two quantities.

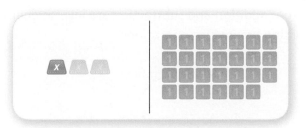

Algebra tiles represent the quantities in the equation.

Example Solving Multiplication Equations from Models

Write the modeled equation. Then solve it.

continued on next page >

Solution

$$3x = 27$$

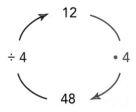

$$x = 9$$

Check

Substitute the value $x = 9$ into the original equation and simplify.

Substitute.

$$3x = 27$$
$$3(9) \stackrel{?}{=} 27$$
$$27 = 27 \checkmark$$

Key Concept

Just as addition and subtraction are inverse operations, multiplication and division are inverse operations.

12   48

÷ 4   • 4   • 4   ÷ 4

48   12

Division undoes multiplication.   Multiplication undoes division.

Multiplication and division are inverse operations.

Part 2

Example Identifying Inverse Operations

Each equation shows an operation. Identify the inverse operation for each equation.

$24 = k \cdot 5$ $75 = t \div 25$ $2(s) = 24$ $t + 16 = 32$

$3w = 27$ $a - 25 = 225$ $200 = 800 - r$ $130 = 50 + d$

$3 + w = 17$ $75 \div x = 35$

Solution

Inverse operations undo each other.

> Addition and subtraction undo each other.

> Multiplication and division undo each other.

Addition	Subtraction	Multiplication	Division
$a - 25 = 225$	$t + 16 = 32$	$75 \div x = 35$	$3w = 27$
$200 = 800 - r$	$130 = 50 + d$	$75 = t \div 25$	$24 = k \cdot 5$
	$3 + w = 17$		$2(s) = 24$

Part 3

Example Solving Division Equations

An octopus's suction cups are evenly divided among its 8 arms.

Solve the equation $s \div 8 = 240$ to find how many suction cups the octopus has in all.

I have 240 suction cups on each arm.

continued on next page >

Part 3

Example continued

Solution

Use inverse operations. Multiply by 8 to undo dividing by 8.

Write the equation.	$s \div 8 = 240$
Multiply each side by the same number.	$(s \div 8) \cdot 8 = 240 \cdot 8$
Simplify.	$s \cdot 1 = 1{,}920$
Solve for s.	$s = 1{,}920$

The octopus has 1,920 suction cups in all.

Check

Substitute the value $s = 1{,}920$ into the original equation and simplify.

Substitute.

$$s \div 8 = 240$$
$$1{,}920 \div 8 \overset{?}{=} 240$$
$$240 = 240 \checkmark$$

1. The bar diagram models the equation $3r = 57$. Solve the equation.

2. The algebra tiles model the equation $2x = 14$. Solve the equation.

Algebra Tiles

3. The local acting group has 35 members. They are carpooling in 5 vans to perform a show. They want each van to carry an equal number of people. Let p be the number of people in each van. The group uses algebra tiles to model the equation $5p = 35$. How many people are in each van?

Algebra Tiles

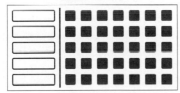

4. Each equation shows an operation. Select all the equations that have multiplication as the inverse operation.

A. $g \cdot 17 = 204$ **B.** $80 = x \div 5$

C. $n + 15 = 78$ **D.** $m \div 7 = 9$

5. Complete the sentence.
Dividing by 12 is the inverse of ■.

6. Solve the equation $x \div 7 = 8$.

7. Kelsey and her 4 sisters spent an equal amount of time cleaning their home. Their parents added their times. They found that the 5 girls spent a total of 15 hours cleaning. Let c be the number of hours each person spent cleaning. Kelsey writes the equation $5c = 15$ to model this situation. To solve for c, which operation should Kelsey use?

8. A physical education teacher divides the class into teams of 5 to play floor hockey. There are a total of 4 teams. How many students, s, are in the class? Solve the equation $s \div 5 = 4$ to find the number of students.

9. **Error Analysis** The director of an animal rescue group wants to evenly share 24 toys between three puppies. Let t be the number of toys each puppy received. The director draws the bar diagram to model the equation $3t = 24$. From this, a worker thinks each puppy should get 5 toys. Wait a minute! This answer does not make sense.

a. What is the error?

A. The worker did not use the bar diagram correctly.

B. The director did not draw the bar diagram correctly.

C. The director did not use the bar diagram correctly.

D. The worker did not draw the bar diagram correctly.

b. How many toys should each puppy receive?

10. a. **Writing** Write a one-step equation that involves multiplication and a one-step equation that involves division.

b. Explain how you would use inverse operations to solve these equations.

c. To correspond to your explanation, which operation would you use to solve $3k = 27$?

A. Division

B. Multiplication

11. a. Reasoning For the equation $z \div 3 = 8$, what must be true about the value of z? Select all that apply.

   A. The value of z must have 3 and 8 as factors.

   B. The value of z must have 3 and 8 as multiples.

   C. The value of z is $8 + 3$.

   D. The value of z is $8 - 3$.

   E. The value of z is $8 \cdot 3$.

   F. The value of z is $8 \div 3$.

   b. Explain your reasoning.

12. Fundraising The fundraising group collected the quarters from the school's wishing well. The group arranged the quarters into 8 piles of 20 quarters. Let q be the number of quarters in the well.

   a. Solve the equation $q \div 8 = 20$ to find the number of quarters in the well.

   b. How much money, in dollars, did the group collect? (Hint: Four quarters equal one dollar.)

13. At its grand opening, a clothing store sold three green shirts for every red shirt sold. The store sold 18 green shirts that day. Let r be the number of red shirts sold. The algebra tiles model the equation $3r = 18$.

Algebra Tiles

   a. The store sold how many red shirts?

   b. The store sold how many red shirts and green shirts?

14. For the equation $(x - 5) \div 2 = 14$, what operation should you use to get $(x - 5)$ alone on the left side?

15. Think About the Process

   a. How should you solve the equation $x \div 15 = 30$?

   A. Multiply each side by 15. Then simplify.

   B. Multiply each side by 30. Then simplify.

   C. Divide each side by x. Then simplify.

   D. Divide each side by 15. Then simplify.

   E. Multiply each side by x. Then simplify.

   F. Divide each side by 30. Then simplify.

   b. What is the resulting equivalent equation?

16. Think About the Process How could you arrange algebra tiles to solve the equation $6x = 24$? Show a correct arrangement of algebra tiles. Then solve the equation.

17. Challenge A teacher evenly shares 45 berries and 125 grapes among 5 students. They use the bar diagrams to model the equations. Let b be the number of berries and g be the number of grapes for each student.

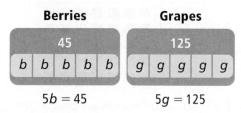

   a. How many berries does each student get?

   b. How many grapes does each student get?

   c. How many pieces of fruit does each student get?

18. Challenge A local softball league has 6 teams. Each team had 11 players at the start of the season and 14 players at the end. Let b be the number of players in the league at the start of the season and c at the end.

   a. Use the equations $b \div 6 = 11$ and $c \div 6 = 14$ to find how many players joined the league during the season.

   b. Describe another way to solve this problem.

CCSS: 6.EE.B.8

Part 1

Intro

An **inequality** is a mathematical sentence that uses $<$, $\leq$, $>$, $\geq$, or $\neq$ to compare two quantities.

Symbol	Meaning	Arithmetic Example	Algebraic Example
$<$	less than	$3 < 16$	$b < 6$
$\leq$	less than or equal to	$12 \leq 12$	$12 \leq m$
$>$	greater than	$15 > 10$	$15 > t$
$\geq$	greater than or equal to	$13 \geq 7$	$a \geq 7$
$\neq$	not equal to	$9 \neq 3$	$x \neq 3$

Symbol	English Sentence
$<$	Children under 6 ride free.
$\leq$	Children ride free through age 6.
$>$	You must be older than 12 to drive a go-cart.
$\geq$	You must be at least 12 to drive a go-cart.
$\neq$	Four apples are not equal to three mice.

Example Differentiating Between Equation and Inequality Situations

Decide whether each situation could be represented with an *equation* or an *inequality*.

You ride your scooter 2 miles.

You must be at least 48 inches tall to ride the bumper cars.

You have less than 3 days to write a book report.

Your movie ticket costs $10.

You have less than $10 to spend on snacks at the movie.

continued on next page >

Part 1

Example continued

Solution ·

Equations have one value, Inequalities, except ≠, have more than one value.

Equations:

- You ride your scooter 2 miles.
- Your movie ticket costs $10.

Inequalities:

- You must be at least 48 inches tall to ride the bumper cars.
- You have less than 3 days to write a book report.
- You have less than $10 to spend on snacks at the movie.

Part 2

Example   Using Inequalities to Describe Situations

Inequalities can describe height requirements, speed limits, time limits, and many other situations. Find the inequality that represents the information given on each sign.

$x \leq 5{,}900$ $x \geq 5{,}900$ $x > 14$ $x < 14$ $6 \leq x \leq 8$ $8 \leq x \leq 18$

a.

b.

c.

Solution ·

a. The height of the bridge is 14 feet so the vehicle must be less than 14 feet tall to pass under it safely. The inequality is $x < 14$.

b. The range for 1-hour parking is from 0800 to 1800 hours. The inequality is $8 \leq x \leq 18$.

c. The highest point in the town of Dinosaur is at 5,900 ft above sea level. The inequality is $x \leq 5{,}900$.

Part 3

Intro

The graph of an inequality is part of a number line.

Graph the inequality $x > 5$ on a number line. x is greater than 5, so all values greater than 5 are solutions of this inequality.

> An **open circle** means 5 is *not* a solution of the inequality.

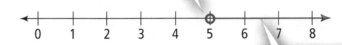

> **Shading to the right** means x is greater than 5.

Graph the inequality $c \le 7$ on a number line. c is less than or equal to 7, so 7 and all values less than 7 are solutions of this inequality.

> A **closed circle** means 7 is a solution of the inequality.

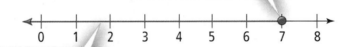

> **Shading to the left** means C is less than 7.

Example Graphing Inequalities to Represent Situations

Graph the inequality that models the situation.

The high temperature today was less than 30 degrees.

Solution

High Temperature Today

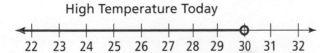

> To graph less than 30 degrees, draw an open circle at 30 and an arrow to the left.

See your complete lesson at MyMathUniverse.com

Key Concept

Inequalities

Symbol	Meaning	Example	Graph
$<$	less than	$b < 16$	graph with open circle at 16, points 8, 16, 24
$\leq$	less than or equal to	$m \leq 12$	graph with closed circle at 12, points 10, 12, 14
$>$	greater than	$t > 15$	graph with open circle at 15, points 5, 15, 25
$\geq$	greater than or equal to	$a \geq 57$	graph with closed circle at 57, points 53, 57, 61
$\neq$	not equal to	$x \neq 3$	graph with open circle at 3, points 1, 3, 5

1. Which of these situations have exactly one solution?

   1. To make some cookies, John needs 4 eggs.
   2. Karen went to more than 5 baseball games last year.
   3. Last year, a teacher gave one test for each of the 8 chapters in the textbook.
   4. Some friends spent more than 3 hours playing their favorite board game.

   a. Select all that apply.
      A. situation 4
      B. situation 3
      C. situation 1
      D. situation 2

   b. Select all of the situations that have more than one solution.
      A. situation 2
      B. situation 4
      C. situation 3
      D. situation 1

2. Which situations can you represent with an equation?

   1. Two friends live 7 blocks apart.
   2. A girl earned $26 babysitting on Saturday night.
   3. Each class must have fewer than 23 students.
   4. The homework took 4 hours to complete.

   a. Select all of the situations that apply.
      A. situation 1
      B. situation 2
      C. situation 3
      D. situation 4

   b. Select all of the situations that you can represent with an inequality.

      A. situation 2
      B. situation 3
      C. situation 1
      D. situation 4

3. The restaurant can seat no more than 171 people. If p is the restaurant's capacity, which of the following inequalities models the given situation?

   A. $p \leq 171$ B. $p > 171$
   C. $p \geq 171$ D. $p < 171$

4. **Vehicle Speed** Write an inequality that represents the situation. Use x for the speed of the truck.

   The speed of the truck must be no less than 34 miles per hour.

   A. $x > 34$ B. $x \geq 34$
   C. $x \leq 34$ D. $x < 34$
   E. $x \neq 34$

5. Which of these situations can you represent with the inequality $x \geq 45$?

   1. You must be at least 45 inches tall to go on this ride.
   2. A loaf of bread must be baked for no more than 45 minutes.
   3. You have at least 45 minutes left on a parking meter.
   4. The bill at a restaurant was no more than $45.

   Select all of the situations that you can represent with the inequality $x \geq 45$.
      A. situation 4   B. situation 1
      C. situation 3   D. situation 2

6. Which inequality has this graph? **(Figure 1)**

   A. $x \leq 5$ B. $x < 5$
   C. $x \geq 5$ D. $x > 5$
   E. $x \neq 5$

(Figure 1)

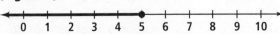

7. a. Multiple Representations For the following situation, decide if there is exactly one or more than one solution. Make one or more drawings to support your answer. A glass holds 9 ounces of juice. A boy overfills the glass and spills some juice. How much juice could he spill?

b. How many solutions are there?

8. Writing Simon has fewer than 8 photographs in an art show. Decide if you can represent this situation with an equation or inequality. Explain your answer.

9. a. Open-Ended Describe a situation that you could represent with the inequality $x > 17$.

b. Is 22 a solution of your situation?

10. a. Reasoning Graph the inequalities $x > 2$ and $x < 2$.

b. Are the graphs the same?

11. Error Analysis Two students were told to find an inequality that has this graph. **(Figure 2)** Andrew says the inequality is $x > 7$. Lauren says the inequality is $x < 7$. Who is incorrect and why?

A. Andrew is incorrect. His inequality symbol points the wrong way.

B. Lauren is incorrect. Her inequality includes 7 as a solution.

C. Lauren is incorrect. Her inequality includes 7 as a solution, and her inequality symbol points the wrong way.

D. Lauren is incorrect. Her inequality symbol points the wrong way.

E. Andrew is incorrect. His inequality includes 7 as a solution, and his inequality symbol point the wrong way.

F. Andrew is incorrect. His inequality includes 7 as a solution.

12. Write an inequality that represents the following situation. A certain airplane must carry no fewer than 134 passengers during a flight.

13. The high temperature yesterday was no greater than 74 degrees. Make a graph that models the situation.

14. Graph the inequality that models the situation. There are at most 33 books in a bookcase. Choose the correct graph below.

A. ⟵―┼┼┼┼┼┼⊕┼┼―→
     0 10 20 30 40 50

B. ⟵―┼┼┼┼┼⊕┼┼┼―→
     0 10 20 30 40 50

C. ⟵―┼┼┼┼┼┼●┼┼―→
     0 10 20 30 40 50

D. ⟵―┼┼┼┼┼●┼┼┼―→
     0 10 20 30 40 50

15. Think About the Process You have to graph the inequality $x < 12$. What is your first step?

The first step is to draw <u>a closed circle/an open circle</u> at 12.

16. Think About the Process You need to find an inequality that has this graph. What inequality symbol should you use? **(Figure 3)**

Choose the correct inequality symbol below.

A. $>$ **B.** $\neq$

C. $<$ **D.** $\geq$

17. Challenge Find an inequality that has this graph. **(Figure 4)**

A. $38 > t$ **B.** $38 \leq c$

C. $38 \geq d$ **D.** $38 < m$

E. $38 \neq y$

(Figure 2)

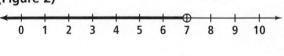

(Figure 3)

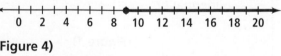

(Figure 4)

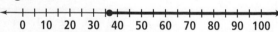

See your complete lesson at MyMathUniverse.com

Vocabulary
equivalent inequalities,
solution of an
inequality

CCSS: 6.EE.B.5, 6.EE.B.8

Part 1

Example Checking If Values Make Inequalities True

Suppose your aunt has a bank account in which she has to keep a balance greater than $150. She has $290 in the account at the moment. For which amounts can your aunt write a check and have the balance stay above $150: $59, $75, $142?

The inequality $290 - c > 150$ models this situation. Decide whether the inequality is true or false for each amount.

Solution

Test each check amount. Substitute each amount for c in the inequality.

$$290 - c > 150 \qquad 290 - c > 150 \qquad 290 - c > 150$$
$$290 - 59 \overset{?}{>} 150 \qquad 290 - 75 \overset{?}{>} 150 \qquad 290 - 142 \overset{?}{>} 150$$
$$231 > 150 ✔ \qquad\quad 215 > 150 ✔ \qquad\quad 148 \not> 150 ✗$$

Your aunt could write a check for $59 or for $75, but not for $142.

Key Concept

In an equation, you can change each side by the same amount to write an equivalent equation.

$$8 + 4 = 12 \text{ and } 8 + 4 - 3 = 12 - 3 \qquad 6 \cdot 2 = 12 \text{ and } 6 \cdot 2 \div 3 = 12 \div 3$$

$$8 + c = 12 \text{ and } 8 + c - 3 = 12 - 3 \qquad 6c = 12 \text{ and } 6c \div 3 = 12 \div 3$$

In an inequality, you can change each side by the same amount to write an equivalent inequality.

$$8 + 4 < 15 \text{ and } 8 + 4 - 3 < 15 - 3 \qquad 6 \cdot 2 < 12 \text{ and } 6 \cdot 2 \div 3 < 12 \div 3$$

$$8 + c > 15 \text{ and } 8 + c + 3 > 15 + 3 \qquad 6c > 15 \text{ and } 6c \div 3 > 15 \div 3$$

See your complete lesson at MyMathUniverse.com

Example Identifying Solutions to Inequalities on Graphs

Solve each inequality by changing each side by the same amount. Then match each inequality to the correct graph.

$$3 > d - 1 \qquad 2 \geq t \div 2 \qquad\qquad b + 6 < 10 \qquad 28 < 7y$$

$$a + 15 \leq 19 \qquad 12 \geq 3r \qquad\qquad x - 4 \geq 0 \qquad 2h > 8$$

a.
2 3 4 5 6

b.
2 3 4 5 6

c.
2 3 4 5 6

d.
2 3 4 5 6

Solution

a.
$$2h > 8$$
$$2h \div 2 > 8 \div 2$$
$$h > 4$$

$$28 < 7y$$
$$28 \div 7 < 7y \div 7$$
$$4 < y$$

c.
$$x - 4 \geq 0$$
$$x - 4 + 4 \geq 0 + 4$$
$$x \geq 4$$

b.
$$3 > d - 1$$
$$3 + 1 > d - 1 + 1$$
$$4 > d$$

$$b + 6 < 10$$
$$b + 6 - 6 < 10 - 6$$
$$b < 4$$

d.
$$2 \geq t \div 2$$
$$2 \cdot 2 \geq t \div 2 \cdot 2$$
$$4 \geq t$$

$$12 \geq 3r$$
$$12 \div 3 \geq 3r \div 3$$
$$4 \geq r$$

$$a + 15 \leq 19$$
$$a + 15 - 15 \leq 19 - 15$$
$$a \leq 4$$

Part 3

Example Determining If Graphs Show Solutions to Inequalities

Look at the graph and then decide whether each statement is *true* or *false*.

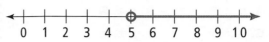

a. The graph shows the solution of $3x \geq 15$.

b. The graph shows the solution of $8 < x + 3$.

c. The graph shows the solution of both $x - 3 > 2$ and $x + 10 > 15$.

Solution

Solve each inequality. Then check whether its solution matches the graph.

a. $3x \geq 15$

$3x \div 3 \geq 15 \div 3$

$x \geq 5$ ✗

> The first statement is *false*.

b. $8 < x + 3$

$8 - 3 < x + 3 - 3$

$5 < x$, or $x > 5$ ✔

> The second statement is *true*.

c.

$x - 3 > 2$	$x + 10 > 15$
$x - 3 + 3 > 2 + 3$	$x + 10 - 10 > 15 - 10$
$x > 5$ ✔	$x > 5$ ✔

> Both inequalities match the graph, so the third statement is *true*.

1. Solve the inequality $p - 5 > 9$. Write the answer to complete your choice.

   A. $p < \blacksquare$ **B.** $p \geq \blacksquare$

   C. $p > \blacksquare$ **D.** $p \leq \blacksquare$

2. Solve the inequality $y + 3 < 5$. Write the answer to complete your choice.

   A. $y \leq \blacksquare$ **B.** $y > \blacksquare$

   C. $y < \blacksquare$ **D.** $y \geq \blacksquare$

3. Solve the inequality $x \div 3 \leq 4$. Write the answer to complete your choice.

   A. $x > \blacksquare$ **B.** $x < \blacksquare$

   C. $x \leq \blacksquare$ **D.** $x \geq \blacksquare$

4. Solve the inequality $3x > 18$. Write the answer to complete your choice.

   A. $x < \blacksquare$ **B.** $x \geq \blacksquare$

   C. $x > \blacksquare$ **D.** $x \leq \blacksquare$

5. Solve the inequality.

   $$21 \geq 3x$$

   A. $x \leq \blacksquare$ **B.** $x < \blacksquare$

   C. $x \geq \blacksquare$ **D.** $x > \blacksquare$

6. Solve the inequality.

   $$x + 32 \geq 47$$

   A. $x \leq \blacksquare$ **B.** $x < \blacksquare$

   C. $x > \blacksquare$ **D.** $x \geq \blacksquare$

7. Sketch a graph that shows the solutions of the inequality $x - 2 < 14$.

8. **Greenhouse** The temperature in a greenhouse should be 65 degrees or higher. One morning, the heater stopped working. The temperature dropped 5 degrees before someone fixed the heater. The temperature was still at least 65 degrees when the heater started working again. How can you best describe the temperature in the greenhouse before the heater stopped working?

9. **Estimation** What is the easiest way to estimate the solutions of the inequality $x \div 9 < 69$?

   A. Multiply 69 by 10 to get $x > 690$.

   B. Multiply 69 by 8 to get $x < 552$.

   C. Multiply 70 by 10 to get $x < 700$.

   D. Multiply 9 by 70 to get $x < 630$.

   E. Multiply 70 by 10 to get $x > 700$.

10. Sketch a graph that shows the solutions of the inequality $49 \geq x + 22$.

11. **Think About the Process** You want to solve the inequality $6z \leq 54$. What is the first step?

    A. Subtract 6 from each side of the inequality.

    B. Add 6 to each side of the inequality.

    C. Subtract $5z$ from each side of the inequality.

    D. Divide each side of the inequality by z.

    E. Divide each side of the inequality by 6.

    F. Multiply each side of the inequality by 6.

12. **Think About the Process** Boris knows that the solutions of $x < 27$ can be shown on a number line. His teacher asks for an inequality that requires multiplying by 9 to find the solutions shown. What should he do to $x < 277$ to meet the teacher's request? What is the result?

    A. He should add 9 to each side of the inequality. The result is $x + 9 < 36$.

    B. He should divide each side of the inequality by 9. The result is $x \div 9 < 3$.

    C. He should multiply each side of the inequality by 9. The result is $9x < 243$.

    D. He should subtract 9 from each side of the inequality. The result is $x - 9 < 18$.

13. **Challenge** Last month, Simon's neighbors paid him to take care of their bird when they went on vacation. He spent $3 of his earnings on an afternoon snack and $17 on a new book. Afterward, he had at most $7 left. How can you describe how much Simon's neighbors paid him? Select the correct choice and write the answer to complete your choice.

A. They paid him at least ■.

B. They paid him at most ■.

C. They paid him exactly ■.

14. **Challenge** You have a bag of x peanuts. You share these peanuts with 3 of your friends. Each of you gets no fewer than 28 peanuts. The inequality $28 < x \div 4$ models this situation. Which graph shows the solutions of this inequality?

A.

B.
28

  0 10 20 30 40 50

C.
112

  0 40 80 120 160 200

D.
112

  0 40 80 120 160 200

E.
7

  0 2 4 6 8 10

F.
112

  0 40 80 120 160 200

G.
112

  0 40 80 120 160 200

H.
28

  0 10 20 30 40 50

15. **a. Writing** Explain what inverse operations are.

  b. Show how to use inverse operations to solve the inequality $x + 16 < 19$.

  c. Solve the inequality $x + 16 < 19$.

  A. $x > $ ■

  B. $x < $ ■

  C. $x = $ ■

16. **Think About the Process** You want to solve the inequality $9z > 54$. What is the first step?

  A. Divide each side of the inequality by 9.

  B. Multiply each side of the inequality by 9.

  C. Add 9 to each side of the inequality.

  D. Subtract $8z$ from each side of the inequality.

  E. Subtract 9 from each side of the inequality.

  F. Divide each side of the inequality by z.

17. **Challenge** Last month, Carla's neighbors paid her to take care of their dog when they went on vacation. She spent $5 of her earnings on an afternoon snack and $14 on a new book. Afterward, she had no more than $9 left. How can you best describe how much Carla's neighbors paid her? Select the correct choice and write the answer to complete your choice.

  A. They paid her exactly $■.

  B. They paid her no more than $■.

  C. They paid her no less than $■.

CCSS: 6.EE.B.7, Also 6.EE.B.5

Key Concept

To model a problem and write an equation, you need to identify the information you know. Here is an example:

A student has collected 37 phone cards to donate to a charity. The goal is to donate 75 cards. How many more cards, c, does the student need to collect?

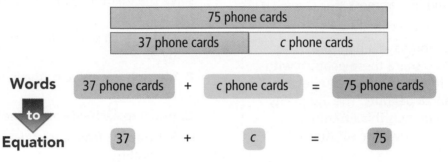

75 phone cards	
37 phone cards	c phone cards

Words | 37 phone cards | + | c phone cards | = | 75 phone cards |

to

Equation | 37 | + | c | = | 75 |

Part 1

Example Representing Situations with Models and Equations

The Mississippi River is 890 miles longer than the Colorado River. The Mississippi River is 2,340 miles long. How long is the Colorado River?

Let r be the length of the Colorado River. Which model and equation could you use to represent the problem?

I.

2,340	
r	890

$$2{,}340 - r = 890$$

II. ├──── 2,340 ────┤

890		
r	...	r

$$2{,}340 = 890 \div r$$

III.

890	
2,340	r

$$890 = 2{,}340 + r$$

Example continued

Solution ·

The model and equation in Choice I match key information in the problem.

The Mississippi River is 890 miles longer than the Colorado River.
The Mississippi River is 2,340 miles long. How long is the Colorado River?

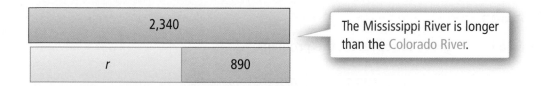

The Mississippi River is longer
than the Colorado River.

The problem compares two lengths with a difference. You can model the situation with subtraction.

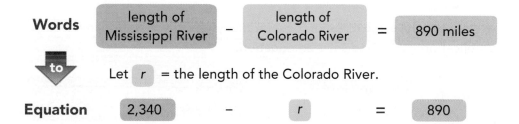

Part 2

Example Using Models and Equations to Solve Problems

An athlete in training for a marathon runs *m* miles every day. After 6 days, the athlete has run 90 miles. How far did the athlete run each day? Draw a model and write an equation to represent the problem. Then solve the equation.

Solution

Draw a bar diagram to represent the problem.

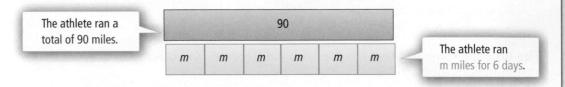

The athlete ran a total of 90 miles.

90

m | m | m | m | m | m

The athlete ran m miles for 6 days.

The athlete ran the same distance for several days, so the operation involved is multiplication. Write and solve an equation.

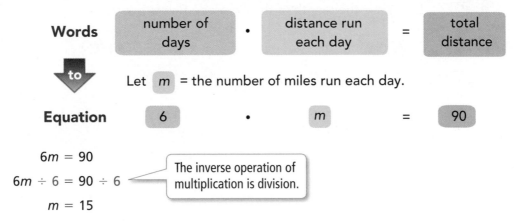

| **Words** | number of days | $\cdot$ | distance run each day | = | total distance |

to

Let *m* = the number of miles run each day.

| **Equation** | 6 | $\cdot$ | m | = | 90 |

$$6m = 90$$
$$6m \div 6 = 90 \div 6$$
$$m = 15$$

The inverse operation of multiplication is division.

The athlete ran 15 miles each day.

Example Writing and Solving Inequalities

A model train runs on a looping track. It makes 7 loops around the track each hour. The train travels at least 28 meters each hour. Let t represent the length of each loop. Write an inequality to represent the situation. Then solve the inequality.

Solution

Use key information from the problem to write an inequality.

A model train runs on a looping track. It makes 7 loops around the track each hour. The train travels at least 28 meters each hour. Let t represent the length of each loop.

The words "at least" mean that the train can travel faster than 28 meters per hour or exactly 28 meters per hour, but not any slower.

| Words | number of loops per hour | • | length of each loop | ≥ | 28 meters per hour |

Let t = the length of each loop.

| Inequality | 7 | • | t | ≥ | 28 |

$$7t \geq 28$$
$$7t \div 7 \geq 28 \div 7$$
$$t \geq 4$$

The inverse operation of multiplication is division.

The track is at least 4 meters long.

1. In a city, Building *P* is 453 feet taller than Building *Q*. The height of Building *P* is 956 feet.

   a. Which diagram and equation represent the problem?

   A.

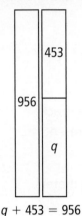

   $q + 453 = 956$

   B.

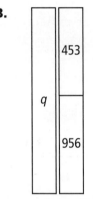

   $q + 956 = 453$

   C.

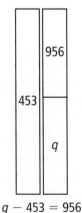

   $q - 453 = 956$

   b. What is the height, *q*, of Building *Q*?

2. The 6th-grade students sold potted flowers and potted vegetables to raise money for a class trip. They raised $289 for the trip. Sales of the flowers raised $153. Let *v* be the number of dollars raised selling the vegetables.

   a. Which bar diagram and equation model the problem?

   A.

153		
v	...	*v*

   $\vdash$ ------------- 289 ------------- $\dashv$

   $153 \div v = 289$

   B.

289		
v	...	*v*

   $\vdash$ ------------- 153 ------------- $\dashv$

   $153v = 289$

   C.

v	
289	153

   $v - 153 = 289$

   D.

289	
v	153

   $v + 153 = 289$

   b. How many dollars did sales of the vegetables raise?

3. A type of fish for your aquarium costs $3 each. You can spend at most $27. Let *f* be the number of fish you can buy.

   a. Which inequality models the problem?

   A. $f + 3 \geq 27$ **B.** $3f \geq 27$

   C. $3f \leq 27$ **D.** $f + 3 \leq 27$

   b. How many of these fish can you buy?

4. Can this bar diagram represent both a multiplication and a division equation? Why?

56						
b	*b*	*b*	*b*	*b*	*b*	*b*

5. The employees at a local business make 4,704 photocopies during a normal month. (Hint: There are about 21 work days per month.) Let *n* be the number of copies made each day.

  a. Which bar diagram and equation model the problem?

  A.
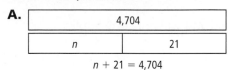
  $n + 21 = 4{,}704$

  B.
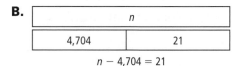
  $n - 4{,}704 = 21$

  C.
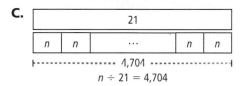
  $n \div 21 = 4{,}704$

  D.
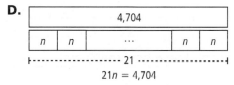
  $21n = 4{,}704$

  b. About how many copies do the employees make each day?

6. A textbook has 370 pages. There are 14 pages in the index. Let *p* be the number of pages not in the index.

  a. What is an addition equation that models the problem?

  b. How many pages of the textbook are not in the index?

7. A teacher writes the inequality $x \div 7 < 14$ on the board. A student solves the inequality incorrectly and gets the result $x < 2$.

  a. What is the correct result?

  b. Why is the student's result incorrect?

8. A traffic helicopter descends 127 meters to be 477 meters above the ground. Let *h* be the original height of the helicopter.

  a. What is a subtraction equation that models the problem?

  b. What was the original height of the helicopter?

9. A group of friends do yardwork to earn extra money. They charge $10 to mow a lawn and $15 an hour to prune trees and shrubs. The group earned $140 last summer. They mowed 8 lawns and earned $80.

  a. Draw a bar diagram and write an equation to model the problem.

  b. How many dollars, *p,* did the group earn pruning?

10. Think About the Process Only 12 students can be in the next school play. Let *t* be the total number of students who tried out. The number of students who tried out but did not get a role is 42. The bar diagram models this situation.

t	
12	42

  a. Explain how the bar diagram and the equation $t - 12 = 42$ model this situation.

  b. Solve the equation to find the total number of students who tried out for the play.

11. Think About the Process A day-care center tries to have at least 2 toys available for each child. The inequality $t \div 19 \geq 2$ models the number of toys *t* the center needs when there are 19 children.

  a. To solve the inequality for *t,* what is the correct inverse operation to use?

  b. How many toys does the center need?

CCSS: 6.EE.C.9

Vocabulary
dependent variable, independent variable

Part 1

Intro

Suppose you are going to buy 12 pieces of fruit and you will only buy apples and pears.

There are two related and unknown quantities in this situation: *number of apples* and *number of pears*. A change in one affects a change in the other. The more apples you buy, the fewer pears you buy.

Example Identifying Related and Unknown Quantities

A fruit basket business takes 103 orders in one month. Orders can be placed online or over the phone.

Identify the related and unknown quantities.

Solution

There are a total of 103 orders placed, but you don't know how many are online orders and how many are phone orders.

The two related are unknown quantities are *number of online orders* and *number of phone orders*.

Part 2

Intro

Suppose again that you are going to buy 12 pieces of fruit and you will only buy apples and pears.

You can assign a variable to each of the related quantities.

a = number of apples
p = number of pears

You can write an equation to represent the relationship.

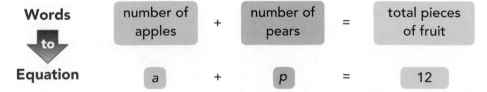

Words	number of apples	+	number of pears	=	total pieces of fruit
Equation	a	+	p	=	12

Part 2

Example Writing Equations to Represent Situations

After-school practice is 90 minutes long. Some of that time is spent doing warm-ups and the rest is spent doing drills.

Write an equation to represent the situation.

Solution ··

Know
- Practice is 90 minutes long.
- All of the practice is spent on warm-ups and drills.

Need
- Equation relating 90 minutes to the time spent on warm-ups and drills

Plan
- Assign variables to the related quantities.

Step 1 Identify the related quantities and assign variables to them.

w = number of minutes spent doing warm-ups
d = number of minutes spent doing drills

Step 2 Write the relationship in words.

The number of minutes spent doing warm-ups plus the number of minutes spent doing drills equals the total number of minutes in practice.

Step 3 Write an equation to represent the relationship.

Words	number of minutes spent doing warm-ups	plus	number of minutes spent doing drills	equals	total number of minutes in practice
to					
Equation	w	+	d	=	90

Key Concept

The growth of a plant depends on how much water it receives.

Amount of growth and amount of water are related and unknown quantities.

The amount of growth is the dependent variable and the amount of water is the independent variable.

A **dependent variable** changes in response to another variable.

An **independent variable** affects change on the dependent variable.

Part 3

Example Classifying Quantities as Dependent or Independent Variables

Classify each highlighted quantity as an *independent* or *dependent variable*. Copy each sentence. Underline the independent variable and then circle the dependent variable.

   a. You biked *m* miles to the store and burned *c* Calories.
   b. The category of a hurricane is related to the wind speed of the hurricane.
   c. The population of a state determines the number of representatives from that state in the U.S. Congress.

Solution ·

   a. You <u>biked *m* miles</u> to the store and (burned *c* Calories).

   The number of Calories burned depends on the number of miles biked.

   b. The (category of a hurricane) is related to the <u>wind speed of the hurricane</u>.

   The category of a hurricane depends on the wind speed of the hurricane.

   c. The <u>population of a state</u> determines the (number of representatives) from that state in the U.S. Congress.

   The number of representatives in the U.S. Congress depends on the population of the state.

1. A college student washes cars to cover his weekly expenses. The student charges $8 for each hour he spends washing cars. Select the two unknown quantities in this situation that are related.

   A. the amount of money the student earns

   B. the number of hours the student spends washing cars

   C. the number of college students washing cars

   D. the number of cars the student washes

2. An athlete plans to exercise for 90 minutes. She will only sprint and swim.

   Let x be the number of minutes the athlete spends sprinting. Let y be the number of minutes swimming. Which equation represents this situation?

   A. $x + y = 90$ **B.** $x - y = 90$

   C. $90 + y = x$ **D.** $90 + x = y$

3. An athlete plans to exercise for 120 minutes. He will only sprint and swim.

   Let x be the number of minutes the athlete spends sprinting. Let y be the number of minutes swimming. Select the three equations that represent this situation.

   A. $120 - x = y$ **B.** $120 - y = x$

   C. $x - y = 120$ **D.** $120 + y = x$

   E. $x + y = 120$ **F.** $120 + x = y$

4. Identify the dependent variable in this relationship.

   A garden hose runs for m minutes and produces g gallons of water.

5. **Open-Ended** The number of oranges in a bag and the cost of the bag of oranges are related.

   a. Identify the independent variable in this relationship.

   A. The cost of a bag of oranges

   B. The number of bags of oranges

   C. The number of oranges in the bag

   D. The cost of each orange

   b. Describe another relationship involving bags of oranges that does not involve cost. Can you identify the independent variable in the relationship? If not, explain why not.

6. The number of cars already parked in a lot and the number of open parking spaces in the lot are related. What is the dependent variable?

   A. The number of cars the parking lot holds

   B. The types of cars in the parking lot

   C. The number of cars already parked in the lot

   D. The number of open parking spaces in the lot

7. **Writing** Last season, a farmer harvested 18 bushels of apples and plums from her orchard.

   a. What are the unknown and related quantities in this relationship?

   b. Describe how you could use values for one of these unknown quantities to find values for the other. Make a table of values to illustrate your description.

8. **Reasoning** Some of the vehicles in a parking lot are two-door cars. The rest are four-door cars. There are 25 two-door cars. Let n be the number of four-door cars in the parking lot. Let T be the total number of cars in the parking lot.

   a. Select the three equations that represent this situation.

   A. $n + 25 = T$ **B.** $T + n = 25$

   C. $T + 25 = n$ **D.** $n - 25 = T$

   E. $T - 25 = n$ **F.** $T - n = 25$

   b. Present at least one other way to show each of these three equations. Is one way better than the others? Explain.

9. **Multiple Representations** A woman owns stock in two companies, company A and company B. She owns 85 shares of stock in company A. Each share of stock in company A is worth $10. Each share of stock in company B is worth $15. Let b be the number of shares of stock in company B the woman owns. Let T be the total number of shares of stock the woman owns.

   a. Write three equations to represent the total number of shares of stock the woman owns.

   b. Present at least one other way to show each of these three equations.

10. **Open-Ended** A man spends $651 to plant 144 flowers in his garden. He plants only red flowers and yellow flowers. The red flowers cost $4 each. The yellow flowers cost $5 each. Let r be the number of red flowers the man plants. Let y be the number of yellow flowers the man plants.

    a. Write an equation for the total number of flowers.

    b. Suppose the man wants to plant three colors of flowers in the garden next year. Write an equation for the total number of flowers for this situation. Be sure to define any variables you use.

11. A local store sells cartons of eggs. The number of eggs in a carton and the cost of the carton of eggs are related. You need 9 eggs. What is the independent variable?

12. **Think About the Process** The 28 members of a club want to make official club sweatshirts with the club's logo printed on them. A local shop charges 2 dollars per sweatshirt to print each color in the logo. One member writes an equation to model the cost to print each sweatshirt. The equation contains two related and unknown quantities.

    a. What is a good first step to identify these quantities?

       A. Decide if there is enough information to write the equation.

       B. Find the cost of printing one member's sweatshirt.

       C. Find the number of colors in the logo.

       D. Identify all three quantities related to the cost of printing each sweatshirt.

    b. What are the two related and unknown quantities?

13. **Think About the Process** Grazielle buys 3 loaves of bread. She buys only rye bread and wheat bread. Grazielle wants to write an equation to represent the number of loaves of bread she buys.

    a. First, identify the two related and unknown quantities for the equation.

       A. The number of loaves of wheat bread, w

       B. The number of loaves of rye bread, y

       C. The price of each loaf of rye bread, y

       D. The price of each loaf of wheat bread, w

    b. Complete the equation for the number of loaves of bread Grazielle buys. $y \ \blacksquare \ w = \blacksquare$

14. **Challenge** The weight of a stack of dishes and the number of dishes in the stack are related.

    a. What is the dependent variable?

       A. the number of dishes in the stack

       B. the weight of each dish

       C. the number of stacks of dishes

       D. the weight of the stack

    b. Describe why the other variable is considered to be independent in this situation.

Analyzing Patterns Using Tables and Graphs

CCSS: 6.NS.C.8, 6.EE.C.9

Part 1

Intro

When you have a problem with two variables, you can organize the variables in a table.

Suppose your friend is two years older than you. A table is one way to record your ages at different points.

Your Age	Friend's Age
0	2
5	7
10	12
15	17

Example Continuing a Pattern Using a Table

Look at the first three figures. Determine the pattern and draw Figure 4.

Figure 1   Figure 2   Figure 3   Figure 4

  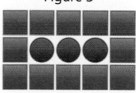

Solution

The fourth figure in the pattern has 4 circles and 14 squares.

Figure 4

continued on next page >

Part 1

Example continued

Complete the table.

Number of Circles	Number of Squares
1	8
2	10
3	☐
4	☐
5	☐
6	☐

Figure 1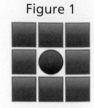

Figure 2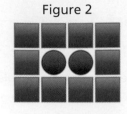

Figure 3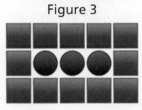

Figure 4

Solution

An additional circle requires two more squares than the previous figure.

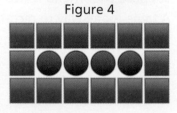

Number of Circles	Number of Squares	
1	8	
2	10	+2
3	12	+2
4	14	+2
5	16	+2
6	18	+2

Key Concept

You can use tables and graphs to analyze patterns. Both tables and graphs will help you see how a change in the independent variable affects the dependent variable.

Time (hours)	Miles
1	500
2	1,000
3	1,500
4	2,000
5	2,500

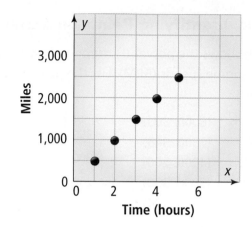

Part 2

Example Graphing Relationships from Tables

In the first eight weeks of its life, a large-breed dog gains 1 kilogram every 2 weeks. Use the table to graph the relationship between weeks and kilograms.

Weeks	Kilograms
2	1
4	2
6	3
8	4

Solution ·

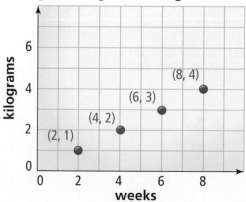

Part 3

Intro

To solve some problems, you can connect the points with a line or curve.

Example Identifying Points on a Graph

The graph shows the power (Horsepower) delivered by a car engine at different engine speeds (RPM). List the points that fall on the curve of the graph.

(2000, 75)   (6000, 300)
(1000, 40)   (7500, 345)
(8000, 400)   (4000, 200)
(3000, 140)   (3000, 350)
(5000, 150)   (2300, 100)

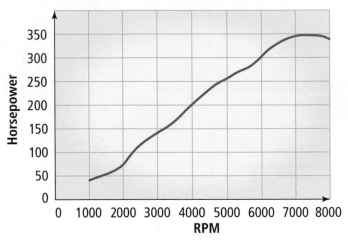

Solution ·

The points (1000, 40), (2000, 75), (2300, 100), (3000, 140), (4000, 200), (6000, 300), and (7500, 345) fall on the curve.

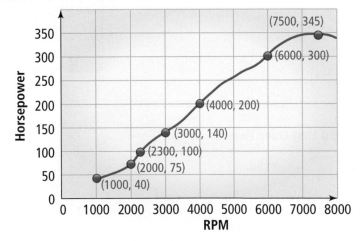

Part 4

Example Completing Tables to Graph Relationships

A landscape architect is designing a greenway. The design calls for 620 trees on every acre of the greenway. Use the given information to complete the table. Then graph the relationship between acres and number of trees.

Acres	Number of Trees
0	0
5	3,100
10	6,200
15	▢
20	▢
25	▢

Solution ·

To complete the table, multiply the number in the "Acres" column by 620. The number of trees increases by 3,100 for every 5 additional acres.

Acres	Number of Acres • 620	Number of Trees
0	0 • 620 = 0	0
5	5 • 620 = 3,100	3,100
10	10 • 620 = 6,200	6,200
15	15 • 620 = 9,300	9,300
20	20 • 620 = 12,400	12,400
25	25 • 620 = 15,500	15,500

Use the completed table to graph the relationship between Acres and Number of Trees.

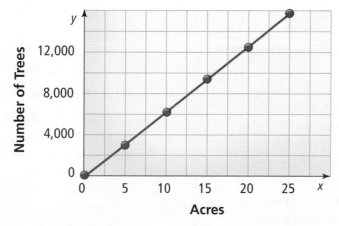

1. **Open-Ended** The three figures below begin a pattern. To help find the pattern, draw the next three figures in the pattern.

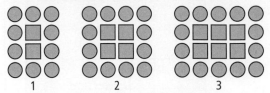

1   2   3

a. Use the pattern to complete the table.

Number of squares	Number of Ovals
20	28
22	■
24	■
26	■
28	■

b. What could these figures represent?

2. The table shows the relationship between the number of correct answers and the total points.

Correct Answer	Total Points
3	9
5	15
7	21
9	27

What is the relationship suggested by the table?

A. Square the number of correct answers to find the total points.

B. Triple the number of correct answers to find the total points.

C. Double the number of correct answers to find the total points.

D. Subtract 2 from each correct answer to find the total points.

3. **Reasoning** The graph shows the relationship between years and the population of a certain town.

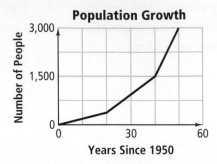

a. Which points fall on the graph? Select all that apply.

A. (30, 900)   B. (40, 1500)
C. (40, 900)   D. (900, 40)

b. What do the numbers for each point represent?

4. **Estimation** The graph shows the number of customers at a pizza place per week. Which points approximate points on the graph? Select all that apply.

A. (51, 1100)   B. (11, 845)
C. (29, 800)   D. (11, 800)
E. (800, 51)   F. (51, 800)

5. Think About the Process Honey bees produce 49 pounds of honey for each beehive in a certain region.

a. Complete the following sentence to describe how to graph points for the relationship shown in the table.

Honey Produced

Hives	Honey (pounds)
1	49
2	98
3	147
4	196

To graph the points, move <u>left / right / up</u> the number of units in the Hives column. Move <u>left / right / up</u> the number of units in the Honey (pounds) column.

b. Which graph shows the relationship between the number of hives and the amount of honey?

A. Honey Produced

B. Honey Produced

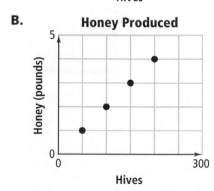

C. Honey Produced

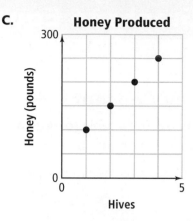

6. Think About the Process In the table as x increases by 1, y increases by 200.

x	0	1	2	3	4	5
y	0			600		

a. What step should you take to complete the table?

A. Divide each value of x by 200.

B. Multiply each value of x by 200.

C. Subtract 200 from each value of x.

D. Add 200 to each value of x.

b. Complete the table.

c. The table shows the relationship between x and y. Which statement expresses that relationship?

A. Each value of y is 200 greater than the corresponding value of x.

B. Each value of y is 200 times the corresponding value of x.

C. Each value of y is 100 greater than the corresponding value of x.

D. Each value of y is 100 times the corresponding value of x.

d. Use the table to sketch a graph that shows this relationship.

CCSS: 6.EE.C.9

Key Concept

You can use a table to write an equation that represents the relationship between two variables.

Look for a pattern in the table that connects the variables.

x		y
0	0 + 3 = 3	3
1	1 + 3 = 4	4
2	2 + 3 = 5	5
3	3 + 3 = 6	6
4	4 + 3 = 7	7
5	5 + 3 = 8	8

Words to Equation

Write the relationship in words.

The number in the x-column + 3 = The number in the y-column

Write the relationship as an equation.

x + 3 = y

Part 1

Example Writing Equations From Tables

Use the table to relate the independent variable x to the dependent variable y. First, describe the relationship in words. Then form an equation.

x	y
0	0
1	3
2	6
3	9
4	12
5	15

continued on next page >

See your complete lesson at MyMathUniverse.com

Solution

Look for a pattern in the table that connects the independent variable *x* to the dependent variable *y*.

x	Pattern	y
0	0 • 3 = 0	0
1	1 • 3 = 3	3
2	2 • 3 = 6	6
3	3 • 3 = 9	9
4	4 • 3 = 12	12
5	5 • 3 = 15	15

Write the relationship in words.

The number in the *x*-column times 3 equals the number in the *y*-column.

Words  **Equation**

number in the x-column	times	3	equals	number in the y-column
x	•	3	=	y

Intro

You can also use a graph to write an equation that represents the relationship between two variables.

x	y
0	10
1	9
2	8
3	7
4	6

To start, use the points on the graph to make a table.

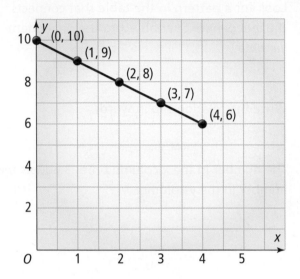

Look for a pattern in the table.

x	Pattern	y
0	0 + 10 = 10	10
1	1 + 9 = 10	9
2	2 + 8 = 10	8
3	3 + 7 = 10	7
4	4 + 6 = 10	6

Write the relationship in words.

Words

 to

Equation

The number in the *x*-column   plus   The number in the *y*-column   equals   10

$$x \quad + \quad y \quad = \quad 10$$

Write the relationship as an equation.

Example Writing Equations From Graphs

Use the graph to write an equation that represents the relationship between x and y. Make a table to start.

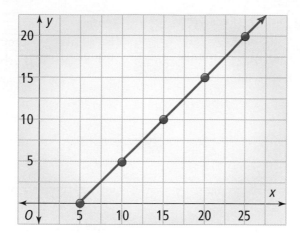

Solution

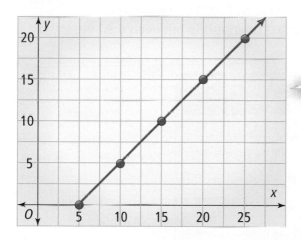

> Use the points on the graph to make a table.

x	y
5	0
10	5
15	10
20	15
25	20

Look for a pattern in the table.

x	Pattern	y
5	$5 - 5 = 0$	0
10	$10 - 5 = 5$	5
15	$15 - 5 = 10$	10
20	$20 - 5 = 15$	15
25	$25 - 5 = 20$	20

Write the relationship in words.

Part 2

Solution continued

The number in the *x*-column minus 5 equals the number in the *y*-column.

Write the relationship as an equation.

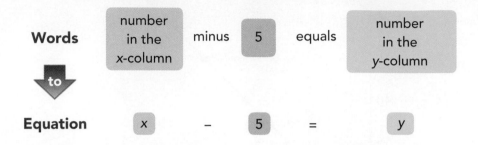

Words	number in the *x*-column	minus	5	equals	number in the *y*-column
Equation	*x*	–	5	=	*y*

Part 3

Intro

Suppose there is a $10 entry fee for a carnival and each game costs an additional $2. Make a table that reflects the relationship between the number of games and the total cost.

Number of Games	Entry Fee Plus $2 Per Game	Total Cost
1	10 + 2(1) = 12	12
2	10 + 2(2) = 14	14
3	10 + 2(3) = 16	16
4	10 + 2(4) = 18	18
5	10 + 2(5) = 20	20

The total cost is the $10 entry fee plus $2 times the number of games.

Example Writing Equations to Represent Total Cost

It costs $3 to bowl a game and $5 to rent shoes.

Make a table and then write an equation that shows the relationship between the number of games bowled and the total cost.

Solution ·

Number of Games	Cost for Games and Shoe Rental	Total Cost
1	3(1) + 5	8
2	3(2) + 5	11
3	3(3) + 5	14
4	3(4) + 5	17
5	3(5) + 5	20

Assign variables to the unknown quantities *number of games* and *total cost*.

g = number of games played
T = total cost for games and shoe rental

Use the second column in the table to write the relationship in words.

The total costs equals $3 times the number of games played, plus $5 for shoe rental.

Write the relationship as an equation.

Words	total cost	equals	$3	times	number of games played	plus	$5 shoe rental

to

Equation	T	=	3	·	g	+	5

1. Suppose each side of a triangle has length x. Let y be the perimeter of the triangle. Use the table to relate the independent variable x to the dependent variable y.

x	0	3	4	5
y	0	9	12	15

   a. Describe the relationship in words.

   b. Write an equation that represents the relationship between x and y.

2. Use the table to relate the independent variable x to the dependent variable y.

x	0	1	2	4
y	0	4	8	16

   a. First describe the relationship in words.

   b. Write an equation.

   c. Extend the table to show three more (x, y) pairs that have the same relationship.

3. **Mental Math** It costs a company $100 to use a machine to make any number of shirts. The materials for each shirt cost $5.

   a. Complete the table.

   Shirt Making Costs

Shirts made	Cost of machine and materials	Total cost ($)
1	100 + 5(1)	■
2	100 + 5(■)	110
■	100 + 5(3)	■
■	■ + 5(4)	120
5	100 + 5(5)	■

   b. Write an equation that shows the relationship between the number of shirts made, s, and the total cost, T.

   c. What will be the total cost if the company wants to make 10 shirts?

4. **Writing** Erin is putting items into a crate. The crate weighs 2 kilograms when empty. Let x be the number of items in the crate. Let y be the total weight of the crate. Use the table to relate the independent variable x to the dependent variable y.

x	0	1	4	7
y	2	3	6	9

   a. Describe the relationship in words.

   b. Write an equation that represents the relationship between x and y.

   c. Explain why Erin might need this information.

5. **Reasoning** Shira put a glass of water in a refrigerator. The graph shows the water's temperature y (in degrees Celsius) after x minutes. Use the graph to complete the table of values for x and y.

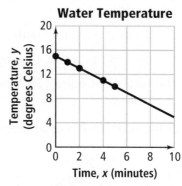

Water Temperature

   a. Use the given information to complete the table.

x	0	1	2	4	5
y	■	■	■	■	■

   b. What would the graph look like if Shira leaves the water in the refrigerator for 24 hours? Explain your reasoning.

   c. Write an equation that represents the relationship between x and y.

6. Error Analysis Anna had this table as part of her homework last night. She had to use it to relate the independent variable x to the dependent variable y. First, she used words and then she wrote an equation. She incorrectly said the value of x times 2 equals the value of y, and that the equation is $y = 2x$.

x	1	4	5	6
y	2	5	6	7

a. Describe the relationship in words correctly.

b. Write an equation that represents the relationship between x and y.

c. Explain Anna's likely error.

   A. She considered only the first (x, y) pair, not all four.

   B. She used the correct number but the incorrect operation.

   C. She used the correct operation but the incorrect number.

   D. She formed the correct equation, but did not give the correct description in words.

7. Think About the Process

a. Use the graph to complete the table of values for x and y.

x	0	2	4	5	6
y	■	■	■	■	■

b. Describe the relationship between x and y in words.

c. Write an equation that represents the relationship between x and y.

d. Mark three new points on the graph and give their x- and y-values.

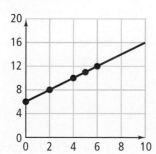

8. Think About the Process To rent a paddle boat, there is a fee of $7. It also costs $9 per hour.

a. Complete the table.

Paddle Boat Rental Costs

Hours rented	Cost of fee and hourly rate	Total cost ($)
1	7 + 9(1)	■
2	7 + 9(■)	25
■	7 + 9(3)	■
■	■ + 9(4)	43
5	7 + 9(5)	■

b. Describe the relationship between the number of hours a paddle boat is rented, r, and the total cost of the rental, C, in words.

9. Challenge A company has 6 workers who make and package barbecue grills. The parts for one grill cost $41. The packing material for one grill costs $2. Each of the workers earns $200 per day. Suppose the workers make and package a total of n grills every day.

a. Write an equation that shows the relationship between n and the total cost of the process, C, for the factory every day.

b. Yesterday, the workers made and packaged a total of 25 grills. What did yesterday's process cost the factory?

See your complete lesson at MyMathUniverse.com

CCSS: 6.EE.A.2c, 6.EE.C.9

Part 1

Example Writing Equations with Two Operations

Suppose you open a bank account and deposit $1. At the end of each year, the bank will pay you $100. Write an equation that relates the year and the amount of money in the account.

Solution ·

Know
- You start with $1.
- At the end of each year, you get an additional $100.

Need

An equation relating the year and the amount of money in the account

Plan
- Make a table to find out how much is in the account in the first few years.
- Look for a pattern in the table, and use the pattern to write an equation.

Step 1 Make a table showing how the account total changes in the first few years.

You start with one dollar. At the end of each year, you get an additional $100.

Year	$100 More Than Previous Year	Account Total
1	1 + 100	101
2	1 + 100 + 100	201
3	1 + 100 + 100 + 100	301
4	1 + 100 + 100 + 100 + 100	401

At the end of the fourth year, you have $401 in the account.

continued on next page >

Step 2 Find a pattern in the table.

Year	$100 More Than Previous Year	Account Total	
1	1 + 100	101	⟩ + 100
2	1 + 100 + 100	201	⟩ + 100
3	1 + 100 + 100 + 100	301	⟩ + 100
4	1 + 100 + 100 + 100 + 100	401	

Step 3 Write the relationship in words.

The Account Total increases by $100 each year. Repeated addition signals multiplication. In this case, the Year is multiplied by 100.

Step 4 Define variables and write the relationship as an equation.

T = account total at the end of a given year

y = year

Words Account total at end of year equals $1 plus $100 times year

to

Equation T = 1 + 100 · y

Part 2

Intro

Remember that repeated multiplication can be written with an exponent.

$$3 \cdot 3 = 3^2$$
$$3 \cdot 3 \cdot 3 = 3^3$$
$$3 \cdot 3 \cdot 3 \cdot 3 = 3^4$$

Example Writing Equations with Powers

Suppose you open a bank account and deposit $1. At the end of each year, the bank will double your money. Write an equation that relates the year and the amount of money in the account.

Solution

Know	Need	Plan
• You start with $1. • At the end of each year, your money is doubled.	An equation relating the year and the amount of money in the account	• Make a table to find out how much is in the account in the first few years. • Look for a pattern in the table, and use the pattern to write an equation.

Step 1 Make a table showing how the account total changes in the first few years.

You start with one dollar and double it at the end of the year.

Year	Double the Amount from the Previous Year	Account Total
1	2	2
2	2 • 2	4
3	2 • 2 • 2	8
4	2 • 2 • 2 • 2	16
5	2 • 2 • 2 • 2 • 2	32

At the end of the fifth year, you have $32 in the account.

continued on next page >

Part 2

Solution continued

Step 2 Find a pattern in the table.

Year	Double the Amount from the Previous Year	Account Total
1	2	2
2	2 • 2	4
3	2 • 2 • 2	8
4	2 • 2 • 2 • 2	16
5	2 • 2 • 2 • 2 • 2	32

Each row in the middle column shows a power of 2.

You can rewrite the amounts with exponents.

Year	Double the Amount from the Previous Year	Account Total
1	$2 = 2^1$	2
2	$2 • 2 = 2^2$	4
3	$2 • 2 • 2 = 2^3$	8
4	$2 • 2 • 2 • 2 = 2^4$	16
5	$2 • 2 • 2 • 2 • 2 = 2^5$	32

The exponent shows the year.

Step 3 Write the relationship in words.

The Account Total at the end of a given year equals 2 raised to the power of that Year.

Step 4 Define variables and write the relationship as an equation.

T = account total at the end of a given year

y = year

Words Account total at end of year equals 2 to the power of the Year

to

Equation T = 2^y

Example Evaluating Equations to Compare Them

You will deposit $1. Which bank should you choose for each of the given situations?

Bank of Lotsabucks

$T = 1 + 100y$

Wahoo Savings and Loan

$T = 2^y$

a. You will withdraw your money after 4 years.
b. You will withdraw your money after 9 years.
c. You will withdraw your money after 10 years.
d. You will withdraw your money after 15 years.

Solution

Evaluate the equations $T = 1 + 100y$ and $T = 2^y$ at each of the years. Compare the results to see which account will have more money. Find the balance in each account after 4, 9, 10, and 15 years.

a. Year 4

Evaluate $T = 1 + 100y$ at $y = 4$.	Evaluate $T = 2^y$ at $y = 4$.
$T = 1 + 100y$	$T = 2^y$
$= 1 + 100(4)$	$= 2^4$
$= 1 + 400$	$= 2 \cdot 2 \cdot 2 \cdot 2$
$= 401$	$= 16$

At the end of Year 4, there will be $401 in Bank of Lotsabucks and $16 in Wahoo Savings and Loan. If you are going to withdraw your money after 4 years, you should choose Bank of Lotsabucks.

b. Year 9

Evaluate $T = 1 + 100y$ at $y = 9$.	Evaluate $T = 2^y$ at $y = 9$.
$T = 1 + 100y$	$T = 2^y$
$= 1 + 100(9)$	$= 2^9$
$= 1 + 900$	$= 512$
$= 901$	

At the end of Year 9, there will be $901 in Bank of Lotsabucks and $512 in Wahoo Savings and Loan. If you are going to withdraw your money after 9 years, you should choose Bank of Lotsabucks.

continued on next page >

Solution continued

   c. Year 10

Evaluate $T = 1 + 100y$ at $y = 10$.   Evaluate $T = 2^y$ at $y = 10$.

$$T = 1 + 100y$$
$$= 1 + 100(10)$$
$$= 1 + 1{,}000$$
$$= 1{,}001$$

$$T = 2^y$$
$$= 2^{10}$$
$$= 1{,}024$$

At the end of Year 10, there will be $1,001 in Bank of Lotsabucks and $1,024 in Wahoo Savings and Loan. If you are going to withdraw your money after 10 years, you should choose Wahoo Savings and Loan. The account totals are dependent on the independent variable, which is time.

   d. Year 15

Evaluate $T = 1 + 100y$ at $y = 15$.   Evaluate $T = 2^y$ at $y = 15$.

$$T = 1 + 100y$$
$$= 1 + 100(15)$$
$$= 1 + 1{,}500$$
$$= 1{,}501$$

$$T = 2^y$$
$$= 2^{15}$$
$$= 32{,}768$$

At the end of Year 15, there will be $1,501 in Bank of Lotsabucks and $32,768 in Wahoo Savings and Loan. If you are going to withdraw your money after 15 years, you should choose Wahoo Savings and Loan.

After 5 years, the account at Bank of Lotsabucks will have more money.

Wahoo Savings and Loan

Y	T
1	2
2	4
...	...
5	32
...	...
10	1,024
...	...
15	32,768

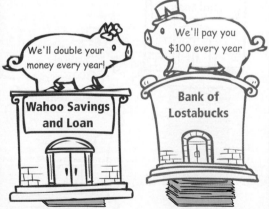

Bank of Lotsabucks

Y	T
1	101
2	201
...	...
5	501
...	...
10	1,001
...	...
15	1,501

continued on next page >

Solution continued

After 10 years, the account at Wahoo Savings and Loan will have slightly more money.

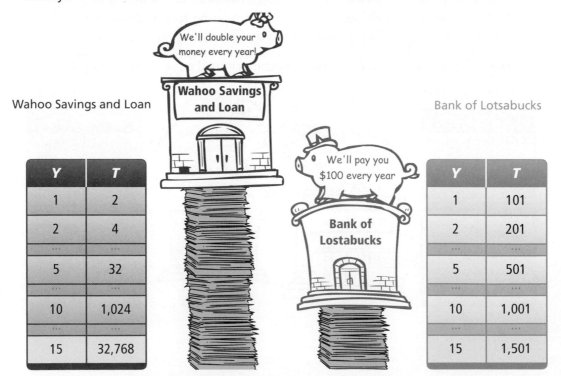

Wahoo Savings and Loan

Y	T
1	2
2	4
...	...
5	32
...	...
10	1,024
...	...
15	32,768

Bank of Lotsabucks

Y	T
1	101
2	201
...	...
5	501
...	...
10	1,001
...	...
15	1,501

We'll double your money every year!

Wahoo Savings and Loan

We'll pay you $100 every year

Bank of Lostabucks

After 15 years, the account at Wahoo Savings and Loan will have much more money.

We'll double your money every year!

Wahoo Savings and Loan

Wahoo Savings and Loan

Y	T
1	2
2	4
...	...
5	32
...	...
10	1,024
...	...
15	32,768

We'll pay you $100 every year

Bank of Lostabucks

Bank of Lotsabucks

Y	T
1	101
2	201
...	...
5	501
...	...
10	1,001
...	...
15	1,501

The amount of money in the accounts depends on how long you leave it in the bank. The account in Bank of Lotsabucks will have more money in the first few years. However, in any year after Year 9, the account in Wahoo Savings and Loan will have more money. The account totals are dependent on the independent variable, which is time.

1. Suppose you open a bank account and deposit $10. Then, every month you deposit $25. Write an equation that relates the total number of dollars deposited, T, and the month, m.

2. In a large city, the number of people with the flu, k, increases every day. On the first day, 9 people have the flu. Each day after the first, there are 9 times as many people who have the flu than there were the previous day. Write an equation that relates the number of people who have the flu, k, and the day, d.

3. Two cell phone companies start up at the same time. Each wants to model, or represent with an equation, the number of people, T, who have signed up for its services after m months. Company A models its number of people using $T = 25 + 20m$. Company B models its number of people using $T = 2^m$. If the models are accurate, which company had more customers after 14 months?

4. Jenice has $2,000. Each week she pays $25 for gas, $30 for food, and $60 for entertainment.

   a. Which equation below relates the total number of dollars, T, and the week, w?

   A. $T = 2{,}000 - 115w$

   B. $T = 2{,}000$

   C. $T = 2{,}000 + 115w$

   D. $T = 2{,}000 - 25w - 30w$

   b. After how many weeks will there be no money left? Explain how you found your answer.

5. You invest $21 in a company. At the end of each year, the company promises to double your investment. Write an equation relating the total value of your investment, T, and the year, y.

   A. $T = 21^y$ B. $T = 2 + 21^y$

   C. $T = 21 \cdot 2^y$ D. $T = 2 \cdot 21^y$

   E. $T = 21 + 2^y$

6. Each year, a cell phone carrier has 18 times as many customers as it had the previous year. The company started with 1 customer. The company incorrectly models its customers, c, using the equation $c = 18y$, where y is the number of years since the company started.

   a. Which of these equations relates the number of customers, c, and the number of years, y?

   A. $c = y \div 2$

   B. $c = y^2$

   C. $c = 18 + y$

   D. $c = 18^y$

   b. Which of the following was the company's likely error?

   A. The company multiplied 18 by y instead of dividing y by 18.

   B. The company multiplied 18 by y instead of using 18^y.

   C. The company multiplied 18 by y instead of adding 18 and y.

   D. The company multiplied 18 by y instead of using y^{18}.

7. The cost, c, for your company to ship a package is related to the package weight, p, in pounds. Last year, there was a flat rate of $3 and an additional rate of $5 per pound. The additional rate increases by $1 per pound this year. Write an equation that relates the cost, c, to ship a package this year and the weight of the package, p.

8. In dollars, it costs a company $59n + 1{,}598$ to make n items of Product A. It costs the company $51n + 1{,}898$ to make n items of Product B.

   a. Estimate the costs of 399 items of each product.

   b. For which product is the cost of 399 items less?

   A. Product B B. Product A

9. You are deciding between two hotels. Hotel A charges $90n$ dollars for n nights. This rate includes breakfast for each morning of your stay. Hotel B charges $80n$ dollars for n nights, but does not include breakfast. To include breakfast at Hotel B, the cost is $80n + 60$. If you want breakfast each day of your stay, which hotel has the better deal for 2 nights? For 10 nights?

10. There are 5 inches of snow on a major road. It will continue to snow at a rate of 3 inches per hour for the next n hours. The town can remove the snow at a rate of 2 inches per hour.

    a. Write an equation that relates the total amount of snow on the road, T, and the number of hours, n.

    b. If the snow keeps falling at a rate of 3 inches per hour, how much snow will there be on the road in 8 hours?

11. **Think About the Process** Each week, a manufacturing company spends $1,400 on bills. It also spends $500 per employee.

    a. Make a table showing the total weekly costs for the company for 1, 2, and 3 employees.

Number of Employees (n)	Total Cost Per Week (T)
1	■
2	■
3	■

    b. Which operation(s) can you use to write an equation relating the company's total weekly cost, T, and its number of employees, n? Select all that apply.

    A. Division

    B. Subtraction

    C. Addition

    D. Multiplication

12. **Think About the Process** You plan to do yardwork this summer. You are thinking about two different rates to charge for w hours of work. With rate A, you will earn $13 + 9w$ dollars. Using rate B, you will earn $10w$ dollars.

    a. For a given number of hours worked, how can you find the rate for which you will earn more money?

    A. Set each expression equal to the number of hours worked. Then solve the equations for w. The rate that corresponds to the greater value of w will earn you more money.

    B. Set each expression equal to the number of hours worked. Then solve the equations for w. The rate that corresponds to the lesser value of w will earn you more money.

    C. Substitute the number of hours worked for w in each expression. Then evaluate the expressions. The rate that corresponds to the lesser value will earn you more money.

    D. Substitute the number of hours worked for w in each expression. Then evaluate the expressions. The rate that corresponds to the greater value will earn you more money.

    b. For which rate will you earn more for 32 hours of work?

    A. rate B   **B.** rate A

13. **Challenge** A sample contains 100 bacteria. This type of bacteria quadruples every hour.

    a. Choose the equation that relates the number of bacteria, b, and the number of hours, n.

    A. $b = 100 + 4^n$ **B.** $b = 4 + 100^n$

    C. $b = 4 \cdot 100^n$ **D.** $b = 100^n$

    E. $b = 100 \cdot 4^n$

    b. How many bacteria will there be after 5 hours?

Multiplying Fractions and Whole Numbers

CCSS: 6.NS.A.1

Part 1

Intro

You can use a model to multiply a fraction and a whole number.

A fraction is a number that describes one or more parts of a whole that is divided into equal parts. This model shows $\frac{2}{5}$.

$\frac{2}{5}$ is two copies of $\frac{1}{5}$, which is $2 \times \frac{1}{5}$.

$$\frac{2}{5} = 2 \times \frac{1}{5}$$

Two times $\frac{2}{5}$ is two copies of $\frac{2}{5}$.

$$2 \times \frac{2}{5} = 2\left(2 \times \frac{1}{5}\right)$$
$$= (2 \times 2) \times \frac{1}{5}$$
$$= 4 \times \frac{1}{5}$$
$$= \frac{4}{5}$$

$$2 \times \frac{2}{5} = \frac{4}{5}$$

Three times $\frac{2}{5}$ is three copies of $\frac{2}{5}$.

$$3 \times \frac{2}{5} = 3\left(2 \times \frac{1}{5}\right)$$
$$= (3 \times 2) \times \frac{1}{5}$$
$$= 6 \times \frac{1}{5}$$
$$= \frac{6}{5}$$

So, $3 \times \frac{2}{5} = \frac{6}{5}$, or $1\frac{1}{5}$.

Part 1

Example Modeling Products of Whole Numbers and Fractions

Match each multiplication equation to its model.

$3 \times \frac{3}{10} = \frac{9}{10}$ $2 \times \frac{5}{12} = \frac{10}{12}$ $4 \times \frac{3}{8} = \frac{12}{8}$ or $1\frac{4}{8}$

Solution

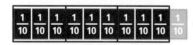

This model shows that 4 copies of $\frac{3}{8}$ is $\frac{12}{8}$, or $1\frac{4}{8}$.

The matching equation is $4 \times \frac{3}{8} = \frac{12}{8}$, or $1\frac{4}{8}$.

This model shows that 3 copies of $\frac{3}{10}$ is $\frac{9}{10}$.

The matching equation is $3 \times \frac{3}{10} = \frac{9}{10}$.

This model shows that 2 copies of $\frac{5}{12}$ is $\frac{10}{12}$.

The matching equation is $2 \times \frac{5}{12} = \frac{10}{12}$.

Part 2

Intro

You can use a model to multiply a fraction and a whole number.

Model $\frac{2}{5} \times 3$.

Step 1 To show $\frac{2}{5} \times 3$, first show 3 ones.

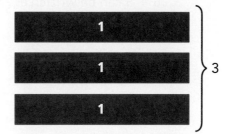

Step 2 Divide each of the 3 ones into 5 equal parts.

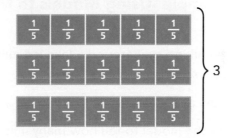

Step 3 One part shows $3 : 5$, or $\frac{1}{5}$ of 3.

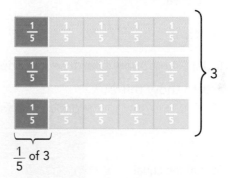

$\frac{1}{5}$ of 3

Step 4 Two parts show $2 \times (3 \div 5)$, or $\frac{2}{5}$ of 3.

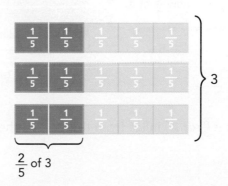

$\frac{2}{5}$ of 3

continued on next page >

Part 2

Step 5 $2 \times (3 \div 5) = (2 \times 3) \div 5$,
or $6 \div 5$.

$6 \div 5$ can be written as $\frac{6}{5}$.

So, $\frac{2}{5} \times 3 = \frac{6}{5}$, or $1\frac{1}{5}$.

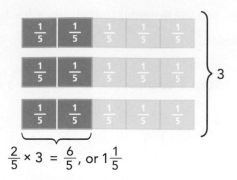

$\frac{2}{5} \times 3 = \frac{6}{5}$, or $1\frac{1}{5}$

Example Using Models to Multiply Whole Numbers and Fractions

The hiking trail around a lake is 4 miles long. There is a picnic area $\frac{2}{3}$ of the way from the start.

Draw a model to show $\frac{2}{3} \times 4$.

Use the model to tell how many miles it is from the start of the trail to the picnic area.

Solution

Model $\frac{2}{3} \times 4$. Show four fraction strips, and then divide each into 3 equal parts to show thirds.

Two of the equal parts show $\frac{2}{3}$ of 4.

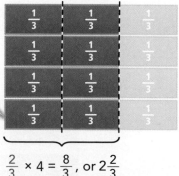

$\frac{2}{3} \times 4 = \frac{8}{3}$, or $2\frac{2}{3}$

It is $\frac{8}{3}$, or $2\frac{2}{3}$ miles from the start of the trail to the picnic area.

Key Concept

General Rule in Words When multiplying fractions and whole numbers:
- Multiply the fraction's numerator by the whole number to find the numerator of the product.
- Keep the fraction's denominator.
- If the product is an improper fraction, rewrite it as a mixed number in simplest form.

$$3 \times \frac{2}{5} = \frac{3 \times 2}{5}$$
$$= \frac{6}{5}, \text{ or } 1\frac{1}{5}$$

$$\frac{2}{5} \times 3 = \frac{2 \times 3}{5}$$
$$= \frac{6}{5}, \text{ or } 1\frac{1}{5}$$

General Rules You can use the general rules for any fraction $\frac{a}{b}$ and any whole number N.

$$N \times \frac{a}{b} = \frac{N \times a}{b}$$

Example:
$$6 \times \frac{4}{5} = \frac{6 \times 4}{5}$$
$$= \frac{24}{5}, \text{ or } 4\frac{4}{5}$$

$$\frac{a}{b} \times N = \frac{a \times N}{b}$$

Example:
$$\frac{4}{7} \times 3 = \frac{4 \times 3}{7}$$
$$= \frac{12}{7}, \text{ or } 1\frac{5}{7}$$

Part 3

Example Finding Products of Whole Numbers and Fractions

Match each factor pair with the correct product.

$6 \times \frac{2}{5}$ $\qquad$ $9 \times \frac{4}{5}$ $\qquad$ $\frac{2}{5} \times 6$ $\qquad$ $\frac{3}{8} \times 5$

$5 \times \frac{3}{8}$ $\qquad$ $\frac{1}{8} \times 7$ $\qquad$ $\frac{4}{5} \times 9$ $\qquad$ $7 \times \frac{1}{8}$

a. ■ and ■ = $\frac{7}{8}$

b. ■ and ■ = $\frac{12}{5}$, or $2\frac{2}{5}$

c. ■ and ■ = $\frac{15}{8}$, or $1\frac{7}{8}$

d. ■ and ■ = $\frac{36}{5}$, or $7\frac{1}{5}$

Solution

To multiply fractions and whole numbers, multiply the numerator of the fraction by the whole number; keep the same denominator as the fraction.

a. $7 \times \frac{1}{8} = \frac{7}{8}$ $\qquad$ and $\qquad$ $\frac{1}{8} \times 7 = \frac{7}{8}$

b. $6 \times \frac{2}{5} = \frac{12}{5}$, or $2\frac{2}{5}$ $\qquad$ and $\qquad$ $\frac{6}{5} \times 2 = \frac{12}{5}$, or $2\frac{2}{5}$

c. $5 \times \frac{3}{8} = \frac{15}{8}$, or $1\frac{7}{8}$ $\qquad$ and $\qquad$ $\frac{3}{8} \times 5 = \frac{15}{8}$, or $1\frac{7}{8}$

d. $9 \times \frac{4}{5} = \frac{36}{5}$, or $7\frac{1}{5}$ $\qquad$ and $\qquad$ $\frac{4}{5} \times 4 = \frac{36}{5}$, or $7\frac{1}{5}$

> If the product is an improper fraction, rewrite it as a mixed number in simplest form.

1. Use the model to find the product $3 \times \frac{2}{11}$.

$$\begin{array}{|c|c|c|c|c|c|c|c|c|c|c|} \hline \frac{1}{11} & \frac{1}{11} & \frac{1}{11} & \frac{1}{11} & \frac{1}{11} & \frac{1}{11} & \frac{1}{11} & \frac{1}{11} & \frac{1}{11} & \frac{1}{11} & \frac{1}{11} \\ \hline \end{array}$$

2. You use $\frac{5}{7}$ of your homework time on math. You spend 3 hours doing homework.

a. Which model shows $\frac{5}{7} \times 3$?

A.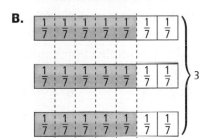

B.

C.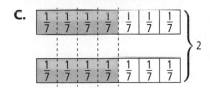

b. How much time do you spend on math?

3. Which multiplication equation matches the model? **(Figure 1)**

A. $2 \times \frac{5}{8} = 1\frac{2}{8}$

B. $5 \times \frac{2}{8} = 1\frac{2}{8}$

C. $2 \times \frac{5}{7} = 1\frac{3}{7}$

D. $5 \times \frac{2}{8} = \frac{8}{10}$

4. **Think About the Process**

a. How do you use the model to find the product $7 \times \frac{3}{5}$? **(Figure 2)**

A. You outline 1 copy of $\frac{21}{5}$.

B. You outline 3 copies of $\frac{7}{5}$. Then find that you have 3×7, or 21, fifths.

C. You outline 7 copies of $\frac{3}{5}$. Then find that you have 7×3, or 21, fifths.

D. You outline 21 copies of $\frac{1}{5}$.

b. Use the model to find the product $7 \times \frac{3}{5}$.

5. Which multiplication equation matches the model?

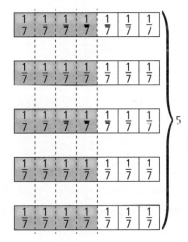

A. $\frac{4}{3} \times 5 = \frac{20}{3}$ or $6\frac{2}{3}$

B. $\frac{5}{7} \times 4 = \frac{7}{20}$

C. $\frac{5}{7} \times 7 = \frac{20}{7}$ or $2\frac{6}{7}$

D. $\frac{4}{7} \times 5 = \frac{20}{7}$ or $2\frac{6}{7}$

(Figure 1)

$$\begin{array}{|c|c|c|c|c|c|c|c|c|c|c|c|c|c|c|} \hline \frac{1}{8} & \frac{1}{8} & \frac{1}{8} & \frac{1}{8} & \frac{1}{8} & \frac{1}{8} & \frac{1}{8} & \frac{1}{8} & \frac{1}{8} & \frac{1}{8} & \frac{1}{8} & \frac{1}{8} & \frac{1}{8} & \frac{1}{8} & \frac{1}{8} \\ \hline \end{array}$$

(Figure 2)

$$\begin{array}{|c|c|c|c|c|c|c|c|c|c|c|c|c|c|c|c|c|c|c|c|c|c|c|} \hline \frac{1}{5} & \frac{1}{5} \\ \hline \end{array}$$

6. Find the product $\frac{1}{9} \times 5$.

7. Find the product $\frac{1}{2} \times 7$.

8. Which multiplication equation matches the model?

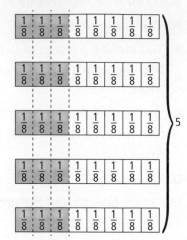

A. $\frac{5}{8} \times 3 = \frac{8}{15}$

B. $\frac{3}{8} \times 5 = \frac{15}{8}$ or $1\frac{7}{8}$

C. $\frac{3}{4} \times 5 = \frac{15}{4}$ or $3\frac{3}{4}$

D. $\frac{5}{8} \times 8 = \frac{15}{8}$ or $1\frac{7}{8}$

9. Reasoning The model below suggests a multiplication equation.

$\frac{1}{2}$	$\frac{1}{2}$	$\frac{1}{2}$	$\frac{1}{2}$

a. Is the product greater than 1?

b. Which multiplication equation matches the model?

A. $1 \times \frac{3}{2} = \frac{2}{3}$ **B.** $1 \times \frac{3}{2} = 2\frac{1}{2}$

C. $2 \times \frac{3}{2} = \frac{2}{3}$ **D.** $3 \times \frac{1}{2} = 1\frac{1}{2}$

c. Describe a situation that the model and equation could represent.

10. Think About the Process This fraction-tile diagram suggests a model for multiplication with a fraction.

a. What are the first steps in using the model to write a multiplication equation?

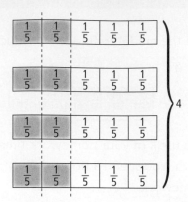

A. Show 5 tiles and divide 5 into 4 equal parts to show fourths.

B. Show 4 tiles and divide 4 into 5 equal parts to show fifths.

C. Show 4 tiles and divide 4 into 2 equal parts to show halves.

D. Show 1 tile and divide 1 into 5 equal parts to show fifths.

b. Which multiplication equation matches the model?

A. $\frac{2}{9} \times 4 = \frac{8}{9}$ **B.** $\frac{2}{5} \times 4 = 1\frac{3}{5}$

C. $\frac{4}{5} \times 2 = \frac{5}{8}$ **D.** $\frac{4}{5} \times 5 = 1\frac{3}{5}$

11. Multiple Representations There are two distinct fraction-tile models for the product of 2 and $\frac{3}{11}$.

a. Which model represents the product $2 \times \frac{3}{11}$?

A.

B.

C.

b. Find the product $2 \times \frac{3}{11}$.

c. Draw the second fraction-tile model for the product.

12. Two friends go for a 3-mile walk. After walking $\frac{2}{5}$ of the way, the friends stop at a store.

a. Draw a model to show $\frac{2}{5} \times 3$.

b. How many miles is it from the start of the walk to the store?

CCSS: 6.NS.A.1

Part 1

Intro

You can use a model to multiply two fractions. Here is how to model the product $\frac{3}{4} \times \frac{2}{3}$.

Step 1 Show $\frac{2}{3}$.

First divide the whole into 3 equal parts and show $\frac{2}{3}$.

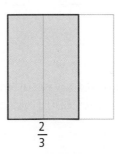

$\frac{2}{3}$

Step 2 Show $\frac{3}{4}$.

Then divide these thirds into 4 equal parts and show $\frac{3}{4}$.

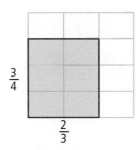

$\frac{3}{4}$

$\frac{2}{3}$

Step 3 Find the product $\frac{3}{4} \times \frac{2}{3}$.

The whole square now has 12 equal parts. The purple parts show $\frac{3}{4}$ of $\frac{2}{3}$. Six of the 12 equal parts are purple, so $\frac{3}{4} \times \frac{2}{3} = \frac{6}{12}$, or $\frac{1}{2}$.

Example Modeling Fraction Multiplication

Each square represents 1 whole. Which multiplication equation matches each given model?

$$\frac{4}{5} \times \frac{2}{3} = \frac{8}{15} \qquad \frac{1}{2} \times \frac{1}{2} = \frac{1}{4} \qquad \frac{1}{3} \times \frac{2}{3} = \frac{2}{9}$$

a.
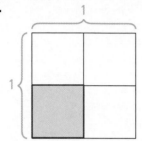

b.
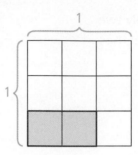

c.
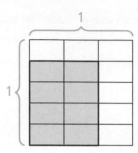

Solution

a. The unit square shows $\frac{1}{2}$ of $\frac{1}{2}$.

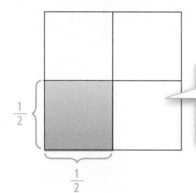

There are 4 equal parts; 1 is shaded.
$$\frac{1}{2} \times \frac{1}{2} = \frac{1}{4}$$

b. The unit square shows $\frac{1}{3}$ of $\frac{2}{3}$.

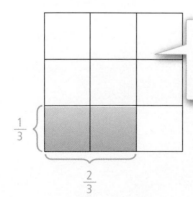

There are 9 equal parts; 2 are shaded.
$$\frac{1}{3} \times \frac{2}{3} = \frac{2}{9}$$

continued on next page >

Part 1

Solution continued

c. The unit square shows $\frac{4}{5}$ of $\frac{2}{3}$.

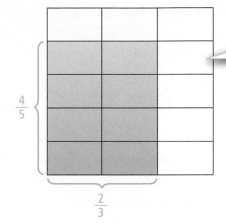

There are 15 equal parts; 8 are shaded.

$$\frac{4}{5} \times \frac{2}{3} = \frac{8}{15}$$

$\frac{4}{5}$

$\frac{2}{3}$

Key Concept

The examples in Part 1 illustrate a general rule that you can always use to multiple two fractions.

$$\frac{1}{3} \times \frac{2}{3} = \frac{2}{9} \qquad \frac{1}{2} \times \frac{1}{2} = \frac{1}{4} \qquad \frac{4}{5} \times \frac{2}{3} = \frac{8}{15}$$

When multiplying two fractions:

- Multiply the fractions' numerators to find the numerator of the product.
- Multiply the fractions' denominators to find the denominator of the product.
- If necessary, rewrite the product in simplest form.

You can use this general rule for any two fractions $\frac{a}{b}$ and $\frac{c}{d}$.

$$\frac{a}{b} \times \frac{c}{d} = \frac{a \times c}{b \times d}$$

Part 2

Example Multiplying Fractions

Which pair of factors result in each product?

$$\frac{5}{11} \times \frac{2}{7} \qquad \frac{3}{4} \times \frac{5}{8} \qquad \frac{5}{6} \times \frac{5}{6} \qquad \frac{4}{9} \times \frac{1}{5} \qquad \frac{5}{9} \times \frac{7}{8} \qquad \frac{1}{2} \times \frac{3}{8}$$

a. $\frac{15}{32}$ **b.** $\frac{35}{72}$ **c.** $\frac{25}{36}$

d. $\frac{3}{16}$ **e.** $\frac{10}{77}$ **f.** $\frac{4}{45}$

continued on next page >

Part 2

Example continued

Solution

- Multiply the numerators of the two factors to find the numerator of the product.
- Multiply the denominators of the two factors to find the denominator of the product.

a. $\frac{3}{4} \times \frac{5}{8} = \frac{15}{32}$ **b.** $\frac{5}{9} \times \frac{7}{8} = \frac{35}{72}$ **c.** $\frac{5}{6} \times \frac{5}{6} = \frac{25}{36}$

d. $\frac{1}{2} \times \frac{3}{8} = \frac{3}{16}$ **e.** $\frac{5}{11} \times \frac{2}{7} \times \frac{10}{77}$ **f.** $\frac{4}{9} \times \frac{1}{5} = \frac{4}{45}$

Part 3

Intro

When multiplying two fractions, such as $\frac{3}{8} \times \frac{2}{5}$, there are two methods you can use to write the product in simplest form.

Method 1 Simplify after multiplying.

Multiply the numerators and denominators.

$$\frac{3}{8} \times \frac{2}{5} = \frac{3 \times 2}{8 \times 5}$$

$$= \frac{6}{40}$$

Divide the numerator and the denominator of the product by their greatest common factor (GCF), 2.

$$= \frac{6 \div 2}{40 \div 2}$$

Write the product in simplest form.

$$= \frac{3}{20}$$

Method 2 Simplify before multiplying.

Divide the numerator and the denominator of either factor by their GCF. Divide 8 and 2 by 2.

Multiply the simplified factors.

$$\frac{3}{4} \times \frac{1}{5} = \frac{3 \times 1}{4 \times 5}$$

Write the product in simplest form.

$$= \frac{3}{20}$$

Part 3

Example Multiplying Fractions to Find Area

Find the area, in square miles, of a rectangular city neighborhood shown in the diagram.

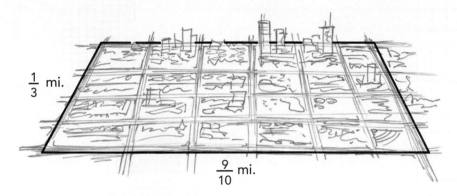

$\frac{1}{3}$ mi.

$\frac{9}{10}$ mi.

Solution

To find the area, multiply the length by the width.

Method 1 Simplify after multiplying.

$$\frac{9}{10} \times \frac{1}{3} = \frac{9 \times 1}{10 \times 3}$$

$$= \frac{9}{30}$$

$$= \frac{9 \div 3}{30 \div 3}$$

$$= \frac{3}{10}$$

Method 2 Simplify before multiplying.

$$\frac{{}^{3}\cancel{9}}{10} \times \frac{1}{\cancel{3}_{1}} = \frac{3}{10}$$

The area is $\frac{3}{10}$ square miles.

1. a. Which area model shows $\frac{1}{2} \times \frac{1}{5}$?

A.

B.

C.

   b. Find the product $\frac{1}{2} \times \frac{1}{5}$.

2. Simplify the factors and multiply.
$\frac{25}{26} \times \frac{13}{15}$

3. Select each pair of factors that has the product $\frac{5}{24}$.

   A. $\frac{5}{6} \times \frac{5}{12}$ **B.** $\frac{1}{4} \times \frac{1}{2}$

   C. $\frac{5}{12} \times \frac{1}{2}$ **D.** $\frac{5}{6} \times \frac{1}{4}$

4. Multiply. Write the product $\frac{3}{10} \cdot \frac{7}{11}$ in simplest form.

5. Multiply. Write the product $\frac{2}{3} \times \frac{3}{4}$ in simplest form.

6. A park worker cuts a rectangular piece of sod measuring $\frac{2}{3}$ ft by $\frac{3}{7}$ ft. Find the area of the piece of sod by finding $\frac{2}{3} \times \frac{3}{7}$.

7. Open-Ended

   a. Find the product $\frac{1}{2} \times \frac{4}{5}$ and then simplify.

   b. Describe a situation that you can model with this product.

8. Writing Find the product $\frac{3}{4} \times \frac{1}{3}$. What do you notice about $\frac{3}{4}$ and $\frac{1}{3}$ that can simplify your work? What does this tell you to watch for when multiplying fractions?

9. a. Reasoning Explain why you can use the unit square shown here to draw an area model for $\frac{7}{9} \times \frac{8}{9}$.

   b. Which area model shows $\frac{7}{9} \times \frac{8}{9}$?

   A.

   B.

   C.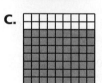

10. Think About the Process Julio wants to find and then simplify the product $\frac{1}{2} \times \frac{2}{3}$. He multiplies the numerators and the denominators of the two factors to get $\frac{1}{2} \times \frac{2}{3} = \frac{2}{6}$.

   a. What should he do to write this product in simplest form?

   A. He should divide the numerator and denominator by 6.

   B. He should multiply the numerator and denominator by 2.

   C. He should subtract 2 from the numerator and denominator.

   D. He should divide the numerator and denominator by 2.

   b. What is the product in simplest form?

11. Select each pair of factors that has the product $\frac{7}{54}$.

   A. $\frac{1}{6} \times \frac{7}{9}$ **B.** $\frac{7}{18} \times \frac{1}{3}$

   C. $\frac{3}{26} \times \frac{3}{4}$ **D.** $\frac{1}{2} \times \frac{7}{27}$

12. Multiple Representations

    a. Which area model shows $\frac{3}{5}$?

    A.

    B.

    C.

    b. Which area model shows $\frac{1}{2}$?

    A.

    B.

    C.

    c. Which area model shows $\frac{3}{5} \times \frac{1}{2}$?

    A.

    B.

    C.

    d. Find the product $\frac{3}{5} \times \frac{1}{2}$.

---

13. Think About the Process This is a model for the multiplication of two fractions.

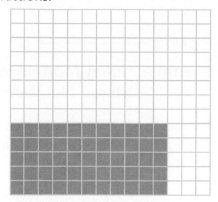

a. What could be the first step in using the model?

    A. Write the fraction $\frac{5}{11}$.

    B. Write the fraction $\frac{5}{13}$.

    C. Write the fraction $\frac{13}{14}$.

    D. Write the fraction $\frac{5}{14}$.

b. Which equation matches the model?

    A. $\frac{5}{13} \times \frac{11}{14} = \frac{55}{182}$

    B. $\frac{5}{13} \times \frac{11}{14} = \frac{16}{27}$

    C. $\frac{5}{13} \times \frac{10}{14} = \frac{50}{182}$

    D. $\frac{11}{13} \times \frac{5}{14} = \frac{55}{182}$

14. a. Challenge Select each product that equals $\frac{9}{52}$.

    A. $\frac{3}{4} \times \frac{3}{13}$

    B. $\frac{9}{26} \times \frac{1}{2}$

    C. $\frac{9}{13} \times \frac{1}{4}$

    D. $\frac{3}{26} \times \frac{3}{4}$

b. List three other pairs of factors whose products are different from $\frac{9}{52}$, but which simplify to $\frac{9}{52}$.

Part 1

> #### Example Using Models to Multiply Fractions and Mixed Numbers

A birdbath can hold $2\frac{1}{2}$ gallons of water. The birdbath is $\frac{3}{4}$ full. How many gallons of water are in the birdbath? Use a grid to draw a model to show and solve the problem.

Solution ···

Draw a model to show $\frac{3}{4} \times 2\frac{1}{2}$.

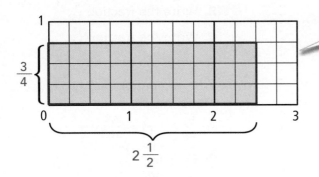

Each grid square is $\frac{1}{4} \times \frac{1}{4} = \frac{1}{16}$.

The model shows 30 grid squares of $\frac{1}{16}$.

Multiply to find the number of gallons of water.

$$30 \times \frac{1}{16} = \frac{30}{16}$$
$$= \frac{30 \div 2}{16 \div 2}$$
$$= \frac{15}{8}, \text{ or } 1\frac{7}{8}$$

There are $1\frac{7}{8}$ gallons of water in the birdbath.

Key Concept

You can use the rules for multiplying fractions to multiply a fraction by a mixed number. Here is how to find $\frac{2}{3} \times 6\frac{1}{2}$.

Step 1 Write the mixed number as an improper fraction: $6\frac{1}{2} = \frac{13}{2}$.

$$\frac{2}{3} \times 6\frac{1}{2} = \frac{2}{3} \times \frac{13}{2}$$

Step 2 Simplify factors, if possible.

$$= \frac{\overset{1}{2}}{3} \times \frac{13}{\underset{1}{2}}$$

Step 3 Multiply the numerators. Multiply the denominators. Write the product.

$$= \frac{13}{3}$$

Step 4 If the product is an improper fraction, rewrite it as a mixed number.

$$= 4\frac{1}{3}$$

Part 2

Example Multiplying Fractions and Mixed Numbers

The road up a mountain is $3\frac{1}{3}$ miles long. The first lookout point is $\frac{1}{4}$ of the way to the top. How far is it from the start to the first lookout point?

Solution ·

Find $\frac{1}{4} \times 3\frac{1}{3}$.

Write the mixed number as an improper fraction.

$$\frac{1}{4} \times 3\frac{1}{3} = \frac{1}{4} \times \frac{10}{3}$$

Simplify the factors by dividing by the GCF.

$$= \frac{1}{\underset{2}{4}} \times \frac{\overset{5}{10}}{3}$$

Multiply the factors.

$$= \frac{5}{6}$$

$\frac{5}{6}$ is a proper fraction.

It is $\frac{5}{6}$ mile from the start to the first lookout point.

Part 3

Example Finding Products of Fractions and Mixed Numbers

An MP3 Player has $7\frac{1}{2}$ gigabytes of memory available. If you use $\frac{3}{5}$ of that memory for music, how many gigabytes are used for music?

Solution

Find $7\frac{1}{2} \times \frac{3}{5}$.

Write the mixed number as an improper fraction.	$7\frac{1}{2} \times \frac{3}{5} = \frac{15}{2} \times \frac{3}{5}$
Simplify the factors by dividing by the GCF.	$= \frac{\overset{3}{\cancel{15}}}{2} \times \frac{3}{\underset{1}{\cancel{5}}}$
Multiply the factors.	$= \frac{9}{2}$
Write the product as a mixed number.	$= 4\frac{1}{2}$

$4\frac{1}{2}$ gigabytes of memory are used for music.

1. a. Which model shows $\frac{1}{2} \times 4\frac{1}{4}$?

A.

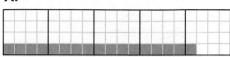

B.

C.

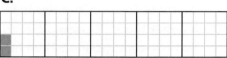

b. Find the product $\frac{1}{2} \times 4\frac{1}{4}$.

2. For a project, you cut paper into strips that are $3\frac{1}{2}$ inches long by $\frac{3}{4}$ inch wide.

a. Which model shows the area of each strip of paper?

A.

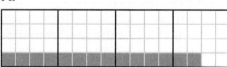

B.

C.

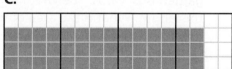

b. What is the area of each strip of paper?

3. Find the product $\frac{1}{4} \times 4\frac{1}{5}$.

4. A model for a proposed computer chip measures $\frac{1}{9}$ inch by $1\frac{8}{9}$ inches. Find its area.

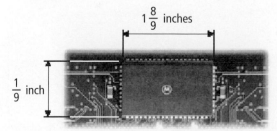

$1\frac{8}{9}$ inches

$\frac{1}{9}$ inch

5. Multiply $\frac{2}{7} \times 9\frac{1}{10}$.

6. You fill a $17\frac{1}{2}$ gallon tub $\frac{1}{7}$ full of water. How many gallons of water are in the tub?

7. New workers at a factory require $13\frac{1}{2}$ hours of training. The workers spend $\frac{5}{7}$ of the training time in a classroom. How many hours are the workers in the classroom?

8. a. Find $\frac{7}{8} \times 8\frac{1}{14}$. Then find $8\frac{1}{14} \times \frac{7}{8}$.

b. Compare the results. Explain why you can compare these expressions before doing the calculations.

9. Writing A farmer has $2\frac{1}{16}$ acres of land unplanted. The farmer plants corn in $\frac{3}{4}$ of the remaining land. How many acres does the farmer use for corn?

10. Think About the Process

a. How do you use the area model to find $\frac{1}{2} \times 4\frac{3}{4}$?

A. Multiply the number of grid squares in the shaded part by the size of each grid square. The size of each grid square is $\frac{1}{4}$.

B. Multiply the total number of grid squares by the size of each grid square. The size of each grid square is $\frac{1}{8}$.

C. Multiply the number of grid squares in the shaded part by the size of each grid square. The size of each grid square is $\frac{1}{16}$.

b. Find the product $\frac{1}{2} \times 4\frac{3}{4}$.

11. Reasoning A recipe calls for $5\frac{1}{3}$ cups of flour. You want to make a new recipe with $\frac{2}{3}$ of the flour. The area model shows the amount of flour in the new recipe.

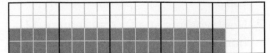

  a. Is the amount of flour in the new recipe greater than the amount of flour in the original recipe?

  b. How much flour is in the new recipe?

  c. Explain why you can answer the first question without answering the second question.

12. Error Analysis The teacher asks students to find $\frac{4}{5} \times 8\frac{2}{5}$. One student incorrectly says the product is $8\frac{8}{25}$.

  a. What is the correct product $\frac{4}{5} \times 8\frac{2}{5}$?

  b. What was the error the student likely made?

  A. The student multiplied the fraction parts without writing the mixed number as an improper fraction.

  B. The student multiplied the fractions without simplifying the factors.

  C. The student multiplied the numerators of the fractions, but not the denominators of the fractions.

13. Mental Math Find the product $\frac{1}{4} \times 8\frac{1}{2}$.

14. Think About the Process

  a. First write $5\frac{1}{4}$ as an improper fraction to find $\frac{2}{7} \times 5\frac{1}{4}$. Then find the product.

  b. After taking the first step mentioned above, describe the second step you would take in finding the simplified product.

15. Find $\frac{3}{10} \times 7\frac{2}{5}$. Explain why you need to rewrite the mixed number as an improper fraction in order to multiply.

16. A writer has a 16-page paper to write. He finished $15\frac{3}{4}$ pages. Then he proofread $\frac{2}{7}$ of the pages.

  a. How many pages did the writer proofread?

  b. Show how to find the fraction of the whole paper that the proofread pages represent.

17. Challenge In a $5\frac{4}{5}$-mile race, there are two water stations. The first water station is $\frac{1}{3}$ of the way from the starting point. The second water station is $\frac{2}{3}$ of the way from the starting point. How far is it from the first water station to the second water station? Show two ways to solve this problem.

18. Challenge The length of a rectangular garden is $2\frac{4}{5}$ yards. The width is $\frac{1}{4}$ of the length. What is the area of the garden?

CCSS: 6.NS.A.1

Part 1

Example Modeling Products of Mixed Numbers

Use an area model to find $2\frac{1}{3} \times 1\frac{3}{4}$.

Solution ·

Step 1 Show $2\frac{1}{3}$ and $1\frac{3}{4}$ as improper fractions.

Step 2 Count the shaded parts.

There are 49 shaded parts.

Each unit square has 12 equal parts.

So each part is $\frac{1}{12}$ of a unit.

Step 3 Find the product.

$$\frac{1}{12} \times 49 = \frac{49}{12}$$

Step 4 Change the improper fraction to a mixed number.

$$\frac{49}{12} = 4\frac{1}{12}$$

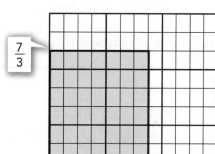

$\frac{7}{3}$

$\frac{7}{4}$

Key Concept

To find the product of two mixed numbers, you can change the mixed numbers to improper fractions and multiply.

$$6\frac{3}{4} \times 7\frac{1}{3} = \frac{27}{4} \times \frac{22}{3}$$

Then you can use the GCF to simplify the factors.

$$= \frac{\overset{9}{\cancel{27}}}{\underset{2}{\cancel{4}}} \times \frac{\overset{11}{\cancel{22}}}{\underset{1}{\cancel{3}}}$$

> The GCF of 27 and 3 is 3.
> The GCF of 4 and 22 is 2.

Multiply the numerators and the denominators. Then rewrite as a mixed number.

$$= \frac{99}{2}$$

$$= 49\frac{1}{2}$$

continued on next page >

Key Concept

continued

Use estimation to check your answer.

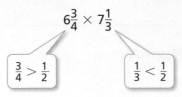

$$6\tfrac{3}{4} \times 7\tfrac{1}{3}$$

$$\boxed{\tfrac{3}{4} > \tfrac{1}{2}} \qquad \boxed{\tfrac{1}{3} < \tfrac{1}{2}}$$

$$7 \times 7 = 49$$

$$6\tfrac{3}{4} \times 7\tfrac{1}{3} \approx 49$$

The answer is reasonable.

Part 2

Example Multiplying Mixed Numbers to Find Areas

An art club is making a mural for the wall space shown. What is the area of the wall space available for the mural?

$5\tfrac{5}{6}$ ft

$4\tfrac{1}{5}$ ft

Solution ·

Multiply length times width to find the area.

Write the factors as improper fractions. $\quad 5\tfrac{5}{6} \times 4\tfrac{1}{5} = \dfrac{35}{6} \times \dfrac{21}{5}$

Simplify. $\quad = \dfrac{\overset{7}{\cancel{35}}}{\underset{2}{\cancel{6}}} \times \dfrac{\overset{7}{\cancel{21}}}{\underset{1}{\cancel{5}}}$

Multiply. $\quad = \dfrac{49}{2}$

Write the improper fraction as a mixed number. $\quad = 22\tfrac{1}{2}$

continued on next page >

Part 2

Solution continued

Use estimation to check your answer for reasonableness.

$$5\tfrac{5}{6} \times 4\tfrac{1}{5} \approx 6 \times 4$$
$$= 24$$

$24\tfrac{1}{2}$ is close to the estimate, 24, so your answer is reasonable.

The area is $24\tfrac{1}{2}$ ft^2.

Part 3

Intro

Using the Distributive Property to multiply mixed numbers:

$$3 \times 5\tfrac{3}{10} = 3\left(5 + \tfrac{3}{10}\right)$$

$$= (3 \times 5) + \left(3 \times \tfrac{3}{10}\right)$$

$$= 15 + \tfrac{9}{10}, \text{ or } 15\tfrac{9}{10}$$

Example Using the Distributive Property to Multiply Mixed Numbers

A volunteer feeds the cats at an animal shelter $5\tfrac{1}{16}$ pounds of food each day.

Use the Distributive Property to find how much food the cats are given each week. Find $7 \times 5\tfrac{1}{16}$.

Solution ·

Use the Distributive Property to find $7 \times 5\tfrac{1}{16}$.

Break the mixed number apart.	$7 \times 5\tfrac{1}{16} = 7\left(5 + \tfrac{1}{16}\right)$
Use the Distributive Property.	$= 7(5) + 7\left(\tfrac{1}{16}\right)$
Multiply.	$= 35 + \tfrac{7}{16}$
Add.	$= 35\tfrac{7}{16}$

The cats are given $35\tfrac{7}{16}$ pounds of food each week.

1. a. Which area model represents $2\frac{1}{3} \times 2\frac{1}{2}$?

A.

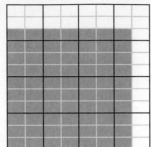

B.

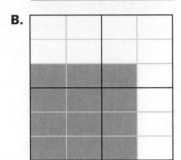

C.

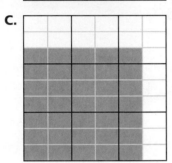

b. Multiply $2\frac{1}{3} \times 2\frac{1}{2}$.

2. Which multiplication of mixed numbers matches this model?

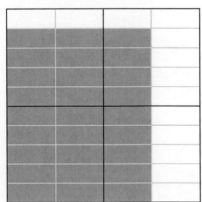

A. $4\frac{1}{2} \times \frac{3}{5} = \frac{10}{27}$

B. $4\frac{1}{2} \times \frac{3}{5} = 2\frac{7}{10}$

C. $1\frac{4}{5} \times 1\frac{1}{2} = 2\frac{7}{10}$

D. $1\frac{4}{5} \times 1\frac{1}{2} = \frac{10}{27}$

3. a. What multiplication expression matches the area model?

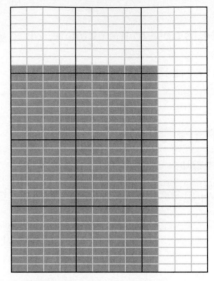

A. $6\frac{1}{4} \times 2\frac{1}{4}$ **B.** $3\frac{1}{8} \times 2\frac{1}{4}$

C. $3\frac{1}{8} \times 1\frac{1}{8}$ **D.** $6\frac{1}{4} \times 1\frac{1}{8}$

b. Use the model to help you find the product.

c. What differences, if any, would the model show if the multiplication had its factors in the opposite order? Explain.

4. Multiply $2\frac{8}{11} \times 1\frac{7}{10}$.

5. A blueprint of a house has a scale in which 1 inch represents $4\frac{1}{2}$ feet. If a living room wall measures $6\frac{1}{8}$ inches on the drawing, what is the actual length of the wall?

6. Think About the Process

a. Use the Distributive Property to rewrite $9 \times 4\frac{5}{7}$.

A. $4 + \left(9 \times \frac{5}{7}\right)$

B. $(9 \times 4) + \frac{5}{7}$

C. $(9 \times 4) + \left(9 \times \frac{5}{7}\right)$

D. $(4 \times 7) + 5$

b. Find the product $9 \times 4\frac{5}{7}$.

See your complete lesson at MyMathUniverse.com

7. Use the Distributive Property to help you find the product $2 \times 6\frac{1}{5}$.

8. **Mental Math** Use the Distributive Property to help you find the product. $6\frac{1}{10} \times 10$

9. A wheel rotates for 2 minutes. If it makes $6\frac{2}{9}$ rotations each minute, how many rotations does it make?

10. **Writing** To train for the cross-country team, Shira runs $6\frac{1}{2}$ miles each day. How far does she run each week? Explain how you can use the Distributive Property to find the answer.

11. **Reasoning** You want to find the product $2\frac{4}{9} \times 1\frac{3}{11}$.
    a. Is the product greater than $2\frac{4}{9}$?
    b. Find the product $2\frac{4}{9} \times 1\frac{3}{11}$.
    c. Explain your reasoning.

12. **Error Analysis** Your friend incorrectly says that $4 \times 9\frac{3}{13} = 36\frac{3}{13}$.
    a. What is the correct product $4 \times 9\frac{3}{13}$?
    b. What mistake did your friend most likely make?
       A. Your friend did not multiply the whole number part of $9\frac{3}{13}$ by 4.
       B. Your friend did not simplify the product correctly.
       C. Your friend did not multiply the fraction part of $9\frac{3}{13}$ by 4.

13. How many pounds of a liquid are contained in a barrel if the barrel holds $18\frac{3}{5}$ gallons, and a gallon of the liquid weighs $7\frac{2}{3}$ lb?

14. a. **Estimation** Use whole numbers to estimate the product $2\frac{1}{3} \times 6\frac{1}{2}$.
    b. Find the exact product $2\frac{1}{3} \times 6\frac{1}{2}$.

15. How wide is a floor made from 44 boards that are each $4\frac{5}{8}$ inches wide?

16. **Mental math** Use mental math to find the product $2\frac{1}{3} \times 3\frac{6}{7}$.

17. **Challenge** A large garbage bag holds $10\frac{1}{3}$ pounds of leaves. Yesterday, you filled $3\frac{4}{5}$ bags with leaves before lunch.
    a. How many pounds of leaves did you bag before lunch?
    b. If you filled another $8\frac{1}{5}$ bags after lunch, how many pounds of leaves did you bag in all yesterday?

18. **Challenge** A mosaic is made up of square tiles. Each tile is $3\frac{1}{16}$ inches on a side. If the mosaic is 15 tiles wide and 11 tiles long, what are the dimensions of the mosaic in inches? Describe in words two ways to find the area of the mosaic.

CCSS: 6.NS.A.1

Part 1

Example Analyzing Products of Mixed Numbers and Variables

Analyze the expression $2\frac{1}{2} \cdot b$. Decide whether the product is greater than $2\frac{1}{2}$ or less than $2\frac{1}{2}$ for each given value of b.

a. $b = 2$ **b.** $b = 1\frac{1}{2}$ **c.** $b = 2\frac{1}{2}$

d. $b = \frac{9}{10}$ **e.** $b = \frac{1}{2}$ **f.** $b = \frac{1}{10}$

Solution ·

Use number sense. If b equals 1, then $2\frac{1}{2} \cdot b = 2\frac{1}{2}$. If b is greater than 1, then $2\frac{1}{2} \cdot b > 2\frac{1}{2}$. If b is less than 1, then $2\frac{1}{2} \cdot b < 2\frac{1}{2}$.

a. 2 is greater than 1, so $2\frac{1}{2} \cdot b > 2\frac{1}{2}$.

If b is a mixed number, then the value of b is greater than 1.

b. $1\frac{1}{2}$ is a mixed number, so $2\frac{1}{2} \cdot b > 2\frac{1}{2}$.

c. $2\frac{1}{2}$ is a mixed number, so $2\frac{1}{2} \cdot b > 2\frac{1}{2}$.

If b is a proper fraction, then its value is less than 1.

d. $\frac{9}{10}$ is a proper fraction, so $2\frac{1}{2} \cdot b < 2\frac{1}{2}$.

e. $\frac{1}{2}$ is a proper fraction, so $2\frac{1}{2} \cdot b < 2\frac{1}{2}$.

f. $\frac{1}{10}$ is a proper fraction, so $2\frac{1}{2} \cdot b < 2\frac{1}{2}$.

Part 2

Example Multiplying Mixed Numbers to Solve Problems

A student is helping the science teacher make a batch of "oobleck" for the class. The teacher says to use $1\frac{5}{8}$ cups of cornstarch for every cup of water used. If the student uses $2\frac{2}{3}$ cups of water, how much cornstarch should he use?

Solution

> **Know**
> Oobleck is made using $1\frac{5}{8}$ cups of cornstarch for every cup of water.

> **Need**
> To find how much cornstarch to use with $2\frac{2}{3}$ cups of water.

> **Plan**
> Find $1\frac{5}{8} \times 2\frac{2}{3}$.

$$1\frac{5}{8} \times 2\frac{2}{3} = \frac{13}{8} \times \frac{8}{3}$$

$$= \frac{13}{\underset{1}{8}} \times \frac{\overset{1}{8}}{3}$$

$$= \frac{13}{3}, \text{ or } 4\frac{1}{3}$$

The student should use $4\frac{1}{3}$ cups of cornstarch.

Part 3

Example Writing Multiplication Equations with Fractions

Each of the string lengths to be filled in below is $\frac{8}{9}$ of the length of the previous string. Write equations to find the missing fraction lengths of the strings below.

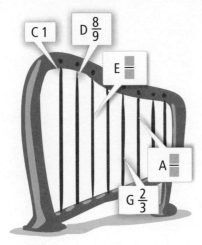

Solution

You know that each string length is $\frac{8}{9}$ of the length of the previous string. Since $D = \frac{8}{9}$, and the D string is above the E string,

$$E = \frac{8}{9} \times \frac{8}{9}$$
$$= \frac{64}{81}$$

> Multiply the length of the D string by $\frac{8}{9}$.

Since $G = \frac{2}{3}$, and the G string is above the A string,

$$A = \frac{2}{3} \times \frac{8}{9}$$
$$= \frac{16}{27}$$

> Multiply the length of the A string by $\frac{8}{9}$.

1. Analyze the expression $2\frac{1}{2} \cdot B$. For which values of B will the product be greater than $2\frac{1}{2}$? Select all that apply.

   A. $B = \frac{1}{2}$ **B.** $B = 1\frac{1}{2}$

   C. $B = 2$ **D.** $B = \frac{1}{8}$

2. A recipe for punch says to use $1\frac{4}{5}$ cups of lemonade for each cup of ginger ale. If you use $1\frac{4}{7}$ cups of ginger ale, how much lemonade should you use?

3. You have two marbles. The smaller marble has $\frac{5}{6}$ the mass of the larger marble. The mass of the larger marble is $1\frac{3}{4}$ grams. Write an equation to find the mass of the smaller marble.

   A. $\frac{5}{6} \cdot 1\frac{3}{4} = 1\frac{11}{24}$ **B.** $\frac{5}{6} \cdot 1\frac{3}{4} = 2\frac{7}{12}$

   C. $\frac{5}{6} + 1\frac{3}{4} = 1\frac{11}{24}$ **D.** $\frac{5}{6} + 1\frac{3}{4} = 2\frac{7}{12}$

4. A rectangle has length that is $\frac{1}{5}$ of the length of a larger rectangle. The length of the larger rectangle is $\frac{4}{5}$ inch. Which equation gives the length of the smaller rectangle?

   A. $\frac{1}{5} + \frac{4}{5} = \frac{1}{25}$ **B.** $\frac{1}{5} \cdot \frac{4}{5} = \frac{4}{25}$

   C. $\frac{1}{5} \cdot \frac{4}{5} = \frac{1}{25}$ **D.** $\frac{1}{5} \cdot \frac{4}{5} = 1$

5. Is the inequality $9\frac{1}{9} \cdot 1\frac{1}{9} < 9\frac{1}{9}$ true or false? Explain.

6. **Think About the Process**

   a. How can you tell if the product $\frac{13}{14} \cdot 4\frac{5}{6}$ is greater than or less than $4\frac{5}{6}$?

   A. Check to see if $4\frac{5}{6}$ is greater than 1.

   B. Check to see if $\frac{13}{14}$ is greater than 1.

   C. Check to see if $4\frac{5}{6}$ is greater than 0.

   D. Check to see if $\frac{13}{14}$ is greater than 0.

   b. Is $\frac{13}{14} \cdot 4\frac{5}{6}$ greater than or less than $4\frac{5}{6}$?

7. Galvin runs and walks for exercise throughout the week. For each mile Galvin runs, he walks $1\frac{1}{10}$ miles.

   a. If Galvin runs $2\frac{3}{5}$ miles, how many miles must he walk?

   b. Galvin incorrectly says that if he runs $2\frac{3}{5}$ miles, he must walk $3\frac{7}{10}$ miles. What mistake did Galvin likely make with the two mixed numbers, $1\frac{1}{10}$ and $2\frac{3}{5}$?

   A. He multiplied the whole numbers, but not the fractions.

   B. He added the two mixed numbers.

   C. He subtracted the two mixed numbers.

8. **Think About the Process** A worker takes $2\frac{3}{5}$ hours to do each project. The worker has to do 6 full projects and $\frac{1}{2}$ of another project.

   a. How should the worker find the total number of hours it takes to do the projects?

   A. Add to find the number of projects, then multiply by the time per project.

   B. Multiply to find the number of projects, then subtract the time per project.

   C. Multiply to find the number of projects, then add the time per project.

   D. Subtract to find the number of projects, then multiply by the time per project.

   b. How many hours does it take to do the projects?

9. In the first hour after opening, a coffee shop used $5\frac{2}{3}$ pounds of unflavored coffee. The shop used $3\frac{2}{3}$ times as much flavored coffee as unflavored. How many pounds of flavored coffee did the shop use?

See your complete lesson at MyMathUniverse.com

10. Cecilia hired an artist to make a painting to hang on a wall of the company library. The dimensions of the mural must be $1\frac{6}{7}$ ft by $1\frac{1}{3}$ ft.

a. Use rounding to estimate the area of the mural.

   A. 2 ft^2 B. 5 ft^2

   C. 4 ft^2 D. 3 ft^2

b. Find the area of the mural.

11. The height of a lamppost is three-eighths of the height of a 72-foot tree.

a. Which equation gives the height of the lamppost?

   A. $\frac{3}{8} \cdot 72 = 27$

   B. $72 - \frac{3}{8} = 71\frac{5}{8}$

   C. $\frac{3}{8} \cdot 72 = \frac{1}{27}$

   D. $72 + \frac{3}{8} = 72\frac{3}{8}$

b. Describe another situation where the size of one object is a fraction of another. Include values for the fraction and the size of the other object in your description.

12. Analyze the expression $\frac{1}{14} \cdot B$. For which values of B will the product be greater than $\frac{1}{14}$? Select all that apply.

   A. $B = \frac{1}{56}$ B. $B = \frac{1}{14}$

   C. $B = \frac{55}{56}$ D. $B = 14$

   E. $B = 14\frac{1}{14}$ F. $B = 1\frac{1}{14}$

13. You have two marbles. The smaller marble has $\frac{5}{6}$ the mass of the larger marble. The mass of the larger marble is $1\frac{2}{3}$ grams. Write an equation to find the mass of the smaller marble.

14. **Think About the Process** A worker takes $5\frac{2}{3}$ hours to do each project. The worker has to do 3 full projects and $\frac{1}{2}$ of another project.

a. How should the worker find the total number of hours it takes to do the projects?

   A. Add to find the number of projects, then multiply by the time per project.

   B. Subtract to find the number of projects, then multiply by the time per project.

   C. Multiply to find the number of projects, then subtract the time per project.

   D. Multiply to find the number of projects, then add the time per project.

b. How many hours does it take to do the projects?

15. **Challenge** The map shows a scaled distance between towns A and B. The map scale shows that 1 inch represents $6\frac{1}{3}$ miles. What is the actual distance between towns A and B?

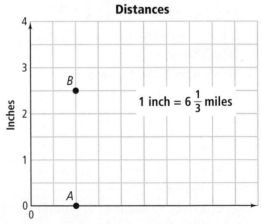

16. **Challenge** There are seven models of a building. Each model after the first is $\frac{3}{5}$ the size of the model before it. Which equation gives the size of the third model as a fraction of the size of the first model?

Dividing Fractions and Whole Numbers

Vocabulary
reciprocals

CCSS: 6.NS.A.1

Part 1

Intro

You can use a model to divide a fraction by a nonzero whole number. Here is how to show $\frac{1}{2} \div 2$.

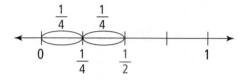

$\frac{1}{2} \div 2 = \frac{1}{4}$ and $\frac{1}{4} \times 2 = \frac{1}{2}$

Example Modeling Fractions Divided by Whole Numbers

Match the division and corresponding multiplication equations with their models.

$$\frac{3}{4} \div 3 = \frac{1}{4} \qquad \frac{1}{2} \div 3 = \frac{1}{6} \qquad \frac{2}{5} \times 2 = \frac{4}{5}$$

$$\frac{1}{6} \times 3 = \frac{1}{2} \qquad \frac{4}{5} \div 2 = \frac{2}{5} \qquad \frac{1}{4} \times 3 = \frac{3}{4}$$

Model	Multiplication	Division
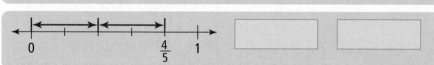		
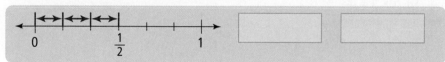		

continued on next page >

Solution ·

Division: $\frac{4}{5}$ is divided into 2 equal segments. Each segment has length $\frac{2}{5}$. So $\frac{4}{5} \div 2 = \frac{2}{5}$.

Division: $\frac{3}{4}$ is divided into 3 equal segments. Each segment has length $\frac{1}{4}$. So $\frac{3}{4} \div 3 = \frac{1}{4}$.

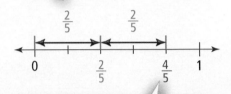

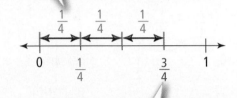

Multiplication: $\frac{2}{5}$ is multiplied 2 times to equal $\frac{4}{5}$. So $\frac{2}{5} \times 2 = \frac{4}{5}$.

Multiplication: $\frac{1}{4}$ is multiplied 3 times to equal $\frac{3}{4}$. So $\frac{1}{4} \times 3 = \frac{3}{4}$.

Division: $\frac{1}{2}$ is divided into 3 equal segments. Each segment has length $\frac{1}{6}$. So $\frac{1}{2} \div 3 = \frac{1}{6}$.

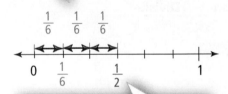

Multiplication: $\frac{1}{6}$ is multiplied 3 times to equal $\frac{1}{2}$. So $\frac{1}{6} \times 3 = \frac{1}{2}$.

Part 2

Intro

You can use a model to divide a whole number by a fraction.

Show $2 \div \frac{1}{2}$.

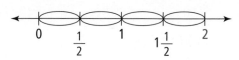

$2 \div \frac{1}{2} = 4$ and $4 \times \frac{1}{2} = 2$

Example Modeling Whole Numbers Divided by Fractions

Match the division and corresponding multiplication equations with their models.

$$8 \times \frac{1}{4} = 2 \qquad\qquad 2 \div \frac{2}{3} - 3 \qquad\qquad 2 \div \frac{1}{3} = 6$$

$$6 \times \frac{1}{3} = 2 \qquad\qquad 3 \times \frac{2}{3} = 2 \qquad\qquad 2 \div \frac{1}{4} - 8$$

Model	Multiplication	Division
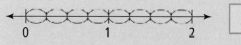		

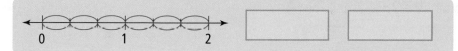		

continued on next page >

Part 2

Example continued

Solution ·

Division: 2 is divided into segments of length $\frac{1}{4}$. There are 8 equal segments. So, $2 \div \frac{1}{4} = 8$.

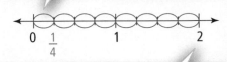

Multiplication: $\frac{1}{4}$ is multiplied 8 times to equal 2. So, $8 \times \frac{1}{4} = 2$.

Division: 2 is divided into segments of length $\frac{2}{3}$. There are 3 equal segments. So, $2 \div \frac{2}{3} = 3$.

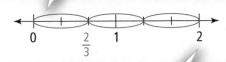

Multiplication: $\frac{2}{3}$ is multiplied 3 times to equal 2. So, $3 \times \frac{2}{3} = 2$.

Division: 2 is divided into segments of length $\frac{1}{3}$. There are 6 equal segments. So, $2 \div \frac{1}{3} = 6$.

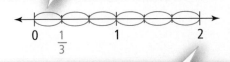

Multiplication: $\frac{1}{3}$ is multiplied 6 times to equal 2. So, $6 \times \frac{1}{3} = 2$.

Key Concept

Two numbers are **reciprocals** if their product is 1.

The reciprocal of $\frac{2}{3}$ is $\frac{3}{2}$. $\longrightarrow$ $\frac{2}{3} \times \frac{3}{2} = \frac{6}{6}$, or 1

The reciprocal of 4, or $\frac{4}{1}$, is $\frac{1}{4}$. $\longrightarrow$ $\frac{4}{1} \times \frac{1}{4} = \frac{4}{4}$, or 1

If a nonzero number is named as a fraction, $\frac{a}{b}$, then its reciprocal is $\frac{b}{a}$.

Rule for Dividing With Fractions To divide a nonzero number, including by a fraction, you can multiply by the divisor's reciprocal.

$$\text{Example: } 2 \div \frac{3}{4} = 2 \times \frac{4}{3}$$

$$= \frac{2 \times 4}{3}$$

$$= \frac{8}{3}, \text{ or } 2\frac{2}{3}$$

Why the Rule Works

Write the division as a fraction. $2 \div \frac{3}{4} = \dfrac{2}{\left(\dfrac{3}{4}\right)}$

Multiply the numerator and denominator by $\frac{4}{3}$, which is the reciprocal of $\frac{3}{4}$. $= \dfrac{2 \times \dfrac{4}{3}}{\dfrac{3}{4} \times \dfrac{4}{3}}$

Simplify the denominator. $= \dfrac{2 \times \dfrac{4}{3}}{1}$, or $2 \times \dfrac{4}{3}$

Example **Dividing Fractions and Whole Numbers to Solve Problems**

Three tenths of an airline's flights are international flights. If the airline's international flights are equally divided among 6 countries, what fraction of the airline's flights are to each country?

Solution ·

Know

- $\frac{3}{10}$ of the flights are international

- International flights are divided evenly among 6 countries.

Need

The fraction of the airline's flights to each country.

Plan

Find $\frac{3}{10} \div 6$.

$$\frac{3}{10} \div 6 = \frac{3}{10} \div \frac{6}{1}$$

> Write the whole number divisor as a fraction.

$$= \frac{3}{10} \times \frac{1}{6}$$

> Change dividing to multiplying by the reciprocal.

$$= \frac{{}^{1}3}{10} \times \frac{1}{6_2}$$

$$= \frac{1}{20}$$

One twentieth of the airline's flights are to each country.

1. a. Which of these models shows $\frac{1}{5} \div 2$?

A.

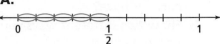

0      $\frac{1}{2}$ 1

B.

0      $\frac{1}{2}$ 1

C.

0   $\frac{1}{5}$ 1

D.

0   $\frac{1}{5}$ 1

b. Find the quotient $\frac{1}{5} \div 2$.

2. a. Which of these models shows $2 \div \frac{1}{5}$?

A.

0   1   2   3   4   5

B.

0   1   2

C.

0   1   2

D.

0   1   2   3   4   5

b. Find the quotient $2 \div \frac{1}{5}$.

3. A carpenter has a board that is $\frac{5}{8}$ yd wide. She cuts the board into 2 pieces. If both the pieces are the same width, how wide is each piece?

4. A construction worker has a rope that is 10 m long. She needs to cut it into pieces that are each $\frac{2}{9}$ m long. How many such pieces can she cut without having any rope left over?

5. You have 8 cups of birdseed. You use $\frac{3}{4}$ cup of birdseed each day. How many days will your birdseed last?

6. Writing Make a model that shows $\frac{1}{4} \div 5$. Describe a real-world situation for which you would want to find that quotient. Describe how you would change the model for $\frac{1}{4} \div 5$ to show $\frac{1}{4} \div 10$.

7. a. Reasoning Which of these models shows $8 \div \frac{4}{5}$?

A.

0   1   2   3   4   5   6   7   8   9   10

B.

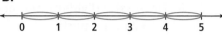

0   1   2   3   4   5

C.

0   1   2   3   4   5   6   7   8

D.

0   1   2   3   4   5

b. How does the model change if the divisor is half as big or twice as big?

8. Think About the Process The first step in using a number line to show $\frac{1}{3} \div 5$ is to locate the dividend on the number line.

a. What is the second step?

     A. Divide the dividend segment into parts that are 5 units long.

     B. Divide the dividend segment into 5 equal parts.

     C. Divide the dividend segment into parts that are $\frac{1}{3}$ of a unit long.

     D. Divide the dividend segment into 3 equal parts.

b. Which of these models shows $\frac{1}{3} \div 5$?

A.

0     $\frac{1}{3}$ 1

B.

0     $\frac{1}{3}$ 1

C.

0     $\frac{1}{5}$ 1

D.

0     $\frac{1}{5}$ 1

c. Find the quotient $\frac{1}{3} \div 5$.

See your complete lesson at MyMathUniverse.com

9. Think About the Process The first step in using a number line to show $2 \div \frac{1}{4}$ is to locate the dividend on the number line.

a. What is the second step?

A. Divide the dividend segment into parts that are 2 units long.

B. Divide the dividend segment into 2 equal parts.

C. Divide the dividend segment into 4 equal parts.

D. Divide the dividend segment into parts that are $\frac{1}{4}$ unit long.

b. Which of these models shows $2 \div \frac{1}{4}$?

A.

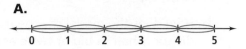

B.

C.

D.

c. Find the quotient $2 \div \frac{1}{4}$.

10. Error Analysis Jennie has 7 cups of milk. A one-batch recipe for pancakes calls for $\frac{3}{4}$ cup of milk. To see how many batches she could make, Jennie finds $7 \div \frac{3}{4}$. She said that because $7 \div \frac{3}{4} = \frac{1}{7} \times \frac{4}{3}$, she could make $\frac{4}{21}$ of a batch.

a. What was Jennie's error?

A. She multiplied the reciprocal of the dividend by the divisor.

B. She multiplied the reciprocal of the dividend by the reciprocal of the divisor.

C. She multiplied the dividend by the divisor.

D. She multiplied the dividend by the reciprocal of the divisor.

b. How many batches could she make?

11. Health Care A pharmacist has $\frac{5}{6}$ qt of cough syrup. She pours it into 3 bottles. If each bottle has the same amount, how much is there in each bottle?

12. A scientist fills 2 jars with a total of $\frac{5}{6}$ kg of a chemical. He puts the same amount in each jar.

a. How much of the chemical does each jar have?

b. Show two different ways you can find the answer.

13. Mental Math Some friends are making cakes for a bake sale. In all, they need 6 cups of sugar. However, they only have a $\frac{1}{4}$-cup measuring cup. How many times will they need to fill the measuring cup?

14. A rectangular piece of paper has area $\frac{1}{4}$ ft² and length 5 ft. Its width in feet is $\frac{1}{4} \div 5$. Find its width. Show how to check your work using the formula for the area of a rectangle.

15. a. What division equation does this model represent?

A. $\frac{2}{5} \div 2 = \blacksquare$

B. $2 \div \frac{2}{5} = \blacksquare$

C. $\frac{2}{5} \div 5 = \blacksquare$

D. $5 \div \frac{2}{5} = \blacksquare$

b. What is the corresponding multiplication equation?

16. Challenge Four-fifteenths of an airline's flights are international. The airline's flights are equally divided among 12 countries.

a. What fraction of the airline's flights are to each country?

b. How many of the airline's flights are international?

c. How many of the airline's flights are not international?

d. How many of the airline's flights are to each of the 12 countries?

17. Challenge A one-serving recipe calls for $\frac{1}{6}$ cup of oil for a marinade and $\frac{1}{2}$ cup of oil for the sauce. You have 6 cups of oil. How many servings can you make?

Dividing Unit Fractions by Unit Fractions

CCSS: 6.NS.A.1

Part 1

Intro

You can use a number line to divide unit fractions.

Find $\frac{1}{2} \div \frac{1}{4}$ on a number line.

Step 1 Draw or use a number line. Because you want to divide by $\frac{1}{4}$, divide the number line into fourths.

Step 2 Label the dividend, $\frac{1}{2}$, on the number line. The number line shows fourths, and $\frac{2}{4} = \frac{1}{2}$.

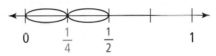

Step 3 Use ovals to divide $\frac{1}{2}$ into segments of length $\frac{1}{4}$.

Step 4 Count the number of equal segments to find the quotient.

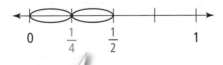

There are 2 segments of length $\frac{1}{4}$.

So $\frac{1}{2} \div \frac{1}{4} = 2$.

Example Using Number Lines to Divide Unit Fractions

If you divide $\frac{1}{2}$ pound of ground beef into patties that weigh $\frac{1}{6}$ pound each, how many patties can you make?

Use a number line to find $\frac{1}{2} \div \frac{1}{6}$. Then use multiplication to check your answer.

Solution ·

Step 1 Draw or use a number line divided into sixths.

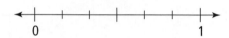

Step 2 Label the dividend, $\frac{1}{2}$, on the number line. The number line shows sixths, and $\frac{3}{6} = \frac{1}{2}$.

Step 3 Use ovals to divide $\frac{1}{2}$ into segments of length $\frac{1}{6}$.

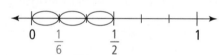

Step 4 Count the number of equal segments to find the quotient.

There are 3 segments of length $\frac{1}{6}$. So $\frac{1}{2} \div \frac{1}{6} = 3$.

You can make 3 patties.

Check ·

$\frac{1}{6} \times 3 = \frac{3}{6}$, or $\frac{1}{2}$, so the answer checks.

See your complete lesson at MyMathUniverse.com

Topic 6   184   Lesson 6-2

Key Concept

To divide unit fractions, you can use the following method.

Find $\frac{1}{2} \div \frac{1}{8}$.

Using Reciprocals To divide unit fractions, you can multiply by the reciprocal of the divisor.

$$\frac{1}{2} \div \frac{1}{8} = \frac{1}{2} \times \frac{8}{1}$$

$$= \frac{1 \times 8}{2 \times 1}$$

$$= \frac{8}{2}, \text{ or } 4$$

Why the Rule Works

Write the division as a fraction.

$$\frac{1}{2} \div \frac{1}{8} = \frac{\left(\frac{1}{2}\right)}{\left(\frac{1}{8}\right)}$$

Multiply the numerator and denominator by $\frac{8}{1}$, which is the reciprocal of $\frac{1}{8}$.

$$= \frac{\left(\frac{1}{2}\right) \times \left(\frac{8}{1}\right)}{\left(\frac{1}{8}\right) \times \left(\frac{8}{1}\right)}$$

Simplify.

$$= \frac{\left(\frac{1}{2}\right) \times \left(\frac{8}{1}\right)}{1}, \text{ or } \frac{1}{2} \times \frac{8}{1}$$

Part 2

Intro

You know that the formula for the area of a rectangle is $A = \ell \times w$.

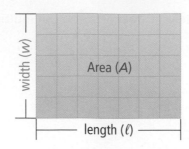

If you know A and either ℓ or w, you can divide A by the known side length to find the missing measure.

Finding Length
$\ell = A \div w$

Finding Width
$w = A \div \ell$

Example Dividing Unit Fractions for Area Problems

A farmer wants to fence off an area of $\frac{1}{32}$ square mile with a length of $\frac{1}{4}$ mile for a pasture. How wide should the area be?

Use division to find the width, in miles. Then use multiplication to check your answer.

Solution

You know that the area of the rectangle is $\frac{1}{32}$ square mile, and the length is $\frac{1}{4}$ mile.

Use the area formula, solved for width.	$w = A \div \ell$
Substitute $\frac{1}{32}$ for A and $\frac{1}{4}$ for ℓ.	$= \frac{1}{32} \div \frac{1}{4}$
Multiply by the reciprocal of $\frac{1}{4}$, which is $\frac{4}{1}$.	$= \frac{1}{32} \times \frac{4}{1}$
Divide by the GCF of 32 and 4, which is 4.	$= \frac{1}{\underset{8}{32}} \times \frac{\overset{1}{4}}{1}$
Multiply.	$= \frac{1}{8}$

The pasture is $\frac{1}{8}$ mile wide.

continued on next page >

Part 2

Solution continued

Check ·

$$\frac{1}{8} \times \frac{1}{4} = \frac{1 \times 1}{8 \times 4}$$

$$= \frac{1}{32} \checkmark$$

The area of the pasture is $\frac{1}{32}$ square mile, so the solution checks.

Part 3

Example Creating Story Problems for Dividing Unit Fractions

Create a story problem that could be solved by finding $\frac{1}{15} \div \frac{1}{3}$.

Solution ·

Think

- The story problem will be solved by finding $\frac{1}{15} \div \frac{1}{3}$.

- I can write a problem about rectanglar area: $\frac{1}{15}$ can be the area, and $\frac{1}{3}$ can be the length.

- The problem can ask to find the width.

Write

A rectangular park has a length of $\frac{1}{3}$ mile and an area of $\frac{1}{15}$ square mile.

What is the width of the park?

1. Use a number line to find $\frac{1}{2} \div \frac{1}{14}$.

2. A shopkeeper cuts a wheel of cheese into 10 equal wedges. A customer buys one-fifth of the wheel. How many wedges does the customer buy? Find $\frac{1}{5} \div \frac{1}{10}$. Use a number line to help find the solution.

3. A radio telescope array is in an unpopulated desert region. The array covers a rectangular area that is $\frac{1}{6}$ square kilometer. The array is $\frac{1}{12}$ kilometer wide. How long is the array?

4. Find $\frac{1}{6} \div \frac{1}{48}$.

5. **a.** Which of the following has $\frac{1}{3} \div \frac{1}{9}$ as the solution?

   A. Find the length of a $\frac{1}{9}$-square-kilometer field that is $\frac{1}{3}$ kilometer wide.

   B. Find the length of a $\frac{1}{3}$-square-mile parking lot that is $\frac{1}{9}$ mile wide.

   C. Find the area of a field that is $\frac{1}{9}$ mile long and $\frac{1}{3}$ mile wide.

   b. Find $\frac{1}{3} \div \frac{1}{9}$.

6. Which of these has $\frac{1}{6} \div \frac{1}{18}$ as the solution?

   A. How many $\frac{1}{6}$-kilogram patties can you make from $\frac{1}{18}$ kilogram of ground beef?

   B. How many $\frac{1}{18}$-kilogram slices can you make from $\frac{1}{6}$ kilogram of cheese?

   C. How much is $\frac{1}{18}$ of $\frac{1}{6}$ kilogram of diced onion?

7. **Multiple Representations**

   a. Which of these situations has $\frac{1}{4} \div \frac{1}{12}$ as the solution?

   A. How many $\frac{1}{4}$-ounce necklaces can a jeweler make from $\frac{1}{12}$ ounce of gold?

   B. How many $\frac{1}{12}$-ounce earrings can a jeweler make from $\frac{1}{4}$ ounce of gold?

   C. How much is $\frac{1}{4}$ of $\frac{1}{12}$ ounce of gold?

   b. Find $\frac{1}{4} \div \frac{1}{12}$.

   c. Draw a model to represent each situation.

8. **a. Writing** Use a number line to find $\frac{1}{5} \div \frac{1}{10}$.

   b. Describe the steps you follow to divide using the number line. Be sure to explain how the fractions relate to what you do in each step.

9. **Reasoning** A circuit board is $\frac{1}{5}$ inch wide.

   a. How many $\frac{1}{15}$-inch-wide circuits fit on the board? Draw a number line to find the solution.

   b. Is the quotient of two unit fractions always greater than the divisor? The dividend? Explain.

10. **Think About the Process** To divide unit fractions, multiply the dividend by the reciprocal of the divisor.

    a. Which fraction in $\frac{1}{6} \div \frac{1}{12}$ is the divisor?

    b. What is the reciprocal of the divisor?

    c. Find the quotient $\frac{1}{6} \div \frac{1}{12}$.

11. **a. Error Analysis** Your friend incorrectly claims that $\frac{1}{5} \div \frac{1}{10} = \frac{1}{50}$. Find $\frac{1}{5} \div \frac{1}{10}$.

    b. Describe what may have been your friend's error.

12. **Accounting** Some accountants still use printing calculators that record each calculation on a long strip of paper which comes in rolls. The area of the paper in one such roll is $\frac{1}{3}$ square meter. The roll is $\frac{1}{12}$ meter wide. How long is the paper in this roll?

13. **Open-Ended** Which of the following is equal to $\frac{1}{5} \div \frac{1}{20}$? Assume the shapes are rectangular.

    A. The length of a $\frac{1}{5}$-square-yard planter that is $\frac{1}{20}$ yard wide.

    B. The length of a $\frac{1}{20}$-square-yard planter that is $\frac{1}{5}$ yard wide.

    C. The area of a tile border that is $\frac{1}{20}$ yard wide and $\frac{1}{5}$ yard long.

14. a. Find $\frac{1}{50} \div \frac{1}{10}$.

b. Find $\frac{1}{10} \div \frac{1}{50}$.

c. Are you surprised by which quotient is greater? Explain why you should know before doing any calculating that the two quotients must be reciprocals of each other.

15. Multiple Representations In a city, 8 schools won a grant to buy equipment needed to improve science education. The schools split the grant money evenly. At one school, the principal split her school's share of the grant money evenly among the science teachers. If each teacher received $\frac{1}{96}$ of the money from the grant, how many science teachers did this school have? Draw a model to represent how the grant money was divided among the schools and the science teachers.

16. Think About the Process A bakery slices a special holiday dessert into 10 pieces. A customer buys one-fifth of the entire dessert.

a. How do you find $\frac{1}{5} \div \frac{1}{10}$?

A. Multiply $\frac{1}{5}$ by the reciprocal of $\frac{1}{10}$.

B. Multiply $\frac{1}{5}$ by $\frac{1}{10}$ and find the reciprocal.

C. Multiply $\frac{1}{10}$ by the reciprocal of $\frac{1}{5}$.

D. Multiply the reciprocal of $\frac{1}{5}$ by the reciprocal of $\frac{1}{10}$.

b. How many pieces of the dessert does the customer buy?

c. Explain why the quotient gives the number of pieces.

17. Challenge A souvenir vendor bought the shirt a pop star wore to a recent music awards ceremony. The vendor cut the shirt into pieces to sell to fans. Each piece was $\frac{1}{45}$ of the shirt. One fan bought enough pieces to make $\frac{1}{5}$ of the shirt. Another fan bought enough pieces to make $\frac{1}{3}$ of the shirt. After these two sales, how many pieces of the shirt did the souvenir vendor have left to sell?

18. a. Challenge Find $\left(\frac{1}{80} \div \frac{1}{8} \right) \div \frac{1}{2}$.

b. Is there an Associative Property for division? Explain.

CCSS: 6.NS.A.1

Part 1

Intro

You can use a number line to divide fractions.

Find $\frac{3}{4} \div \frac{3}{16}$ on a number line.

Step 1 Draw or use a number line. Because you want to divide by $\frac{3}{16}$, divide the number line into sixteenths.

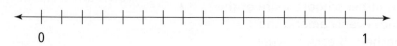

Step 2 Label the dividend, $\frac{3}{4}$, on the number line. The number line shows sixteenths, and $\frac{12}{16} = \frac{3}{4}$.

Step 3 Use ovals to divide $\frac{3}{4}$ into segments of length $\frac{3}{16}$.

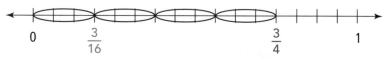

Step 4 Count the number of equal segments to find the quotient.

> There are 4 segments of length $\frac{3}{16}$.
>
> So $\frac{3}{4} \div \frac{3}{16} = 4$.

Part 1

Example Using Number Lines to Divide Fractions by Fractions

If you pour $\frac{3}{4}$ gallon of milk into pitchers that can hold $\frac{3}{8}$ gallon, how many pitchers of milk can you fill?

Use a number line to divide. Then use multiplication to check your answer.

Solution ·

Use a number line to find $\frac{3}{4} \div \frac{3}{8}$.

Step 1 Draw or use a number line divided into eighths.

Step 2 Label the dividend, $\frac{3}{4}$, on the number line. Then number line shows eighths, and $\frac{6}{8} = \frac{3}{4}$.

Step 3 Use ovals to divide $\frac{3}{4}$ into equal segments of length $\frac{3}{8}$.

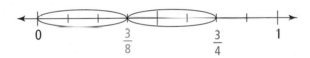

Step 4 Then count the number of equal segments to find the quotient.

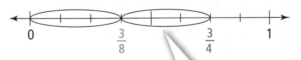

There are 2 segments of length $\frac{3}{8}$. So $\frac{3}{4} \div \frac{3}{8} = 2$.

You can fill 2 pitchers of milk.

Check ·

$\frac{3}{8} \times 2 = \frac{6}{8}$, or $\frac{3}{4}$. ✔

Key Concept

You can use reciprocals to divide any fraction.

Find $\frac{3}{5} \div \frac{9}{10}$.

Using Reciprocals To divide unit fractions, you can multiply by the reciprocal of the divisor.

$$\frac{3}{5} \div \frac{9}{10} = \frac{3}{5} \times \frac{10}{9}$$

$$= \frac{3 \times 10}{5 \times 9}$$

$$= \frac{30}{45}, \text{ or } \frac{2}{3}$$

Why Reciprocals Work These steps show that $\frac{3}{5} \div \frac{9}{10} = \frac{3}{5} \times \frac{10}{9}$.

Write the division as a fraction.

$$\frac{3}{5} \div \frac{9}{10} = \frac{\left(\frac{3}{5}\right)}{\left(\frac{9}{10}\right)}$$

Multiply the numerator and denominator by $\frac{10}{9}$, which is the reciprocal of $\frac{9}{10}$.

$$= \frac{\left(\frac{3}{5}\right) \times \left(\frac{10}{9}\right)}{\left(\frac{9}{10}\right) \times \left(\frac{10}{9}\right)}$$

Simplify the denominator.

$$= \frac{\left(\frac{3}{5}\right) \times \left(\frac{10}{9}\right)}{1}$$

Simplify.

$$= \frac{3}{5} \times \frac{10}{9}$$

Rule in Symbols In general, for any two fractions $\frac{a}{b}$ and $\frac{c}{d}$:

$$\frac{a}{b} \div \frac{c}{d} = \frac{a}{b} \times \frac{d}{c}, \text{ or } \frac{ad}{bc}$$

Part 2

Example Dividing Fractions by Fractions

Match each expression to its value. Then use multiplication to check your answer.

$$1\frac{7}{25} \qquad\qquad 2\frac{1}{3} \qquad\qquad 4 \qquad\qquad \frac{4}{25}$$

a. $\frac{7}{8} \div \frac{3}{8}$ **b.** $\frac{4}{5} \div 5$ **c.** $\frac{4}{5} \div \frac{5}{8}$ **d.** $\frac{10}{19} \div \frac{5}{38}$

Solution

Use the rule for dividing any two fractions $\frac{a}{b}$ and $\frac{c}{d}$.

$$\frac{a}{b} \div \frac{c}{d} = \frac{a}{b} \times \frac{d}{c}, \text{ or } \frac{ad}{bc}$$

a. $\dfrac{7}{8} \div \dfrac{3}{8} = \dfrac{7}{8} \times \dfrac{8}{3}$

$\qquad = \dfrac{7}{\underset{1}{\cancel{8}}} \times \dfrac{\overset{1}{\cancel{8}}}{3}$

$\qquad = \dfrac{7}{3}, \text{ or } 2\dfrac{1}{3}$

b. $\dfrac{4}{5} \div 5 = \dfrac{4}{5} \div \dfrac{5}{1}$

$\qquad = \dfrac{4}{5} \times \dfrac{1}{5}, \text{ or } \dfrac{4}{25}$

c. $\dfrac{4}{5} \div \dfrac{5}{8} = \dfrac{4}{5} \times \dfrac{8}{5}$

$\qquad = \dfrac{4}{5} \times \dfrac{8}{5}$

$\qquad = \dfrac{32}{25}, \text{ or } 1\dfrac{7}{25}$

d. $\dfrac{10}{19} \div \dfrac{5}{38} = \dfrac{10}{19} \times \dfrac{38}{5}$

$\qquad = \dfrac{\overset{2}{\cancel{10}}}{\underset{1}{\cancel{19}}} \times \dfrac{\overset{2}{\cancel{38}}}{\underset{1}{\cancel{5}}}$

$\qquad = \dfrac{4}{1}, \text{ or } 4$

Check

a. $2\dfrac{1}{3} \times \dfrac{3}{8} = \dfrac{7}{\underset{1}{\cancel{3}}} \times \dfrac{\overset{1}{\cancel{3}}}{8}, \text{ or } \dfrac{7}{8}$ ✔

b. $5 \times \dfrac{4}{25} = \dfrac{20}{25}$

$\qquad\quad = \dfrac{20 \div 5}{25 \div 4}, \text{ or } \dfrac{4}{5}$ ✔

c. $1\dfrac{7}{25} \times \dfrac{5}{8} = \dfrac{32}{25} \times \dfrac{5}{8}$

$\qquad\quad = \dfrac{\overset{4}{\cancel{32}}}{\underset{5}{\cancel{25}}} \times \dfrac{\overset{1}{\cancel{5}}}{\underset{1}{\cancel{8}}}, \text{ or } \dfrac{4}{5}$ ✔

d. $4 \times \dfrac{5}{38} = \dfrac{4}{1} \times \dfrac{5}{38}$

$\qquad\quad = \dfrac{\overset{2}{\cancel{4}}}{1} \times \dfrac{5}{\underset{19}{\cancel{38}}}, \text{ or } \dfrac{10}{19}$ ✔

Intro

How can you create a story problem for $\frac{2}{3} \div \frac{3}{4}$?

You can make this story about yogurt. Yogurt is packed in different sizes and shapes. For this story, use the fraction $\frac{3}{4}$, or three-quarters of a cup, as the size for one serving of yogurt. Now use the fraction $\frac{2}{3}$, or two-thirds of a cup, as part of a serving.

How many $\frac{3}{4}$ cup servings are in $\frac{2}{3}$ cup of yogurt?

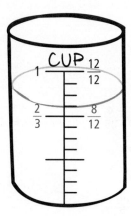 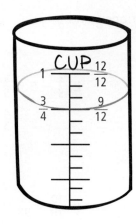

$$\frac{2}{3} \div \frac{3}{4} = \frac{2}{3} \times \frac{4}{3}$$
$$= \frac{2 \times 4}{3 \times 3}$$
$$= \frac{8}{9}$$

That means there is $\frac{8}{9}$ of a $\frac{3}{4}$ cup serving in $\frac{2}{3}$ of a cup of yogurt.

Example Creating Story Problems for Dividing Fractions

Create a story problem that could be solved by finding $\frac{3}{8} \div \frac{1}{2}$.

Solution

Think

- The story problem will be solved by finding $\frac{3}{8} \div \frac{1}{2}$.

- I can write a problem where $\frac{1}{2}$ is a measure of a whole and $\frac{3}{8}$ is the part used.

Write

What part of a $\frac{1}{2}$-mile race is complete when you reach the $\frac{3}{8}$-mile mark?

1. Use a number line to find $\frac{5}{6} \div \frac{5}{24}$.

2. You have a $\frac{4}{5}$-quart bottle of orange juice. How many $\frac{4}{45}$-quart pitchers can you fill? Use a number line to help you find the number of pitchers.

3. Divide to find the value of the expression $\frac{5}{7} \div \frac{2}{7}$.

4. Find $\frac{2}{11} \div \frac{3}{4}$. Use multiplication to check your result.

5. Which story problem can you solve by finding $\frac{3}{9} \div \frac{7}{9}$?

   A. How many $\frac{7}{9}$-cup servings are in $\frac{3}{9}$ of a cup of cream cheese?

   B. How many $\frac{3}{9}$-cup servings are in $\frac{7}{9}$ of a cup of jam?

   C. How many cups is $\frac{7}{9}$ of a $\frac{3}{9}$-cup serving of jelly?

6. Which story problem could be solved by finding $\frac{2}{3} \div \frac{2}{9}$?

   A. What is $\frac{2}{9}$ of a piece of wood that is $\frac{2}{3}$ meter long?

   B. How many $\frac{2}{9}$-meter pieces of wire can you cut from a piece that is $\frac{2}{3}$ meter long?

   C. How many $\frac{2}{3}$-meter pieces of paper can you cut from a piece that is $\frac{2}{9}$ meter long?

7. **Writing** Use a number line to find $\frac{8}{9} \div \frac{8}{45}$. Show how to model this division on a number line.

8. a. **Reasoning** Find $\frac{3}{7} \div \frac{13}{14}$.

   b. Would the result be the same for the quotient $\frac{13}{14} \div \frac{3}{7}$? Explain how you can answer this without doing any calculations.

9. **Error Analysis** A student incorrectly claims that $\frac{2}{3} \div \frac{5}{9} = \frac{5}{6}$.

   a. Find the correct quotient.

   b. What was the student's likely error?

      A. The student multiplied the reciprocal of the dividend by the divisor.

      B. The student multiplied the dividend by the divisor.

   C. The student multiplied the dividend by the reciprocal of the divisor.

   D. The student multiplied the reciprocal of the dividend by the reciprocal of the divisor.

10. **Writing a Paper** Which story problem could you solve by finding $\frac{5}{8} \div \frac{3}{4}$?

    A. What part of a $\frac{5}{8}$-page paper is complete when you reach $\frac{3}{4}$ of a page?

    B. What part of a $\frac{3}{4}$-page paper is complete when you reach $\frac{5}{8}$ of a page?

    C. What is $\frac{5}{8}$ of a $\frac{3}{4}$-page paper?

11. **Open-Ended** Which question does the quotient $\frac{9}{11} \div \frac{2}{11}$ answer?

    A. How many $\frac{9}{11}$ are there in $\frac{2}{11}$?

    B. How many $\frac{2}{11}$ are there in $\frac{11}{9}$?

    C. How many $\frac{2}{11}$ are there in $\frac{9}{11}$?

12. Find $\frac{3}{11} \div \frac{7}{33}$. Before you begin to calculate, explain how you can tell that there will be common factors to remove while you calculate.

13. Find the value of the expression $\frac{17}{23} \div \frac{4}{69}$. Check your results by multiplying.

14. **Multiple Representations** Which problems can you solve by finding $\frac{3}{7} \div \frac{11}{14}$? Select all that apply.

    A. What is the area of a rectangle with length $\frac{11}{14}$ feet and width $\frac{3}{7}$ feet?

    B. What is the width of a rectangle with length $\frac{11}{14}$ feet and area $\frac{3}{7}$ feet?

    C. What is the length of a rectangle with width $\frac{11}{14}$ feet and area $\frac{3}{7}$ feet?

15. **a. Multiple Representations** Which story problems can you solve by finding $\frac{7}{15} \div \frac{3}{4}$? Select all that apply.

   A. How many ounces of salsa is $\frac{3}{4}$ of a $\frac{7}{15}$-ounce serving of salsa?

   B. How many $\frac{3}{4}$-ounce servings are in $\frac{7}{15}$ of an ounce of guacamole?

   C. How many $\frac{3}{4}$-ounce servings are in $\frac{7}{15}$ of an ounce of sour cream?

   b. Find $\frac{7}{15} \div \frac{3}{4}$. Simplify your answer.

16. **Think About the Process** You are finding the quotient $\frac{16}{27} \div \frac{8}{9}$ using the rule $\frac{a}{b} \div \frac{c}{d} = \frac{a}{b} \times \frac{d}{c}$.

   a. Write the rule $\frac{a}{b} \div \frac{c}{d} = \frac{a}{b} \times \frac{d}{c}$ using words.

   A. To divide fractions, divide the dividend by the divisor.

   B. To divide fractions, multiply the reciprocal of the dividend by the reciprocal of the divisor.

   C. To divide fractions, multiply the dividend by the reciprocal of the divisor.

   D. To divide fractions, multiply the divisor by the reciprocal of the dividend.

   b. Find $\frac{16}{27} \div \frac{8}{9}$.

17. **Think About the Process**
   a. Find $\frac{7}{11} \div \frac{8}{33}$.

   b. What step can you take to check that your result is correct?

   A. Multiply your result by $\frac{7}{11}$.

   B. Multiply your result by $\frac{11}{7}$.

   C. Multiply your result by $\frac{33}{8}$.

   D. Multiply your result by $\frac{8}{33}$.

18. **Challenge** A recipe calls for $\frac{4}{25}$ of a cup of any kind of nuts. A cook wants to mix pecans and peanuts. If the cook has one-fifth of a cup of pecans and three-fifths of a cup of peanuts, how many batches can the cook make? Use a number line to answer.

19. **a. Challenge** Find $\frac{18}{23} \div \frac{13}{115}$.

   b. Find $\frac{13}{115} \div \frac{18}{23}$.

   c. Tell how the results compare. Will this always happen when you switch the dividend and divisor? Explain.

6-4 | Dimidiating Mixed Numbers

6-4 | Dividing Mixed Numbers

CCSS: 6.NS.A.1

Part 1

Intro

You can extend what you know about dividing whole numbers and fractions to divide mixed numbers.

Find $2\frac{2}{5} \div \frac{4}{5}$.

Using a Number Line The number line model shows $2\frac{2}{5} \div \frac{4}{5}$.

$2\frac{2}{5}$ is divided into segments of length $\frac{4}{5}$. There are 3 equal segments.

So $2\frac{2}{5} \div \frac{4}{5} = 3$.

Using Reciprocals You can also divide mixed numbers by first writing the mixed numbers as improper fractions. Then multiply by the reciprocal of the divisor.

$$2\frac{2}{5} \div \frac{4}{5} = \frac{12}{5} \div \frac{4}{5}$$

Change any mixed number to an improper fraction.

$$= \frac{12}{5} \times \frac{5}{4}$$

Change dividing to multiplying by the reciprocal.

$$= \frac{^3\cancel{12}}{_1\cancel{5}} \times \frac{\cancel{5}^1}{\cancel{4}_1}$$

$$= \frac{3}{1}, \text{ or } 3$$

Example Finding Quotients with Mixed Numbers

Each expression below has a value of $\frac{2}{3}$, $1\frac{3}{4}$, or $2\frac{1}{4}$.
Match each expression to its value.

$$1\frac{5}{9} \div \frac{8}{9} \qquad\qquad 1\frac{2}{7} \div \frac{4}{7} \qquad\qquad 1\frac{1}{15} \div 1\frac{3}{5}$$

$$\frac{5}{6} \div 1\frac{1}{4} \qquad\qquad 2\frac{1}{2} \div 1\frac{3}{7} \qquad\qquad 6\frac{3}{4} \div 3$$

continued on next page >

Example continued

Solution $\cdots\cdots\cdots\cdots\cdots\cdots\cdots\cdots\cdots\cdots\cdots\cdots\cdots\cdots\cdots\cdots\cdots\cdots\cdots\cdots\cdots\cdots\cdots$

Use reciprocals to find each quotient.

Equal to $\frac{2}{3}$:

$$\frac{5}{6} \div 1\frac{1}{4} = \frac{5}{6} \div \frac{5}{4}$$

$$= \frac{5}{6} \times \frac{4}{5}$$

$$= \frac{1\cancel{5}}{3\cancel{6}} \times \frac{\cancel{4}^2}{\cancel{5}_1}$$

$$= \frac{2}{3}$$

$$1\frac{1}{15} \div 1\frac{3}{5} = \frac{16}{15} \div \frac{8}{5}$$

$$= \frac{16}{15} \times \frac{5}{8}$$

$$= \frac{^2\cancel{16}}{3\cancel{15}} \times \frac{\cancel{5}^1}{\cancel{8}_1}$$

$$= \frac{2}{3}$$

Equal to $1\frac{3}{4}$:

$$2\frac{1}{2} \div 1\frac{3}{7} = \frac{5}{2} \div \frac{10}{7}$$

$$= \frac{5}{2} \times \frac{7}{10}$$

$$= \frac{1\cancel{5}}{2} \times \frac{7}{\cancel{10}_2}$$

$$= \frac{7}{4}, \text{ or } 1\frac{3}{4}$$

$$1\frac{5}{9} \div \frac{8}{9} = \frac{14}{9} \div \frac{8}{9}$$

$$= \frac{14}{9} \times \frac{9}{8}$$

$$= \frac{^7\cancel{14}}{_1\cancel{9}} \times \frac{\cancel{9}^1}{\cancel{8}_4}$$

$$= \frac{7}{4}, \text{ or } 1\frac{3}{4}$$

Equal to $2\frac{1}{4}$:

$$1\frac{2}{7} \div \frac{4}{7} = \frac{9}{7} \div \frac{4}{7}$$

$$= \frac{9}{7} \times \frac{7}{4}$$

$$= \frac{9}{_1\cancel{7}} \times \frac{\cancel{7}^1}{4}$$

$$= \frac{9}{4}, \text{ or } 2\frac{1}{4}$$

$$6\frac{3}{4} \div 3 = \frac{27}{4} \div \frac{3}{1}$$

$$= \frac{27}{4} \times \frac{1}{3}$$

$$= \frac{^9\cancel{27}}{4} \times \frac{1}{\cancel{3}_1}$$

$$= \frac{9}{4}, \text{ or } 2\frac{1}{4}$$

Example Writing and Evaluating Division Expressions with Mixed Numbers

Use division to write the distance of the sweet spot from the large end of the bat as a fraction of the length of the bat.

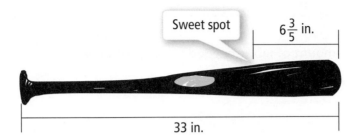

Sweet spot

$6\frac{3}{5}$ in.

33 in.

Solution

Think

Distance to the sweet spot.

$\dfrac{\left(6\frac{3}{5}\right)}{33}$

Length of bat

- A fraction bar means "divide"; so dividing $6\frac{3}{5}$ by 33 gives the distance of the sweet spot from the large end of the bat as a fraction of the length of the bat.

Write

$$6\frac{3}{5} \div 33 = \frac{33}{5} \div \frac{33}{1}$$

$$= \frac{33}{5} \times \frac{1}{33}$$

$$= \frac{\overset{1}{\cancel{33}}}{5} \times \frac{1}{\cancel{33}_{1}}$$

$$= \frac{1}{5}$$

The distance of the sweet spot from the large end of the bat is $\frac{1}{5}$ the length of the bat.

Example Dividing and Adding Mixed Numbers

A tailor has $13\frac{1}{2}$ yards of fabric to use for making costumes. For each costume, she needs $1\frac{1}{2}$ yards of fabric for the top, and $\frac{3}{4}$ yard for the bottom. How many costumes can she make?

Solution ·

Step 1 Find the amount of fabric needed for one costume.

fabric for one costume = fabric for top + fabric for bottom

$$= 1\frac{1}{2} + \frac{3}{4}$$

$$= \frac{3}{2} + \frac{3}{4}$$

$$= \frac{6}{4} + \frac{3}{4}$$

$$= \frac{9}{4}, \text{ or } 2\frac{1}{4} \text{ yd}$$

Step 2 Find the number of costumes that the tailor can make.

number of costumes = total amount of fabric ÷ fabric for one costume

$$= 13\frac{1}{2} \div 2\frac{1}{4}$$

$$= \frac{27}{2} \div \frac{9}{4}$$

$$= \frac{27}{2} \times \frac{4}{9}$$

Change the division to multiplication using the reciprocal of $\frac{9}{4}$.

$$= \frac{{}^{3}\cancel{27}}{{}_{1}\cancel{2}} \times \frac{\cancel{4}^{2}}{\cancel{9}_{1}}$$

$$= \frac{6}{1}, \text{ or } 6$$

So the tailor can make 6 costumes.

1. Divide $1\frac{2}{5} \div \frac{1}{3}$.

2. Divide $\frac{8}{25} \div 2\frac{3}{5}$.

3. Divide $11\frac{1}{5} \div 7$.

4. A trip to a nearby island takes $2\frac{1}{4}$ hours by boat and $\frac{1}{4}$ hour by airplane. How many times as fast as the boat is the plane?

5. The weight of water is $62\frac{1}{2}$ lb per cubic foot. Water that weighs 300 lb will fill how many cubic feet?

6. A baby outfit uses $\frac{2}{9}$ square yard of fabric for the hat and $\frac{5}{9}$ square yard of fabric for the bib. A tailor has $6\frac{2}{9}$ square yards of fabric. How many baby outfits can she make?

7. A family prepares an emergency kit for their home. The kit contains 66 gallons of drinking water. The family's daily drinking water needs are $4\frac{1}{2}$ gallons for the adults and $3\frac{3}{4}$ gallons for the children. For how many days would this emergency water supply last the family?

8. a. **Writing** Find $6 \div 3\frac{3}{5}$. Then explain how you know, without calculating, that $6 \div 3\frac{3}{5}$ must be less than 6.

   b. Is there any number for which the quotient of 6 and that number is greater than 6? Explain.

9. **Reasoning** A restaurant is making hamburgers. The cooks use $\frac{2}{3}$ pound of beef for each hamburger.

   a. If the cooks have $32\frac{2}{3}$ pounds of beef, how many hamburgers can they make?

   b. How does the answer change if the cooks have twice as much beef? Half as much beef? Explain your reasoning.

10. **Error Analysis** Your friend says that $6\frac{2}{3} \div 2 = 13\frac{1}{3}$.

    a. What is the correct quotient?

    b. What error did your friend likely make?

A. Your friend multiplied the two numbers and then took the reciprocal.

B. Your friend multiplied by the divisor, not by its reciprocal.

C. Your friend multiplied by the reciprocal of the dividend.

D. Your friend changed the mixed number to an improper fraction incorrectly.

c. Explain how you can tell that there must be an error without doing any calculating.

11. **Think About the Process**

    a. What step should you take first to find $13\frac{2}{3} \div 2\frac{3}{8}$?

    A. Multiply by the reciprocal of the dividend.

    B. Multiply by the reciprocal of the divisor.

    C. Divide the whole number parts of the mixed numbers.

    D. Write any mixed numbers as improper fractions.

    b. What is the quotient $13\frac{2}{3} \div 2\frac{3}{8}$?

12. **Animal Migration** Last weekend, a herd of antelope moved to better grazing land. The herd traveled $13\frac{9}{10}$ miles on Friday, $11\frac{1}{5}$ miles on Saturday, and $15\frac{1}{5}$ miles on Sunday.

    a. How far did the herd migrate to the better grazing land?

    b. If the herd had traveled the total distance in equal parts, how far would the herd have moved each day?

13. **Estimation** A town recorded $5\frac{5}{7}$ in. of rainfall in 7 weeks, with the same amount falling each week.

    a. About how many inches of rain fell each week?

    A. about 6 in.   B. about 7 in.

    C. about $\frac{7}{6}$ in.   D. about $\frac{6}{7}$ in.

    b. Find the exact amount.

14. For an art project, Marco cuts a $14\frac{4}{5}$ ft piece of string into 8 equal pieces. Maria cuts her string into 8 equal pieces of length $2\frac{17}{20}$ ft.

    a. How long is each of Marco's 8 pieces of string?

    b. Which student started with the longer piece of string? How much longer was it?

15. A car travels 399 miles using $11\frac{2}{5}$ gallons of gas.

    a. How many miles did the car travel on each gallon of gas?

    b. How much gas did the car use to travel each mile?

16. On a recent trip, Jeremy and Frank drove 790 miles on $33\frac{1}{3}$ gallons of gas.

    a. How many miles per gallon did their car get on this trip?

    b. How many gallons of gas are needed for their car to travel 1,896 miles?

17. **Think About the Process** A small business makes rain gutters that attach to the edges of roofs. One type of gutter uses three strips of metal that are all the same length. The width of the strips are $5\frac{5}{8}$ inches, $8\frac{3}{8}$ inches, and $9\frac{3}{8}$ inches.

    a. What is the first step to find the number of gutters the business can make from a sheet of metal that is the right length for the strips?

       A. Divide the amount of sheet metal by the total width needed for each gutter.

       B. Multiply the widths of the strips by 3.

       C. Add the widths of the strips.

       D. Subtract the widths of the strips from the length of the sheet of metal.

    b. What is the next step to find the number of gutters the business can make?

       A. Divide the amount of sheet metal by the total width needed for each gutter.

       B. Multiply the widths of the strips by 3.

       C. Add the widths of the strips.

       D. Subtract the widths of the strips from the length of the sheet of metal.

    c. Assuming there is no waste, how many gutters can the business make from 374 inches of sheet metal?

18. **Challenge** A rancher stretched barbed wire between 38 new fence posts, but is concerned that people and animals cannot see the wire. She has $365\frac{1}{8}$ inches of bright orange ribbon. She decides to tie equal lengths of the ribbon to the wire between adjacent posts. How long should the rancher make each piece of ribbon to use all the ribbon?

19. **Challenge** To help a city's superhero protect her identity, the citizens of the city start to wear copies of the superhero's outfit. Each superhero outfit uses $1\frac{1}{3}$ yards of red cloth and $3\frac{3}{4}$ yards of blue cloth. A tailor has 12 yards of red cloth and 60 yards of blue cloth. How many copies of the superhero's outfit can the tailor make?

CCSS: 6.NS.A.1

Part 1

Example **Dividing Whole Numbers and Mixed Numbers to Solve Problems**

Today, penny sizes are abbreviated using "d," which refers to the length of the nail. A carpenter chose the size of nail shown below for a job she is doing. The nail length is 3 times the thickness of the boards she is nailing. What is the thickness of the boards she is nailing?

Penny Size	2d	3d	4d	6d	7d	9d
Length (in.)	1	$1\frac{1}{4}$	$1\frac{1}{2}$	2	$2\frac{1}{4}$	$2\frac{3}{4}$

7d Nail

Thickness of board

Solution

First, find the length of the nail. A 7-penny nail is $2\frac{1}{4}$ inches long. The nail length is 3 times the thickness of the boards. Use the inverse relationship between multiplication and division to find $2\frac{1}{4} \div 3$.

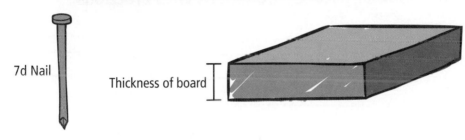

$$2\frac{1}{4} \div 3 = \frac{9}{4} \div \frac{3}{1}$$
$$= \frac{9}{4} \times \frac{1}{3}$$
$$= \frac{{}^{3}\cancel{9}}{4} \times \frac{1}{\cancel{3}_{1}}$$
$$= \frac{3}{4}$$

The boards are $\frac{3}{4}$ inch thick.

> ## Intro

You have solved equations of the form $px = q$ by dividing each side by p. You can also solve such equations by multiplying each side by the reciprocal of p. Solve $\frac{2}{3}x = \frac{4}{7}$.

Method 1 Use Division

$$\frac{2}{3}x = \frac{4}{7}$$

$$\left(\frac{2}{3} \div \frac{2}{3}\right)x = \frac{4}{7} \div \frac{2}{3}$$

$$1 \cdot x = \frac{4}{7} \cdot \frac{3}{2}$$

$$x = \frac{6}{7}$$

Method 2 Use Multiplication

$$\frac{2}{3}x = \frac{4}{7}$$

$$\left(\frac{3}{2} \cdot \frac{2}{3}\right)x = \frac{3}{2} \cdot \frac{4}{7}$$

$$1 \cdot x = \frac{3}{2} \cdot \frac{4}{7}$$

$$x = \frac{6}{7}$$

> ## Example Solving Multiplication Equations with Fractions

Solve each equation.

a. $\frac{1}{3}x = \frac{1}{5}$ **b.** $\frac{2}{3}x = \frac{5}{9}$ **c.** $1\frac{1}{5}x = \frac{3}{5}$

Solution

a.

$$\frac{1}{3}x = \frac{1}{5}$$

$$\left(\frac{1}{3}x\right) \times \frac{3}{1} = \frac{1}{5} \times \frac{3}{1}$$

$$\left(\frac{1}{3} \times \frac{3}{1}\right)x = \frac{1}{5} \times \frac{3}{1}$$

$$1 \cdot x = \frac{3}{5}$$

$$x = \frac{3}{5}$$

> Multiply both sides by the reciprocal of $\frac{1}{3}$, which is $\frac{3}{1}$.

b.

$$\frac{2}{3}x = \frac{5}{9}$$

$$\left(\frac{2}{3}x\right) \div \frac{2}{3} = \frac{5}{9} \div \frac{2}{3}$$

$$\left(\frac{2}{3} \div \frac{2}{3}\right)x = \frac{5}{9} \times \frac{3}{2}$$

$$1 \cdot x = \frac{5}{3\cancel{9}} \times \frac{\cancel{3}^1}{2}$$

$$x = \frac{5}{6}$$

> Divide each side by the coefficient of x, which is $\frac{2}{3}$.

c.

$$1\frac{1}{5}x = \frac{3}{5}$$

$$\frac{6}{5}x = \frac{3}{5}$$

$$\left(\frac{6}{5}x\right) \div \frac{6}{5} = \frac{3}{5} \div \frac{6}{5}$$

$$\left(\frac{6}{5} \div \frac{6}{5}\right)x = \frac{3}{5} \times \frac{5}{6}$$

$$1x = \frac{1\cancel{3}}{1\cancel{5}} \times \frac{\cancel{5}^1}{\cancel{6}_2}$$

$$x = \frac{1}{2}$$

> Write the mixed number as an improper fraction.

> Divide each side by the coefficient of x, which is $\frac{6}{5}$.

Example Writing and Solving Equations with Fractions and Mixed Numbers

A rod is a measure of length. Rods are sometimes used on canoe maps to show portages. A portage is a place where canoes must be carried, such as around dams. A rod is about the length of a typical canoe.

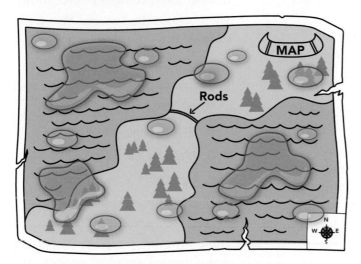

The canoe map shows a portage between two lakes, but the map has gotten wet. The length of the portage is 330 yards, and 1 rod equals $5\frac{1}{2}$ yards. Write and solve an equation to find the length of the portage in rods.

Solution ·

Words

| length of 1 rod | times | length in rods | equals | length in yards |

↓ **to**

Let r = the length of the portage in rods.

Equation

| $5\frac{1}{2}$ | × | r | = | 330 |

$$5\frac{1}{2}r = 330$$

> Divide by the coefficient of r to get the variable alone on one side of the equation.

$$5\frac{1}{2}r \div 5\frac{1}{2} = 330 \div 5\frac{1}{2}$$

$$r = 330 \div \frac{11}{2}$$

$$r = \frac{330}{1} \times \frac{2}{11}$$

$$r = \frac{^{30}\cancel{330}}{1} \times \frac{2}{\cancel{11}_1}$$

$$r = 60$$

The length of the portage is 60 rods.

1. A carpenter bought bolts to finish a project. In all, the bolts weighed 4 pounds. There are 16 ounces in 1 pound. If each bolt weighed $\frac{1}{8}$ ounce, how many bolts did the carpenter buy?

2. Solve the equation $\frac{2}{5}d = \frac{2}{7}$ for d.

3. A rod equals $5\frac{1}{2}$ yards. If a bridge is 220 yards long, how long is it in rods?

4. A rectangle has area $3\frac{3}{8}$ in.^{2} and length 9 in.

   a. Divide its area by its length to find its width.

   b. Find dimensions of a second rectangle that has the same area as this rectangle. Show two different ways to do this.

5. On last night's homework, Malcolm incorrectly said 4 is the solution of $\frac{2}{3}d = 6$.

   a. What is the correct solution?

   b. What was Malcolm's error?

   A. He divided the right side by $\frac{2}{3}$ instead of dividing by the reciprocal of $\frac{2}{3}$.

   B. He divided the right side by $\frac{2}{3}$ instead of dividing by the reciprocal of 6.

   C. He multiplied the right side by $\frac{2}{3}$ instead of multiplying by the reciprocal of 6.

   D. He multiplied the right side by $\frac{2}{3}$ instead of multiplying by the reciprocal of $\frac{2}{3}$.

6. Today, Otto put $12\frac{4}{9}$ pounds of electrical supplies into crates. Each crate held $1\frac{7}{9}$ pounds of supplies.

   a. How many crates did he use?

   b. If it took Otto half an hour to pack each crate, how long did the entire project take him?

7. Solve the equation $\frac{5}{6}n = 30$ for n. Explain how you can use mental math to find the solution.

8. The length of a certain rectangle is $1\frac{1}{2}$ times its width. Suppose the rectangle's length is $9\frac{5}{8}$ in.

   a. Use whole numbers to estimate the rectangle's width.

   b. Find the rectangle's exact width.

9. **Think About the Process** You want to solve this equation for y.

   $$\left(4\frac{4}{5}\right)y = \frac{4}{5}$$

   a. Which of these could be the first step? Select all that apply.

   A. Divide each side by $4\frac{4}{5}$.

   B. Multiply each side by $4\frac{4}{5}$.

   C. Multiply each side by $\frac{5}{24}$.

   D. Divide each side by $\frac{5}{24}$.

   b. What is the solution?

10. **Think About the Process** A gallon of water weighs about $8\frac{2}{5}$ pounds. The water in a certain container weighs 30 pounds. You want to find the number of gallons of water in the container.

    a. Let g be the number of gallons of water in the container. Which of these equations should you solve to find the number of gallons of water in the container?

    A. $g + 8\frac{2}{5} = 30$

    B. $g = \left(8\frac{2}{5}\right)(30)$

    C. $30g = 8\frac{2}{5}$

    D. $\left(8\frac{2}{5}\right)g = 30$

    b. How many gallons of water are there in the container?

11. Last summer, a woman went on a camping vacation. She hiked $8\frac{3}{4}$ miles each day.

    a. If she hiked a total of 35 miles, how long did her vacation last?

    b. If she spent 4 hours hiking steadily each day, about how many miles did she hike each hour?

12. Last week, a sporting goods store had a big sale. During the sale, shoppers bought $\frac{1}{9}$ of the store's skateboards. After the sale, there were 176 skateboards left. How many skateboards were there originally?

13. **Challenge** A wheat farmer has a storage bin that holds $6,846\frac{1}{4}$ cubic feet.

  a. If a bushel of wheat fills $1\frac{1}{4}$ cubic feet, how many bushels can the storage bin hold?

  b. If a farmer wants to make a new storage bin $1\frac{1}{4}$ times as large, how many cubic feet will it hold?

  c. How many bushels will the new bin hold?

14. Last summer, a man went on a camping vacation. He hiked $8\frac{1}{2}$ miles each day.

  a. If he hiked a total of 68 miles, how long did his vacation last?

  b. If he spent 6 hours hiking steadily each day, about how many miles did he hike each hour?

15. The length of a certain rectangle is $1\frac{3}{4}$ times its width. Suppose the rectangle's length is $19\frac{1}{2}$ in.

  a. Use whole numbers to estimate the rectangle's width.

  b. Find the rectangle's exact width.

16. **Think About the Process** A gallon of water weighs about $8\frac{2}{5}$ pounds. The water in a certain container weighs 56 pounds. You want to find the number of gallons of water in the container.

  a. Let g be the number of gallons of water in the container. Which of these equations should you solve to find the number of gallons of water in the container?

  A. $\left(8\frac{2}{5}\right)g = 56$

  B. $56g = 8\frac{2}{5}$

  C. $g + 8\frac{2}{5} = 56$

  D. $g = \left(8\frac{2}{5}\right)(56)$

  b. How many gallons of water are there in the container?

17. **Challenge** A bookcase has a shelf that is $28\frac{1}{2}$ in. long. Each book is $1\frac{1}{8}$ in. thick.

  a. How many books, at most, would fit entirely on the shelf? Draw a diagram of the situation.

  b. Calculate how much longer the shelf would have to be for one more book to fit entirely on the shelf.

Adding and Subtracting Decimals

Vocabulary
decimal, whole number

CCSS: 6.NS.B.3

Part 1

Intro

You can use what you know about adding whole numbers to add decimals.

$$15.09 + 0.741$$

Step 1 Write the addition in a column, using the decimal point to align the ones place and other place values.

$$
\begin{array}{r}
15.09 \\
+\ \ 0.741 \\
\end{array}
$$

Step 2 Write zeros, if needed, so that the decimals have the same number of decimal place values to add.

$$
\begin{array}{r}
15.09 \\
+\ \ 0.741 \\
\end{array}
$$

> There is a blank space in the thousandths place of the first number.

$$
\begin{array}{r}
15.090 \\
+\ \ 0.741 \\
\end{array}
$$

> Writing a zero in the thousandths place as a placeholder does not change the value.

Step 3 Add from right to left as you would add whole numbers, regrouping place-value amounts as needed. Place the decimal point in the sum, aligned with the decimal points of the addends.

$$
\begin{array}{r}
\overset{1}{}15.090 \\
+\ \ 0.741 \\
\hline
15.831 \\
\end{array}
$$

Example Adding Decimals

The diagram below shows the length of the main span of the Golden Gate Bridge. Together, the side spans add 0.686 km to the suspended portion of the bridge. What is the length of the suspended portion of the bridge?

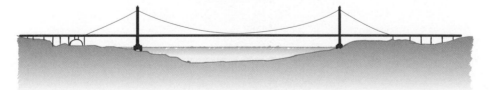

continued on next page >

Part 1

Example continued

Solution

Add to find the length of the suspended portion of the bridge:

$$1.28 + 0.686$$

Write addition in a column, aligning the decimal points.

Write a zero as a placeholder.

$$
\begin{array}{r}
\overset{1}{} \\
1.280 \\
+\ 0.686 \\
\hline
1.966
\end{array}
$$

Add from right to left, regrouping place-value amounts as needed.

The length of the suspended portion is 1.966 km.

Part 2

Intro

You can use what you know about subtracting whole numbers to subtract decimals.

$$22.7 \qquad 1.53$$

Step 1 Write the subtraction in a column, using the decimal point to align the ones place and other place values.

$$
\begin{array}{r}
22.7 \\
-\ \ 1.53 \\
\end{array}
$$

Step 2 Write zeros, if needed, so that the decimals have the same number of decimal place values to subtract.

$$
\begin{array}{r}
22.70 \\
-\ \ 1.53 \\
\end{array}
$$

Writing a zero in the hundredths place as a placeholder does not change the value.

Step 3 Subtract from right to left as you would subtract whole numbers, regrouping place-value amounts as needed. Place the decimal point in the difference, aligned with the decimal points of the other numbers.

$$
\begin{array}{r}
{\scriptstyle 6\ 10} \\
22.7\cancel{0} \\
-\ \ 1.53 \\
\hline
21.17
\end{array}
$$

Part 2

Example Subtracting Decimals

The 10-second barrier in the 100-meter dash was first broken in the 1968 Olympics, when the winning time was 9.95 seconds. A gym teacher ran the 100-meter dash in 14.7 seconds. How much faster was the 1968 Olympic time than the gym teacher's time?

Solution

Subtract to find the difference: $14.7 - 9.95$.

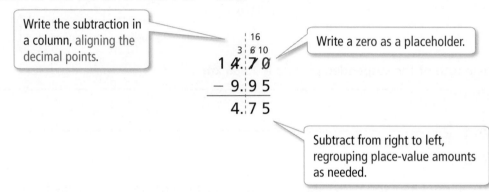

Write the subtraction in a column, aligning the decimal points.

Write a zero as a placeholder.

$$
\begin{array}{r}
1\,4.7\,0 \\
-\ 9.9\,5 \\
\hline
4.7\,5
\end{array}
$$

Subtract from right to left, regrouping place-value amounts as needed.

The Olympic time was 4.75 seconds faster.

Part 3

Example Finding Sums and Differences of Decimals

Find each sum or difference.

a. $2.57 + 7.706$ **b.** $1.5 - 1.056$ **c.** $3.284 + 11.9$

Solution

Write each calculation in a column, aligning the decimal points and including zeros as placeholders if needed.

Work from right to left, regrouping place-value amounts as needed.

$$
\textbf{a.} \quad
\begin{array}{r}
\overset{1}{2.570} \\
+\;\; 7.706 \\
\hline
10.276
\end{array}
\qquad
\textbf{b.} \quad
\begin{array}{r}
\overset{9}{} \\[-4pt]
\overset{4\;\;\cancel{10}\;\;10}{1.\cancel{5}\,\cancel{0}\,\cancel{0}} \\
-\;\; 1.056 \\
\hline
0.444
\end{array}
\qquad
\textbf{c.} \quad
\begin{array}{r}
\overset{1}{3.284} \\
+\;11.900 \\
\hline
15.184
\end{array}
$$

Key Concept

In this lesson, you extended what you knew about place value and adding and subtracting whole numbers to add and subtract decimals just as easily.

Addition	Subtraction

$$15.09 + 0.741 \qquad\qquad 22.7 - 1.53$$

$$
\begin{array}{r}
\overset{1}{} \\
15.090 \\
+\;\;0.741 \\
\hline
15.831
\end{array}
\qquad\qquad
\begin{array}{r}
\overset{6\;\;10}{} \\
22.7\cancel{0} \\
-\;\;1.53 \\
\hline
21.17
\end{array}
$$

1. You are shopping and spend $5.99 in one store and $7.54 in another. How much did you spend in all?

2. You are on your way to work. You drive 1.8 miles to a gas station and buy gas. Your workplace is 2.31 miles from the gas station. What is the distance of your commute to work?

3. You went to the store with $7.75 and spent $4.97. How much money do you have left?

4. You and a friend are buying lemons and sugar for a lemonade stand. You spend $15.89 to buy lemons and your friend spends $8.57 to buy sugar. How much does it cost to make the lemonade?

5. You are on a 4.7-mile run and have already run 2.85 miles. How many more miles do you need to run?

6. A plumber uses two copper pipes to repair a drain. Pipe A is 2.43 in. long. Pipe B is 0.97 in. long. How much longer is Pipe A than Pipe B?

7. Find $4.6 + 1.95$.

8. Find $7.6 - 3.71$.

9. **Reasoning** When adding decimals, you can write additional zeros, if needed, so that the decimals have the same number of decimal places.

   a. Find $7.9 + 8.41$.

   b. Explain why you can write additional zeros to the right of a decimal point but not to the left.

10. **Mental Math** A man wants to hike two trails. The length of one trail is 6.308 km. The length of the other trail is 7.0808 km. What is the total length of the two trails?

11. **Temperature** The average high temperature in a town for the month of July is 37.56°C. One day in July the temperature reached a record high of 39.45°C. How much higher is the record high temperature than the average high temperature?

12. **Think About the Process** Find $14.5 - 5.34$. Why must you line up the decimal points when writing the subtraction of decimal numbers?

13. **Error Analysis** A carpenter needs 35.5 meters of wood to complete a certain project. He has 28.65 meters on the jobsite. He calculates that he needs another 68.5 meters of wood, but realizes this is incorrect.

   a. Find the amount of wood that the carpenter needs to complete the project.

   b. What mistake might the carpenter have made?

      A. The carpenter subtracted incorrectly in the tenths place.

      B. The carpenter subtracted incorrectly in the hundredths place.

      C. The carpenter placed the decimal point in the difference incorrectly.

      D. The carpenter did not align the decimal points correctly before subtracting.

14. **a.** Find the difference $6.6 - 3.96$.

   b. How is subtracting decimals easier than subtracting fractions?

15. Think About the Process A cell phone company is offering a $75 instant rebate on any phone that costs more than $150. You decide to purchase a phone that costs $162.58.

   a. How would you set up the subtraction to find the actual cost of the phone?

     A. Subtract the rebate from the cost of the phone by writing the subtraction in a column and aligning the decimal points. Add two zeros as place holders in front of the decimal point of the rebate.

     B. Subtract the rebate from the cost of the phone by writing the subtraction in a column and aligning the numbers from right to left.

     C. Subtract the rebate from the cost of the phone by writing the subtraction in a column and aligning the numbers from right to left. Add three zeros as place holders after the decimal point of the rebate.

     D. Subtract the rebate from the cost of the phone by writing the subtraction in a column and aligning the decimal points. Add two zeros as place holders after the decimal point of the rebate.

   b. How much money will you have to pay for your phone?

16. Find the sum $6.31 + 37.5 + 0.925 + 4$.

17. You are at the mall and spend $15.99 for a T-shirt, $8.34 on a poster, and $7.86 on snacks at the food court. How much money did you spend altogether?

18. Think About the Process Find $44.2 - 38.96$. Explain why you must line up the decimal points when writing the subtraction of decimal numbers.

19. Error Analysis A carpenter needs 35.3 meters of wood to complete a certain project. He has 28.55 meters on the jobsite. He calculates that he needs another 67.5 meters of wood, but realizes this is incorrect.

   a. Find the amount of wood that the carpenter needs to complete the project.

   b. What mistake might the carpenter have made?

     A. The carpenter placed the decimal point in the difference incorrectly.

     B. The carpenter subtracted incorrectly in the hundredths place.

     C. The carpenter did not align the decimal points correctly before subtracting.

     D. The carpenter subtracted incorrectly in the tenths place.

20. Challenge Some friends took a road trip. They decided to stop for food after driving 61.94 miles. Later, they stopped for gas after driving an additional 79.3 miles. What was the total distance of the road trip if they drove another 137.9 miles before reaching the final stop?

21. Challenge You volunteered to help set up water stations for a marathon. The first station is 3.54 miles from the starting point. The second station is 5.7 miles from the first station. The third station is 4.97 miles from the second station. The last station is 7 miles from the third station. What is the distance of the last station to the finish line if a marathon is approximately 26.2 miles long?

CCSS: 6.NS.B.3

Key Concept

You can use what you know about multiplying whole numbers to multiply decimals.

Step 1 Write the multiplication in a column as you would to multiply whole numbers.

$$
\begin{array}{r}
48.23 \\
\times\ 3.9 \\
\hline
\end{array}
$$

Step 2 Find the product in the same way you do when multiplying whole numbers.

$$
\begin{array}{r}
48.23 \\
\times\ 3.9 \\
\hline
{\scriptstyle 1} \\
43407 \\
+\ 144690 \\
\hline
188097
\end{array}
$$

Step 3 Add the number of decimal places in the factors, and use that sum to place the decimal point in the product.

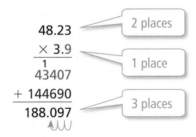

$$
\begin{array}{r}
48.23 \quad \text{2 places} \\
\times\ 3.9 \quad \text{1 place} \\
\hline
{\scriptstyle 1} \\
43407 \\
+\ 144690 \\
\hline
188.097 \quad \text{3 places}
\end{array}
$$

Sometimes you need to write zeros as placeholders in the product. Here is another example.

$$
\begin{array}{r}
0.43 \quad \text{2 places} \\
\times\ 0.22 \quad \text{2 places} \\
\hline
86 \\
+\ 860 \\
\hline
0.0946 \quad \text{4 places}
\end{array}
$$

The product has 4 decimal places so you need to write zeros as placeholders.

Part 1

Example Multiplying Decimals

Find each product.

    a. 0.7×0.08 **b.** $4.29(5.03)$ **c.** 4.8×3.235

Solution

Multiply as you would with whole numbers. Then add the number of decimal places in the factors to place the decimal point in the product.

Sample multiplications:

   a.

$$
\begin{array}{r}
0.08 \quad \longleftarrow \text{2 places} \\
\times\ 0.7 \quad \longleftarrow \text{1 place} \\
\hline
0.056 \quad \longleftarrow \text{3 places}
\end{array}
$$

   b.

$$
\begin{array}{r}
4.29 \quad \longleftarrow \text{2 places} \\
\times\ 5.03 \quad \longleftarrow \text{2 places} \\
\hline
1287 \\
0000 \\
+\ 214500 \\
\hline
21.5787 \quad \longleftarrow \text{4 places}
\end{array}
$$

   c.

$$
\begin{array}{r}
3.235 \quad \longleftarrow \text{3 places} \\
\times\ 4.8 \quad \longleftarrow \text{1 place} \\
\hline
25880 \\
+\ 129400 \\
\hline
15.5280 \quad \longleftarrow \text{4 places}
\end{array}
$$

        or 15.528

Part 2

Example Multiplying Decimals to Find Area

What is the area of the screen for the mini-TV shown below?

3.43 in.

6.1 in.

Solution

Think

You know the formula for the area of a rectangle is $A = \ell \cdot w$; so find 6.1×3.43.

Write

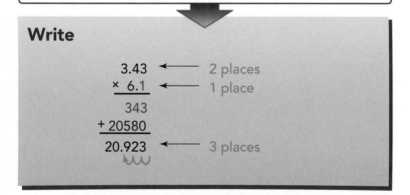

```
       3.43  ←——— 2 places
    ×   6.1  ←——— 1 place
        343
    + 20580
     20.923  ←——— 3 places
```

The area of the screen is 20.923 square inches or about 21 square inches.

Intro

Rounding money to the nearest penny means rounding to the hundredths place.

$$
\begin{array}{r}
\$2.36 \quad \longleftarrow \text{2 places} \\
\times\ 3.1 \quad \longleftarrow \text{1 place} \\
\hline
236 \\
+\ 7080 \\
\hline
\$7.316 \quad \longleftarrow \text{3 places}
\end{array}
$$

Look at the thousandths place: $6 \geq 5$, so round $7.316 to $7.32.

Example Rounding Products of Decimals

If you buy a bag of apples at the market that weigh 3.24 pounds, what is the price of the apples? Round your answer to the nearest cent.

| Bananas | Apples | Pears |
| 69¢/lb | $1.39/lb | $1.49/lb |

Solution

Know
- The apples weigh 3.24 pounds.
- The price for each pound is $1.39.

Need

The total price of the apples

Plan

Find 1.39 × 3.24.

$$
\begin{array}{r}
1.39 \quad \longleftarrow \text{2 places} \\
\times\ 3.24 \quad \longleftarrow \text{2 places} \\
\hline
21 \\
556 \\
2780 \\
+\ 41700 \\
\hline
\$4.5036 \quad \longleftarrow \text{4 places}
\end{array}
$$

The apples cost $4.50.

> Look at the thousandths place: $3 < 5$; so round $4.5036 to $4.50.

1. Find the product 76.6 × 0.08.

2. Find the product 3.2 × 0.03.

3. Find the product 37.07 × 0.087.

4. Find the product 2.22 × 0.005.

5. What is the area of the rectangular bottom of the cardboard box shown?

5.8 in.

7.9 in.

6. A square piece of fabric has side length 2.2 cm. Find the area of the piece of fabric.

7. Arpi has a glass that holds 9.75 fluid ounces. She drinks 1.5 glasses of juice in one day. To the nearest hundredth of a fluid ounce, how much juice does Arpi drink?

8. You buy 3.9 pound of trail mix. The mix costs $2.73 per pound. What is the total price for the trail mix?

9. Multiple Representations Multiply 5.58 × 2.35. Draw an area model that represents the product.

10. Error Analysis Stephen claims the product 0.06 × 0.76 is 0.456.

  a. Find the product 0.06 × 0.76.

  b. What mistake might Stephen have made?

   A. Stephen added instead of multiplied.

   B. Stephen used too many decimal places in the product.

   C. Stephen used too few decimal places in the product.

   D. Stephen divided instead of multiplied.

11. Stamp Dimensions A rectangular stamp has length 3.85 cm and width 2.6 cm. What is the area of the stamp?

12. Reasoning A square plot of land is 102.4 yards on each side.

  a. Find the area of the plot of land.

  b. Explain the relationship between the number of decimal places in the side length and the number of decimal places in the area.

13. Writing The cost of gas at a local gas station is $3.49 per gallon. Marty buys 8.48 gallons.

  a. What is the total cost?

  b. Explain how to estimate the cost if he buys double the number of gallons.

14. A rectangular garden has width 4.1 ft. The length of the garden is 3 ft greater than the width. Find the area of the garden.

15. A cubic foot of water weighs about 62.4 lb. A water storage tank holds 28.33 cubic feet of water. How much does the water in the storage tank weigh when the tank is full?

16. Think About the Process An onion cell has length 0.36 mm and width 0.07 mm. Assume the shape of the cell is approximately rectangular.

  a. Which expression represents the area of the onion cell?

   A. 0.36 ÷ 0.07

   B. 0.36 × 0.07

   C. 0.36 + 0.07

   D. 0.36 − 0.07

  b. What is the area?

17. Think About the Process A snail travels at a speed of 0.029 miles per hour. The product 0.029 × 1.8 represents the distance the snail travels in 1.8 hours.

  a. What is the first step in finding the product 0.029 × 1.8?

    A. Multiply 290 and 180

    B. Multiply 2.9 and 1.8

    C. Multiply 0.029 and 1.8

    D. Multiply 29 and 18

  b. How far does the snail travel in 1.8 hours?

18. Error Analysis Stephen claims the product 0.02 × 0.79 is 0.00158.

  a. Find the product 0.02 × 0.79.

  b. What mistake might Stephen have made?

    A. Stephen added instead of multiplied.

    B. Stephen divided instead of multiplied.

    C. Stephen used too many decimal places in the product.

    D. Stephen used too few decimal places in the product.

19. Challenge You are making 4 identical square paintings that are 10.4 in. on each side.

  a. What is the total area of the paintings?

  b. Suppose you have enough paint to cover 400 in.^{2}. Will you have enough paint?

20. Challenge You buy 3.17 pounds of apples, 1.25 pounds of peaches, and 2.56 pounds of oranges. What is your total bill?

Grocery Store Prices

Item	Cost
Apples	$0.99 per pound
Peaches	$1.19 per pound
Oranges	$1.09 per pound

Vocabulary
compatible numbers, quotient

CCSS: 6.NS.B.2

Key Concept

Standard Long Division

Find $437 \div 20$.

First, rewrite as $20\overline{)437}$ (the dividend is inside the symbol and the divisor is to the left).

Then estimate the quotient to help determine where to place the first digit. Estimate using **compatible numbers,** which are numbers that are easy to compute with mentally:

$$437 \div 20 \approx 400 \div 20$$
$$= 207$$

> This symbol means approximately equal to.

So start by dividing the tens. Use the 4-step method, repeating as needed.

4-step method

   Step 1 Divide

   Step 2 Multiply

   Step 3 Subtract

   Step 4 Compare

```
        21 R17
   20)437
     -40
       37
      -20
       17
```

Check ·

```
        21
      × 20
       420
      + 17
       437 ✓
```

Part 1

Example Finding Quotients of Multi-Digit Numbers

Find each quotient. Check your answers.

    a. 254 ÷ 29   **b.** 784 ÷ 25

Solution

Use long division. Apply the four-step standard method:

1. Divide
2. Multiply
3. Subtract
4. Compare

    a. 254 ÷ 29   **b.** 784 ÷ 25

$$
\begin{array}{r}
8\,R22 \\
29\overline{)254} \\
-232 \\
\hline
22
\end{array}
$$

$$
\begin{array}{r}
31\,R9 \\
25\overline{)784} \\
-75\downarrow \\
\hline
34 \\
-25 \\
\hline
9
\end{array}
$$

Check

a.
$$
\begin{array}{r}
29 \\
\times\ 8 \\
\hline
232
\end{array}
\longrightarrow
\begin{array}{r}
232 \\
+\ 22 \\
\hline
254\ \checkmark
\end{array}
$$

b.
$$
\begin{array}{r}
25 \\
\times\ 31 \\
\hline
25 \\
+750 \\
\hline
775
\end{array}
\longrightarrow
\begin{array}{r}
775 \\
+\ \ 9 \\
\hline
784\ \checkmark
\end{array}
$$

Part 2

Intro

Some divisions have a zero in the quotient. For example, find $4,875 \div 24$.

Example:

$$24\overline{)4,875}$$

Estimate:

$$4,875 \div 24 \approx 5,000 \div 25$$
$$= 200$$

Example:

4-step method

    Step 1 Divide

    Step 2 Multiply

    Step 3 Subtract

    Step 4 Compare

```
      203 R3
24)4,875
   -48↓↓
      075
     -72
        3
```

Check

```
      203
   ×   24
    4,872
   +    3
    4,875 ✓
```

Example Dividing Multi-Digit Numbers for Quotients with a Zero

Find each quotient. Multiply to check your answers.

    a. $4,410 \div 63$ **b.** $9,799 \div 32$

Solution

Use long division. Apply the four-step standard method:

1. Divide
2. Multiply
3. Subtract
4. Compare

    a. $4,410 \div 63$ **b.** $9,799 \div 32$

```
       70              306 R7
63)4,410           32)9,799
  - 441↓              -96↓↓
      00                199
                       -192
                          7
```

continued on next page >

Part 2

Example continued

Check ·

a.
```
      63
  ×   70
   4,410 ✓
```

b.
```
       306
   ×    32
       612
   +  9,180
     9,792 ──────→ 9,792
                  +    7
                   9,799 ✓
```

Part 3

Example Dividing Multi-Digit Numbers to Solve Area Problems

Use the information in the diagram of the Reflecting Pool to find the Reflecting Pool's length.

167 ft | Area = 338,843 ft²

Solution ·

Think

You know $\ell = A \div w$, so find $338,843 \div 167$.

Write

```
            2,029
  167) 338,843
      − 334↓↓
          4 84
        − 334
          1503
        − 1503
             0
```

The Reflecting Pool is reported to be 2,029 feet long.

1. Find the quotient.
   974 ÷ 18 = ■ R ■

2. Use long division to find the quotient.
   5,579 ÷ 17 = ■ R ■

3. Find the quotient.
   5,547 ÷ 18 = ■ R ■

4. Divide.
   16,161 ÷ 20 = ■ R ■

5. Simplify the expression.
   12,419 ÷ 395 = ■ R ■

6. A construction company is in charge of building a new mall. The plot of land available for the mall building is a rectangle with an area of 811,397 ft². The width of the plot of land is 787 ft. If the mall will cover the entire plot of land, how long will it be?

7. **Think About the Process**
   a. Find the quotient 3,328 ÷ 11. What is the quotient?
      A. 302 R 6   **B.** 302
      C. 303   **D.** 303 R 6
   b. Which of the following operations would you use to check your answer? Select all that apply.
      A. Multiplication
      B. Subtraction
      C. Addition
      D. Division

8. a. **Writing** Use long division to find the quotient 5,673 ÷ 18. Use multiplication and, if necessary, addition to check your answer.
   b. Explain when you would use addition along with multiplication to check your answer.

9. **Reasoning** A truck at a granite quarry has a maximum weight capacity of 9,653 pounds.
   a. If each granite block weighs 421 pounds, how many blocks can the truck carry?
   b. Describe what the remainder represents in this problem.

10. **Think About the Process** A building needs 14,658 ft of electrical wire to be constructed. Each roll of wire contains 349 ft or wire.
    a. What is the first step in finding the number of rolls of wire needed to construct the building?
       A. Multiply   **B.** Subtract
       C. Compare   **D.** Divide
    b. How many rolls of wire are needed?

11. **Mental Math** Find the quotient 6,342 ÷ 21.

12. **Error Analysis** Your friend incorrectly says the quotient of the expression 23,456 ÷ 26 is 92 R 4.
    a. What is the quotient?
       A. 903   **B.** 902 R 4
       C. 920 R 4   **D.** 902
    b. What mistake might your friend have made?
       A. Your friend did not include the zero in the ones place of the quotient.
       B. Your friend did not include the zero in the hundreds place of the quotient.
       C. Your friend included a remainder in the quotient.
       D. Your friend did not include the zero in the tens place of the quotient.

13. **Distance** An airplane is traveling at 555 miles per hour. How long will it take the airplane to travel 24,975 miles?

14. A hole is 223 inches deep. How deep is the hole in yards?
    A. The hole is 7 yards deep.
    B. The hole is 6 yards, 7 inches deep.
    C. The hole is 7 yards, 7 inches deep.
    D. The hole is 6 yards deep.

15. A student read a book in 39 days. The book is 429 pages long. If the student read the same whole number of pages each day, how many pages per day did the student read?

16. A library has 20,930 books that have spines of about the same width. If 26 books can fit on one bookshelf, how many bookshelves would it take to hold the library's books?

   A. 804   **B.** 84

   C. 805   **D.** 85

17. A small airplane can hold 11 people per trip. How many trips would it take the airplane to transport 7,717 people?

18. **Think About the Process**

   a. Find the quotient 2,228 ÷ 11. What is the quotient?

   A. 202 R 6

   B. 202

   C. 203 R 6

   D. 203

   b. Which of the following operations would you use to check your answer? Select all that apply.

   A. Addition

   B. Subtraction

   C. Multiplication

   D. Division

19. **a. Writing** Use long division to find the quotient 4,109 ÷ 19. Use multiplication and, if necessary, addition to check your answer.

   A. 217

   B. 216 R 5

   C. 217 R 5

   D. 216

   b. Explain when you would use addition along with multiplication to check your answer.

20. **Challenge** In 40 days, a ferry transports 12,240 people. The ferry makes 3 trips per day.

   a. If the ferry transports the same number of people each trip, how many people does the ferry transport each day?

   b. How many people does the ferry transport per trip?

21. **Challenge** A glider is gliding at an altitude of 256 ft. An airplane is flying at an altitude of 39,168 ft.

   a. How many times higher is the airplane than the glider?

   b. How many times higher would the airplane be than the glider if the altitude of the glider was only 153 ft?

22. **Error Analysis** Your friend incorrectly says the quotient of the expression 23,289 ÷ 29 is 83 R 2.

   a. What is the quotient?

   b. What mistake might your friend have made?

   A. Your friend did not include the zero in the ones place of the quotient.

   B. Your friend did not include the zero in the tens place of the quotient.

   C. Your friend included a remainder in the quotient.

   D. Your friend did not include the zero in the hundreds place of the quotient.

7-4 | Dividing Decimals

CCSS: 6.NS.B.3

Part 1

Intro

You can use what you know about dividing whole numbers to divide a decimal by a whole number.

To illustrate, here is how to find $364.2 \div 12$.

First, write the division using the standard long-division symbol.

Use compatible numbers to estimate the quotient to decide where to place the first digit.

$$\text{Estimate:} \quad 364.2 \div 12 \approx 360 \div 12$$
$$= 30$$

4-Step Method

Step 1 Divide

Step 2 Multiply

Step 3 Subtract

Step 4 Compare

```
        3 0.3 5
   12)3 6 4.2 0
      - 3 6
          0 4 2
          - 3 6
              6 0
            - 6 0
                0
```

Check

```
      30.35
    ×    12
      6070
  + 30350
    364.20  ✔
```

Example Dividing Decimals

Find each quotient. Multiply or use a calculator to check your answers.

a. $97.5 \div 6$ **b.** $5.43 \div 15$

Solution

Apply standard long division, using two additional steps:

Step 1 Place the decimal point in the quotient above the decimal point in the dividend.

Step 2 Instead of writing a remainder, write a zero at the end of the dividend as a placeholder, and continue the division.

continued on next page >

Part 1

Solution continued

a. 97.5 ÷ 6

Place the decimal point in the quotient above the decimal point in the dividend.

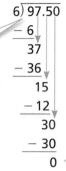

$$
\begin{array}{r}
16.25 \\
6\overline{)97.50} \\
\underline{-6} \\
37 \\
\underline{-36} \\
15 \\
\underline{-12} \\
30 \\
\underline{-30} \\
0
\end{array}
$$

Divide using the standard method.

There is no remainder, so you do not need to write a zero placeholder to continue the division.

The same method is used for part b.

b. 5.43 ÷ 15

$$
\begin{array}{r}
0.362 \\
15\overline{)5.430} \\
\underline{-45} \\
93 \\
\underline{-90} \\
30 \\
\underline{-30} \\
0
\end{array}
$$

Check

a.
$$
\begin{array}{r}
16.25 \\
\times\quad 6 \\
\hline
97.50 \ ✔
\end{array}
$$

b.
$$
\begin{array}{r}
0.362 \\
\times\quad 15 \\
\hline
1.810 \\
+\ 3.620 \\
\hline
5.430 \ ✔
\end{array}
$$

Key Concept

Dividing a Decimal by a Decimal

You can extend what you know about dividing to divide a decimal by a decimal.

First, write the division using the standard long-division symbol.

For example, $0.5\overline{)2.25}$.

Then, multiply the divisor by the power of ten needed to change it to a whole number.

$05.\overline{)2.25}$

To keep the division equal, multiply the dividend by the same power of ten.

$05.\overline{)2\,2.5}$

Then use standard long-division. Place the decimal in the quotient above the decimal point in the dividend.

$5\overline{)22.5}$

Example

$2.25 \div 0.5$

$$
\begin{array}{r}
4.5 \\
5\overline{)2\,2.5} \\
-2\,0\!\downarrow \\
\hline
2\,5 \\
-2\,5 \\
\hline
0
\end{array}
$$

Another Example

$0.141 \div 2.35$

$$
\begin{array}{r}
0.06 \\
235\overline{)14.10} \\
-14\,10 \\
\hline
0
\end{array}
$$

Example Finding Quotients of Decimals

Find each quotient. Use a calculator to check your answers.

     a. 2.4 ÷ 0.3   **b.** 38.27 ÷ 4.3   **c.** 0.144 ÷ 0.96

Solution

     a. 2.4 ÷ 0.3   **b.** 38.27 ÷ 4.3

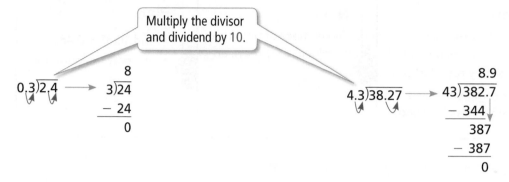

Multiply the divisor and dividend by 10.

     c. 0.144 ÷ 0.96

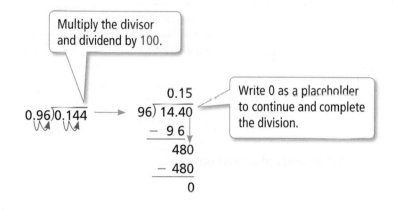

Multiply the divisor and dividend by 100.

Write 0 as a placeholder to continue and complete the division.

Part 3

Example Dividing Decimals to Solve Problems

Last week, a 6th grade class received $10.32 for aluminum cans they recycled. The scrap yard paid them $.48 for each pound. How many pounds of aluminum cans did the class recycle?

Solution

Know	Need	Plan
• The class received $10.32 for aluminum cans they recycled. • The scrap yard paid $0.48 for each pound.	The number of pounds of aluminum cans recycled	• Find $10.32 \div 0.48$. • Interpret the quotient.

Use a long division symbol to write the division.

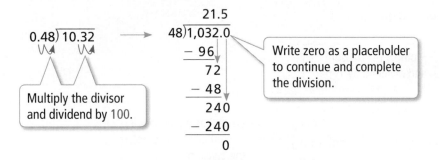

Multiply the divisor and dividend by 100.

Write zero as a placeholder to continue and complete the division.

The class recycled 21.5 pounds of aluminum cans.

1. Find the quotient 38.8 ÷ 4.
2. Find the quotient 3.1 ÷ 5.
3. Divide 3.3 ÷ 1.1.
4. Divide 93.9 ÷ 1.5.
5. Find 117.6 ÷ 14.
6. A store had apples on sale for $1.20 a pound. Joan spent $5.28 on apples. How many pounds did she buy?
7. Danny goes to the store to get more paper plates for a neighborhood cookout. Each package of paper plates sells for $1.70. Danny has $15.64 to spend. What is the maximum number of packages of paper plates he can buy?
8. **Reasoning** Find the quotient for 18.4 ÷ 4. Decide whether the quotient will be greater than or less than the dividend before dividing. Explain your reasoning.
9. **Multiple Representations** Find 32.4 ÷ 9. Without performing calculations, find another division expression which has the same value as the given expression. Explain your answer.
10. **Writing** Find the quotient 0.056 ÷ 0.008. Explain what you need to multiply the dividend by and why.
11. **Error Analysis** A question on a math test was to find the value of 15.12 ÷ 2.4. Steve said the answer is 0.63.
    a. Find the quotient 15.12 ÷ 2.4.
    b. What mistake might Steve have made?
       A. Steve did not multiply the decimals by a power of 10.
       B. Steve multiplied only the dividend by a power of 10.
       C. Steve multiplied only the divisor by a power of 10.
       D. Steve divided each decimal by a power of 10.

12. **Clothes** Patty goes to a store to buy T-shirts. The store has T-shirts on sale for $5.90 each. Patty has $84.96 left on a gift card. What is the maximum number of T-shirts she can buy using only the gift card?
13. The area of a rectangle is 5.472 m². If the length of the rectangle is 0.72 m, what is the width of the rectangle?
14. Find 69.2 ÷ 8. Explain what would happen to the quotient if one of the numbers was multiplied by a power of 10.
15. **Think About the Process**
    a. When finding the quotient for 2.38 ÷ 5, where do you place the decimal in the quotient?
       A. There is no decimal point in the quotient.
       B. The decimal point should be placed one place to the right of the decimal point in the dividend.
       C. The decimal point should be placed above the decimal point in the dividend.
       D. The decimal point should be placed one place to the left of the decimal point in the dividend.
    b. Find 2.38 ÷ 5.
16. **a.** Simplify the expression 12.85 ÷ 2.5.
    b. What is an equivalent expression with divisor 0.25?
17. **Think About the Process**
    a. What quotient might you rewrite 80.4 ÷ 1.5 as to find its value?
       A. 804 ÷ 1.5
       B. 80.4 ÷ 15
       C. 80.4 × 1.5
       D. 804 ÷ 15
    b. Find 80.4 ÷ 1.5.

18. Challenge Do the expressions
$(32.4 \div 3.6) \div 0.3$ and
$32.4 \div (3.6 \div 0.3)$ have the same
value?

19. Challenge A librarian puts books on a
bookshelf. The shelf is 38.1 in. long.
Each book is 1.5 in. thick.

a. What is the maximum number of
books that fit on the shelf?

b. How much longer would the shelf
have to be to fit the next book?

CCSS: 6.NS.C.7

Part 1

Intro

You can use what you know about the word form of numbers to write decimals as fractions.

Tenths The word form of 0.6 is "zero and six-tenths," or just "six-tenths."

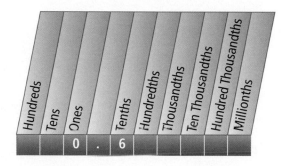

$0.6 = \dfrac{6}{10}$

$\quad = \dfrac{6 \div 2}{10 \div 2}$, or $\dfrac{3}{5}$ ◄—— simplest form

Hundredths The word form of 0.24 is "zero and twenty-four hundredths," or just "twenty-four hundredths."

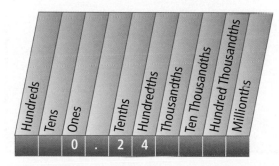

$0.24 = \dfrac{24}{100}$

$\quad = \dfrac{24 \div 4}{100 \div 4}$, or $\dfrac{6}{25}$ ◄—— simplest form

continued on next page >

Part 1

Thousandths The word form of 0.225 is "zero and two hundred twenty-five thousandths," or just "two hundred twenty-five thousandths."

$$0.225 = \frac{225}{1,000}$$

$$= \frac{225 \div 25}{1,000 \div 25}, \text{ or } \frac{9}{40} \longleftarrow \text{simplest form}$$

Example Converting Decimals to Fractions

Merritt Island National Wildlife Refuge, surrounding the Kennedy Space Center, is a sanctuary for green turtles, bald eagles, Florida panthers, and hundreds of other animals. About 0.625 of the total area of the refuge is water. What fraction of the total area is water?

Solution ·

Think

The word form of 0.625 is "zero and six hundred twenty-five thousandths." I need to write the word form as a fraction and then simplify.

Write

$$0.625 = \frac{625}{1,000}$$

$$= \frac{625 \div 125}{1,000 \div 125}$$

$$= \frac{5}{8}$$

About $\frac{5}{8}$ of the total area is water.

Key Concept

You can use what you know about fractions and division to write fractions as decimals.

Write $\frac{3}{4}$ as a decimal. The fraction bar means *divide*.

```
        0.7 5
    4)3.0 0
     −2 8↓
        2 0
       −2 0
          0
```

So, $\frac{3}{4} = 0.75$.

Part 2

Example Converting Fractions to Decimals

Use division to write each fraction as a decimal.

a. $\frac{1}{2}$ **b.** $\frac{3}{8}$ **c.** $\frac{29}{40}$

Solution ·

Divide each fraction's numerator by its denominator.

a. $\frac{1}{2} \longrightarrow$
```
      0.5
   2)1.0
    − 1 0
        0
```

b. $\frac{3}{8} \longrightarrow$
```
      0.3 7 5
   8)3.0 0 0
    −2 4↓
       6 0
      −5 6↓
         4 0
        −4 0
           0
```

c. $\frac{29}{40} \longrightarrow$
```
       0.7 2 5
   40)29.0 0 0
     −28 0↓
        1 0 0
       − 8 0↓
          2 0 0
         −2 0 0
              0
```

So $\frac{1}{2} = 0.5$.   So $\frac{3}{8} = 0.375$.   So $\frac{29}{40} = 0.725$.

Part 3

Intro

Some fractions have decimal forms that repeat without end. You can use rounding to approximate these decimals.

Write $\frac{2}{3}$ as a decimal rounded to the nearest hundredth.

Step 1 Write the fraction as division.

$$3\overline{)2}$$

Step 2 Place a decimal point in the dividend and write a zero in the tenths place as a placeholder.

$$3\overline{)2.0}$$

Step 3 Begin dividing.

$$\begin{array}{r} 0.6 \\ 3\overline{)2.0} \\ -1\,8 \\ \hline 2 \end{array}$$

Step 4 Continue dividing. The digit six in the quotient appears to be repeating. You can round to the nearest hundredth: two thirds is approximately equal to zero-point-six-seven.

$$\begin{array}{r} 0.6\,6\,6 \\ 3\overline{)2.0\,0\,0} \\ -1\,8 \\ \hline 2\,0 \\ -1\,8 \\ \hline 2\,0 \\ -1\,8 \\ \hline 2 \end{array}$$

> The decimal is repeating. $6 > 5$, so round the decimal to 0.67.

So $\frac{2}{3} \approx 0.67$.

Example Rounding Decimal Forms of Fractions

Lake Superior contains about $\frac{1}{9}$ of the world's fresh surface water.

Write $\frac{1}{9}$ as a decimal rounded to the nearest hundredth.

continued on next page >

Example continued

Solution ·

Divide the numerator of the fraction by its denominator to write the fraction as a decimal.

$$\frac{1}{9} \longrightarrow \begin{array}{r} 0.1\ 1\ 1 \\ 9)\overline{1.0\ 0\ 0} \\ \underline{-\ 9} \downarrow \\ 1\ 0 \\ \underline{-\ 9} \downarrow \\ 1\ 0 \\ \underline{-\ 9} \\ 1 \end{array}$$

> The decimal is repeating.
> $1 < 5$, so round the decimal to 0.11.

So $\frac{1}{9} \approx 0.11$.

1. a. What is the word form of 0.59?

   A. Fifty-nine tenths

   B. Fifty-nine hundredths

   C. Fifty-nine hundred

   D. Fifty-nine thousandths

   b. What is the fraction form of 0.59?

   A. $\frac{59}{100}$ **B.** $\frac{59}{10}$

   C. $\frac{59}{1,000}$ **D.** $\frac{1}{59}$

2. Write the word form and fraction form of 0.654.

3. A study found that 0.153 of the people surveyed like tomato juice. What fraction of those surveyed like tomato juice?

   A. $\frac{153}{10}$ **B.** $\frac{153}{1,000}$

   C. $\frac{153}{100}$ **D.** $\frac{1}{153}$

4. Write $\frac{19}{20}$ as a decimal without using long division.

5. Convert $\frac{13}{25}$ to a decimal.

6. a. Use division to write each fraction as a decimal.

   $\frac{3}{20}$ $\frac{27}{40}$

   b. Explain how you can tell, without using long division, that the decimal for either fraction will not be a repeating decimal.

7. Which decimal below is equivalent to $\frac{1}{9}$? The dots indicate that the repeating digits repeat without end.

   A. 0.222...   **B.** 0.111...

   C. 0.11   **D.** 0.111

8. A supply closet contains $\frac{5}{9}$ of a school's crayons. Write $\frac{5}{9}$ as a decimal rounded to the nearest hundredth.

9. a. Reasoning Write 0.394 as a fraction.

   b. Could you use the same method to write 0.394 as a mixed number? As an improper fraction? Explain.

10. Error Analysis Kyra tried to write $\frac{197}{250}$ as a decimal without using long division. Her result, 0.197, is not equivalent to $\frac{197}{250}$.

   a. What is the correct decimal equivalent?

   b. What could possibly be Kyra's mistake?

   A. Kyra meant to multiply the numerator and denominator by 4 to make an equivalent fraction with denominator 1,000 but multiplied only the denominator by 4.

   B. Kyra meant to divide the numerator and denominator by 2.5 to make an equivalent fraction with denominator 100 but divided only the denominator by 2.5.

   C. Kyra meant to divide the numerator and denominator by 2.5 to make an equivalent fraction with denominator 100 but divided only the numerator by 2.5.

   D. Kyra meant to multiply the numerator and denominator by 4 to make an equivalent fraction with denominator 1,000 but multiplied only the numerator by 4.

11. a. Which decimal is equivalent to $\frac{20}{30}$? The dots indicate that the repeating digits repeat without end.

   A. 0.7222...   **B.** 0.7272...

   C. 0.6000...   **D.** 0.6060...

   b. Writing Describe a possible problem using dots to represent repeating digits in a decimal. Describe, if you can, a different way to represent repeating digits in a decimal.

12. Open-Ended Fractions with denominator 41 have decimal forms in which 5 digits repeat without end. Which decimal is equivalent to $\frac{13}{41}$? A calculator may be used to find your answer.

   A. 0.34707...   **B.** 0.31707...

   C. 0.31407...   **D.** 0.34407...

13. **Buying Chicken** A package of chicken weighs $\frac{2}{3}$ kg.
    a. Use a decimal to approximate $\frac{2}{3}$.
    b. If chicken costs $6.30 per kilogram, what is the price of this package?

14. A supermarket chain had a taste test between the store-brand plain yogurt and the best-selling brand. The test showed that 0.86 of the people surveyed preferred the store-brand and 0.14 of the people preferred the best-selling brand.
    a. What fraction of the people preferred the store-brand?
    b. What fraction of the people preferred the best-selling brand?

15. a. Which decimal is equivalent to $\frac{25}{37}$? The dots indicate that the repeating digits repeat without end.
    A. 0.675675...   **B.** 0.67575...
    C. 0.6755...   **D.** 0.675
    b. Which decimal is equivalent to $\frac{55}{74}$?
    A. 0.7432432...
    B. 0.743232...
    C. 0.74327432...
    D. 0.74322...
    c. Compare the fractions $\frac{25}{37}$ and $\frac{55}{74}$ using a greater than or less than symbol.

16. **Think About the Process**
    a. What is a first step in writing the decimal 0.85 as a fraction?
    A. Write a fraction with the decimal as the numerator and 10 as the denominator.
    B. Find the word for the decimal place farthest to the right.
    b. Use the word form to write 0.85 as a fraction. Simplify your answer.

17. **Think About the Process**
    a. What is a good first step in writing $\frac{42}{60}$ as a decimal without using long division?
    A. Multiply the numerator and denominator of the fraction by 6.
    B. Divide the numerator and denominator of the fraction by 6.
    C. Multiply the numerator and denominator of the fraction by 7.
    D. Divide the numerator and denominator of the fraction by 7.
    b. Write $\frac{42}{60}$ as a decimal.

18. **Challenge** A chef's specialty calls for one-fiftieth of an ounce of a spice per serving. The chef has a digital scale that shows the weight as a decimal. What scale reading does the chef need to see for this spice when preparing the specialty for 17 people?

19. **Challenge** A man has an $\frac{11}{15}$-oz gold ring and a $\frac{17}{18}$-oz gold chain. He asks a jeweler to use the ring and chain to make a bracelet. The jeweler needs 1.6 oz of gold to make the bracelet.
    a. What is the combined weight of the ring and chain as a decimal?
    b. Is this enough gold to make the bracelet?
    c. Explain.

| # Comparing and Ordering Decimals and Fractions

CCSS: 6.NS.C.7

Part 1

Example Ordering Decimals

Order the numbers from greatest to least.

| 35.435 | 35.44 | 35.43 | 35.451 |

Solution

Write numbers in a column, using the decimal point to align the ones place and other place values. Compare the digits from left to right.

35.43 ⟵ least
35.435 ⟵ next least
35.44 ⟵ next greatest
35.451 ⟵ greatest

So the numbers ordered from greatest to least are 35.451, 35.44, 35.435, 35.43.

Key Concept

Intro

There are two ways to compare decimals and fractions.

Compare 0.85 and $\frac{5}{6}$.

One way to compare is as fractions.

$$0.85 = \frac{85}{100}$$

$$= \frac{85 \div 5}{100 \div 5}$$ ⟵ Divide the numerator and denominator by 5.

$$= \frac{17}{20}$$

To compare $\frac{17}{20}$ and $\frac{5}{6}$, find the least common denominator of 20 and 6 to use as a common denominator.

Multiples of 20: 20, 40, 60
Multiples of 6: 6, 12, 18, 24, 30, 36, 42, 48, 54, 60

continued on next page >

Key Concept

Intro continued

60 is the least common multiple. Write both fractions with a denominator of 60.

$$0.85 = \frac{17 \times 3}{20 \times 3}$$

> Multiply the numerator and denominator by 3.

$$= \frac{51}{60}$$

$$\frac{5}{6} = \frac{5 \times 10}{6 \times 10}$$

> Multiply the numerator and denominator by 10.

$$= \frac{50}{60}$$

Compare the fractions: $\frac{51}{60} > \frac{50}{60}$. So, $0.85 > \frac{5}{6}$.

Another way to compare 0.85 and $\frac{5}{6}$ is as decimals.

We can write $\frac{5}{6}$ as a decimal.

$$\frac{5}{6} \rightarrow 6\overline{)5.000} \begin{array}{r} 0.833 \\ \hline \end{array}$$

```
          0.8 3 3
  5
  ─  →  6)5.0 0 0
  6
        −4 8
         ───
          2 0
         −1 8
          ───
           2 0
          −1 8
           ───
            2
```

We have the decimal 0.85, and we know that $\frac{5}{6} \approx 0.83$.

Compare: $0.85 > 0.83$.

So, $0.85 > \frac{5}{6}$.

Example Comparing Decimals and Fractions

Compare each pair of numbers.

a. 0.27 and $\frac{2}{7}$ **b.** 0.6 and $\frac{5}{8}$ **c.** 0.45 and $\frac{4}{9}$

Solution ·

a. 0.27 and $\frac{2}{7}$

$$\frac{2}{7} \rightarrow 7)\overline{\begin{array}{l} 0.2\ 8\ 5 \\ 2.0\ 0\ 0 \end{array}}$$

$$\begin{array}{r} -1\ 4 \downarrow \\ \hline 6\ 0 \\ -5\ 6 \downarrow \\ \hline 4\ 0 \\ -3\ 5 \\ \hline 5 \end{array}$$

$\frac{2}{7} \approx 0.29.$

$0.27 < 0.29$

So, $0.27 < \frac{2}{7}$.

c. 0.45 and $\frac{4}{9}$

$$\frac{4}{9} \rightarrow 9)\overline{\begin{array}{l} 0.4\ 4\ 4 \\ 4.0\ 0\ 0 \end{array}}$$

$$\begin{array}{r} -3\ 6 \downarrow \\ \hline 4\ 0 \\ -3\ 6 \downarrow \\ \hline 4\ 0 \\ -3\ 6 \\ \hline 4 \end{array}$$

$\frac{4}{9} \approx 0.44$

$0.45 > 0.44$

So, $0.45 > \frac{4}{9}$.

b. 0.6 and $\frac{5}{8}$

$0.6 = \frac{6}{10}$

$\frac{6 \times 4}{10 \times 4} = \frac{24}{40}$

$\frac{5 \times 5}{8 \times 5} = \frac{25}{40}$

> 40 is the LCM of 10 and 8.

$\frac{24}{40} < \frac{25}{40}$

So, $0.6 < \frac{5}{8}$

Part 3

Example Ordering Decimals and Fractions

Order the numbers from greatest to least.

$$\frac{7}{11} \qquad\qquad 0.69 \qquad\qquad \frac{6}{9} \qquad\qquad 0.711$$

Solution

These numbers appear difficult to compare as fractions, so write the two fractions, $\frac{7}{11}$ and $\frac{6}{9}$, as decimals.

Divide: $\frac{7}{11} \rightarrow$

$$\begin{array}{r} 0.6\ 3\ 6 \\ 11\overline{)7.0\ 0\ 0} \\ -6\ 6 \\ \hline 4\ 0 \\ -3\ 3 \\ \hline 7\ 0 \\ -6\ 6 \\ \hline 4 \end{array}$$

Round: $\frac{7}{11} \approx 0.64$

Simplify: $\frac{6}{9} = \frac{6 \div 3}{9 \div 3}$

$$= \frac{2}{3}$$

Recall that: $\frac{2}{3} \approx 0.67$

Now, write the 4 decimals in a column to make them easy to compare and order.

0.69
0.711
0.64
0.67

Then, compare place values from left to right: 0.711 is the greatest; use hundredths to order the remaining numbers from greatest to least.

0.711
0.69
0.67
0.64

Lastly, substitute the fractions back and write the order.

$0.711, 0.69, \frac{6}{9}, \frac{7}{11}$

1. Compare 9.95 and 9.91 using a greater than or less than symbol.

2. Order the numbers 0.125, 0.129, and 0.12 from least to greatest.

3. Use a greater than, less than, or equals symbol to compare $\frac{2}{5}$ and 0.4. Change the decimal to a fraction first.

4. Use a greater than, less than, or equals symbol to compare 0.31 and $\frac{1}{3}$. Change the fraction to a decimal first.

5. Order the numbers 0.56, 0.53, and $\frac{1}{2}$ from greatest to least.

6. Order the numbers $\frac{2}{7}$, 0.26, and 0.21 from least to greatest.

7. **Reasoning** Compare the decimals 7.131 and 7.134 using a greater than or less than symbol. Explain how you can use a number line to compare the two values.

8. **Construction** Zach wants to drill a hole with diameter no more than 0.5 inch. Can he use a $\frac{2}{5}$-inch drill bit? Answer this question by changing the decimal to a fraction.

9. **a. Writing** Compare 0.93 and $\frac{11}{12}$ using a greater than or less than symbol. Change the fraction to a decimal first.

   b. When comparing a decimal and a fraction, do you prefer to change the decimal to a fraction or change the fraction to a decimal? Why?

10. **Estimation** Round the decimals to the nearest tenth. Then use these rounded values to order the numbers 0.37, 0.31, $\frac{3}{5}$, and $\frac{7}{20}$ from greatest to least.

11. **a. Error Analysis** Suzie claims that the greatest of the numbers 0.49, 0.41, $\frac{4}{9}$, $\frac{4}{7}$ is $\frac{4}{7}$ and the least is $\frac{4}{9}$. Order the numbers from least to greatest.

    b. What was Suzie's likely error?

    A. She stopped dividing after only one place when finding the decimal equivalent of $\frac{4}{7}$.

    B. She divided the denominator of $\frac{4}{9}$ by its numerator to find the decimal equivalent.

    C. She stopped dividing after only one place when finding the decimal equivalent of $\frac{4}{9}$.

    D. She switched the order of the two fractions.

12. Which of the following numbers could be placed between the numbers 4.14 and 4.28 so that the three numbers are ordered from least to greatest? Select all that apply.

    A. 4.158   **B.** 4.29

    C. 4.2   **D.** 4.13

    E. 4.343   **F.** 4.2034

13. Keisha has a new puppy that weighs 4.64 pounds. Leon also has a new puppy, and his weighs 4.73 pounds. After one month, Keisha's puppy has gained 1.23 pounds, while Leon's has gained 1.11 pounds. Whose puppy currently weighs more?

    A. The puppies currently have the same weight.

    B. Leon's puppy currently weighs more.

    C. Keisha's puppy currently weighs more.

14. You want to buy a new cell phone. You are deciding between two different models. Model X weighs $\frac{5}{16}$ pound and model Y weighs 0.33 pound. You think the one that weighs less will be better. Which model should you buy? Answer this question by changing the fraction to a decimal.

    A. You could buy either model because $\frac{5}{16} = 0.33$.

    B. You should buy model X because $\frac{5}{16} < 0.33$.

    C. You should buy model Y because $\frac{5}{16} > 0.33$.

15. You ordered $\frac{1}{4}$ pound of cheese at the market. The digital scale used to weigh the cheese read 0.25 pound.

   a. Did you get less than, more than, or exactly the amount you requested? Answer this question by changing the decimal to a fraction.

   b. The cheese cost $3 per pound. Multiply this price by the amount you received to find the total cost of your order.

16. Think About the Process Lucy ran the 100-yard dash in 12.81 seconds. Ami ran it in 12.9 seconds. Robin ran it in 12.92 seconds.

   a. Is the fastest time the least time or the greatest time?

   b. Order the runners from fastest to slowest.

17. Think About the Process Review the numbers below.

$$0.9 \qquad 0.8 \qquad \frac{7}{10} \qquad \frac{17}{20} \qquad \frac{3}{5}$$

   a. What process would you use to order the given numbers? Explain.

     A. Change the decimals to fractions since there are fewer decimals than fractions.

     B. Change the fractions to decimals since there are fewer fractions than decimals.

     C. Change the fractions to decimals since changing to fractions will result in fairly large denominators.

     D. Change the decimals to fractions since the lowest common denominator of all resulting fractions will be fairly small and easy to find.

   b. Order the numbers from greatest to least.

18. Challenge Sarah's geography textbook is $\frac{13}{16}$ in. thick and her history textbook is 0.820 in. thick.

   a. Which textbook is thicker? Answer this question by changing the fraction to a decimal.

     A. Her geography textbook is thicker since $\frac{13}{16} > 0.820$.

     B. Her history textbook is thicker since $\frac{13}{16} < 0.820$.

     C. The textbooks are equally thick since $\frac{13}{16} = 0.820$.

   b. If there are 21 students in Sarah's history class, will all of their textbooks fit on a shelf that is 20.9 in. long?

     A. Yes, because the total thickness of all 21 books is ■ in.

     B. No, because the total thickness of all 21 books is ■ in.

19. a. Challenge Of the numbers 0.26, $\frac{10}{17}$, 0.24, and $\frac{4}{11}$, which could replace the number line in the list below so that the numbers are ordered from least to greatest?

$$\frac{1}{4} \qquad \blacksquare \qquad 0.38 \qquad \frac{5}{7}$$

   b. Order the numbers 0.26, $\frac{10}{17}$, 0.24, and $\frac{4}{11}$ from least to greatest.

   c. Suppose there were a fifth number, with denominator 11, in the list of numbers 0.26, $\frac{10}{17}$, 0.24, and $\frac{4}{11}$. Explain how to find all possible numerators between 1 and 10 so that the list is still ordered correctly.

CCSS: 6.NS.C.7, Also 6.EE.B.7

Part 1

Intro

You have written and solved equations of the form $x + p = q$ by subtracting p from each side. This process works if p and q are decimals or fractions.

Decimal Example

$$x + 0.25 = 1.5$$

$$x + 0.25 - 0.25 = 1.5 - 0.25$$

$$x + 0 = 1.25$$

$$x = 1.25$$

Fraction Example

$$x + \frac{1}{4} = 1\frac{1}{2}$$

$$x + \frac{1}{4} - \frac{1}{4} = 1\frac{1}{2} - \frac{1}{4}$$

$$x + 0 = 1\frac{2}{4} - \frac{1}{4}$$

$$x = 1\frac{1}{4}$$

Example Solving Problems with Mixed Numbers and Decimals

The Lafayette Dollar measures $11\frac{3}{5}$ mm longer cross its center than the Washington Dollar. Write and solve an equation to find the measurement of the Washington Dollar across its center.

├─── 38.1 mm ───┤

├─── ? ───┤

Solution

Know

- The Lafayette Dollar measures $11\frac{3}{5}$ mm more across its center than the Washington Dollar.

- The Lafayette Dollar measures 38.1 mm across its center.

Need

The measurement of the Washington Dollar across its center

Plan

- Let x = the measurement of the Washington Dollar across its center.

- Solve $x + 11\frac{3}{5} = 38.1$ by using decimals or by using fractions.

continued on next page >

Solution continued

Method 1 Solve $x + 11\frac{3}{5} = 38.1$ by using decimals.

Step 1 Write $11\frac{3}{5}$ as a decimal.

$$11\frac{3}{5} = 11\frac{6}{10}, \text{ or } 11.6$$

Step 2 Substitute 11.6 into the equation $x + 11\frac{3}{5} = 38.1$.

$$x + 11.6 = 38.1$$
$$x + 11.6 - 11.6 = 38.1 - 11.6$$

> Subtract 11.6 from each side.

$$x = 38.1 - 11.6$$
$$x = 26.5$$

The Washington Dollar measures 26.5 mm across the center.

Method 2 Solve $x + 11\frac{3}{5} = 38.1$ by using fractions.

Step 1 Write 38.1 as a mixed number.

$$38.1 = 38\frac{1}{10}$$

Step 2 Substitute $38\frac{1}{10}$ into the equation $x + 11\frac{3}{5} = 38.1$.

$$x + 11\frac{3}{5} = 38\frac{1}{10}$$
$$x + 11\frac{3}{5} - 11\frac{3}{5} = 38\frac{1}{10} - 11\frac{3}{5}$$

> Subtract $11\frac{3}{5}$ from each side.

$$x = 38\frac{1}{10} - 11\frac{3}{5}$$
$$x = 37\frac{11}{10} - 11\frac{6}{10}$$
$$x = 26\frac{5}{10}$$
$$x = 26\frac{1}{2}$$

The Washington Dollar measures $26\frac{1}{2}$ mm across the center.

Example Solving Area Problems with Decimals

A carpenter is installing a solar attic fan. The area of a rectangular hole that he cut for the fan is 420.25 square inches. The hole is 20.5 inches long. Write and solve an equation to find the width.

Solution ·

Know	Need	Plan
• The hole is rectangular. • The area is 420.25 in². • The hole is 20.5 in. long. • $A = \ell \cdot w$	The width of the hole	• w = width • Solve the equation $420.25 = 20.5w$

$$420.25 = 20.5w$$

$$\frac{420.25}{20.5} = \frac{20.5w}{20.5}$$

$$\frac{420.25}{20.5} = 1w$$

$$20.5 = w$$

$$20.5\overline{)420.25} \quad = \quad 205\overline{)4202.5}$$

Multiply the divisor and dividend by 10.

$$
\begin{array}{r}
2\,0.5 \\
205\overline{)4\,2\,0\,2.5} \\
-\ 4\,1\,0 \\
\hline
1\,0\,2\,5 \\
-\ 1\,0\,2\,5 \\
\hline
0
\end{array}
$$

The hole is also 20.5 inches wide. The rectangular area is a square.

Part 3

Example Finding Equivalent Quotients, Fractions, and Decimals

Decide if each expression or number is equivalent to $4\overline{)3}$.

a. $\frac{3}{4}$ **b.** $\frac{12}{16}$ **c.** $\frac{75}{100}$

d. 0.75 **e.** $0.4\overline{)0.3}$ **f.** $4 \div 3$

g. $0.004\overline{)0.003}$

Solution

Sample explanations are shown below.

a. $\frac{3}{4}$: A fraction bar means divide, so $\frac{3}{4} = 4\overline{)3}$.

b. $\frac{12}{16} = \frac{12 \div 4}{16 \div 4}$, or $\frac{3}{4}$, and $\frac{3}{4} = 4\overline{)3}$.

c. $\frac{75}{100} = \frac{75 \div 25}{100 \div 25}$, or $\frac{3}{4}$, and $\frac{3}{4} = 4\overline{)3}$.

d. 0.75 is 75 hundredths, or $\frac{75}{100}$; as shown above, $\frac{75}{100} = 4\overline{)3}$.

e. and **g.** $0.4\overline{)0.3} = 4\overline{)3}$ and $0.004\overline{)0.003} = 4\overline{)3}$.

> Multiply the divisor and dividend by 10.

> Multiply the divisor and dividend by 1,000.

f. $4 \div 3 = 3\overline{)4}$, not $4\overline{)3}$.

1. If you increase your bicycle speed by 9.1 miles per hour, the speed will be 18.2 miles per hour. What is your bicycle speed now?

2. You have two identical pieces of rope. The combined length of the two pieces is $\frac{1}{4}$ yards. What is the length of each piece?

3. Write $3 \div 5$ as a fraction and a decimal.

4. Of the students in a class, $\frac{1}{4}$ prefer apple juice. In total, $\frac{7}{12}$ of the students prefer apple juice or orange juice.

   a. Solve the equation $n + \frac{1}{4} = \frac{7}{12}$ to find the fraction of students n who prefer orange juice.

   b. One student who did this claimed that $\frac{5}{6}$ of the students prefer orange juice. What was that student's possible error?

      A. In solving the equation, the student subtracted $\frac{1}{4}$ from each side of the equation.

      B. In solving the equation, the student multiplied each side of the equation by 4.

      C. In solving the equation, the student added $\frac{1}{4}$ to each side of the equation.

      D. In solving the equation, the student subtracted $\frac{7}{12}$ from each side of the equation.

5. Two friends start an exercise program. The two friends spend a combined 42.2 hours at the gym each month. The first friend spends 20.8 hours at the gym.

   a. Estimate the number of hours the second friend spends at the gym by rounding each value to the nearest whole number.

   b. Find the exact number of hours.

6. **Think About the Process** Talen took x dollars to the flower shop. He bought several roses for a total of $14.75 and had $23.75 left over.

   a. Which equation would help you find how much money Talen took to the flower shop?

      A. $x - 14.75 = 23.75$

      B. $x + 14.75 = 23.75$

      C. $x \times 14.75 = 23.75$

      D. $14.75 \div x = 23.75$

   b. How much money did Talen take to the flower shop?

7. Lee-Ann takes a test in 75 minutes.

   a. If Lee-Ann completes each problem in 2.5 minutes, how many problems are on the test?

   b. If Lee-Ann works at a faster rate, how would that change the time she would take on the test? Explain.

8. You have a case of watermelons. Each watermelon weighs 7.5 pounds. The watermelons have a combined weight of 30 pounds. How many watermelons do you have?

9. Benny paid $73.00 for 4 gallons of a particular kind of paint. What is the price of one gallon of that paint?

10. A gardener measures the height of a plant to be $\frac{9}{10}$ inch. Which of the expressions or numbers can you use to also represent the height of the plant? Select all that apply.

    A. 0.9

    B. $9 \div 10$

    C. $9\overline{)10}$

    D. $\frac{27}{3}$

11. Think About the Process

a. How can you check that $\frac{3}{4}$ and $520\overline{)390}$ represent the same value?

A. Write $520\overline{)390}$ as $\frac{520}{390}$ and divide the numerator by the denominator.

B. Write $520\overline{)390}$ as $\frac{390}{520}$ and divide the numerator by the denominator.

C. Write $520\overline{)390}$ as $\frac{390}{520}$ and write the fraction in simplest form.

D. Write $520\overline{)390}$ as $\frac{520}{390}$ and write the fraction in simplest form.

b. How can you check that $0.52\overline{)0.39}$ and $520\overline{)390}$ represent the same value?

A. Divide the divisor and dividend in $0.52\overline{)0.39}$ by 1,000.

B. Multiply the divisor and dividend in $0.52\overline{)0.39}$ by 1,000.

C. Multiply the divisor and dividend in $0.52\overline{)0.39}$ by 100.

D. Divide the divisor and dividend in $0.52\overline{)0.39}$ by 1,000.

12. A rectangle has an area of 4.5 m². The rectangle has width $\frac{1}{5}$ m. Find the length.

13. Challenge Robot A can manufacture 855 items each hour. Robot A can manufacture $10\frac{3}{4}$ more items than Robot B each minute. How many items can Robot B manufacture each minute? Use the fact that there are 60 minutes in 1 hour.

14. Challenge Check all the expressions or numbers that represent 10 times the value of $9.5 \div 7.6$.

A. $7.6\overline{)95}$

B. $\dfrac{95}{76}$

C. $76\overline{)95}$

D. 1.25

E. 12.5

CCSS: 6.NS.C.5, 6.NS.C.6a, Also 6.NS.C.6c

Key Concept

Positive Numbers Any numbers to the right of zero are positive numbers. Numbers without a sign symbol are assumed to be positive.

Negative Numbers Any numbers to the left of zero are negative numbers. Negative numbers are written with a negative sign.

Zero The number zero is neither positive nor negative.

Opposites Two numbers that are the same distance from 0 on a number line but in opposite directions are called **opposites**. The opposite of 0 is 0. For example, −4 and 4 are opposites.

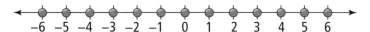

Integers The **integers** are the set of positive whole numbers, their opposites, and zero.

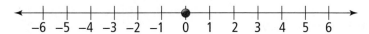

Example Naming Integers and Their Opposites

Use an integer to name the location of each point. Find the opposite of the integer represented by each point.

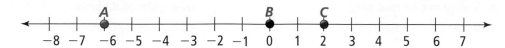

Solution ·

The opposite of a number is the same distance from 0 but on the other side of the number line.

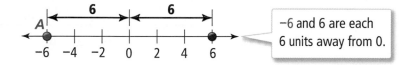

−6 and 6 are each 6 units away from 0.

The opposite of point A at −6 is 6.

0 is 0 units away from 0.

The opposite of point B at 0 is 0.

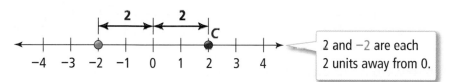

2 and −2 are each 2 units away from 0.

The opposite of point C at 2 is −2.

Example Representing Situations with Integers

What integer represents each situation? Explain your answer using a number line.

   a. 5 degrees below zero   **b.** a gain of 8 yards
   c. a loss of 6 dollars   **d.** 3 steps backwards

Solution ·

The ideas of below, behind, and loss are represented by negative numbers.
The ideas of ahead, in front, and gain are represented by positive numbers.

   a. 5 degrees below zero is represented by −5.

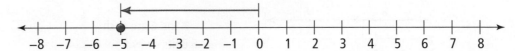

   b. A gain of 8 years is represented by 8.

   c. A loss of 6 dollars is represented by −6.

   d. 3 steps backward is represented by −3.

Part 3

Example Expressing Elevations as Integers

The highest point on land on Earth is the peak of Mount Everest. Its elevation is 29,028 ft above sea level. The lowest point on land on Earth is in the Dead Sea. Its elevation is 1,312 ft below sea level. Express each elevation as an integer.

Solution

A place located at sea level has an elevation of 0 ft.

Mount Everest is 29,028 ft above sea level.

> Use positive numbers to represent elevations above sea level.

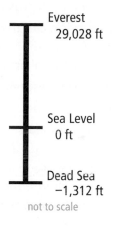

Everest
29,028 ft

Sea Level
0 ft

Dead Sea
−1,312 ft

not to scale

The elevation of Mount Everest expressed as an integer is 29,028.

The Dead Sea is 1,312 ft below sea level.

> Use negative numbers to represent elevations below sea level.

The elevation of the Dead Sea expressed as an integer is −1,312.

1. **a.** What integer does point *A* in **Figure 1** represent?

   b. What is the opposite of the integer represented by point *A*?

2. Find the opposite of −9.

3. Determine which integers correspond to the situations.

   a. On Wednesday, the temperature was 25° above zero.

   b. On Thursday, it was 7° below zero.

4. Which situation can the integer −10 represent?

   A. spending 10 dollars

   B. walking up 10 stairs

   C. gaining 10 yards

   D. earning 10 dollars

5. A point on the side of a mountain is 7,039 m above sea level. Express this elevation as an integer.

6. Which situation can the integer 11 represent?

   A. A fish swims 11 ft below sea level.

   B. A bird flies 11 ft above sea level.

   C. You scuba dive 11 ft below sea level.

7. **a.** **Writing** What is the opposite of 73?

   b. What is the reciprocal of 73?

   c. Describe any similarities and differences between the opposite of a nonzero number and the reciprocal of that number.

8. **Error Analysis** Your friend incorrectly says that point *A* and point *B* in **Figure 2** represent opposite integers.

   a. What is the opposite of the integer represented by point *A*?

   b. What is the opposite of the integer represented by point *B*?

   c. Why is your friend incorrect?

   A. The distance from 0 to *A* is greater than the distance from 0 to *B*.

   B. The distance from 0 to *A* is less than the distance from 0 to *B*.

   C. *A* and *B* are not on opposite sides of 0.

   D. *A* and *B* are not the same point.

9. **Think About the Process** You are given a number line with labels for −100, 0, 100, and a point plotted for an integer *A*. How can you plot the point for the opposite of the integer *A*? (**Figure 3**)

   A. Draw any point to the right of 0 on the number line.

   B. Draw any point to the left of 0 on the number line.

   C. Draw a point to the left of 0 on the number line at the same distance from 0 as *A* is to the right.

   D. It is not possible to plot the opposite of point *A*.

(Figure 1)

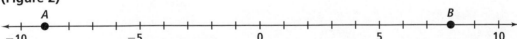

(Figure 2)

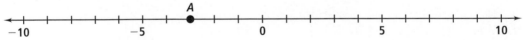

(Figure 3)

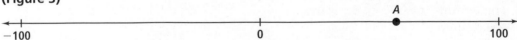

10. **Open-Ended** Which situations(s) could be represented by −104? Select all that apply.

   A. skiing 104 ft down a mountain

   B. a bird flying 104 ft above the ground

   C. spending $104 on vacation

   D. earning $104 at your summer job

11. **Reasoning** Two people are scuba diving. One diver is 36 ft below the surface. The other is 44 ft below the surface.

   a. What integers represent where the divers are with respect to the surface?

   b. Which diver is deeper?

12. A meteorologist forecasts the temperature to be 6°C below zero. The integer −6 represents this situation.

   a. Find the opposite of this integer.

   b. Which of the following represents the opposite of the situation?

   A. The meteorologist forecasts the temperature to be 5°C degrees above zero.

   B. The meteorologist forecasts the temperature to be 6°C degrees below zero.

   C. The meteorologist forecasts the temperature to be 7°C degrees below zero.

   D. The meteorologist forecasts the temperature to be 6°C degrees above zero.

13. **Air Travel** An airplane traveling at an altitude of 6,400 m changes its altitude by 1,400 m. Which situation describes the change in altitude?

   A. The altitude is 1,400 m higher after the change.

   B. The altitude is 1,400 m lower after the change.

   C. The altitude is 6,400 m higher after the change.

   D. The altitude is 6,400 m lower after the change.

14. **Think About the Process** A contestant in a game show has 9,000 points. The contestant answers the next question incorrectly and loses 750 points.

   a. Does the word "lose" suggest a positive integer or a negative integer?

   A. A negative integer

   B. A positive integer

   b. What integer represents a loss of 750 points?

15. The news reports that the temperature today is 16°F colder than yesterday. You dress for the weather and go to meet a friend at the cinema. You forgot your wallet, so your friend gives you $10 to buy your ticket. What integer best represents the change in temperature?

16. **Multiple Representations** You and a friend are hiking up a mountain. At one point your friend is 54 ft higher up than you are. What integer represents your elevation relative to your friend's? Your friend's elevation relative to yours?

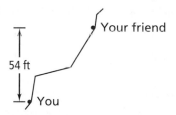

17. **Multiple Representations** Four gliders circle above a field. Glider A is at an altitude of 8,134 feet. Glider B is at an altitude of 4,573 feet. Glider C is at an altitude of 6,467 feet. Glider D is at an altitude of 2,878 feet.

   a. What integer represents the altitude of Glider A relative to Glider D?

   b. What integer represents the altitude of Glider D relative to Glider A?

18. a. **Challenge** What integer represents the opposite of the expression 11 · (34 − 13) + 36?

   b. Suppose you plot the value of this expression and the opposite of the value on a number line. What would be true about the two plotted points?

CCSS: 6.NS.C.7a, 6.NS.C.7b, Also 6.NS.C.7

Key Concept

Remember, the symbol > means "greater than" and the symbol < means "less than". On a number line, the numbers increase from left to right.

If $a > b$, then a is to the right of b on a number line.

b a

If $c < b$, then c is to the left of b on a number line.

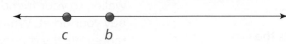

c b

Part 1

Example Comparing Integers

Complete each statement with the symbol < or >.

a. 6 ■ 9   **b.** −8 ■ −5   **c.** −3 ■ −4

d. 2 ■ −1   **e.** −2 ■ 0   **f.** −7 ■ −9

Solution

a.

The number on the left is less than the number on the right.

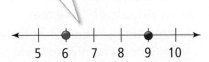

Since 6 is to the left of 9, 6 is less than 9.

$$6 < 9$$

b.

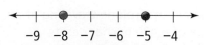

Since −8 is to the left of −5, −8 is less than −5.

$$-8 < -5$$

continued on next page >

c.

The number on the right is greater than the number on the left.

Since −3 is to the right of −4, −3 is greater than −4.

$$-3 > -4$$

d.

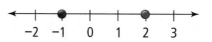

Since 2 is to the right of −1, 2 is greater than −1.

$$2 > -1$$

e.

Since −2 is to the left of 0, −2 is less than 0.

$$-2 < 0$$

f.

Since −7 is to the right of −9, −7 is greater than −9.

$$-7 > -9$$

Example Writing Inequalities With Integers

During January, in Montréal, Canada, the temperature at 1 P.M. was −8°C. The temperature at 11 P.M. was −12°C. Write an inequality to compare the two temperatures. When was it warmer?

Solution ·

Know	**Need**	**Plan**
• Temperature at 1 P.M.: −8°C • Temperature at 11 P.M.: −12°C	The time when it was warmer	Use a number line to find the greater integer.

On a vertical number line, one number is greater than another number if is location is higher.

An inequality that compares the two temperatures is $-8 > -12$.

−8°C is warmer than −12°C, so it was warmer at 1 P.M. than at 11 P.M.

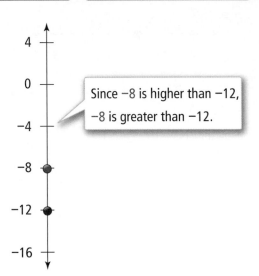

Since −8 is higher than −12, −8 is greater than −12.

Example Ordering Integers

The table shows the number of yards gained or lost by a high school football team during the first play in each game. Order the results of the plays from least yards gained to most yards gained.

Yards Gained and Lost

	Play	Result
Game 1	Sack	−10 yards
Game 2	Run	5 yards
Game 3	Pass	3 yards
Game 4	Run	−4 yards
Game 5	Pass	−1 yard

Solution ·

The number line shows the plays from least to greatest as you read from left to right.

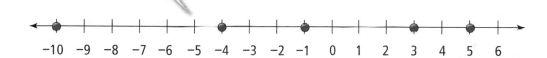

The results of the plays from least yards gained to most yards gained are −10, −4, −1, 3, 5.

1. **a.** Which inequality below compares 1 and −7 correctly?

   A. $1 > -7$ **B.** $1 < -7$

   b. Explain how you can make the comparison without plotting points on a number line.

2. Which inequality compares −3 and −1 correctly?

   A. $-3 < -1$ **B.** $-3 > -1$

3. **Figure 1** shows the number of yards gained or lost by a football team on its first play with the ball in each of five games. Positive numbers represent yards gained. Negative numbers represent yards lost.

   a. Which list shows the numbers ordered from greatest to least?

   A. −8, 4, 12, −12, 9
   B. 12, 4, −12, −8, 9
   C. −12, −8, 4, 9, 12
   D. 12, 9, 4, −8, −12

   b. In which game did the team do best on its first play?

4. Five friends played a board game. **Figure 2** shows their scores at the end of the game.

   a. Which list shows the numbers ordered from least to greatest?

   A. 9, 8, 7, −2, −3
   B. −3, −2, 7, 8, 9
   C. −2, 7, 9, −3, 8
   D. 9, 7, −3, −2, 8

   b. If the person with the highest score won, who finished in second place?

5. **Mental Math** Five people started an exercise program. Each person ran 10 laps around a track and recorded the time. After doing this daily for two months, each person ran another 10 laps around the same track and recorded the time. The table shows the change from the first time to the second time for each person.

Changes in Times

Person	Change (seconds)
A	20
B	−30
C	−20
D	30
E	−10

   a. Which list below shows the numbers ordered from least to greatest?

   A. 30, 20, −10, −20, −30
   B. −20, −10, 30, −30, 20
   C. −30, −20, −10, 20, 30
   D. 30, −10, −30, −20, 20

   b. Which person's time decreased the most?

(Figure 1)

First-Play Results					
Game	1	2	3	4	5
Result	−12 yards	12 yards	−8 yards	9 yards	4 yards

(Figure 2)

Scores					
Person	Adam	Brenda	Carrie	Daniel	Emily
Score	−3 points	7 points	−2 points	8 points	9 points

See your complete lesson at MyMathUniverse.com

6. **Think About the Process** One day, a boy found $17. The next day, he spent $12. Find two integers to represent these situations. How do you know which integers to use?

   a. Since the word "found" suggests a positive/negative number, use the integer 17/−17 to represent the situation "a boy found $17."

   Since the word "spent" suggests a positive/negative number, use the integer 12/−12 to represent the situation "he spent $12."

   b. Which inequality below compares the two integers?
      A. 17 > −12   **B.** −17 > −12
      C. 17 < 12   **D.** −17 < −12
      E. 17 > 12   **F.** 17 < −12
      G. −17 < 12   **H.** 17 > 12

7. **Think About the Process** Last winter, a neighbor recorded the outside temperature each day at 8 A.M. for a week. The table shows these temperatures.

   a. Think about how you arrange numbers in order by plotting them on a number line. Which list below shows the numbers ordered from greatest to least?

   Temperatures at 8 A.M.

Day	Temperature (°C)
Sun.	−5
Mon.	2
Tues.	−3
Wed.	6
Thurs.	4
Fri.	−7
Sat.	−4

   A. −7, −5, −4, −3, 2, 4, 6
   B. 6, 2, −4, −5, −3, −7, 4
   C. 6, 4, 2, −3, −4, −5, −7
   D. −5, −3, 2, −7, 6, −4, 4

   b. How can you always tell which day was the coldest?
      A. Find the day that corresponds to the number farthest right on the number line.
      B. Find the day that corresponds to the middle number on the number line.
      C. Find the day that corresponds to the number farthest from 0 on the number line.
      D. Find the day that corresponds to the number farthest left on the number line.

   c. Which day was coldest?

8. **Writing Figure 3** shows the lowest temperatures last year for five cities.

   a. Which list shows the numbers ordered from least to greatest?
      A. 10, −4, −8, −18, −24
      B. 10, −8, −24, −18, −4
      C. −24, −18, −8, −4, 10
      D. −18, −8, 10, −24, −4

   b. Which city had the lowest temperature?

   c. Describe two methods you can use to order this set of numbers.

(Figure 3)

Lowest Temperatures Recorded Last Year					
City	A	B	C	D	E
Temperature	−18°C	−24°C	10°C	−8°C	−4°C

See your complete lesson at MyMathUniverse.com

CCSS: 6.NS.C.7b, 6.NS.C.7c, 6.NS.C.7d, Also 6.NS.C.7

Key Concept

The **absolute value** of a number is its distance from 0 on a number line. Since absolute value is a distance, an absolute value is never negative. The symbol for the absolute value of a number n is $|n|$.

The absolute value of 5 is the distance from 0 to 5.

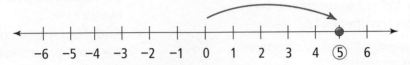

5 is 5 units from 0, so $|5| = 5$.

The absolute value of -5 is the distance from 0 to -5.

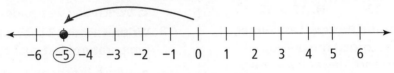

-5 is 5 units from 0, so $|-5| = 5$.

Notice that opposite numbers have the same absolute value.

Example Finding Absolute Values

Find each absolute value.

  a. $|9|$ **b.** $|-3|$ **c.** $|0|$

Solution ·

  a. $|9| = 9$

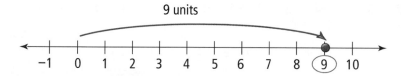

9 units

  b. $|-3| = 3$

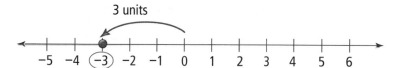

3 units

  c. $|0| = 0$

0 is 0 units from 0.

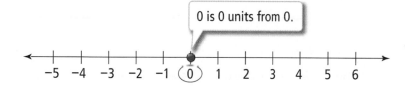

Part 2

Example Ordering Integers and Absolute Values

Order the values from greatest to least.

$$|-3| \qquad -3 \qquad |-7| \qquad -7 \qquad |0| \qquad -1 \qquad |1|$$

Solution ·

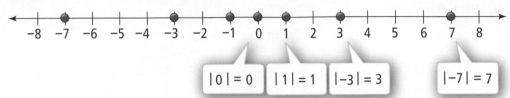

$|0| = 0 \qquad |1| = 1 \qquad |-3| = 3 \qquad\qquad |-7| = 7$

To give the numbers in order from greatest to least, read the values on the number line from right to left. The values in order from greatest to least are:

$$|-7|, \ |-3|, \ |1|, \ |0|, \ -1, \ -3, \ -7$$

Part 3

Intro

You can represent the *positions* of the divers relative to sea level using the integers −2 and −5.

However, *depth* is a positive quantity, so the depths of the divers are given by $|-2|$ and $|-5|$.

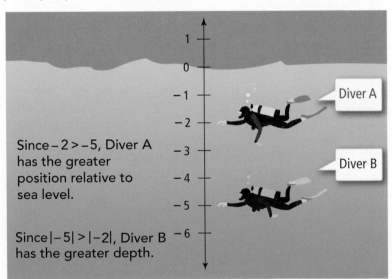

Since −2 > −5, Diver A has the greater position relative to sea level.

Since $|-5| > |-2|$, Diver B has the greater depth.

Part 3

Example Using Absolute Values in Problems

A college student is working during the summer to save money for the upcoming school year. She deposits the money she earns working. The money she withdraws she uses to pay for her living expenses.

In which month did the college student spend the most money?

Month	Deposits	Withdrawals
May	$925	−$400
June	$875	−$325
July	$1,300	−$450
August	$1,250	−$550

Solution ·

You want to find the month when the college student withdrew the most money. In order to compare the relative size of the withdrawals, you need to compare the absolute values of the withdrawals.

Find the month when the absolute value of the withdrawals is the greatest.

May: $|-\$400| = \$400$
June: $|-\$325| = \$325$
July: $|-\$450| = \$450$
August: $|-\$550| = \$550$

Since $550 is the greatest value, the college student withdrew the most money in August.

1. Plot −8 on a number line.

2. Find |−11|.

3. Order these numbers from greatest to least.

   |−12|, −12, |−7|, −7, 0, |3|, −3

4. Order these numbers from least to greatest.

   −13, |−13|, −23, 23, 0

5. Two goldfish swim in a tank. The position of fish A, relative to the top of the tank, is −13 cm. The position of fish B is −78 cm. Use |−13| and |−78| to represent the depths of the fish.

   a. Compare the depths |−13| and |−78| using a greater than or less than symbol.

   b. Which fish is closer to the top of the tank?

6. **Error Analysis** Your friend incorrectly plotted the numbers −10, −1, |6|, |−3|, and 10 on the number line in **Figure 1** as shown.

   a. Which number line shows the numbers plotted correctly?

   A.

   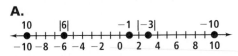

   B.

   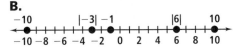

   C.

   D.

   D.

   b. What was your friend's mistake?

   A. Your friend plotted negative numbers to the right of zero, instead of to the left.

   B. Your friend confused the definitions of opposite and absolute value.

   C. Your friend plotted the absolute values as negative numbers.

   D. Your friend plotted two values incorrectly.

   c. Order the numbers from greatest to least.

7. Order the numbers from greatest to least.

   −|16|, |−16|, −|54|, |−54|, 0

   A. −|54|, −|16|, 0, |−16|, |−54|

   B. 0, −|16|, |−16|, −|54|, |−54|

   C. |−54|, |−16|, 0, −|16|, −|54|

   D. |−54|, −|54|, |−16|, −|16|, 0

8. **Think About the Process** You want to write these numbers in order from least to greatest. Which number comes immediately after |19| − 1 in the ordered list?

   |57|, |−32|, |19|, |−71|, |19| − 1

9. **Track Meet** Four friends compete against each other in a track meet. All four run two races and find the differences between their times in the first and second race.

   Differences in Times

Runner	Difference (seconds)
W	−11
X	9
Y	−7
Z	−4

   a. Which runner had the greatest change in times for the two races?

   b. Which runners ran faster in the second race than the first? Explain your reasoning.

(Figure 1)

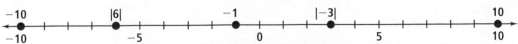

10. **Reasoning** You and a friend dropped two water balloons out a window while another friend watched safely from the ground. The elevation (relative to the window) of the first balloon was −22 ft when it burst. The elevation of the second balloon was −34 ft when it burst. Use |−22| and |−34| to represent the distances the balloons fell.

a. Which balloon fell farther?

b. Is it possible to find how far from the ground the second balloon was when it burst?

   A. Yes, it is the distance between the two when they burst.

   B. Yes, it is two times the distance from the second balloon to the window.

   C. Yes, it is the same as the distance from the second balloon to the window.

   D. No, the distance from the ground to the window is not known.

11. **Mental Math** Contestants on a game show compete head-to-head in 3 rounds. After each round, the number of points each contestant gained or lost is recorded as a positive or negative integer (see **Figure 2**).

a. What is Contestant A's greater change in score during the first 2 rounds?

b. Which contestant's score changed more in that round?

   A. Contestant A's score changed more.

   B. Contestant A's score changed the same amount as Contestant B's.

   C. Contestant B's score changed more.

12. **Mental Math** Contestants on a game show compete in 3 rounds. After each round, the number of points each contestant gains or loses is recorded as a positive or negative integer (see **Figure 3**).

a. During which of the first two rounds did Contestant B's score change more?

b. Compare this change in score with the change in score from Round 3. In which of these rounds did Contestant B's score change more? Explain your reasoning.

13. **Think About the Process** You want to solve the equation $|x| + 32 = 77$.

a. How many values of x are there that are solutions to the equation $|x| + 32 = 77$?

b. Which values of x are solutions to the equation $|x| + 32 = 77$? Select all that apply.

14. **Challenge** Find the values of x for which the equation $2 \cdot |x| + 16 = 124$ is true.

(Figure 2)

Points Per Round

Contestant	Round 1	Round 2	Round 3
A	−500 points	−200 points	300 points
B	300 points	350 points	−400 points

(Figure 3)

Points Per Round

Contestant	Round 1	Round 2	Round 3
A	−150 points	300 points	−200 points
B	200 points	400 points	−300 points

See your complete lesson at MyMathUniverse.com

Integers and the Coordinate Plane

CCSS: 6.NS.C.6b, Also 6.NS.C.6c and 6.NS.C.8

Vocabulary
coordinate plane,
image, line of reflection,
ordered pair, origin,
quadrant, reflection,
transformation, x-axis,
x-coordinate, y-axis,
y-coordinate

Key Concept

The **coordinate plane** is a surface formed by the intersection of two number lines. The horizontal number line is called the **x-axis**. The vertical number line is called the **y-axis**. The point where the two number lines intersect is called the **origin**.

The axes divide the coordinate plane into four regions, called **quadrants**. The quadrants are named in a counter-clockwise direction. The points on the axes do not lie in any of the quadrants.

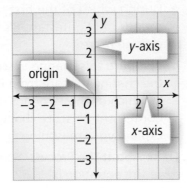

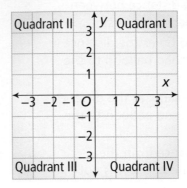

An **ordered pair** is a pair of numbers that describe the location of a point in the coordinate plane.

(x, y)

The *x*-coordinate tells the position along the *x*-axis.

The *y*-coordinate tells the position along the *y*-axis.

Intro

You can graph points if you know their coordinates.

(x, y)

> The *x*-coordinate tells you how far to move right or left from the origin.

> The *y*-coordinate tells you how far to move up or down from the *x*-axis.

When the *x*-coordinate is positive, move right from the origin.
When the *x*-coordinate is negative, move left from the origin.

When the *y*-coordinate is positive, move up from the *x*-axis.
When the *y*-coordinate is negative, move down from the *x*-axis.

Graph the point *A*(−2, 1).

The *x*-coordinate is −2. Move left 2 units from the origin.

The *y*-coordinate is 1. Move up 1 unit from the *x*-axis.

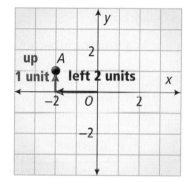

Example Plotting Points in Four Quadrants

Plot each point on a coordinate plane. Identify the quadrant.

   A(3, 4)   *B*(−8, −4)   *C*(−6, 5)   *D*(1, −7)   *E*(0, −2)

Solution

Graph the point *A*(3, 4). Start at the origin. The *x*-coordinate is 3. Move 3 units to the right from the origin. The *y*-coordinate is 4. Move 4 units up from the *x*-axis.

Graph the point *B*(−8, −4). Start at the origin. The *x*-coordinate is −8. Move 8 units to the left from the origin. The *y*-coordinate is −4. Move 4 units down from the *x*-axis.

Graph the point *C*(−6, 5). Start at the origin. The *x*-coordinate is −6. Move 6 units to the left from the origin. The *y*-coordinate is 5. Move 5 units up from the *x*-axis.

continued on next page >

Graph the point $D(1, -7)$. Start at the origin. The x-coordinate is 1. Move 1 unit to the right from the origin. The y-coordinate is -7. Move 7 units down from the x-axis.

Graph the point $E(0, -2)$. Start at the origin. The x-coordinate is 0. Stay at the origin. The y-coordinate is -2. Move 2 units down from the x-axis.

Point A in Quadrant I.

Point B in Quadrant III.

Point C in Quadrant II.

Point D in Quadrant IV.

Point E is not in a quadrant because it lies on an axis.

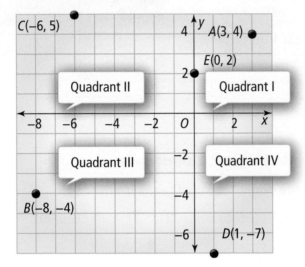

Intro

(x, y) is an ordered pair.

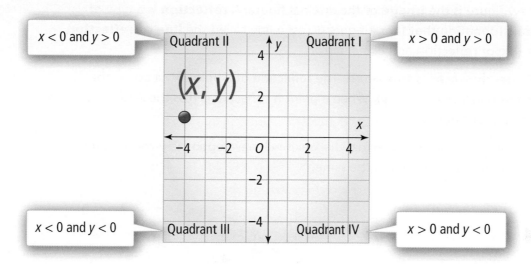

$x < 0$ and $y > 0$

Quadrant II

Quadrant I

$x > 0$ and $y > 0$

$x < 0$ and $y < 0$

Quadrant III

Quadrant IV

$x > 0$ and $y < 0$

Example Identifying Quadrants Where Points Lie

Identify the quadrant where each point lies. Then plot the points on a coordinate plane.

$(1, -2)$ $(4, -1)$ $(-1, -3)$ $(-3, 4)$ $(2, 1)$

$(-4, -4)$ $(2, -5)$ $(-2, 5)$ $(3, 5)$ $(-5, 2)$

Solution

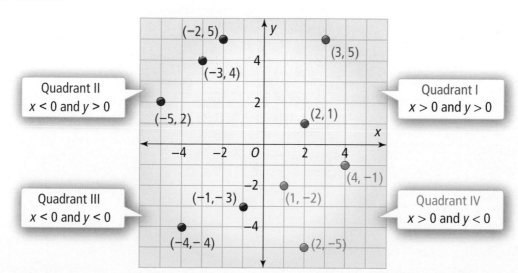

Quadrant II
$x < 0$ and $y > 0$

Quadrant I
$x > 0$ and $y > 0$

Quadrant III
$x < 0$ and $y < 0$

Quadrant IV
$x > 0$ and $y < 0$

A **transformation** of a figure is a change in its position, shape, or size. The new figure is the **image** of the original figure. A **reflection** is a type of transformation that flips a figure across a line called the **line of reflection**. A line of reflection acts like a mirror.

Reflection across the x-axis The reflection of a point (x, y) across the x-axis is located at $(x, -y)$. When a point is reflected across the x-axis, only the y-coordinate changes.

A point at its reflection across the x-axis will have opposite y-coordinates. The x-coordinates remain the same.

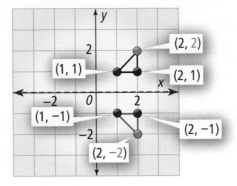

Reflection across the y-axis When a point is reflected across the y-axis, only the x-coordinate changes. A point and its reflection across the y-axis will have opposite x-coordinates. The y-coordinates remain the same.

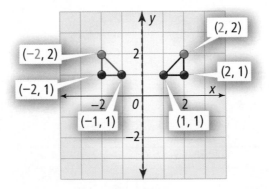

Example Identifying Reflections of Points

Complete each statement, using the following ordered pairs.

(−3, −2)   (2, 3)   (3, −2)   (−2, −3)   (2, −3)

a. ■ is the reflection of the point (3, 2) across the x-axis.
b. ■ is the reflection of the point (3, 2) across the y-axis.
c. ■ is the reflection of the point (−2, 3) across the x-axis.
d. ■ is the reflection of the point (−2, 3) across the y-axis.

Solution ·

> A reflection across the x-axis changes the sign of the y-coordinate.

a. (3, −2) is the reflection of the point (3, 2) across the x-axis.

> A reflection across the y-axis changes the sign of the x-coordinate.

b. (−3, 2) is the reflection of the point (3, 2) across the y-axis.

> A reflection across the x-axis changes the sign of the y-coordinate.

c. (−2, −3) is the reflection of the point (−2, 3) across the x-axis.

> A reflection across the y-axis changes the sign of the x-coordinate.

d. (2, 3) is the reflection of the point (−2, 3) across the y-axis.

1. **Think About the Process** To plot the point (7, 2) on the coordinate plane, start at the origin, (0, 0). What are the next steps?

   Select the correct choice below and fill in the blanks to complete your choice.

   A. Move ■ unit(s) to the left and ■ unit(s) up.

   B. Move ■ unit(s) to the left and ■ unit(s) down.

   C. Move ■ unit(s) to the right and ■ unit(s) down.

   D. Move ■ unit(s) to the right and ■ unit(s) up.

2. Plot the point (−2, 1) on the coordinate plane.

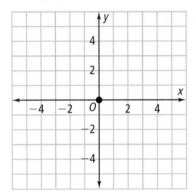

3. In which quadrant is the point (3, 1) located?

   A. Quadrant I   **B.** Quadrant II

   C. Quadrant III   **D.** Quadrant IV

   E. The point is not in a quadrant.

4. What ordered pair could be the coordinates of point *B*? Explain your answer.

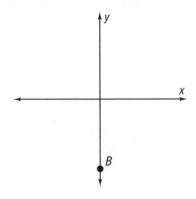

   A. (22, 12)   **B.** (0, −45)

   C. (−21, −36)   **D.** (15, −43)

   E. (−12, 46)

5. What is the reflection of the point (3, −4) across the *x*-axis?

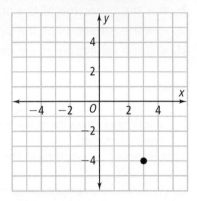

6. **Think About the Process** The coordinate plane shows a point and its reflection.

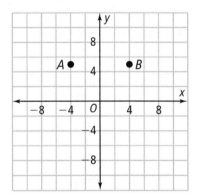

   a. How do the coordinates of points *A* and *B* compare?

   A. The *y*-coordinates are the same. The *x*-coordinates are opposites.

   B. The *x*-coordinates and the *y*-coordinates are switched.

   C. The *x*-coordinates are the same. The *y*-coordinates are opposites.

   D. The *x*-coordinates are opposites. The *y*-coordinates are opposites.

   b. Point *B* is the reflection of point *A* across which axis?

See your complete lesson at MyMathUniverse.com

7. The coordinate plane shows a point and its reflection. What is the relationship between point *A* and point *B*?

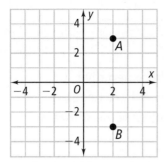

8. Find the coordinates of point *A*.

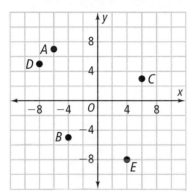

9. Map Coordinates The coordinate plane shows certain locations in a town. Find the coordinates of the hospital.

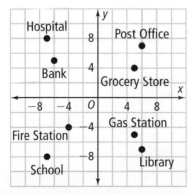

10. Writing Suppose you have to find the quadrant in which the point $(-5, y)$ is located.

   a. Describe how you can find the quadrant given only that $y > 0$.

   b. In which quadrant is the point $(-5, y)$ located?

11.a. Find a point that is not in any quadrant.

   A. $(-3, -8)$ **B.** $(6, 6)$
   C. $(5, -3)$ **D.** $(-8, 0)$
   E. $(-8, 8)$

   b. Open-Ended List at least 5 more points that are not in any quadrant. Explain what all the points have in common.

12. Reasoning The coordinate plane shows figures formed from connecting four points.

   How could you reflect the points in figure *A* to get figure *B*?

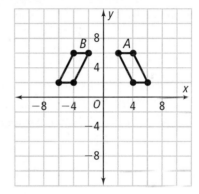

13. Find the coordinates of each point

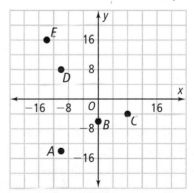

The coordinates of point *A* are ■.
The coordinates of point *B* are ■.
The coordinates of point *C* are ■.
The coordinates of point *D* are ■.
The coordinates of point *E* are ■.

8-5 | Distance

CCSS: 6.NS.C.8, 6.G.A.3

Part 1

Intro

There are some measurements, such as temperature, where negative numbers have a meaning. There are other measurements where negative numbers are meaningless. Distance is an example of a measurement that is always nonnegative.

Recall that absolute value measures the distance a number is from zero on a number line. Absolute value is never negative. Distance cannot be measured in negative units.

Example Finding Vertical Distance Between Points

a. What is the distance between point X and point Y?

b. What is the distance between point Y and point Z?

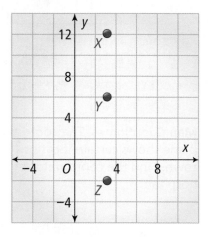

Solution

Each of the points has the same x-coordinate. So, find the distance between the y-coordinates.

a. Find the distance between point X and point Y.

$$|12| - |6|$$

> Since the points are on the same side of the x-axis, subtract the distances.

The distance between point X and point Y is 6 units.

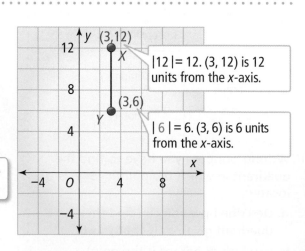

> $|12| = 12.$ (3, 12) is 12 units from the x-axis.

> $|6| = 6.$ (3, 6) is 6 units from the x-axis.

continued on next page >

Part 1

Solution continued

b. Find the distance between point Y and point Z.

$$|6| + |-2|$$

> Since the points are on different sides of the x-axis, add the distances.

The distance between point Y and point Z is 8 units.

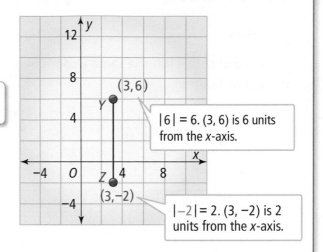

> $|6| = 6$. (3, 6) is 6 units from the x-axis.

> $|-2| = 2$. (3, −2) is 2 units from the x-axis.

Part 2

Example Finding Horizontal Distance Between Points

Your cousin rides the subway to work. His trip is shown on the coordinate plane. Each grid line represents 1 block.

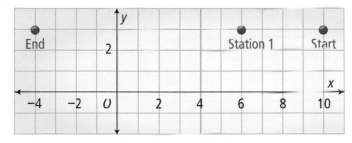

a. What is the distance between the Start and Station 1?

b. What is the distance between Station 1 and the End?

continued on next page >

Solution ·

Each of the points has the same *y*-coordinate. So, find the distance between the *x*-coordinates.

a.

(10, 3) is $|10|$ = 10 units from the *y*-axis.

(6, 3) is $|6|$ = 6 units from the *y*-axis.

> Since the points are on the same side of the *y*-axis, subtract the distances.

$|10| - |6|$ = 4 units

It is 4 blocks between the start of your cousin's ride and Station 1.

b.

(6, 3) is $|6|$ = 6 units from the *y*-axis.

(−4, 3) is $|-4|$ = 4 units from the *y*-axis.

> Since the points are on opposite sides of the *y*-axis, add the distances.

$|6| + |-4|$ = 10 units

It is 10 blocks between Station 1 and the end of your cousin's ride.

Example Finding Areas in the Coordinate Plane

A city planner is using a coordinate plane to plan a new city park.
The four corners of a rectangular dog park will be located at
$A(-3, 1)$, $B(-3, 8)$, $C(5, 8)$, and $D(5, 1)$. What is the area of the dog park?

Solution ·

The area of a rectangle is equal to the length times the width. Find the
dimensions of the rectangle and multiply.

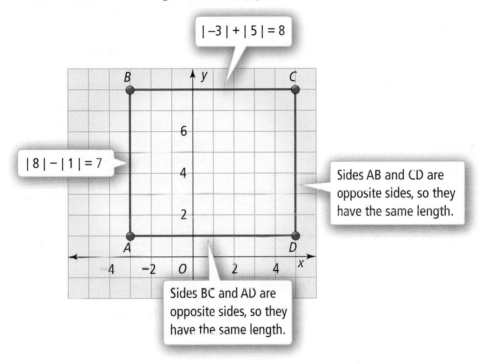

$|-3| + |5| = 8$

$|8| - |1| = 7$

Sides AB and CD are
opposite sides, so they
have the same length.

Sides BC and AD are
opposite sides, so they
have the same length.

$A = \ell w$
$= (8)(7)$
$= 56 \text{ units}^2$

The dog park has an area of 56 units².

1. What is the distance between the points (5, 2) and (5, 18)?

2. What is the distance between (−4, −1) and (−26, −1)?

3. You are competing in a foot race. You are at point *B* (8, 5) and the finish line is at point *A* (−5, 5). Each unit represents 100 feet. How far are you from the finish line?

4. A fish is swimming 4 m below the surface of a lake. A bird is flying 10 m above the surface of the lake, directly over the fish.

   What is the distance between the bird and the fish?

5. **Writing** Begin with point *A*(−8, 3). Reflections across the axes will produce points *B*, *C*, and *D* so that *ABCD* is a rectangle.

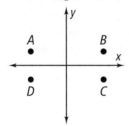

   a. What are the coordinates of point *D*?

   b. What is the length of side *AD*?

   c. Explain how to use what you know about reflections to find the coordinates of the remaining 2 vertices.

   d. Explain how you can find the perimeter of the rectangle.

6.

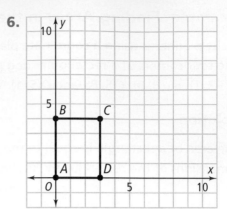

   a. **Reasoning** Find the lengths of sides of rectangle *ABCD* shown on the coordinating plane.

   b. Suppose you double the length of each side. What would be the new coordinates of point *C* if the coordinates of point *A* stay the same? Explain your reasoning.

7. **Error Analysis** Your friend incorrectly says that the distance between (4, 22) and (4, 11) is 26 units.

   a. What is the correct distance?

   b. What mistake did your friend make?

      A. Your friend added the absolute values instead of subtracting.

      B. Your friend used the x-coordinates instead of the y-coordinates.

      C. Your friend added the absolute values of the coordinates of the first point.

8. Air Travel Airport *A* is located on a grid at the point (−18, 14). Airport *B* is located at the point (8, 14). Each unit on the grid represents 50 km.

a. How far apart are the airports?

b. Which airport is closer to Airport *C* at (0, 14)?

   A. Airport *B* is closer to Airport *C*.

   B. Airport *A* is closer to Airport *C*.

   C. The airports are the same distance from Airport *C*.

9. Think About the Process *ABC* is an equilateral triangle.

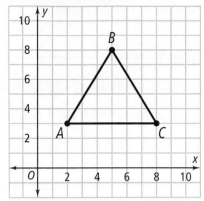

a. Which expression could you use to find the length of side *BC*?

   A. $|8| - |2|$ **B.** $|5| - |2|$

   C. $|8| + |2|$ **D.** $|3| - |3|$

b. What is the length of side *BC*?

10. Think About the Process You want to find the height of triangle *ABC*.

(Figure 1)

a. What are the coordinates of *D*, the point on side *AB* directly under *C*?

b. What is the height of triangle *ABC*?

(Figure 1)

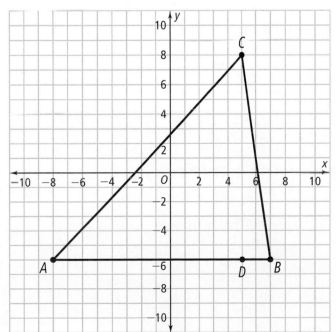

See your complete lesson at MyMathUniverse.com

CCSS: 6.NS.C.6b, 6.NS.C.7c, Also 6.G.A.4

Part 1

Example Finding Distance Using Integers

The elevator starts on the first floor.

    a. What is the total distance the elevator traveled?

    b. Which trip was the longest?

    c. On what floor does the elevator end?

Elevator Distance

Trip	Floors
First	+8
Second	−2
Third	+5
Fourth	−9

Solution

a. The find the total distance the elevator traveled, find the sum of all of the distances traveled.

> Distances cannot be negative, so use absolute values.

$$|+8| = 8 \text{ floors}$$
$$|-2| = 2 \text{ floors}$$
$$|+5| = 5 \text{ floors}$$
$$|-9| = 9 \text{ floors}$$

The elevator traveled $8 + 2 + 5 + 9 = 24$ floors.

b. The trip that was the longest is the trip with the greatest absolute value.

> Put the absolute values in order from greatest to least.

$$|-9| > |+8| > |+5| > |-2|$$

> $|-9|$ corresponds to the fourth trip.

The fourth trip was the longest trip.

continued on next page >

Part 1

Solution continued

c. The signs indicate the direction the elevator traveled. To find where the elevator was located after the fourth trip, find how each trip changed its location.

First the elevator travels up 8 floors from the 1st floor to the 9th floor.

Then the elevator travels down 2 floors to the 7th floor.

Then the elevator travels up 5 floors to the 12th floor.

Then the elevator travels down 9 floors to the 3rd floor.

The elevator ended on the 3rd floor.

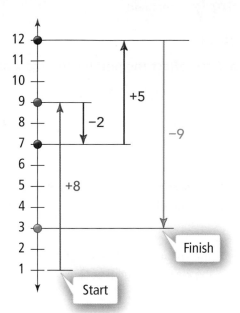

Part 2

Example Exploring Reflections and Distances

Start with the point (2, 3).

a. You reflect the point (2, 3) across the *x*-axis and then reflect that image across the *y*-axis. In which quadrant is the final image of your reflections located?

b. You reflect the point (2, 3) across the *y*-axis and then reflect that image across the *x*-axis. In which quadrant is the final image of your reflection located?

c. What is the distance between the final images in parts *a* and *b*?

continued on next page >

Example continued

Solution ·

a. First reflect the point across the *x*-axis.

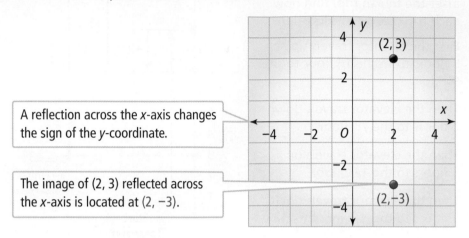

A reflection across the *x*-axis changes the sign of the *y*-coordinate.

The image of (2, 3) reflected across the *x*-axis is located at (2, −3).

Then reflect the image across the *y*-axis.

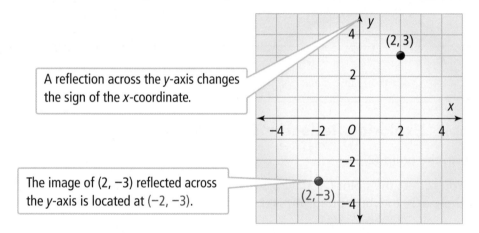

A reflection across the *y*-axis changes the sign of the *x*-coordinate.

The image of (2, −3) reflected across the *y*-axis is located at (−2, −3).

continued on next page >

b. First reflect the point across the *y*-axis.

A reflection across the *y*-axis changes the sign of the *x*-coordinate.

The image of (2, 3) reflected across the *y*-axis is located at (−2, 3).

Then reflect the image across the *x*-axis.

A reflection across the *x*-axis changes the sign of the *y*-coordinate.

The image of (−2, 3) reflected across the *x*-axis is located at (−2, −3).

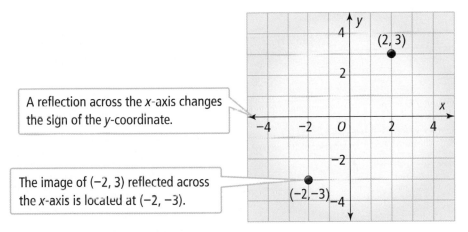

continued on next page >

Solution continued

    c. The distance between the two images is 0 units.

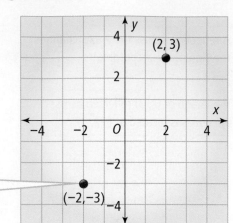

Both final images are at (−2, −3).

1. At dawn, the temperature was −8°C. By noon, it had warmed up to 5°C. By how many degrees had the temperature risen?

2. You reflect the point (−7, −6) across the x-axis and then reflect that image across the y-axis. What are the coordinates of the final image?

3. There are four parks located along the longest street in a large city. The Park Department's equipment yard is centrally located at 0 on the number line in **Figure 1** and the parks are represented by the points A, B, C, and D. Each unit on the number line is 1 km.

   a. Which two parks are the same distance from the equipment yard?

   A. A and D **B.** A and B
   C. A and C **D.** B and D
   E. B and C **F.** C and D

   b. How far are these two parks from the equipment yard?

4. a. A student reflected the point (8, −9) across the y-axis and then reflected the image across the x-axis. The student incorrectly claims that the final image is the same as the original point. What are the correct coordinates of the final image?

   b. What mistake did the student likely make?

   A. The student reflected the point across the same axis twice.

   B. The student reflected the point across the y-axis, then the x-axis, then the y-axis.

   C. The student incorrectly reflected the point across the x-axis.

   D. The student incorrectly reflected the point across the y-axis.

5. A police officer drives out of the station to patrol the East/West Highway. The officer first travels 10 miles east, then reverses directions and travels 16 miles west to help with an accident. From there, the officer travels 8 more miles west, then reverses direction and travels 26 miles to help with traffic around a construction site. The trips are summarized in the table below.

   Patrolling the East/West Highway

Westbound (Miles)	Eastbound (Miles)
−16 (Trip 2)	+10 (Trip 1)
−8 (Trip 3)	+26 (Trip 4)

   a. How many miles has the officer traveled?

   b. How many miles, and in which direction, must the officer travel to return to the station?

6. Reflect the point (−6, −4) across the x-axis. Reflect its image across the y-axis. Then reflect across the x-axis again.

   a. What are the coordinates of the final image?

   b. What is the distance between the original point and the final image?

7. Reflect the point (−3, −8) across the y-axis. Reflect its image across the x-axis. Then reflect across the y-axis again.

   a. What are the coordinates of the final image? Describe another way to get from the original point to the final image using reflection.

   b. In which quadrant is the final image located?

   A. Quadrant I **B.** Quadrant II
   C. Quadrant IV **D.** Quadrant III

(Figure 1)

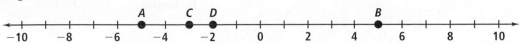

8. Think About the Process

  a. When you reflect a point across the *x*-axis, how do the coordinates of the image and the original point differ?

   A. The *y*-coordinates are the same. The *x*-coordinates are opposites.

   B. The *x*-coordinates are opposites. The *y*-coordinates are opposites.

   C. The *x*-coordinates and the *y*-coordinates are switched.

   D. The *x*-coordinates are the same. The *y*-coordinates are opposites.

  b. When you reflect a point across the *y*-axis, how do the coordinates of the image and the original point differ?

   A. The *x*-coordinates and the *y*-coordinates are switched.

   B. The *y*-coordinate stays the same. The *x*-coordinates are opposites.

   C. The *x*-coordinates are opposites. The *y*-coordinates are opposites.

   D. The *x*-coordinate stays the same. The *y*-coordinates are opposites.

  c. What are the coordinates of the final image when you reflect the point (−8, −16) across the *x*-axis and then reflect its image across the *y*-axis?

9. A worker drives into the parking garage of a bank building in a large city. She enters the garage on the first floor, and then drives 4 floors down to park. She then gets into an elevator and goes to her office on the building's eighth floor. Each floor of the building is about 10 feet high. How far did the worker travel on the elevator?

10. Yesterday's 7 A.M. temperature for four towns in ski country are shown in the table.

Ski Country Temperatures

Town	Temperatures (°F)
Icy Falls	−8
Snow Mountain	5
Winterville	−7
Cold Valley	−6

  a. Which town was the coldest?

  b. Which town was the warmest?

  c. Which town had a temperature closest to 0°F?

   A. Cold Valley

   B. Snow Mountain

   C. Winterville

   D. Icy Falls

  d. How much colder was the coldest town than the warmest town?

11. Think About the Process The players in a bowling league wanted to see whose score improved the most, and whose score changed the most, from last week's scores. The table below shows the changes.

Bowling League Changes in Scores

Name	Change	Name	Change
Andrew	−11	Deanna	−19
Brianna	−4	Ellie	−10
Cassie	−25	Frank	24

  a. Which player's score increased the most from last week?

   A. Ellie   **B.** Deanna

   C. Frank   **D.** Andrew

   E. Brianna   **F.** Cassie

  b. Which player's score changed the most from last week?

   A. Deanna   **B.** Andrew

   C. Frank   **D.** Brianna

   E. Cassie   **F.** Ellie

Rational Numbers and the Number Line

Vocabulary
rational numbers

CCSS: 6.NS.C.5, 6.NS.C.6a, Also 6.NS.C.6c

Key Concept

Rational numbers are numbers that can be written in the form $\frac{a}{b}$ or $-\frac{a}{b}$, where a is a whole number and b is a positive whole number.

- Rational numbers include all of the integers: zero, positive whole numbers, and their opposites.
- Rational numbers include all positive fractions and their opposites.
- Rational numbers include all positive mixed numbers and their opposites.
- Rational numbers include positive decimals and their opposites.

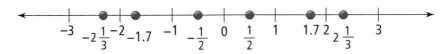

Part 1

Example Locating Rational Numbers and Their Opposites on a Number Line

Name the location of each point as both a decimal and as a fraction or mixed number. Then name the opposite of each point, and position each opposite point on the number line.

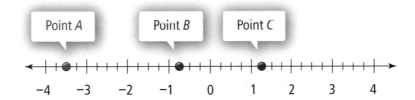

continued on next page >

Example continued

Solution ·

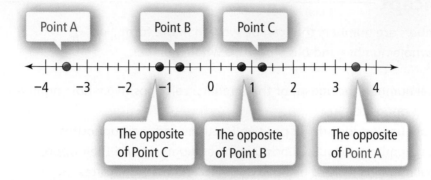

Point *A* is located at −3.5.

−3.5 can be rewritten as $-3\frac{1}{2}$, or $-\frac{7}{2}$.

The opposite of Point *A* is located at 3.5.

3.5 can be rewritten as $3\frac{1}{2}$, or $\frac{7}{2}$.

Point *B* is located at −0.75.

−0.75 can be rewritten as $-\frac{3}{4}$.

The opposite of Point *B* is located at 0.75.

0.75 can be rewritten as $\frac{3}{4}$.

Point *C* is located at 1.25.

1.25 can be rewritten as $1\frac{1}{4}$, or $\frac{5}{4}$.

The opposite of Point *C* is located at −1.25.

−1.25 can be rewritten as $-1\frac{1}{4}$, or $-\frac{5}{4}$.

Part 2

Example Using Rational Numbers and Zero to Represent Situations

Explain what the number 0 represents in each situation. Then write a rational number to represent the situation.

    a. The pant legs shrunk $\frac{2}{3}$ inch after washing.

    b. Dad gained $1\frac{1}{4}$ pounds during vacation.

    c. It is 10 seconds before blastoff.

Solution ·

    a. Zero represents the length of the pant legs before washing. Shrink means decrease, so use a negative sign to represent the situation:

$$-\frac{2}{3} \text{ inch.}$$

    b. Zero represents Dad's weight before vacation. Gain means increase. A positive sign is understood:

$$1\frac{1}{4} \text{ pounds.}$$

    c. Zero represents blastoff. Use a negative sign to represent time before blastoff:

$$-10 \text{ seconds.}$$

Part 3

Example Using Rational Numbers and Zero to Represent Elevations

In South America, the highest point is the peak of Mt. Aconcagua, at 22,834 feet above sea level. The lowest point on land is in the Valdes Peninsula, 131 feet below sea level. Explain the meaning of 0 in this situation, and write each elevation as a rational number in yards.

continued on next page >

Example continued

Solution ·

Know	**Need**	**Plan**
• Highest point is 22,834 feet above sea level • Lowest point is 131 feet below sea level • 1 yd = 3 ft	• To explain 0 in this situation • To write each elevation as a rational number in yards	Use a positive rational number to write a point above sea level. Use a negative rational number to write a point below sea level. Use division to write feet as yards.

In this situation zero represents sea level, which has an elevation of 0 ft.

Highest point:

Since the highest point is 22,834 ft above sea level, write it as a positive number, 22,834.

$$22{,}834 \text{ ft} = \frac{22{,}834}{3} \text{ yd}$$

To change feet to yards, divide by 3.

$$= 7{,}611\tfrac{1}{3} \text{ yd}$$

Rewrite the fraction as a mixed number.

The highest point is $\frac{22{,}834}{3}$ yd, or $7{,}611\tfrac{1}{3}$ yd.

Lowest point:

Since the lowest point is 131 ft below sea level, write it as a negative number, −131.

$$-131 \text{ ft} = -\frac{131}{3} \text{ yd}$$

To change feet to yards, divide by 3.

$$= -43\tfrac{2}{3} \text{ yd}$$

Rewrite the fraction as a mixed number.

The lowest point is $-\frac{131}{3}$ yd, or $-43\tfrac{2}{3}$ yd.

1. a. Graph $-2\frac{1}{2}$.

   b. Graph the opposite of $-2\frac{1}{2}$.

2. Find the opposite of the number -3.5.

3. There are 22 seconds before a space shuttle takes off.

   a. What does 0 represent in this situation?

      A. It represents when the shuttle will takeoff.

      B. It represents the current height of the space shuttle.

      C. It represents the amount of time before takeoff.

   b. Which rational number represents the time before takeoff?

      A. -22 seconds

      B. 22 seconds

4. Of the statements below, which one describes a situation that you could represent by the rational number 389, but not by -389?

   a. A ball drops 389 ft.

   b. A diver is 389 ft below the surface of the water.

   c. A baseball travels 389 ft.

   d. A person withdraws $389 from a bank account.

5. The highest point in a country is a mountain peak 20,653 feet above sea level. The lowest point on land is 145 feet below sea level.

   a. What does 0 represent in this situation?

      A. The elevation of the highest point is 0 feet.

      B. The elevation of the lowest point is 0 feet.

      C. The elevation of sea level is 0 feet.

      D. The average elevation of the country is 0 feet.

   b. Write the highest elevation as a rational number.

   c. Write the lowest elevation as a rational number.

6. Of the statements below, which one describes a situation that you could represent by the rational number -141, but not by 141?

   A. The lowest point on land is 141 feet above the snow line.

   B. A submarine is 141 feet above the ocean floor.

   C. The lowest point on land is 141 feet below sea level.

   D. The peak of a mountain is 141 feet above the snow line.

7. a. Writing Which situation could you represent with the rational number 2.58, but not with -2.58?

      A. A student needs $2.58 more to buy a fruit salad.

      B. A student grew 2.58 inches over the course of one year.

      C. A student cut off 2.58 of their hair.

      D. A student is 2.58 minutes early for class.

   b. Describe two more situations that the given rational number could represent. Give situations that use units other than those used above.

8. Error Analysis Mary incorrectly claims that $-2\frac{1}{2}$ has no opposite because it is already a negative.

   a. What is the opposite of $-2\frac{1}{2}$?

   b. Why is Mary incorrect?

      A. Mary is incorrect because the opposite of a number is always a positive.

      B. Mary is incorrect because the opposite of a negative number is a negative number.

      C. Mary is incorrect because the opposite of a negative number is a positive number.

      D. Mary is incorrect because the opposite of a number is always negative.

9. Think About the Process

  a. When finding the opposite of a number, how can you check that your answer is correct?

    A. On a number line, the original number and the answer will be on the same side of 0 and have different distances from 0.

    B. On a number line, the original number and the answer will be on opposite sides of 0 and have different distances from 0.

    C. On a number line, the original number and the answer will be on opposite sides of 0 and have the same distance from 0.

    D. On a number line, the original number and the answer will be on the same side of 0 and have the same distance from 0.

  b. What is the opposite of $-2\frac{1}{8}$?

10. While a student was walking to school he accidentally dropped $2.63. He could only find $2.08. Let 0 represent the number of dollars the student had before dropping the money. Write a rational number to represent the change in the value of the student's money.

    A. −$0.55   **B.** $2.08

    C. $0.55   **D.** −$2.08

11. Complete the sentence to suggest a result that you can represent by the rational number $-6\frac{2}{3}$.

  A football team ■ $3\frac{2}{3}$ yards in one play, then ■ $10\frac{1}{3}$ yards in the next play.

12. Multiple Representations A robotic submarine dives to a depth of 23,437 ft below sea level.

  A. If 0 represents sea level, what rational number represents the submarine's position?

  B. If 0 represents the ocean floor, 27,459 ft below sea level, what rational number represents the submarine's position?

  C. Draw a picture that represents the elevation of the submarine if 0 represents sea level.

  D. Draw a picture that represents the elevation of the submarine if 0 represents the ocean floor.

13. Think About the Process A person hikes to the top of a mountain. After hiking halfway back down the mountain, the person's elevation is 3,649 ft above sea level.

  a. How can you find the height of the mountain?

    A. Divide the person's current elevation by 2.

    B. Quadruple the person's current elevation.

    C. Double the person's current elevation.

    D. There is not enough information to find the height of the mountain.

  b. Write the elevation of the mountain as a rational number.

CCSS: 6.NS.C.6c, 6.NS.C.7a, Also 6.NS.C.7b, 6.NS.C.7c

Part 1

Intro

You can compare negative rational numbers by using a number line in the same way that you compare positive rational numbers.

Comparing One-Third and One-Half

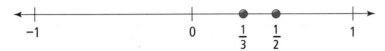

$\frac{1}{3}$ is to the left of $\frac{1}{2}$ on the number line. So $\frac{1}{3}$ is less than $\frac{1}{2}$.

$\frac{1}{2}$ is to the right of $\frac{1}{3}$ on the number line. So $\frac{1}{2}$ is greater than $\frac{1}{3}$.

$$\frac{1}{3} < \frac{1}{2} \text{ and } \frac{1}{2} > \frac{1}{3}$$

Comparing Negative One-Third and Negative One-Half

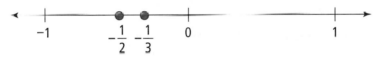

$-\frac{1}{3}$ is to the right of $-\frac{1}{2}$ on the number line. So $-\frac{1}{3}$ is greater than $-\frac{1}{2}$.

$-\frac{1}{2}$ is to the left of $-\frac{1}{3}$ on the number line. So $-\frac{1}{2}$ is less than $-\frac{1}{3}$.

$$-\frac{1}{3} > -\frac{1}{2} \text{ and } -\frac{1}{2} < -\frac{1}{3}$$

On a number line, numbers increase from left to right. They decrease from right to left.

Part 1

Example Using Number Lines to Compare
Rational Numbers

Use a number line to plot the rational numbers given in each problem below. Then use an inequality sign to compare each pair of numbers.

a. $1.1 \ \blacksquare \ 1\frac{1}{6}$ **b.** $-1\frac{1}{3} \ \blacksquare \ -1.6$ **c.** $-0.75 \ \blacksquare \ -\frac{2}{3}$

d. $\frac{1}{4} \ \blacksquare \ 0.35$ **e.** $-\frac{2}{3} \ \blacksquare \ -\frac{4}{3}$ **f.** $\frac{1}{4} \ \blacksquare \ -0.75$

Solution

a.

Since 1.1 is to the left of $1\frac{1}{6}$, $1.1 < 1\frac{1}{6}$.

b.

Since $-1\frac{1}{3}$ is to the right of -1.6, $-1\frac{1}{3} > -1.6$.

c.

Since -0.75 is to the left of $-\frac{2}{3}$, $-0.75 < -\frac{2}{3}$.

d.

Since $\frac{1}{4}$ is to the left of 0.35, $\frac{1}{4} < 0.35$.

e.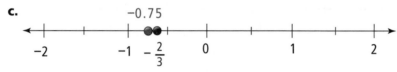

Since $-\frac{2}{3}$ is to the right of $-\frac{4}{3}$, $-\frac{2}{3} > -\frac{4}{3}$.

f.

Since $\frac{1}{4}$ is to the right of -0.75, $\frac{1}{4} > -0.75$.

Intro

The absolute value of any rational number is its distance from 0.

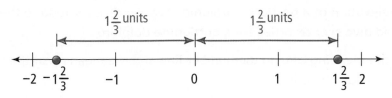

$1\frac{2}{3}$ units $1\frac{2}{3}$ units

-2 $-1\frac{2}{3}$ -1 0 1 $1\frac{2}{3}$ 2

Example Comparing Absolute Values

Compare each pair.

a. $\left|1.25\right|$ ■ $\left|1\frac{1}{2}\right|$ **b** $\left|-\frac{1}{3}\right|$ ■ $\left|-0.67\right|$ **c.** $\left|1\frac{1}{2}\right|$ ■ $\left|-1\frac{1}{2}\right|$

d. $\left|-1\frac{1}{2}\right|$ ■ $\left|-1.8\right|$ **e.** $\left|\frac{1}{2}\right|$ ■ $\left|-\frac{1}{3}\right|$ **f.** $\left|-1.8\right|$ ■ $\left|0\right|$

Solution

a. $\left|1.25\right| = 1.25$ and $\left|1\frac{1}{2}\right| = 1\frac{1}{2}$.

$1.25 < 1\frac{1}{2}$, so $\left|1.25\right| < \left|1\frac{1}{2}\right|$.   *1.25 is closer to 0 than $1\frac{1}{2}$.*

b. $\left|-\frac{1}{3}\right| = \frac{1}{3}$ and $\left|-0.67\right| = 0.67$.

$\frac{1}{3} < 0.67$, so $\left|-\frac{1}{3}\right| < \left|-0.67\right|$.   *$\frac{1}{3}$ is closer to 0 than -0.67.*

c. $\left|1\frac{1}{2}\right| = 1\frac{1}{2}$ and $\left|-1\frac{1}{2}\right| = 1\frac{1}{2}$.

$1\frac{1}{2} = 1\frac{1}{2}$, so $\left|1\frac{1}{2}\right| = \left|-1\frac{1}{2}\right|$.   *The points are the same distance from 0.*

d. $\left|-1\frac{1}{2}\right| = 1\frac{1}{2}$ and $\left|-1.8\right| = 1.8$.

$1\frac{1}{2} < 1.8$, so $\left|-1\frac{1}{2}\right| < \left|-1.8\right|$.   *$-1\frac{1}{2}$ is closer to 0 than -1.8.*

e. $\left|\frac{1}{2}\right| = \frac{1}{2}$ and $\left|-\frac{1}{3}\right| = \frac{1}{3}$.

$\frac{1}{2} > \frac{1}{3}$, so $\left|\frac{1}{2}\right| > \left|-\frac{1}{3}\right|$.   *$\frac{1}{2}$ is farther from 0 than $-\frac{1}{3}$.*

f. $\left|-1.8\right| = 1.8$ and $\left|0\right| = 0$.

$1.8 > 0$, so $\left|-1.8\right| > \left|0\right|$.   *1.8 is farther than 0.*

Example Using Rational Numbers to Compare Elevations

Compare the elevation of a bottlenose dolphin's regular dive for food to the deepest trained dive ever recorded for a bottlenose dolphin.

Then explain the meaning of 0 on the number line and the meaning of the rational numbers you compared.

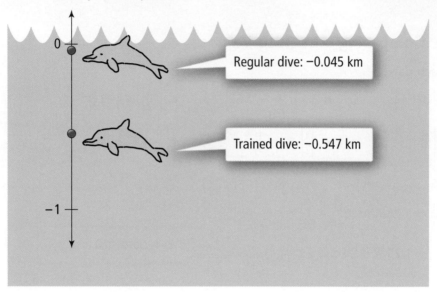

Regular dive: −0.045 km

Trained dive: −0.547 km

Solution ·

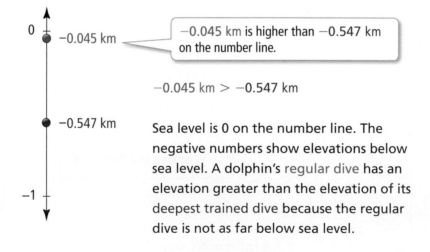

−0.045 km

−0.045 km is higher than −0.547 km on the number line.

$$-0.045 \text{ km} > -0.547 \text{ km}$$

−0.547 km

Sea level is 0 on the number line. The negative numbers show elevations below sea level. A dolphin's regular dive has an elevation greater than the elevation of its deepest trained dive because the regular dive is not as far below sea level.

1. Use =, <, or > to make a true statement about 3.5 and $5\frac{1}{2}$.

2. Use =, <, or > to compare |27.2| and |−27.5|.

3. Use the inequality symbols > and < to compare $\left|-2\frac{1}{6}\right|$ and $|-2.6|$.

4. During a very cold weekend in January the temperature at sunrise on Saturday was −3.2°C. The temperature at sunrise on Sunday was −2.7°C.

a. Compare the temperatures at sunrise on both days using a greater than or less than symbol.

b. What is the meaning of zero on the number line?

   A. the freezing temperature

   B. the boiling temperature

   C. the greatest possible temperature at sunrise

   D. the least possible temperature at sunrise

5. The table shows possible elevations, expressed as rational numbers relative to sea level, of an eel and an anglerfish.

Animal	Elevation (km)
Eel	−1.19
Anglerfish	−2.05

a. Compare the absolute values of the elevations for the eel and anglerfish using a greater than or less than symbol.

b. What do the absolute values for these elevations mean?

6. a. Writing Compare the absolute values of $-3\frac{1}{10}$ and −2.7 using a greater than or less than symbol.

b. Describe a situation you can model using these numbers.

7. Reasoning The number line shows −0.5 and $\frac{3}{11}$. **(Figure 1)**

a. Compare these numbers using =, < or >.

b. Justify in two different ways the inequality symbol you chose.

8. Which symbol correctly compares the numbers −3.35 and $-3\frac{3}{5}$? Use the number line below if necessary. **(Figure 2)**

9. Accounting Accountants create income statements that show how much money a business earns or loses. During the month of February Business X shows an income of $−424 and Business Y shows an income of $−474.

a. Compare the income statements of businesses X and Y using a greater than or less than symbol.

b. What is the meaning of zero in this situation?

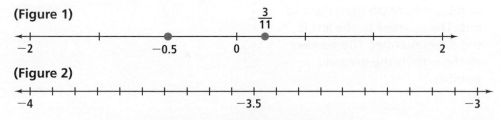

(Figure 1)

$$-2 \qquad -0.5 \qquad 0 \qquad \frac{3}{11} \qquad 2$$

(Figure 2)

$$-4 \qquad\qquad -3.5 \qquad\qquad -3$$

10. **Mental Math** Compare $\left|-\frac{7}{9}\right|$ and $\left|-\frac{4}{9}\right|$ using the inequality symbols, $>$ or $<$.

11. **a.** Which number line correctly displays -4.7 and $-3\frac{1}{4}$?

    A.

    B.

    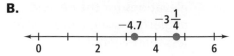

    C.

    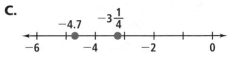

    D.

    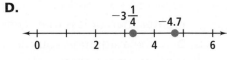

    b. Compare the numbers -4.7 and $-3\frac{1}{4}$ using a greater than or less than symbol.

12. **Estimation** Samantha is training to run the 100-m dash, and hopes to break the record for running the fastest time. The record is currently 9.58 s. On her first try she was -1.44 s relative to her goal. On the second try she was -0.78 s relative to her goal.

    a. On which try was Samantha closer to her goal?

    b. Estimate the difference in time between her first try and her second try by rounding each of her times to the nearest tenth.

    c. Find the actual difference between the two tries.

13. **Think About the Process**

    a. Is -0.4 to the left or to the right of $-\frac{1}{4}$ on a number line?

    b. How can you use a number line to compare two numbers?

    A. On a number line, numbers increase from left to right and numbers decrease from right to left. The number to the left is the lesser number. The number to the right is the greater number.

    B. On a number line, numbers increase from left to right and numbers decrease from right to left. The number to the left is the greater number. The number to the right is the lesser number.

    C. On a number line, numbers decrease from left to right and numbers increase from right to left. The number to the left is the lesser number. The number to the right is the greater number.

    D. On a number line, numbers decrease from left to right and numbers increase from right to left. The number to the left is the greater number. The number to the right is the lesser number.

14. **Estimation** Carla and Brian are at basketball practice. Their goal is to have a 30.1-in. vertical leap. The elevation of Carla's jump is -10.11 compared to the goal. The elevation of Brian's jump is -7.59 compared to the goal.

    a. Estimate Carla's current vertical leap by rounding each height to the nearest inch.

    b. Estimate Brian's current vertical leap.

    c. Who is closer to reaching the goal?

15. **Think About the Process**

    a. What symbol correctly compares the absolute values below?
    $$\left|-7\frac{1}{2}\right| \blacksquare \left|-7.9\right|$$

    b. How is comparing the absolute values of two rational numbers different from comparing the actual values?

See your complete lesson at MyMathUniverse.com

CCSS: 6.NS.C.6c, 6.NS.C.7a, Also 6.NS.C.7b, 6.NS.C.7c, 6.NS.C.7d

Part 1

Intro

A number line is a helpful tool to order a set of rational numbers from greatest to least or least to greatest.

←———Order greatest to least from right to left.←———

Least ←————————————————————————→ Greatest

0

———→ Order least to greatest from left to right.———→

You can draw or use a number line when you are asked to order a group of rational numbers.

Example Ordering Rational Numbers

Order -5, 2.1, 0.75, and $-\frac{1}{2}$ from least to greatest.

Solution

To order the numbers from least to greatest, plot them on a number line.

Least to greatest is from left to right on the number line.
The order is:

$$-5, -\frac{1}{2}, 0.75, 2.1$$

Part 2

Example Ordering Rational Numbers in a Real-World Situation

The table shows possible elevations, expressed as rational numbers relative to sea level, of 4 ocean animals.

Order those animals swimming deeper than 1 km, from least depth to greatest depth. Explain your reasoning.

Ocean Animal Elevations

Animal	Elevation (km)
Deep sea anglerfish	$-\frac{2}{3}$
Fanfin anglerfish	$-2\frac{1}{4}$
Gulper eel	-1.19
Pacific blackdragon	$-\frac{3}{10}$

Solution

Deeper than 1 km means absolute value *greater* than 1 km. The two animals with elevations that have absolute values greater than 1 km are the gulper eel at -1.19 km and the fanfin anglerfish at $-2\frac{1}{4}$ km.

Find the absolute values. $|-1.19| = 1.19$

$$\left|-2\frac{1}{4}\right| = 2\frac{1}{4}$$

Compare 1.19 and $2\frac{1}{4}$. $1.19 < 2\frac{1}{4}$

The absolute values from least to greatest are $|-1.19|, \left|-2\frac{1}{4}\right|$.

So for animals swimming deeper than 1 km, their order is, from least to greatest: gulper eel and fanfin anglerfish.

Part 3

Intro

Accountants use parentheses as negative signs.

   Example: ($209) means −209 dollars.

Whenever you see an accounting number is parentheses, you can write it as a negative number, showing a loss or negative balance. (Outside of accounting, however, you should *not* interpret a number in parentheses to be a negative number.)

Example Comparing Absolute Values of Rational Numbers

Use rational numbers to write an expression that compares an income of ($41.16) to an income of ($14.61), interpreted as size of loss.

Solution

Think	Write
Parentheses mean negative numbers. Absolute values show the size of the debts. 41.16 > 14.61	(41.16) = −41.16 (14.61) = −14.61 $\lvert -41.16 \rvert = 41.16$ $\lvert -14.61 \rvert = 14.61$ $\lvert -41.16 \rvert > \lvert -14.61 \rvert$

($41.16), or −$41.16, is a greater loss than ($14.61), or −$14.61.

1. Which number line in **Figure 1** correctly displays each number from greatest to least?

2. **a.** Order -1.78, $1\frac{1}{3}$, $-\frac{7}{9}$, and $\frac{1}{6}$ from greatest to least.

   b. Which number line correctly displays each number?

   A.

   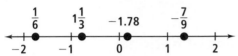

   B.

   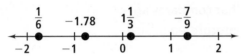

   C.

   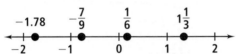

   D.

   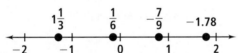

3. The table shows the elevations, in km, of four different fish. Order those fish swimming at a depth below 1 km from greatest depth to least depth.

Fish Elevations				
Fish	F	I	S	H
Elevations (km)	-1.88	$-2\frac{1}{5}$	$-\frac{3}{4}$	$-\frac{1}{5}$

4. A researcher recorded the temperature for five consecutive days in December. See the table.

Temperature at Sunrise					
Day	1	2	3	4	5
Temperature (°F)	$\frac{29}{2}$	$5\frac{1}{10}$	29.4	36.2	$33\frac{1}{3}$

   a. Order the temperatures below freezing from greatest to least.

   A. $36.2, 5\frac{1}{10}, \frac{29}{2}, 33\frac{1}{3}$

   B. $5\frac{1}{10}, \frac{29}{2}, 29.4$

   C. $29.4, \frac{29}{2}, 5\frac{1}{10}$

   D. $5\frac{1}{10}, \frac{29}{2}, 29.4, 33\frac{1}{3}, 36.2$

   b. Which day was the temperature closest to freezing?

5. While grocery shopping, Cindy spent $56.14 and Andy spent $45.61.

   a. Which expression correctly compares the number of dollars each friend spent?

   A. $|-56.14| > |-45.61|$

   B. $|-56.14| < |-45.61|$

   C. $56.14 > 45.61$

   D. $56.14 < 45.61$

   b. Which friend spent less on groceries?

(Figure 1)

a.
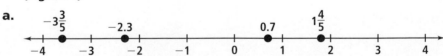

b.
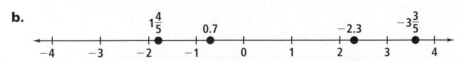

6. A bird flies $13\frac{7}{10}$ feet above sea level. A fish swims $16\frac{1}{5}$ feet below sea level.

a. Which expression compares the locations of the bird and the fish?

A. $13\frac{7}{10} < 16\frac{1}{5}$ B. $13\frac{7}{10} < -16\frac{1}{5}$

C. $13\frac{7}{10} > 16\frac{1}{5}$ D. $13\frac{7}{10} > -16\frac{1}{5}$

b. Compare the distances $\left|13\frac{7}{10}\right|$ and $\left|-16\frac{1}{5}\right|$ from sea level to each creature.

c. Which is farther from sea level?

7. Of the numbers below, order those numbers with absolute value greater than 2 from least to greatest.

$-3\frac{1}{6}, -3.6, -\frac{7}{4}, -0.52$

8. **Think About the Process** At the beginning of the month, Mary and Paul each deposit $100 into their checking accounts. At the end of the month, Mary's bank account shows a total change of $36.77 and Paul's bank account shows a total change of –$39.43.

a. Which values should you compare to decide whose account balance is lesser?

A. Compare |36.77| and |−39.43|.

B. Compare 36.77 and −39.43.

C. You can compare either pair of values.

b. Whose account shows the lesser balance?

c. Whose account balance had the greater change?

9. **Think About the Process** The masses of five objects are shown in the table. See **Figure 2**.

a. How can you order the objects based on how close their mass is to the mass of Object X?

A. Ignore X in the expression for each mass and find the absolute value of the signed number.

B. Ignore X in the expression for each mass and use the signed number to order.

C. Find the absolute value of each mass expression.

D. Plot the masses on a number line.

b. Order the objects that have a mass that is within 10 kg of the mass of Object X from least to greatest difference from the mass of Object X. Choose the correct answer below.

A. Object Z, Object V

B. Object W, Object Y

C. Object V, Object Z

D. Object Y, Object W, Object V, Object Z

E. Object Y, Object W

(Figure 2)

Object Masses					
Object	V	W	X	Y	Z
Mass (kg)	$X - 10.1$	$X - 5\frac{5}{8}$	X	$X + 5.275$	$X + 10\frac{1}{10}$

See your complete lesson at MyMathUniverse.com

Rational Numbers and the Coordinate Plane

CCSS: 6.NS.C.6b, Also 6.NS.C.6c

Part 1

▶ Intro

The coordinate plane shows point $P\left(-1\frac{1}{2}, \frac{3}{4}\right)$.

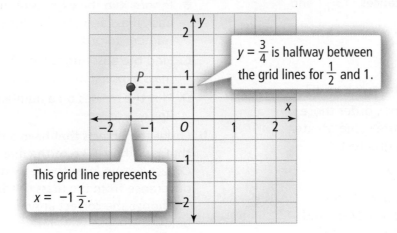

$y = \frac{3}{4}$ is halfway between the grid lines for $\frac{1}{2}$ and 1.

This grid line represents $x = -1\frac{1}{2}$.

▶ Example Writing Ordered Pairs with Fractions and Mixed Numbers

Use fractions or mixed numbers to write the ordered pair for each point on the grid. Identify the quadrant for each point.

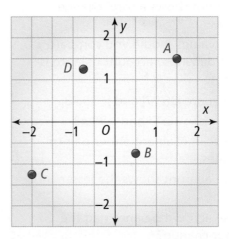

continued on next page >

Example continued

Solution ·

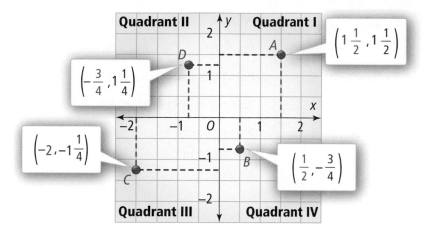

Point $A\left(1\frac{1}{2},\ 1\frac{1}{2}\right)$ is in Quadrant I.

Point $B\left(\frac{1}{2},\ -\frac{3}{4}\right)$ is in Quadrant IV.

Point $C\left(-2,\ -1\frac{1}{4}\right)$ is in Quadrant III.

Point $D\left(-\frac{3}{4},\ 1\frac{1}{4}\right)$ is in Quadrant II.

Part 2

Example Plotting Points with Rational Coordinates

Plot each point on a coordinate plane. Identify the quadrant for each point.

$A(1.5, 4)$ $B(-2, -2.3)$ $C(-1.7, 1.5)$ $D(1, -0.7)$ $E(0, 2.5)$

Solution ·

To graph each on the coordinate plane:

Step 1 Start at the origin $(0, 0)$.

Step 2 Use the x-coordinate to move right (if positive) or left (if negative) along the x-axis.

continued on next page >

Part 2

Solution continued

Step 3 Use the *y*-coordinate to move up (if positive) or down (if negative) along the *y*-axis.

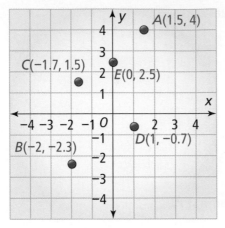

Point *A* is in Quadrant I.

Point *B* is in Quadrant III.

Point *C* is in Quadrant II.

Point *D* is in Quadrant IV.

Point *E* is not in any quadrant because it lies on an axis.

Part 3

Intro

When two ordered pairs differ only by the signs of their coordinates, you know that they are related by reflections across the *x*-axis, the *y*-axis, or both axes.

Reflection across the *x*-axis When a point is reflected across the *x*-axis, the sign of the *y*-coordinate of the ordered pair changes.

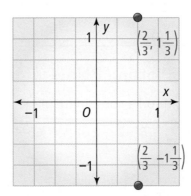

continued on next page >

Part 3

Intro continued

Reflection across the *y*-axis When a point is reflected across the *y*-axis, the sign of the *x*-coordinate of the ordered pair changes.

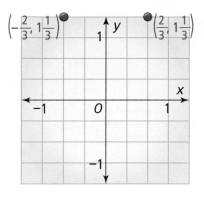

Reflection across both axes When a point is reflected across both axes, the sign of both the *x*-coordinate and the *y*-coordinate of the ordered pair change.

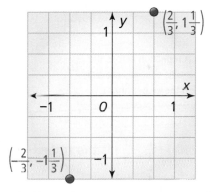

Example Identifying Reflections of Points with Rational Coordinates

Complete each statement, using the following ordered pairs.

$\left(\frac{1}{2}, \frac{1}{3}\right)$ $\left(\frac{1}{2}, -\frac{1}{3}\right)$ $\left(-\frac{1}{2}, -\frac{1}{3}\right)$ $\left(-\frac{1}{3}, \frac{1}{2}\right)$ $\left(-\frac{1}{3}, -\frac{1}{2}\right)$ $\left(-\frac{1}{2}, -\frac{1}{3}\right)$

a. ■ is the reflection of $\left(-\frac{1}{2}, \frac{1}{3}\right)$ across the *x*-axis.

b. ■ is the reflection of $\left(-\frac{1}{2}, \frac{1}{3}\right)$ across the *y*-axis.

c. ■ is the reflection of $\left(-\frac{1}{2}, \frac{1}{3}\right)$ across both axes.

continued on next page >

Solution ·

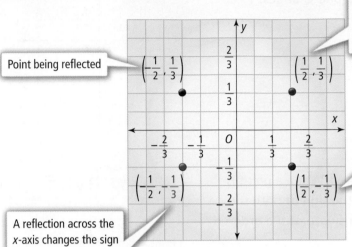

Point being reflected

$\left(-\dfrac{1}{2}, \dfrac{1}{3}\right)$

A reflection across the y-axis changes the sign of the x-coordinate.

$\left(\dfrac{1}{2}, \dfrac{1}{3}\right)$

$\left(-\dfrac{1}{2}, -\dfrac{1}{3}\right)$

A reflection across both axes changes the sign of both the x-coordinate and the y-coordinate.

$\left(\dfrac{1}{2}, -\dfrac{1}{3}\right)$

A reflection across the x-axis changes the sign of the y-coordinate.

a. $\left(-\dfrac{1}{2}, -\dfrac{1}{3}\right)$ is the reflection of $\left(-\dfrac{1}{2}, \dfrac{1}{3}\right)$ across the x-axis.

b. $\left(\dfrac{1}{2}, \dfrac{1}{3}\right)$ is the reflection of $\left(-\dfrac{1}{2}, \dfrac{1}{3}\right)$ across the y-axis.

c. $\left(\dfrac{1}{2}, -\dfrac{1}{3}\right)$ is the reflection of $\left(-\dfrac{1}{2}, \dfrac{1}{3}\right)$ across both axes.

1. Which ordered pair corresponds to point *G*?

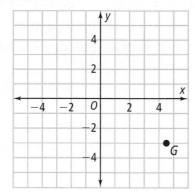

A. $\left(5\frac{1}{2}, -3\right)$ B. $\left(4\frac{1}{2}, -3\right)$

C. $\left(4\frac{1}{2}, -2\right)$ D. $\left(-3, 4\frac{1}{2}\right)$

2. Identify the ordered pair for each point on the grid.

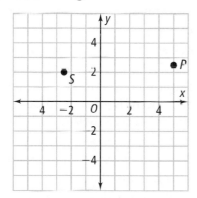

a. Which ordered pair corresponds to point *S*?

A. (−2.5, 3)   B. (−1.5, 2)

C. (2, −2.5)   D. (−2.5, 2)

b. Which ordered pair corresponds to point *P*?

A. (2.5, 5)   B. (5, 2.5)

C. (6, 2.5)   D. (5, 3.5)

3. **Think About the Process** To plot the point (−1, 5.5) on the coordinate plane, start at the origin, (0,0). What is the next step?

A. Move ■ unit(s) to the left and ■ unit(s) down.

B. Move ■ unit(s) to the right and ■ unit(s) up.

C. Move ■ unit(s) to the left and ■ unit(s) up.

D. Move ■ unit(s) to the right and ■ unit(s) down.

4. The coordinate plane shows a point and its reflection. What is the relationship between point *A* and point *B*?

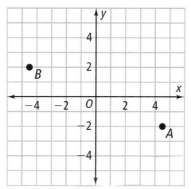

5. **Think About the Process** The coordinate plane shows a point and its reflection.

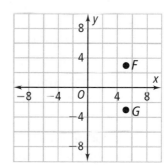

a. How do the coordinates of points *F* and *G* compare?

A. The *x*-coordinates are the same. The *y*-coordinates are opposites.

B. The *y*-coordinates are the same. The *x*-coordinates are opposites.

C. The *x*-coordinates and the *y*-coordinates are switched.

D. The *x*-coordinates are opposites. The *y*-coordinates are opposites.

b. Point *G* is the reflection of point *F* across which axis?

6. a. Reasoning Plot and label the points $S(-3.7, 4.1)$ and $P(2.6, -3.3)$ on a coordinate plane.

b. How do you know these points are not in the same quadrant without plotting them?

7. a. Open-Ended Find the reflection of the point $(-3.5, 4\frac{2}{5})$ across the y-axis.

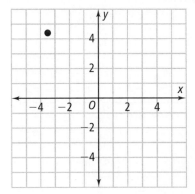

b. Find a point for which the sign of neither coordinate changes with a reflection across the x-axis.

c. Find a point for which the sign of neither coordinate changes with a reflection across the y-axis.

d. Find a point for which the sign of neither coordinate changes with a reflection across both axes, one after the other.

8. Identify the quadrant and ordered pair for each point on the graph.

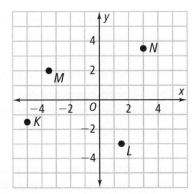

a. In which quadrant is point K?

b. Which ordered pair corresponds to point K?
   A. $(-1.5, -5)$ **B.** $(-5, -1.5)$
   C. $(-5, -0.5)$ **D.** $(-4, -1.5)$

c. In which quadrant is point L?

d. Which ordered pair corresponds to point L?
   A. $(-3, 1.5)$ **B.** $(2.5, -3)$
   C. $(1.5, -3)$ **D.** $(1.5, -2)$

e. In which quadrant is point M?

f. Which ordered pair corresponds to point M?
   A. $(-3.5, 2)$ **B.** $(-3.5, 3)$
   C. $(-2.5, 2)$ **D.** $(2, -3.5)$

g. In which quadrant is point N?

h. Which ordered pair corresponds to point N?
   A. $(3.5, 3)$ **B.** $(3, 3.5)$
   C. $(3, 4.5)$ **D.** $(4, 3.5)$

9. a. Plot the points on a coordinate plane.
   $K(4.9, -1)$ $L(3, 3.3)$
   $M(-3, -2.3)$ $N(-2.5, 4)$

b. Determine the quadrant where each point is located. Choose the correct answer below.

   A. K is in quadrant II. L is in quadrant IV. M is in quadrant I. N is in quadrant III.

   B. K is in quadrant I. L is in quadrant III. M is in quadrant II. N is in quadrant IV.

   C. K is in quadrant IV. L is in quadrant I. M is in quadrant III. N is in quadrant II.

   D. K is in quadrant III. L is in quadrant II. M is in quadrant IV. N is in quadrant I.

Polygons in the Coordinate Plane

CCSS: 6.G.A.3

Key Concept

A **polygon** is a closed figure formed by three or more line segments that do not cross.

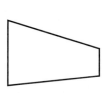

Polygon

Polygon

Not a polygon

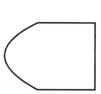

Not a polygon

A **vertex** of a polygon is any point where two sides of the polygon meet. This trapezoid is a polygon with four vertices.

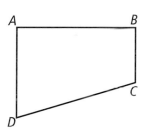

You can use a coordinate plane to draw a polygon.

$A\left(-3\frac{1}{2}, -1\right)$

$B\ (2, 4)$

$C\ (4, -3)$

Triangle *ABC*

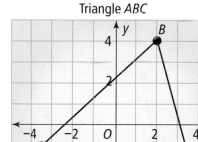

See your complete lesson at MyMathUniverse.com

Example Drawing Polygons in the Coordinate Plane

Draw a polygon with vertices $A\left(-2\frac{1}{2}, 1\frac{1}{2}\right)$, $B\left(2, 2\frac{1}{2}\right)$, $C\left(3\frac{1}{2}, -1\right)$, $D(0, -3)$, and $E\left(-3, -1\frac{1}{2}\right)$.

Name the polygon.

Solution ·

Step 1 Plot each point:

Estimate halfway to plot fraction parts of x and y-coordinates.

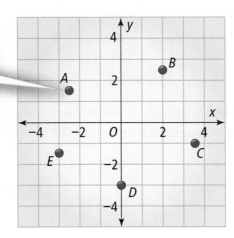

Step 2 Use a straightedge to connect the vertices and draw the polygon.

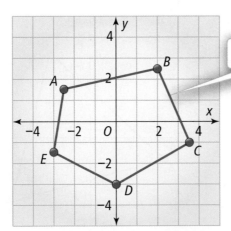

The polygon is pentagon *ABCDE*.

Intro

You can use what you know about finding distance in the coordinate plane to find the length of a segment with endpoints that have the same x-coordinate or y-coordinate.

Length of Segment AC Since points A and C are on different sides of the y-axis, add the distances on each side of the y-axis. Add the absolute values of the x-coordinates of the points.

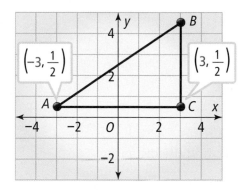

$$|-3| + |3| = 3 + 3$$
$$= 6$$

Segment AC is 6 units long.

Length of Segment BC Since points B and C are on the same side of the x-axis, subtract the distances from the x-axis. Subtract the absolute values of the y-coordinates of the points.

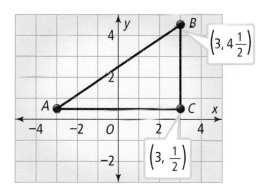

$$\left|4\tfrac{1}{2}\right| - \left|\tfrac{1}{2}\right| = 4\tfrac{1}{2} - \tfrac{1}{2}$$
$$= 4$$

Segment BC is 4 units long.

Example Finding Segment Lengths in the Coordinate Plane

Find the lengths of segment *AB* and segment *CD*.

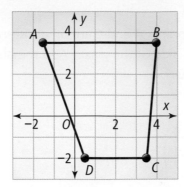

Solution

To find the lengths of segment *AB* and segment *CD*, find the distance between the end points of each segment.

Step 1 Find the coordinates of the points *A*, *B*, *C*, and *D*.

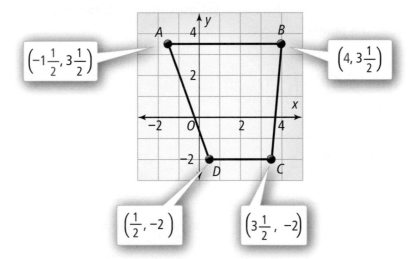

continued on next page >

Part 2

Solution continued

Step 2 Find the length of segment *AB*.

Since points *A* and *B* are on different sides of the *y*-axis, add the distances on each side of *y*-axis.

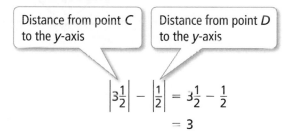

Distance from point *A* to the *y*-axis

Distance from point *B* to the *y*-axis

$$\left| -1\frac{1}{2} \right| + |4| = 1\frac{1}{2} + 4$$

$$= 5\frac{1}{2}$$

Segment *AB* is $5\frac{1}{2}$ units long.

Step 3 Find the length of segment *CD*.

Since points *C* and *D* are on same side of the *y*-axis, subtract the distances from the *y*-axis.

Distance from point *C* to the *y*-axis

Distance from point *D* to the *y*-axis

$$\left| 3\frac{1}{2} \right| - \left| \frac{1}{2} \right| = 3\frac{1}{2} - \frac{1}{2}$$

$$= 3$$

Segment *CD* is 3 units long.

Example Representing Polygon-Shaped Objects in the Coordinate Plane

Use the ordered pairs $A\left(-8\frac{1}{2}, 8\frac{1}{2}\right)$, $B\left(-8\frac{1}{2}, 0\right)$, $C\left(0, -8\frac{1}{2}\right)$, $D\left(8\frac{1}{2}, 0\right)$, and $E\left(8\frac{1}{2}, 8\frac{1}{2}\right)$ to draw a picture of home plate in baseball.

Solution ·

Step 1 Plot the vertices of home plate.

Step 2 Use a straightedge to connect the vertices and draw a picture of home plate.

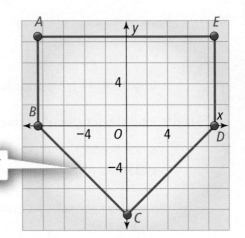

Pentagon *ABCDE*

1. Which ordered pair represents a vertex of polygon *KLMN*?

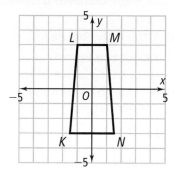

A. $(1, -3)$ **B.** $\left(1\frac{1}{2}, 3\right)$

C. $\left(-1\frac{1}{2}, -3\right)$ **D.** $(-1, -3)$

2. The graph shows a drawing of a mountain. Each unit represents 1,000 ft.

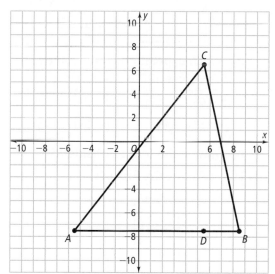

a. What is the distance between *C* and *D* in units?

b. What is the height of the mountain?

3. a. Writing Which ordered pairs represent the vertices of *EFGH*? Select all that apply.

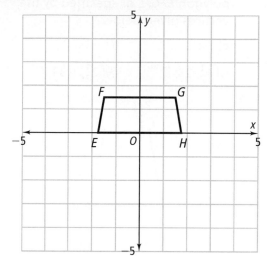

A. $(-3, 3)$ **B.** $\left(3\frac{1}{2}, 3\right)$

C. $(3, 0)$ **D.** $\left(-3\frac{1}{2}, 0\right)$

E. $(-3, 0)$

b. Explain how you could rule out one or more choices without graphing the points.

4. Reasoning The rectangle *ABCD* shown on the coordinate plane represents an overhead view of a piece of land. Each unit represents 1,000 ft.

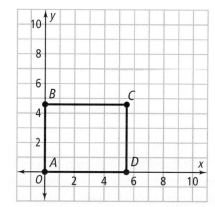

a. What is the length of segment *AD* in units?

b. How long is the piece of land in feet?

c. Describe the relationship between the length of *AD* and the coordinates of vertex *C*.

5. a. Which is the correct graph of the polygon *EFGH*, as specified by the vertices given below?

$$E\left(-2\tfrac{1}{2}, -3\right), \qquad F\left(-1\tfrac{1}{2}, 2\right),$$

$$G\left(1\tfrac{1}{2}, 2\right), \qquad H\left(2\tfrac{1}{2}, -3\right)$$

A.

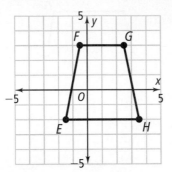

B.

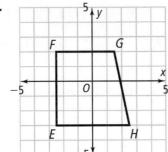

C.

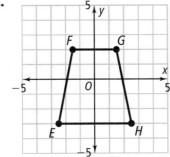

b. Explain what makes a figure a polygon.

6. The following is a sketch of a wall of a house that is going to be built. Each unit represents 5 feet.

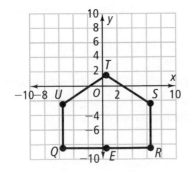

a. What is the distance between *Q* and *R*?

b. How long is the house?

c. What is the distance between *T* and *E*?

d. How tall is the house?

7. Think About the Process An equilateral triangle is a triangle in which all sides have the same length. *QRS* is an equilateral triangle.

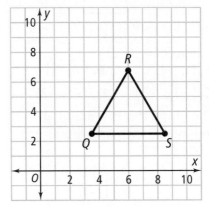

a. Which expression could you use to find the length of side *RS*?

A. $\left|2\tfrac{1}{2}\right| - \left|2\tfrac{1}{2}\right|$ **B.** $\left|6\tfrac{1}{2}\right| - \left|3\tfrac{1}{2}\right|$

C. $\left|8\tfrac{1}{2}\right| + \left|3\tfrac{1}{2}\right|$ **D.** $\left|8\tfrac{1}{2}\right| - \left|3\tfrac{1}{2}\right|$

b. What is the length of side *RS*?

8. Think About the Process

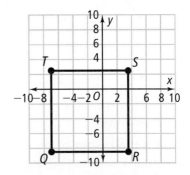

a. Write an expression you could use to find the length of the side *QT*.

A. $-\left|2\tfrac{1}{2}\right| + \left|-8\tfrac{1}{2}\right|$

B. $\left|2\tfrac{1}{2}\right| + \left|-8\tfrac{1}{2}\right|$

C. $\left|2\tfrac{1}{2}\right| - \left|-8\tfrac{1}{2}\right|$

D. $2\tfrac{1}{2} + \left(-8\tfrac{1}{2}\right)$

b. Find the length of side *QT*.

CCSS: 6.NS.C.6b, Also 6.NS.C.6c, 6.NS.C.7b, and 6.G.A.3

Part 1

Example Ordering Absolute Values of Rational Numbers

A quality engineer checks the lengths of 5 portable music players and records differences from the standard specified lengths. Order the players from closest to farthest from standard.

Player 1
–0.01 cm

Player 2
+0.05 cm

Player 3
+0.02 cm

Player 4
–0.04 cm

Player 5
0.00 cm

Solution

The absolute value of a player's difference from the standard length determines how close the player is to the standard. Find the absolute values of the differences, and order them from least to greatest.

Player 1: $|-0.01| = 0.01$

Player 2: $|+0.05| = 0.05$

Player 3: $|+0.02| = 0.02$

Player 4: $|-0.04| = 0.04$

Player 5: $|0.00| = 0.00$

> The ones places and the tenths places are all zeros, so use the hundredths place to order the absolute values. From least to greatest the order is: 0.00, 0.01, 0.02, 0.04, 0.05.

The order from closest to farthest from standard is Player 5, Player 1, Player 3, Player 4, and Player 2.

Example Finding Missing Vertices in the Coordinate Plane

A student started to draw a 3 × 4 rectangle. She got interrupted after she graphed only two vertices at (−3.5, −1) and (−0.5, 3). Draw the rectangle that she was drawing. Label the coordinates for each vertex. Check your drawing.

Solution

Know	Need	Plan
• Rectangle is 3 x 4 • Angles are all right angles • Opposites sides are equal • Two vertices: (−3.5, −1), (−0.5, 3)	• To draw the rectangle • To label the coordinates for each vertex	Use grid paper to draw a coordinate plane and plot the vertices (−3.5, −1) and (−0.5, 3). Use reasoning to find the coordinates of the other two vertices.

Step 1 Use grid paper to draw a coordinate plane and plot the vertices (−3.5, −1) and (−0.5, 3).

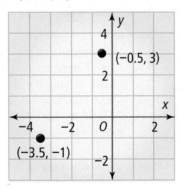

Step 2 Use reasoning to find the two missing points.

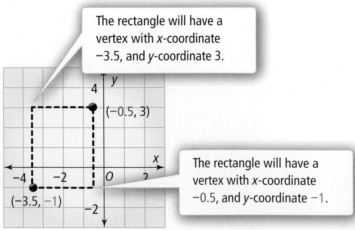

The rectangle will have a vertex with x-coordinate −3.5, and y-coordinate 3.

The rectangle will have a vertex with x-coordinate −0.5, and y-coordinate −1.

continued on next page >

Solution continued

Step 3 Draw the rectangle and label the points.

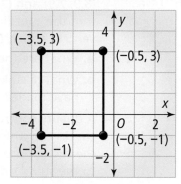

(−3.5, 3) (−0.5, 3)

(−3.5, −1) (−0.5, −1)

Check Find the lengths of the sides of the figure.
The points (−3.5, 3) and (−0.5, 3) have the same y-coordinate. Find
the length of the side connecting the two points.

$$|-3.5| - |-0.5| = 3.5 - 0.5$$
$$= 3.0, \text{ or } 3 \text{ units } \checkmark$$

> The points are on the same side of the y-axis. Subtract the absolute values of their x-coordinates to find the distance between them.

The points (−3.5, 3) and (−3.5, −1) have the
same x-coordinate. Find the length of the
side connecting the two points.

$$|3| + |-1| = 3 + 1$$
$$= 4 \text{ units } \checkmark$$

> The points are on different sides of the x-axis. Add the absolute values of their y-coordinates to find the distance between them.

The rectangle's length and width check.

1. From their nest 5 m off the ground, two birds fly to separate branches in the same tree. Bird 1 flies to a branch $2\frac{3}{5}$ m off the ground, and Bird 2 flies to a branch 7.45 m off the ground.

   a. Use the given information to complete the table, expressing each bird's change in elevation with a positive or a negative number.

Bird	Starting Elevation (m)	Change in Elevation (m)
Bird 1	■	■
Bird 2	■	■

   b. Which bird's elevation changed more?

   A. Bird 1's elevation changed more.

   B. Bird 2's elevation changed more.

   C. Their elevations changed the same amount.

2. David and Sarah opened savings accounts on the same day, each with an initial deposit of $100.00. After two months, David's account shows a balance of $61.62 and Sarah's account shows a balance of $142.45. Which account balance changed by the greatest amount? Why?

   A. Sarah's changed by the greatest amount because $|-\$38.38| < |\$42.45|$.

   B. David's changed by the greatest amount because $|-\$38.38| > |\$42.45|$.

   C. Sarah's changed by the greatest amount because $\$61.62 < \$142.45$.

   D. David's changed by the greatest amount because $-\$38.38 > \$42.45$.

3. You and your friend are each drawing a 3.9 by 6.9 rectangle with vertices (5.9, 7.9) and (2, 1). Your friend says that the coordinates of the missing vertices are (1, 5.9) and (7.9, 2).

   a. What are the correct coordinates?

   b. What mistake might your friend have made?

4. A quality control engineer at a factory checks the weight of each widget the factory produces and compares it to the standard specified weight. The difference between the actual weight and the standard weight is recorded for four widgets (See **Figure 1**).

   a. Order the widgets from closest to farthest from the standard weight.

   b. Which widget's weight is the farthest from the standard?

5. Think About the Process The table shows the first quarter averages of two students. The class average is 82.4.

   First Quarter Averages

Student	Average
Andy	77.2
Alice	93.6

   a. Which values should you use to decide which student's average is farther from the class average?

   A. $|-5.2|$ and $|11.2|$

   B. -5.2 and 11.2

   C. $|77.2|$ and $|93.6|$

   D. 77.2 and 93.6

   b. Which student's average is farther from the class average?

(Figure 1)

Widget Weights				
Widget	W	X	Y	Z
Weight Difference (kg)	−1.8	2	−1	$-1\frac{3}{5}$

See your complete lesson at MyMathUniverse.com

6. **Think About the Process**

a. Suppose (q, r) and (s, t) are two vertices at opposite corners of a rectangle. What are the coordinates of the other two vertices?

   A. $(q, -r)$ and $(s, -t)$

   B. (r, q) and (t, s)

   C. (q, s) and (r, t)

   D. (q, t) and (s, r)

b. A rectangle has width $5\frac{1}{2}$ units, length $4\frac{3}{4}$ units, and vertices $\left(-5\frac{1}{2}, 2\right)$ and $\left(\frac{1}{4}, 6\frac{3}{4}\right)$. Find the coordinates of the other two vertices.

   A. $\left(-5\frac{1}{4}, 6\frac{3}{4}\right)$ and $\left(\frac{1}{4}, 2\right)$

   B. $\left(-5\frac{1}{4}, -2\right)$ and $\left(\frac{1}{4}, -6\frac{3}{4}\right)$

   C. $\left(-5\frac{1}{4}, \frac{1}{4}\right)$ and $\left(2, 6\frac{3}{4}\right)$

   D. $\left(2, -5\frac{1}{4}\right)$ and $\left(6\frac{3}{4}, \frac{1}{4}\right)$

c. Which graph shows the given rectangle?

   A.
   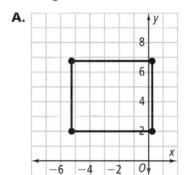

B.
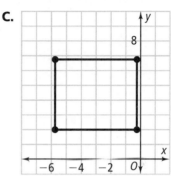

C.
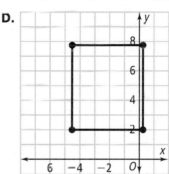

D.

7. Five identical seedlings are planted in a garden. After 1 month, they are measured, and their change in height is recorded in the table in **Figure 2**. Negative numbers indicate that a plant has shrunk since it was planted.

   a. Which plant is tallest?

      A. plant 2   **B.** plant 3

      C. plant 1   **D.** plant 5

      E. plant 4

   b. Why do you think some of the plants are shorter than when they were planted?

(Figure 2)

Plant Heights					
Plant	1	2	3	4	5
Change in Height (cm)	$\frac{4}{5}$	2.3	1.2	$-2\frac{1}{5}$	-0.9

See your complete lesson at MyMathUniverse.com

English/Spanish Glossary

A

Absolute deviation from the mean Absolute deviation measures the distance that the data value is from the mean. You find the absolute deviation by taking the absolute value of the deviation of a data value. Absolute deviations are always nonnegative.

Desviación absoluta de la media La desviación absoluta mide la distancia a la que un valor se encuentra de la media. Para hallar la desviación absoluta, tomas el valor absoluto de la desviación de un valor. Las desviaciones absolutas siempre son no negativas.

Absolute value The absolute value of a number a is the distance between a and zero on a number line. The absolute value of a is written as $|a|$.

Valor absoluto El valor absoluto de un número a es la distancia entre a y cero en la recta numérica. El valor absoluto de a se escribe como $|a|$.

Accuracy The accuracy of an estimate or measurement is the degree to which it agrees with an accepted or actual value of that measurement.

Exactitud La exactitud de una estimación o medición es el grado de concordancia con un valor aceptado o real de esa medición.

Action In a probability situation, an action is a process with an uncertain result.

Acción En una situación de probabilidad, una acción es el proceso con un resultado incierto.

Acute angle An acute angle is an angle with a measure between 0° and 90°.

Ángulo agudo Un ángulo agudo es un ángulo que mide entre 0° y 90°.

Acute triangle An acute triangle is a triangle with three acute angles.

Triángulo acutángulo Un triángulo acutángulo es un triángulo que tiene tres ángulos agudos.

Addend Addends are the numbers that are added together to find a sum.

Sumando Los sumandos son los números que se suman para hallar un total.

English/Spanish Glossary

Additive inverses Two numbers that have a sum of 0.

Inversos de suma Dos números cuya suma es 0.

Adjacent angles Two angles are adjacent angles if they share a vertex and a side, but have no interior points in common.

Ángulos adyacentes Dos ángulos son adyacentes si tienen un vértice y un lado en común, pero no comparten puntos internos.

Algebraic expression An algebraic expression is a mathematical phrase that consists of variables, numbers, and operation symbols.

Expresión algebraica Una expresión algebraica es una frase matemática que consiste en variables, números y símbolos de operaciones.

Analyze To analyze is to think about and understand facts and details about a given set of information. Analyzing can involve providing a written summary supported by factual information, diagrams, charts, tables, or any combination of these.

Analizar Analizar es pensar en los datos y detalles de cierta información y comprenderlos. El análisis puede incluir la presentación de un resumen escrito sustentado por información objetiva, diagramas, tablas o una combinación de esos elementos.

Angle An angle is a figure formed by two rays with a common endpoint.

Ángulo Un ángulo es una figura formada por dos semirrectas que tienen un extremo en común.

Angle of rotation The angle of rotation is the number of degrees a figure is rotated.

Ángulo de rotación El ángulo de rotación es el número de grados que se rota una figura.

Annual salary The amount of money earned at a job in one year.

Salario annual La cantidad de dinero ganó en un trabajo en un año.

Area The area of a figure is the number of square units the figure encloses.

Área El área de una figura es el número de unidades cuadradas que ocupa.

English/Spanish Glossary

Area of a circle The formula for the area of a circle is $A = \pi r^2$, where A represents the area and r represents the radius of the circle.

Área de un círculo La fórmula del área de un círculo es $A = \pi r^2$, donde A representa el área y r representa el radio del círculo.

Area of a parallelogram The formula for the area of a parallelogram is $A = bh$, where A represents the area, b represents a base, and h is the corresponding height.

Área de un paralelogramo La fórmula del área de un paralelogramo es $A = bh$, donde A representa el área, b representa una base y h es la altura correspondiente.

Area of a rectangle The formula for the area of a rectangle is $A = bh$, where A represents the area, b represents the base, and h represents the height of the rectangle.

Área de un rectángulo La fórmula del área de un rectángulo es $A = bh$, donde A representa el área, b representa la base y h representa la altura del rectángulo.

Area of a square The formula for the area of a square is $A = s^2$, where A represents the area and s represents a side length.

Área de un cuadrado La fórmula del área de un cuadrado es $A = s^2$, donde A representa el área y l representa la longitud de un lado.

Area of a trapezoid The formula for the area of a trapezoid is $A = \frac{1}{2}h(b_1 + b_2)$, where A represents the area, b_1 and b_2 represent the bases, and h represents the height between the bases.

El área de un trapezoide La fórmula para el área de un trapezoide es $A = \frac{1}{2}h(b_1 + b_2)$, donde A representa el área, b_1 y b_2 representan las bases, y h representa la altura entre las bases.

Area of a triangle The formula for the area of a triangle is $A = \frac{1}{2}bh$, where A represents the area, b represents the length of a base, and h represents the corresponding height.

Área de un triángulo La fórmula del área de un triángulo es $A = \frac{1}{2}bh$, donde A representa el área, b representa la longitud de una base y h representa la altura correspondiente.

Asset An asset is money you have or property of value that you own.

Ventaja Una ventaja es dinero que tiene o la propiedad de valor que usted posee.

English/Spanish Glossary

Associative Property of Addition For any numbers a, b, and c:
$$(a + b) + c = a + (b + c)$$

Propiedad asociativa de la suma Para los números cualesquiera a, b y c:
$$(a + b) + c = a + (b + c)$$

Associative Property of Multiplication For any numbers a, b, and c:
$$(a \cdot b) \cdot c = a \cdot (b \cdot c)$$

Propiedad asociativa de la multiplicación Para los números cualesquiera a, b y c:
$$(a \cdot b) \cdot c = a \cdot (b \cdot c)$$

Average of two numbers The average of two numbers is the value that represents the middle of two numbers. It is found by adding the two numbers together and dividing by 2.

Promedio de dos números El promedio de dos números es el valor que está justo en el medio de esos dos números. Se halla sumando los dos números y dividiendo el resultado por 2.

B

Balance The balance in an account is the principal amount plus the interest earned.

Saldo El saldo de una cuenta es el capital más el interés ganado.

Balance of a checking Account The balance of a checking account is the amount of money in the checking account.

El equilibrio de una Cuenta Corriente Bancaria El equilibrio de una cuenta corriente bancaria es la cantidad de dinero en la cuenta corriente bancaria.

Balance of a loan The balance of a loan is the remaining unpaid principal.

El equilibrio de un préstamo El equilibrio de un préstamo es el director impagado restante.

Bar diagram A bar diagram is a way to represent part to whole relationships.

Diagrama de barras Un diagrama de barras es una forma de representar una relación de parte a entero.

Base The base is the repeated factor of a number written in exponential form.

Base La base es el factor repetido de un número escrito en forma exponencial.

English/Spanish Glossary

Base area of a cone The base area of a cone is the area of a circle. Base Area = πr^2.

Área de la base de un cono El área de la base de un cono es el área de un círculo. El área de la base = πr^2.

Base of a cone The base of a cone is a circle with radius r.

Base de un cono La base de un cono es un círculo con radio r.

Base of a cylinder A base of a cylinder is one of a pair of parallel circular faces that are the same size.

Base de un cilindro Una base de un cilindro es una de dos caras circulares paralelas que tienen el mismo tamaño.

Base of a parallelogram A base of a parallelogram is any side of the parallelogram.

Base de un paralelogramo La base de un paralelogramo es cualquiera de los lados del paralelogramo.

Base of a prism A base of a prism is one of a pair of parallel polygonal faces that are the same size and shape. A prism is named for the shape of its bases.

Base de un prisma La base de un prisma es una de las dos caras poligonales paralelas que tienen el mismo tamaño y la misma forma. El nombre de un prisma depende de la forma de sus bases.

Base of a pyramid A base of a pyramid is a polygonal face that does not connect to the vertex.

Base de una pirámide La base de una pirámide es una cara poligonal que no se conecta con el vértice.

Base of a triangle The base of a triangle is any side of the triangle.

Base de un triángulo La base de un triángulo es cualquiera de los lados del triángulo.

Benchmark A benchmark is a number you can use as a reference point for other numbers.

Referencia Una referencia es un número que usted puede utilizar como un punto de referencia para otros números.

English/Spanish Glossary

Bias A bias is a tendency toward a particular perspective that is different from the overall perspective of the population.

Sesgo Un sesgo es una tendencia hacia una perspectiva particular que es diferente de la perspectiva general de la población.

Biased sample In a biased sample, the number of subjects in the sample with the trait that you are studying is not proportional to the number of members in the population with that trait. A biased sample does not accurately represent the population.

Muestra sesgada En una muestra sesgada, el número de sujetos de la muestra que tiene la característica que se está estudiando no es proporcional al número de miembros de la población que tienen esa característica. Una muestra sesgada no representa con exactitud la población.

Bivariate categorical data Bivariate categorical data pairs categorical data collected about two variables of the same population.

Datos bivariados por categorías Los datos bivariados por categorías agrupan pares de datos obtenidos acerca de dos variables de la misma población.

Bivariate data Bivariate data is comprised of pairs of linked observations about a population.

Datos bivariados Los datos bivariados se forman a partir de pares de observaciones relacionadas sobre una población.

Box plot A box plot is a statistical graph that shows the distribution of a data set by marking five boundary points where data occur along a number line. Unlike a dot plot or a histogram, a box plot does not show frequency.

Diagrama de cajas Un diagrama de cajas es un diagrama de estadísticas que muestra la distribución de un conjunto de datos al marcar cinco puntos de frontera donde se hallan los datos sobre una recta numérica. A diferencia del diagrama de puntos o el histograma, el diagrama de cajas no muestra la frecuencia.

Budget A budget is a plan for how you will spend your money.

Presupuesto Un presupuesto es un plan para cómo gastará su dinero.

English/Spanish Glossary

C

Categorical data Categorical data consist of data that fall into categories.

Datos por categorías Los datos por categorías son datos que se pueden clasificar en categorías.

Center of a circle The center of a circle is the point inside the circle that is the same distance from all points on the circle. Name a circle by its center.

Centro de un círculo El centro de un círculo es el punto dentro del círculo que está a la misma distancia de todos los puntos del círculo. Un círculo se identifica por su centro.

Center of a regular polygon The center of a regular polygon is the point that is equidistant from its vertices.

Centro de un polígono regular El centro de un polígono regular es el punto equidistante de todos sus vértices.

Center of rotation The center of rotation is a fixed point about which a figure is rotated.

Centro de rotación El centro de rotación es el punto fijo alrededor del cual se rota una figura.

Check register A record that shows all of the transactions for a bank account, including withdrawals, deposits, and transfers. It also shows the balance of the account after each transaction.

Verifique registro Un registro que muestra todas las transacciones para una cuenta bancaria, inclusive retiradas, los depósitos, y las transferencias. También muestra el equilibrio de la cuenta después de cada transacción.

Circle A circle is the set of all points in a plane that are the same distance from a given point, called the center.

Círculo Un círculo es el conjunto de todos los puntos de un plano que están a la misma distancia de un punto dado, llamado centro.

Circle graph A circle graph is a graph that represents a whole divided into parts.

Gráfica circular Una gráfica circular es una gráfica que representa un todo dividido en partes.

English/Spanish Glossary

Circumference of a circle The circumference of a circle is the distance around the circle. The formula for the circumference of a circle is $C = \pi d$, where C represents the circumference and d represents the diameter of the circle.

Circunferencia de un círculo La circunferencia de un círculo es la distancia alrededor del círculo. La fórmula de la circunferencia de un círculo es $C = \pi d$, donde C representa la circunferencia y d representa el diámetro del círculo.

Cluster A cluster is a group of points that lie close together on a scatter plot.

Grupo Un grupo es un conjunto de puntos que están agrupados en un diagrama de dispersión.

Coefficient A coefficient is the number part of a term that contains a variable.

Coeficiente Un coeficiente es la parte numérica de un término que contiene una variable.

Common denominator A common denominator is a number that is the denominator of two or more fractions.

Común denominador Un común denominador es un número que es el denominador de dos o más fracciones.

Common multiple A common multiple is a multiple that two or more numbers share.

Múltiplo común Un múltiplo común es un múltiplo que comparten dos o más números.

Commutative Property of Addition For any numbers a and b: $a + b = b + a$

Propiedad conmutativa de la suma Para los números cualesquiera a y b: $a + b = b + a$

Commutative Property of Multiplication For any numbers a and b: $a \cdot b = b \cdot a$

Propiedad conmutativa de la multiplicación Para los números cualesquiera a y b: $a \cdot b = b \cdot a$

Comparative inference A comparative inference is an inference made by interpreting and comparing two sets of data.

Inferencia comparativa Una inferencia comparativa es una inferencia que se hace al interpretar y comparar dos conjuntos de datos.

English/Spanish Glossary

Compare To compare is to tell or show how two things are alike or different.

Comparar Comparar es describir o mostrar en qué se parecen o en qué se diferencian dos cosas.

Compatible numbers Compatible numbers are numbers that are easy to compute mentally.

Números compatibles Los números compatibles son números fáciles de calcular mentalmente.

Complementary angles Two angles are complementary angles if the sum of their measures is 90°. Complementary angles that are adjacent form a right angle.

Ángulos complementarios Dos ángulos son complementarios si la suma de sus medidas es 90°. Los ángulos complementarios que son adyacentes forman un ángulo recto.

Complex fraction A complex fraction is a fraction $\frac{A}{B}$ where A and/or B are fractions and B is not zero.

Fracción compleja Una fracción compleja es una fracción $\frac{A}{B}$ donde A y/o B son fracciones y B es distinto de cero.

Compose a shape To compose a shape, join two (or more) shapes so that there is no gap or overlap.

Componer una figura Para componer una figura, debes unir dos (o más) figuras de modo que entre ellas no queden espacios ni superposiciones.

Composite figure A composite figure is the combination of two or more figures into one object.

Figura compuesta Una figura compuesta es la combinación de dos o más figuras en un objeto.

Composite number A composite number is a whole number greater than 1 with more than two factors.

Número compuesto Un número compuesto es un número entero mayor que 1 con más de dos factores.

Compound event A compound event is an event associated with a multi-step action. A compound event is composed of events that are the outcomes of the steps of the action.

Evento compuesto Un evento compuesto es un evento que se relaciona con una acción de varios pasos. Un evento compuesto se compone de eventos que son los resultados de los pasos de una acción.

English/Spanish Glossary

Compound interest Compound interest is interest paid on both the principal and the interest earned in previous interest periods. To calculate compound interest, use the formula $B = p(1 + r)^n$, where B is the balance in the account, p is the principal, r is the annual interest rate, and n is the time in years that the account earns interest.

Interés compuesto El interés compuesto es el interés que se paga sobre el capital y el interés obtenido en períodos de interés anteriores. Para calcular el interés compuesto, usa la fórmula $B = c(1 + r)^n$ donde B es el saldo de la cuenta, c es el capital, r es la tasa de interés anual y n es el tiempo en años en que la cuenta obtiene un interés.

Cone A cone is a three-dimensional figure with one circular base and one vertex.

Cono Un cono es una figura tridimensional con una base circular y un vértice.

Congruent figures Two two-dimensional figures are congruent $\cong$ if the second can be obtained from the first by a sequence of rotations, reflections, and translations.

Figuras congruentes Dos figuras bidimensionales son congruentes $\cong$ si la segunda puede obtenerse a partir de la primera mediante una secuencia de rotaciones, reflexiones y traslaciones.

Conjecture A conjecture is a statement that you believe to be true but have not yet proved to be true.

Conjetura Una conjetura es un enunciado que crees que es verdadero, pero que todavía no has comprobado que sea verdadero.

Constant A constant is a term that only contains a number.

Constante Una constante es un término que solamente contiene un número.

Constant of proportionality In a proportional relationship, one quantity y is a constant multiple of the other quantity x. The constant multiple is called the constant of proportionality. The constant of proportionality is equal to the ratio $\frac{y}{x}$.

Constante de proporcionalidad En una relación proporcional, una cantidad y es un múltiplo constante de la otra cantidad x. El múltiplo constante se llama constante de proporcionalidad. La constante de proporcionalidad es igual a la razón $\frac{y}{x}$.

English/Spanish Glossary

Construct To construct is to make something, such as an argument, by organizing ideas. Constructing an argument can involve a written response, equations, diagrams, charts, tables, or a combination of these.

Construir Construir es hacer o crear algo, como se construye un argumento al organizar ideas. Para construir un argumento puede usarse una respuesta escrita, ecuaciones, diagramas, tablas o una combinación de esos elementos.

Convenience sampling Convenience sampling is a sampling method in which a researcher chooses members of the population that are convenient and available. Many researchers use this sampling technique because it is fast and inexpensive. It does not require the researcher to keep track of everyone in the population.

Muestra de conveniencia Una muestra de conveniencia es un método de muestreo en el que un investigador escoge miembros de la población que están convenientemente disponibles. Muchos investigadores usan esta técnica de muestreo porque es rápida y no es costosa. No requiere que el investigador lleve un registro de cada miembro de la población.

Cost of attendance The cost of attendance of one year of college is the sum of all of your expenses during the year.

El costo de asistencia El costo de asistencia de un año del colegio es la suma de todos sus gastos durante el año.

Cost of credit The cost of credit for a loan Is the difference between the total cost and the principal.

El costo de crédito El costo de crédito para un préstamo es la diferencia entre el coste total y el director.

Converse of the Pythagorean Theorem If the sum of the squares of the lengths of two sides of a triangle equals the square of the length of the third side, then the triangle is a right triangle. If $a^2 + b^2 = c^2$, then the triangle is a right triangle.

Expresión recíproca del Teorema de Pitágoras Si la suma del cuadrado de la longitud de dos lados de un triángulo es igual al cuadrado de la longitud del tercer lado, entonces el triángulo es un triángulo rectángulo. $a^2 + b^2 = c^2$, entonces el triángulo es un triángulo rectángulo.

Conversion factor A conversion factor is a rate that equals 1.

Factor de conversión Un factor de conversión es una tasa que es igual a 1.

English/Spanish Glossary

Coordinate plane A coordinate plane is formed by a horizontal number line called the *x*-axis and a vertical number line called the *y*-axis.

Plano de coordenadas Un plano de coordenadas está formado por una recta numérica horizontal llamada eje de las *x* y una recta numérica vertical llamada eje de las *y*.

Corresponding angles Corresponding angles lie on the same side of a transversal and in corresponding positions.

Ángulos correspondientes Los ángulos correspondientes se ubican al mismo lado de una secante y en posiciones correspondientes.

Counterexample A counterexample is a specific example that shows that a conjecture is false.

Contraejemplo Un contraejemplo es un ejemplo específico que muestra que una conjetura es falsa.

Counting Principle If there are *m* possible outcomes of one action and *n* possible outcomes of a second action, then there are *m · n* outcomes of the first action followed by the second action.

Principio de conteo Si hay *m* resultados posibles de una acción y *n* resultados posibles de una segunda acción, entonces hay *m · n* resultados de la primera acción seguida de la segunda acción.

Coupon A coupon is part of a printed or online advertisement entitling the holder to a discount at checkout.

Cupón Un cupón forma parte de un anuncio impreso o en línea que permite al poseedor a un descuento en comprueba.

Credit card A credit card is a card issued by a lender that can be used to borrow money or make purchases on credit.

Tarjeta de crédito Una tarjeta de crédito es una tarjeta publicada por un prestamista que puede ser utilizado para pedir dinero prestado o compras de marca a cuenta.

Credit history A credit history shows how a consumer has managed credit in the past.

Acredite la historia Una historia del crédito muestra cómo un consumidor ha manejado crédito en el pasado.

English/Spanish Glossary

Credit report A report that shows personal information about a consumer and details about the consumer's credit history.

Acredite reporte Un reporte que muestra información personal sobre un consumidor y detalles acerca de la historia del crédito del consumidor.

Critique A critique is a careful judgment in which you give your opinion about the good and bad parts of something, such as how a problem was solved.

Crítica Una crítica es una evaluación cuidadosa en la que das tu opinión acerca de las partes positivas y negativas de algo, como la manera en la que se resolvió un problema.

Cross section A cross section is the intersection of a three-dimensional figure and a plane.

Corte transversal Un corte transversal es la intersección de una figura tridimensional y un plano.

Cube A cube is a rectangular prism whose faces are all squares.

Cubo Un cubo es un prisma rectangular cuyas caras son todas cuadrados.

Cube root The cube root of a number, n, is a number whose cube equals n.

Raíz cúbica La raíz cúbica de un número, n, es un número que elevado al cubo es igual a n.

Cubic unit A cubic unit is the volume of a cube that measures 1 unit on each edge.

Unidad cúbica Una unidad cúbica es el volumen de un cubo en el que cada arista mide 1 unidad.

Cylinder A cylinder is a three-dimensional figure with two parallel circular bases that are the same size.

Cilindro Un cilindro es una figura tridimensional con dos bases circulares paralelas que tienen el mismo tamaño.

D

Data Data are pieces of information collected by asking questions, measuring, or making observations about the real world.

Datos Los datos son información reunida mediante preguntas, mediciones u observaciones sobre la vida diaria.

English/Spanish Glossary

Debit card A debit card is a card issued by a bank that is linked a customer's bank account, normally a checking account. A debit card can normally be used to withdraw money from an ATM or to make a purchase.

Tarjeta de débito Una tarjeta de débito es una tarjeta publicada por un banco que es ligado la cuenta bancaria de un cliente, normalmente una cuenta corriente bancaria. Una tarjeta de débito puede ser utilizada normalmente retirar dinero de una ATM o para hacer una compra.

Decimal A decimal is a number with one or more places to the right of a decimal point.

Decimal Un decimal es un número que tiene uno o más lugares a la derecha del punto decimal.

Decimal places The digits after the decimal point are called decimal places.

Lugares decimales Los dígitos que están después del punto decimal se llaman lugares decimales.

Decompose a shape To decompose a shape, break it up to form other shapes.

Descomponer una figura Para descomponer una figura, debes separarla para formar otras figuras.

Deductive reasoning Deductive reasoning is a process of reasoning logically from given facts to a conclusion.

Razonamiento deductivo El razonamiento deductivo es un proceso de razonamiento lógico que parte de hechos dados hasta llegar a una conclusión.

Denominator The denominator is the number below the fraction bar in a fraction.

Denominador El denominador es el número que está debajo de la barra de fracción en una fracción.

Dependent events Two events are dependent events if the occurrence of the first event affects the probability of the second event.

Eventos dependientes Dos eventos son dependientes si el resultado del primer evento afecta la probabilidad del segundo evento.

Deposit A transaction that adds money to a bank account is a deposit.

Depósito Una transacción que agrega dinero a una cuenta bancaria es un depósito.

English/Spanish Glossary

Dependent variable A dependent variable is a variable whose value changes in response to another (independent) variable.

Variable dependiente Una variable dependiente es una variable cuyo valor cambia en respuesta a otra variable (independiente).

Describe To describe is to explain or tell in detail. A written description can contain facts and other information needed to communicate your answer. A diagram or a graph may also be included.

Describir Describir es explicar o indicar algo en detalle. Una descripción escrita puede incluir hechos y otra información necesaria para comunicar tu respuesta. También puede incluir un diagrama o una gráfica.

Design To design is to make using specific criteria.

Diseñar Diseñar es crear algo a partir de criterios específicos.

Determine To determine is to use the given information and any related facts to find a value or make a decision.

Determinar Determinar es usar la información dada y cualquier otro dato relacionado para hallar un valor o tomar una decisión.

Deviation from the mean Deviation indicates how far away and in which direction a data value is from the mean. Data values that are less than the mean have a negative deviation. Data values that are greater than the mean have a positive deviation.

Desviación de la media La desviación indica a qué distancia y en qué dirección un valor se aleja de la media. Los valores menores que la media tienen una desviación negativa. Los valores mayores que la media tienen una desviación positiva.

Diagonal A diagonal of a figure is a segment that connects two nonconsecutive vertices of the figure.

Diagonal La diagonal de una figura es un segmento que conecta dos vértices no consecutivos de la figura.

Diameter A diameter is a segment that passes through the center of a circle and has both endpoints on the circle. The term diameter can also mean the length of this segment.

Diámetro Un diámetro es un segmento que atraviesa el centro de un círculo y tiene sus dos extremos en el círculo. El término diámetro también puede referirse a la longitud de este segmento.

English/Spanish Glossary

Difference The difference is the answer you get when subtracting two numbers.

Diferencia La diferencia es la respuesta que obtienes cuando restas dos números.

Dilation A dilation is a transformation that moves each point along the ray through the point, starting from a fixed center, and multiplies distances from the center by a common scale factor. If a vertex of a figure is the center of dilation, then the vertex and its image after the dilation are the same point.

Dilatación Una dilatación es una transformación que mueve cada punto a lo largo de la semirrecta a través del punto, a partir de un centro fijo, y multiplica las distancias desde el centro por un factor de escala común. Si un vértice de una figura es el centro de dilatación, entonces el vértice y su imagen después de la dilatación son el mismo punto.

Direct variation A linear relationship that can be represented by an equation in the form $y = kx$, where $x \neq 0$.

Dirija variación Una relación lineal que puede ser representada por una ecuación en la forma $y = kx$, donde x no iguale 0.

Distribution (of a data set) The distribution of a data set describes the way that its data values are spread out over all possible values. This includes describing the frequencies of each data value. The shape of a data display shows the distribution of a data set.

Distribución (de un conjunto de datos) La distribución de un conjunto de datos describe la manera en que sus valores se esparcen sobre todos los valores posibles. Eso incluye la descripción de las frecuencias de cada valor. La forma de una exhibición de datos muestra la distribución de un conjunto de datos.

Distributive Property Multiplying a number by a sum or difference gives the same result as multiplying that number by each term in the sum or difference and then adding or subtracting the corresponding products.
$a \cdot (b + c) = a \cdot b + a \cdot c$ and
$a \cdot (b - c) = a \cdot b - a \cdot c$

Propiedad distributiva Multiplicar un número por una suma o una diferencia da el mismo resultado que multiplicar ese mismo número por cada uno de los términos de la suma o la diferencia y después sumar o restar los productos obtenidos.
$a \cdot (b + c) = a \cdot b + a \cdot c$ and
$a \cdot (b - c) = a \cdot b - a \cdot c$

Dividend The dividend is the number to be divided.

Dividendo El dividendo es el número que se divide.

English/Spanish Glossary

Divisible A number is divisible by another number if there is no remainder after dividing.

Divisible Un número es divisible por otro número si no hay residuo después de dividir.

Divisor The divisor is the number used to divide another number.

Divisor El divisor es el número por el cual se divide otro número.

Dot plot A dot plot is a statistical graph that shows the shape of a data set with stacked dots above each data value on a number line. Each dot represents one data value.

Diagrama de puntos Un diagrama de puntos es una gráfica estadística que muestra la forma de un conjunto de datos con puntos marcados sobre cada valor de una recta numérica. Cada punto representa un valor.

E

Earned wages Earned wages are the income you receive from an employer for doing a job. Earned wages are also called gross pay.

Sueldos ganados Los sueldos ganados son los ingresos que usted recibe de un empleador para hacer un trabajo. Los sueldos ganados también son llamados la paga bruta.

Easy-access loan The term easy-access loan refers to a wide variety of loans with a streamlined application process. Many easy-access loans are short-term loans of relatively small amounts of money. They often have high interest rates.

Préstamo de fácil-acceso El préstamo del fácil-acceso del término se refiere a una gran variedad de préstamos con un proceso simplificado de aplicación. Muchos préstamos del fácil-acceso son préstamos a corto plazo de cantidades relativamente pequeñas de dinero. Ellos a menudo tienen los tipos de interés altos.

Edge of a three-dimensional figure An edge of a three-dimensional figure is a segment formed by the intersection of two faces.

Arista de una figura tridimensional Una arista de una figura tridimensional es un segmento formado por la intersección de dos caras.

English/Spanish Glossary

Enlargement An enlargement is a dilation with a scale factor greater than 1. After an enlargement, the image is bigger than the original figure.

Aumento Un aumento es una dilatación con un factor de escala mayor que 1. Después de un aumento, la imagen es más grande que la figura original.

Equation An equation is a mathematical sentence that includes an equals sign to compare two expressions.

Ecuación Una ecuación es una oración matemática que incluye un signo igual para comparar dos expresiones.

Equilateral triangle An equilateral triangle is a triangle whose sides are all the same length.

Triángulo equilátero Un triángulo equilátero es un triángulo que tiene todos sus lados de la misma longitud.

Equivalent equations Equivalent equations are equations that have exactly the same solutions.

Ecuaciones equivalentes Las ecuaciones equivalentes son ecuaciones que tienen exactamente la misma solución.

Equivalent expressions Equivalent expressions are expressions that always have the same value.

Expresiones equivalentes Las expresiones equivalentes son expresiones que siempre tienen el mismo valor.

Equivalent fractions Equivalent fractions are fractions that name the same number.

Fracciones equivalentes Las fracciones equivalentes son fracciones que representan el mismo número.

Equivalent inequalities Equivalent inequalities are inequalities that have the same solution.

Desigualdades equivalentes Las desigualdades equivalentes son desigualdades que tienen la misma solución.

Equivalent ratios Equivalent ratios are ratios that express the same relationship.

Razones equivalentes Las razones equivalentes son razones que expresan la misma relación.

Estimate To estimate is to find a number that is close to an exact answer.

Estimar Estimar es hallar un número cercano a una respuesta exacta.

English/Spanish Glossary

Evaluate a numerical expression To evaluate a numerical expression is to follow the order of operations.

Evaluar una expresión numérica Evaluar una expresión numérica es seguir el orden de las operaciones.

Evaluate an algebraic expression To evaluate an algebraic expression, replace each variable with a number, and then follow the order of operations.

Evaluar una expresión algebraica Para evaluar una expresión algebraica, reemplaza cada variable con un número y luego sigue el orden de las operaciones.

Event An event is a single outcome or group of outcomes from a sample space.

Evento Un evento es un resultado simple o un grupo de resultados de un espacio muestral.

Expand an algebraic expression To expand an algebraic expression, use the Distributive Property to rewrite a product as a sum or difference of terms.

Desarrollar una expresión algebraica Para desarrollar una expresión algebraica, usa la propiedad distributiva para reescribir el producto como una suma o diferencia de términos.

Expected family contribution The amount of money a student's family is expected to contribute towards the student's cost of attendance for school.

Contribución familiar esperado La cantidad de dinero que la familia de un estudiante es esperada contribuir hacia el estudiante es costado de asistencia para la escuela.

Expense Money that a business or a person needs to spend to pay for or buy something.

Gasto El dinero que un negocio o una persona debe gastar para pagar por o comprar algo.

Experiment To experiment is to try to gather information in several ways.

Experimentar Experimentar es intentar reunir información de varias maneras.

English/Spanish Glossary

Experimental probability You find the experimental probability of an event by repeating an experiment many times and using this ratio: $P(\text{event}) = \dfrac{\text{number of times event occurs}}{\text{total number of trials}}$

Probabilidad experimental Para hallar la probabilidad experimental de un evento, debes repetir un experimento muchas veces y usar esta razón: $P(\text{evento}) = \dfrac{\text{número de veces que sucede el evento}}{\text{número total de pruebas}}$

Explain To explain is to give facts and details that make an idea easier to understand. Explaining can involve a written summary supported by a diagram, chart, table, or a combination of these.

Explicar Explicar es brindar datos y detalles para que una idea sea más fácil de comprender. Para explicar algo se puede usar un resumen escrito sustentado por un diagrama, una tabla o una combinación de esos elementos.

Exponent An exponent is a number that shows how many times a base is used as a factor.

Exponente Un exponente es un número que muestra cuántas veces se usa una base como factor.

Expression An expression is a mathematical phrase that can involve variables, numbers, and operations. See algebraic expression or numerical expression.

Expresión Una expresión es una frase matemática que puede tener variables, números y operaciones. Ver expresión algebraica o expresión numérica.

Exterior angle of a triangle An exterior angle of a triangle is an angle formed by a side and an extension of an adjacent side.

Ángulo externo de un triángulo Un ángulo externo de un triángulo es un ángulo formado por un lado y una extensión de un lado adyacente.

F

Face of a three-dimensional figure A face of a three-dimensional figure is a flat surface shaped like a polygon.

Cara de una figura tridimensional La cara de una figura tridimensional es una superficie plana con forma de polígono.

English/Spanish Glossary

Factor an algebraic expression To factor an algebraic expression, write the expression as a product.

Descomponer una expresión algebraica en factores Para descomponer una expresión algebraica en factores, escribe la expresión como un producto.

Factors Factors are numbers that are multiplied to give a product.

Factores Los factores son los números que se multiplican para obtener un producto.

False equation A false equation has values that do not equal each other on each side of the equals sign.

Ecuación falsa Una ecuación falsa tiene valores a cada lado del signo igual que no son iguales entre sí.

Financial aid Financial aid is any money offered to a student to assist with the cost of attendance.

Ayuda financiera La ayuda financiera es cualquier dinero ofreció a un estudiante para ayudar con el costo de asistencia.

Financial need A student's financial need is the difference between the student's cost of attendance and the student's expected family contribution.

Necesidad financiera Una necesidad financiera del estudiante es la diferencia entre el estudiante es costada de asistencia y la contribución esperado de familia de estudiante.

Find To find is to calculate or determine.

Hallar Hallar es calcular o determinar.

First quartile For an ordered set of data, the first quartile is the median of the lower half of the data set.

Primer cuartil Para un conjunto ordenado de datos, el primer cuartil es la mediana de la mitad inferior del conjunto de datos.

Fixed expenses Fixed expenses are expenses that do not change from one budget period to the next.

Gastos fijos Los gastos fijos son los gastos que no cambian de un período económico al próximo.

English/Spanish Glossary

Fraction A fraction is a number that can be written in the form $\frac{a}{b}$, where a is a whole number and b is a positive whole number. A fraction is formed by a parts of size $\frac{1}{b}$.

Fracción Una fracción es un número que puede expresarse de forma $\frac{a}{b}$, donde a es un entero y b es un número entero positivo. La fracción está formada por a partes de tamaño $\frac{1}{b}$.

Frequency Frequency describes the number of times a specific value occurs in a data set.

Frecuencia La frecuencia describe el número de veces que aparece un valor específico en un conjunto de datos.

Function A function is a rule for taking each input value and producing exactly one output value.

Función Una función es una regla por la cual se toma cada valor de entrada y se produce exactamente un valor de salida.

G

Gap A gap is an area of a graph that contains no data points.

Espacio vacío o brecha Un espacio vacío o brecha es un área de una gráfica que no contiene ningún valor.

Grant A type of monetary award a student can use to pay for his or her education. The student does not need to repay this money.

Grant Un tipo de premio monetario que un estudiante puede utilizar para pagar por su educación. El estudiante no debe devolver este dinero.

Greater than $>$ The greater-than symbol shows a comparison of two numbers with the number of greater value shown first, or on the left.

Mayor que $>$ El símbolo de mayor que muestra una comparación de dos números con el número de mayor valor que aparece primero, o a la izquierda.

Greatest common factor The greatest common factor (GCF) of two or more whole numbers is the greatest number that is a factor of all of the numbers.

Máximo común divisor El máximo común divisor (M.C.D.) de dos o más números enteros no negativos es el número mayor que es un factor de todos los números.

English/Spanish Glossary

H

Height of a cone The height of a cone, *h*, is the length of a segment perpendicular to the base that joins the vertex and the base.

Altura de un cono La altura de un cono, *h*, es la longitud de un segmento perpendicular a la base que une el vértice y la base.

Height of a cylinder The height of a cylinder is the length of a perpendicular segment that joins the planes of the bases.

Altura de un cilindro La altura de un cilindro es la longitud de un segmento perpendicular que une los planos de las bases.

Height of a parallelogram A height of a parallelogram is the perpendicular distance between opposite bases.

Altura de un paralelogramo La altura de un paralelogramo es la distancia perpendicular que existe entre las bases opuestas.

Height of a prism The height of a prism is the length of a perpendicular segment that joins the bases.

Altura de un prisma La altura de un prisma es la longitud de un segmento perpendicular que une a las bases.

Height of a pyramid The height of a pyramid is the length of a segment perpendicular to the base that joins the vertex and the base.

Altura de una pirámide La altura de una pirámide es la longitud de un segmento perpendicular a la base que une al vértice con la base.

Height of a triangle The height of a triangle is the length of the perpendicular segment from a vertex to the base opposite that vertex.

Altura de un triángulo La altura de un triángulo es la longitud del segmento perpendicular desde un vértice hasta la base opuesta a ese vértice.

Hexagon A hexagon is a polygon with six sides.

Hexágono Un hexágono es un polígono de seis lados.

English/Spanish Glossary

Histogram A histogram is a statistical graph that shows the shape of a data set with vertical bars above intervals of values on a number line. The intervals are equal in size and do not overlap. The height of each bar shows the frequency of data within that interval.

Histograma Un histograma es una gráfica de estadísticas que muestra la forma de un conjunto de datos con barras verticales encima de intervalos de valores en una recta numérica. Los intervalos tienen el mismo tamaño y no se superponen. La altura de cada barra muestra la frecuencia de los datos dentro de ese intervalo.

Hundredths One hundredth is one part of 100 equal parts of a whole.

Centésima Una centésima es 1 de las 100 partes iguales de un todo.

Hypotenuse In a right triangle, the longest side, which is opposite the right angle, is the hypotenuse.

Hipotenusa En un triángulo rectángulo, el lado más largo, que es opuesto al ángulo recto, es la hipotenusa.

I

Identify To identify is to match a definition or description to an object or to recognize something and be able to name it.

Identificar Identificar es unir una definición o una descripción con un objeto, o reconocer algo y poder nombrarlo.

Identity Property of Addition The sum of 0 and any number is that number. For any number n, $n + 0 = n$ and $0 + n = n$.

Propiedad de identidad de la suma La suma de 0 y cualquier número es ese número. Para cualquier número n, $n + 0 = n$ and $0 + n = n$.

Identity Property of Multiplication The product of 1 and any number is that number. For any number n, $n \cdot 1 = n$ and $1 \cdot n = n$.

Propiedad de identidad de la multiplicación El producto de 1 y cualquier número es ese número. Para cualquier número n, $n \cdot 1 = n$ and $1 \cdot n = n$.

Illustrate To illustrate is to show or present information, usually as a drawing or a diagram. You can also illustrate a point using a written explanation.

Ilustrar Ilustrar es mostrar o presentar información, generalmente en forma de dibujo o diagrama. También puedes usar una explicación escrita para ilustrar un punto.

English/Spanish Glossary

Image An image is the result of a transformation of a point, line, or figure.

Imagen Una imagen es el resultado de una transformación de un punto, una recta o una figura.

Improper fraction An improper fraction is a fraction in which the numerator is greater than or equal to its denominator.

Fracción impropia Una fracción impropia es una fracción en la cual el numerador es mayor que o igual a su denominador.

Included angle An included angle is an angle that is between two sides.

Ángulo incluido Un ángulo incluido es un ángulo que está entre dos lados.

Included side An included side is a side that is between two angles.

Lado incluido Un lado incluido es un lado que está entre dos ángulos.

Income Money that a business receives. The money that a person earns from working is also called income.

Ingresos El dinero que un negocio recibe. El dinero que una persona gana de trabajar también es llamado los ingresos.

Income tax Income tax is money collected by the government based on how much you earn.

Impuesto de renta El impuesto de renta es dinero completo por el gobierno basado en cuánto gana.

Independent events Two events are independent events if the occurrence of one event does not affect the probability of the other event.

Eventos independientes Dos eventos son eventos independientes cuando el resultado de un evento no altera la probabilidad del otro.

Independent variable An independent variable is a variable whose value determines the value of another (dependent) variable.

Variable independiente Una variable independiente es una variable cuyo valor determina el valor de otra variable (dependiente).

Indicate To indicate is to point out or show.

Indicar Indicar es señalar o mostrar.

English/Spanish Glossary

Indirect measurement Indirect measurement uses proportions and similar triangles to measure distances that would be difficult to measure directly.

Medición indirecta La medición indirecta usa proporciones y triángulos semejantes para medir distancias que serían difíciles de medir de forma directa.

Inequality An inequality is a mathematical sentence that uses $<$, $\leq$, $>$, $\geq$, or $\neq$ to compare two quantities.

Desigualdad Una desigualdad es una oración matemática que usa $<$, $\leq$, $>$, $\geq$, o $\neq$ para comparar dos cantidades.

Inference An inference is a judgment made by interpreting data.

Inferencia Una inferencia es una opinión que se forma al interpretar datos.

Infinitely many solutions A linear equation in one variable has infinitely many solutions if any value of the variable makes the two sides of the equation equal.

Número infinito de soluciones Una ecuación lineal en una variable tiene un número infinito de soluciones si cualquier valor de la variable hace que los dos lados de la ecuación sean iguales.

Initial value The initial value of a linear function is the value of the output when the input is 0.

Valor inicial El valor inicial de una función lineal es el valor de salida cuando el valor de entrada es 0.

Integers Integers are the set of positive whole numbers, their opposites, and 0.

Enteros Los enteros son el conjunto de los números enteros positivos, sus opuestos y 0.

Interest When you deposit money in a bank account, the bank pays you interest for the right to use your money for a period of time.

Interés Cuando depositas dinero en una cuenta bancaria, el banco te paga un interés por el derecho a usar tu dinero por un período de tiempo.

Interest period The length of time on which compound interest is based. The total number of interest periods that you keep the money in the account is represented by the variable n.

Período de interés La cantidad de tiempo sobre la que se calcula el interés compuesto. El número total de períodos de interés que mantienes el dinero en la cuenta se representa con la variable n.

English/Spanish Glossary

Interest rate Interest is calculated based on a percent of the principal. That percent is called the interest rate (r).

Tasa de interés El interés se calcula con base en un porcentaje del capital. Ese porcentaje se llama tasa de interés, (r).

Interest rate for an interest period The interest rate for an interest period is the annual interest rate divided by the number of interest periods per year.

El tipo de interés por un período de interés El tipo de interés por un período de interés es el tipo de interés anual dividido por el número de períodos de interés por año.

Interquartile range The interquartile range (IQR) is the distance between the first and third quartiles of the data set. It represents the spread of the middle 50% of the data values.

Rango intercuartil El rango intercuartil es la distancia entre el primer y el tercer cuartil del conjunto de datos. Representa la ubicación del 50% del medio de los valores.

Interval An interval is a period of time between two points of time or events.

Intervalo Un intervalo es un período de tiempo entre dos puntos en el tiempo o entre dos sucesos.

Invalid inference An invalid inference is false about the population, or does not follow from the available data. A biased sample can lead to invalid inferences.

Inferencia inválida Una inferencia inválida es una inferencia falsa acerca de una población, o no se deduce a partir de los datos disponibles. Una muestra sesgada puede llevar a inferencias inválidas.

Inverse operations Inverse operations are operations that undo each other.

Operaciones inversas Las operaciones inversas son operaciones que se cancelan entre sí.

Inverse property of addition Every number has an additive inverse. The sum of a number and its additive inverse is zero.

Propiedad inversa de la suma Todos los números tienen un inverso de suma. La suma de un número y su inverso de suma es cero.

English/Spanish Glossary

Irrational numbers An irrational number is a number that cannot be written in the form $\frac{a}{b}$, where a and b are integers and $b \neq 0$. In decimal form, an irrational number cannot be written as a terminating or repeating decimal.

Números irracionales Un número irracional es un número que no se puede escribir en la forma $\frac{a}{b}$ donde a y b, son enteros y $b \neq 0$. Los números racionales en forma decimal no son finitos y no son periódicos.

Isolate a variable When solving equations, to isolate a variable means to get a variable with a coefficient of 1 alone on one side of an equation. Use the properties of equality and inverse operations to isolate a variable.

Aislar una variable Cuando resuelves ecuaciones, aislar una variable significa poner una variable con un coeficiente de 1 sola a un lado de la ecuación. Usa las propiedades de igualdad y las operaciones inversas para aislar una variable.

Isosceles triangle An isosceles triangle is a triangle with at least two sides that are the same length.

Triángulo isósceles Un triángulo isósceles es un triángulo que tiene al menos dos lados de la misma longitud.

J

Justify To justify is to support your answer with reasons or examples. A justification may include a written response, diagrams, charts, tables, or a combination of these.

Justificar Justificar es apoyar tu respuesta con razones o ejemplos. Una justificación puede incluir una respuesta escrita, diagramas, tablas o una combinación de esos elementos.

L

Lateral area of a cone The lateral area of a cone is the area of its lateral surface. The formula for the lateral area of a cone is L.A. $= \pi r \ell$, where r represents the radius of the base and ℓ represents the slant height of the cone.

Área lateral de un cono El área lateral de un cono es el área de su superficie lateral. La fórmula del área lateral de un cono es A.L. $= \pi r \ell$, donde r representa el radio de la base y ℓ representa la altura inclinada del cono.

English/Spanish Glossary

Lateral area of a cylinder The lateral area of a cylinder is the area of its lateral surface. The formula for the lateral area of a cylinder is L.A. = $2\pi rh$, where r represents the radius of a base and h represents the height of the cylinder.

Área lateral de un cilindro El área lateral de un cilindro es el área de su superficie lateral. La fórmula del área lateral de un cilindro es A.L. = $2\pi rh$, donde r representa el radio de una base y h representa la altura del cilindro.

Lateral area of a prism The lateral area of a prism is the sum of the areas of the lateral faces of the prism. The formula for the lateral area, L.A., of a prism is L.A. = ph, where p represents the perimeter of the base and h represents the height of the prism.

Área lateral de un prisma El área lateral de un prisma es la suma de las áreas de las caras laterales del prisma. La fórmula del área lateral, A.L., de un prisma es A.L. = ph, donde p representa el perímetro de la base y h representa la altura del prisma.

Lateral area of a pyramid The lateral area of a pyramid is the sum of the areas of the lateral faces of the pyramid. The formula for the lateral area, L.A., of a pyramid is L.A. = $\frac{1}{2}p\ell$ where p represents the perimeter of the base and ℓ represents the slant height of the pyramid.

Área lateral de una pirámide El área lateral de una pirámide es la suma de las áreas de las caras laterales de la pirámide. La fórmula del área lateral, A.L., de una pirámide es A.L. = $\frac{1}{2}p\ell$ donde p representa el perímetro de la base y ℓ representa la altura inclinada de la pirámide.

Lateral face of a prism A lateral face of a prism is a face that joins the bases of the prism.

Cara lateral de un prisma La cara lateral de un prisma es la cara que une a las bases del prisma.

Lateral face of a pyramid A lateral face of a pyramid is a triangular face that joins the base and the vertex.

Cara lateral de una pirámide La cara lateral de una pirámide es una cara lateral que une a la base con el vértice.

Lateral surface of a cone The lateral surface of a cone is the curved surface that is not included in the base.

Superficie lateral de un cono La superficie lateral de un cono es la superficie curva que no está incluida en la base.

English/Spanish Glossary

Lateral surface of a cylinder The lateral surface of a cylinder is the curved surface that is not included in the bases.

Superficie lateral de un cilindro La superficie lateral de un cilindro es la superficie curva que no está incluida en las bases.

Least common multiple The least common multiple (LCM) of two or more numbers is the least multiple shared by all of the numbers.

Mínimo común múltiplo El mínimo común múltiplo (MCM) de dos o más números es el múltiplo menor compartido por todos los números.

Leg of a right triangle In a right triangle, the two shortest sides are legs.

Cateto de un triángulo rectángulo En un triángulo rectángulo, los dos lados más cortos son los catetos.

Less than $<$ The less-than symbol shows a comparison of two numbers with the number of lesser value shown first, or on the left.

Menor que $<$ El símbolo de menor que muestra una comparación de dos números con el número de menor valor que aparece primero, o a la izquierda.

Liability A liability is money that you owe.

Obligación Una obligación es dinero que usted debe.

Lifetime income The amount of money earned over a lifetime of working.

Ingresos para toda la vida La cantidad de dinero ganó sobre una vida de trabajar.

Like terms Terms that have identical variable parts are like terms.

Términos semejantes Los términos que tienen partes variables idénticas son términos semejantes.

Line of reflection A line of reflection is a line across which a figure is reflected.

Eje de reflexión Un eje de reflexión es una línea a través de la cual se refleja una figura.

Linear equation An equation is a linear equation if the graph of all of its solutions is a line.

Ecuación lineal Una ecuación es lineal si la gráfica de todas sus soluciones es una línea recta.

English/Spanish Glossary

Linear function A linear function is a function whose graph is a straight line. The rate of change for a linear function is constant.

Función lineal Una función lineal es una función cuya gráfica es una línea recta. La tasa de cambio en una función lineal es constante.

Linear function rule A linear function rule is an equation that describes a linear function.

Regla de la función lineal La ecuación que describe una función lineal es la regla de la función lineal.

Loan A loan is an amount of money borrowed for a period of time with the promise of paying it back.

Préstamo Un préstamo es una cantidad de dinero pedido prestaddo por un espacio de tiempo con la promesa de pagarlo apoya.

Loan length Loan length is the period of time set to repay a loan.

Preste longitud La longitud del préstamo es el conjunto de espacio de tiempo de devolver un préstamo.

Loan term The term of a loan is the period of time set to repay the loan.

Preste término El término de un préstamo es el conjunto de espacio de tiempo de devolver el préstamo.

Locate To locate is to find or identify a value, usually on a number line or coordinate graph.

Ubicar Ubicar es hallar o identificar un valor, generalmente en una recta numérica o en una gráfica de coordenadas.

Loss When a business's expenses are greater than the business's income, there is a loss.

Pérdida Cuando los gastos de un negocio son más que los ingresos del negocio, hay una pérdida.

English/Spanish Glossary

M

Mapping diagram A mapping diagram describes a relation by linking the input values to the corresponding output values using arrows.

Diagrama de correspondencia Un diagrama de correspondencia describe una relación uniendo con flechas los valores de entrada con sus correspondientes valores de salida.

Markdown Markdown is the amount of decrease from the selling price to the sale price. The markdown as a percent decrease of the original selling price is called the percent markdown.

Rebaja La rebaja es la cantidad de disminución de un precio de venta a un precio rebajado. La rebaja como una disminución porcentual del precio de venta original se llama porcentaje de rebaja.

Markup Markup is the amount of increase from the cost to the selling price. The markup as a percent increase of the original cost is called the percent markup.

Margen de ganancia El margen de ganancia es la cantidad de aumento del costo al precio de venta. El margen de ganancia como un aumento porcentual del costo original se llama porcentaje del margen de ganancia.

Mean The mean represents the center of a numerical data set. To find the mean, sum the data values and then divide by the number of values in the data set.

Media La media representa el centro de un conjunto de datos numéricos. Para hallar la media, suma los valores y luego divide por el número de valores del conjunto de datos.

Mean absolute deviation The mean absolute deviation is a measure of variability that describes how much the data values are spread out from the mean of a data set. The mean absolute deviation is the average distance that the data values are spread around the mean.

mean absolute deviation =

$$\frac{\text{sum of the absolute deviations of the data values}}{\text{total number of data values}}$$

Desviación absoluta media La desviación absoluta media es una medida de variabilidad que describe cuánto se alejan los valores de la media de un conjunto de datos. La desviación absoluta media es la distancia promedio que los valores se alejan de la media. desviación absoluta media =

$$\frac{\text{suma de las desviaciones absolutas de los valores}}{\text{número total de valores}}$$

English/Spanish Glossary

Measure of variability A measure of variability describes the spread of values in a data set. There may be more than one measure of variability for a data set.

Medida de variabilidad Una medida de variabilidad describe la distribución de los valores de un conjunto de datos. Puede haber más de una medida de variabilidad para un conjunto de datos.

Measurement data Measurement data consist of data that are measures.

Datos de mediciones Los datos de mediciones son datos que son medidas.

Measures of center A measure of center is a value that represents the middle of a data set. There may be more than one measure of center for a data set.

Medida de tendencia central Una medida de tendencia central es un valor que representa el centro de un conjunto de datos. Puede haber más de una medida de tendencia central para un conjunto de datos.

Median The median represents the center of a numerical data set. For an odd number of data values, the median is the middle value when the data values are arranged in numerical order. For an even number of data values, the median is the average of the two middle values when the data values are arranged in numerical order.

Mediana La mediana representa el centro de un conjunto de datos numéricos. Para un número impar de valores, la mediana es el valor del medio cuando los valores están organizados en orden numérico. Para un número par de valores, la mediana es el promedio de los dos valores del medio cuando los valores están organizados en orden numérico.

Median-median line The median-median line, or median trend line, is a method of finding a fit line for a scatter plot that suggests a linear association. This method involves dividing the data into three subgroups and using medians to find a summary point for each subgroup. The summary points are used to find the equation of the fit line.

Recta mediana-mediana La recta mediana-mediana es un método que se usa para hallar una línea de ajuste para un diagrama de dispersión que sugiere una asociación lineal. Este método implica dividir los datos en tres subgrupos y usar medianas para hallar un punto medio para cada subgrupo. Los puntos medios se usan para hallar la ecuación de la línea de ajuste.

Million Whole numbers in the millions have 7, 8, or 9 digits.

Millón Los números enteros no negativos que están en los millones tienen 7, 8 ó 9 dígitos.

English/Spanish Glossary

Mixed number A mixed number combines a whole number and a fraction.

Número mixto Un número mixto combina un número entero no negativo con una fracción.

Mode The item, or items, in a data set that occurs most frequently.

Modo El artículo, o los artículos, en un conjunto de datos que ocurre normalmente.

Model To model is to represent a situation using pictures, diagrams, or number sentences.

Demostrar Demostrar es usar ilustraciones, diagramas o enunciados numéricos para representar una situación.

Monetary incentive A monetary incentive is an offer that might encourage customers to buy a product.

Estímulo monetario Un estímulo monetario es una oferta que quizás favorezca a clientes para comprar un producto.

Multiple A multiple of a number is the product of the number and a whole number.

Múltiplo El múltiplo de un número es el producto del número y un número entero no negativo.

N

Natural numbers The natural numbers are the counting numbers.

Números naturales Los números naturales son los números que se usan para contar.

Negative exponent property For every nonzero number a and integer n, $a^{-n} = \frac{1}{a^n}$.

Propiedad del exponente negativo Para todo número distinto de cero a y entero n, $a^{-n} = \frac{1}{a^n}$.

Negative numbers Negative numbers are numbers less than zero.

Números negativos Los números negativos son números menores que cero.

English/Spanish Glossary

Net A net is a two-dimensional pattern that you can fold to form a three-dimensional figure. A net of a figure shows all of the surfaces of that figure in one view.

Modelo plano Un modelo plano es un diseño bidimensional que puedes doblar para formar una figura tridimensional. Un modelo plano de una figura muestra todas las superficies de la figura en una vista.

Net worth Net worth is the total value of all assets minus the total value of all liabilities.

Patrimonio neto El patrimonio neto es el valor total de todas las ventajas menos el valor total de todas las obligaciones.

Net worth statement Net worth is the total value of all assets minus the total value of all liabilities.

Declaración de patrimonio neto El patrimonio neto es el valor total de todas las ventajas menos el valor total de todas las obligaciones.

No solution A linear equation in one variable has no solution if no value of the variable makes the two sides of the equation equal.

Sin solución Una ecuación lineal en una variable no tiene solución si ningún valor de la variable hace que los dos lados de la ecuación sean iguales.

Nonlinear function A nonlinear function is a function that does not have a constant rate of change.

Función no lineal Una función no lineal es una función que no tiene una tasa de cambio constante.

Numerator The numerator is the number above the fraction bar in a fraction.

Numerador El numerador es el número que está arriba de la barra de fracción en una fracción.

Numerical expression A numerical expression is a mathematical phrase that consists of numbers and operation symbols.

Expresión numérica Una expresión numérica es una frase matemática que contiene números y símbolos de operaciones.

English/Spanish Glossary

O

Obtuse angle An obtuse angle is an angle with a measure greater than 90° and less than 180°.

Ángulo obtuso Un ángulo obtuso es un ángulo con una medida mayor que 90° y menor que 180°.

Obtuse triangle An obtuse triangle is a triangle with one obtuse angle.

Triángulo obtusángulo Un triángulo obtusángulo es un triángulo que tiene un ángulo obtuso.

Octagon An octagon is a polygon with eight sides.

Octágono Un octágono es un polígono de ocho lados.

Online payment system An online payment system allows money to be exchanged electronically between buyer and seller, usually using credit card or bank account information.

Sistema en línea de pago Un sistema en línea del pago permite dinero para ser cambiado electrónicamente entre comprador y vendedor, utilizando generalmente información de tarjeta de crédito o cuenta bancaria.

Open sentence An open sentence is an equation with one or more variables.

Enunciado abierto Un enunciado abierto es una ecuación con una o más variables.

Opposites Opposites are two numbers that are the same distance from 0 on a number line, but in opposite directions.

Opuestos Los opuestos son dos números que están a la misma distancia de 0 en la recta numérica, pero en direcciones opuestas.

Order of operations The order of operations is the order in which operations should be performed in an expression. Operations inside parentheses are done first, followed by exponents. Then, multiplication and division are done in order from left to right, and finally addition and subtraction are done in order from left to right.

Orden de las operaciones El orden de las operaciones es el orden en el que se deben resolver las operaciones de una expresión. Las operaciones que están entre paréntesis se resuelven primero, seguidas de los exponentes. Luego, se multiplica y se divide en orden de izquierda a derecha, y finalmente se suma y se resta en orden de izquierda a derecha.

English/Spanish Glossary

Ordered pair An ordered pair identifies the location of a point in the coordinate plane. The *x*-coordinate shows a point's position left or right of the *y*-axis. The *y*-coordinate shows a point's position up or down from the *x*-axis.

Par ordenado Un par ordenado identifica la ubicación de un punto en el plano de coordenadas. La coordenada *x* muestra la posición de un punto a la izquierda o a la derecha del eje de las *y*. La coordenada *y* muestra la posición de un punto arriba o abajo del eje de las *x*.

Origin The origin is the point of intersection of the *x*- and *y*-axes on a coordinate plane.

Origen El origen es el punto de intersección del eje de las *x* y el eje de las *y* en un plano de coordenadas.

Outcome An outcome is a possible result of an action.

Resultado Un resultado es un desenlace posible de una acción.

Outlier An outlier is a piece of data that doesn't seem to fit with the rest of a data set.

Valor extremo Un valor extremo es un valor que parece no ajustarse al resto de los datos de un conjunto.

P

Parallel lines Parallel lines are lines in the same plane that never intersect.

Rectas paralelas Las rectas paralelas son rectas que están en el mismo plano y nunca se intersecan.

Parallelogram A parallelogram is a quadrilateral with both pairs of opposite sides parallel.

Paralelogramo Un paralelogramo es un cuadrilátero en el cual los dos pares de lados opuestos son paralelos.

Partial product A partial product is part of the total product. A product is the sum of the partial products.

Producto parcial Un producto parcial es una parte del producto total. Un producto es la suma de los productos parciales.

English/Spanish Glossary

Pay period Wages for many jobs are paid at regular intervals, such a weekly, biweekly, semimonthly, or monthly. The interval of time is called a pay period.

Pague el período Los sueldos para muchos trabajos son pagados con regularidad, tal semanal, quincenal, quincenal, o mensual. El intervalo de tiempo es llamado un período de la paga.

Payroll deductions Your employer can deduct your income taxes from your wages before you receive your paycheck. The amounts deducted are called payroll deductions.

Deducciones de nómina Su empleador puede descontar sus impuestos de renta de sus sueldos antes que reciba su cheque de pago. Las cantidades descontadas son llamadas nómina deducciones.

Percent A percent is a ratio that compares a number to 100.

Porcentaje Un porcentaje es una razón que compara un número con 100.

Percent bar graph A percent bar graph is a bar graph that shows each category as a percent of the total number of data items.

Gráfico de barras de por ciento Un gráfico de barras del por ciento es un gráfico de barras que muestra cada categoría como un por ciento del número total de artículos de datos.

Percent decrease When a quantity decreases, the percent of change is called a percent decrease. percent decrease =

$$\frac{\text{amount of decrease}}{\text{original quantity}}$$

Disminución porcentual Cuando una cantidad disminuye, el porcentaje de cambio se llama disminución porcentual. disminución porcentual =

$$\frac{\text{cantidad de disminución}}{\text{cantidad original}}$$

Percent equation The percent equation describes the relationship between a part and a whole. You can use the percent equation to solve percent problems. part = percent · whole

Ecuación de porcentaje La ecuación de porcentaje describe la relación entre una parte y un todo. Puedes usar la ecuación de porcentaje para resolver problemas de porcentaje. parte = por ciento · todo

Percent error Percent error describes the accuracy of a measured or estimated value compared to an actual or accepted value.

Error porcentual El error porcentual describe la exactitud de un valor medido o estimado en comparación con un valor real o aceptado.

English/Spanish Glossary

Percent increase When a quantity increases, the percent of change is called a percent increase.

Aumento porcentual Cuando una cantidad aumenta, el porcentaje de cambio se llama aumento porcentual.

Percent of change Percent of change is the percent something increases or decreases from its original measure or amount. You can find the percent of change by using the equation: percent of change = amount of change original quantity

Porcentaje de cambio El porcentaje de cambio es el porcentaje en que algo aumenta o disminuye en relación a la medida o cantidad original. Puedes hallar el porcentaje de cambio con la siguiente ecuación: porcentaje de cambio = cantidad de cambio cantidad original

Perfect cube A perfect cube is the cube of an integer.

Cubo perfecto Un cubo perfecto es el cubo de un entero.

Perfect square A perfect square is a number that is the square of an integer.

Cuadrado perfecto Un cuadrado perfecto es un número que es el cuadrado de un entero.

Perlmeter Perimeter is the distance around a figure.

Perímetro El perímetro es la distancia alrededor de una figura.

Period A period is a group of 3 digits in a number. Periods are separated by a comma and start from the right of a number.

Período Un período es un grupo de 3 dígitos en un número. Los períodos están separados por una coma y empiezan a la derecha del número.

Periodic savings plan A periodic savings plan is a method of saving that involves making deposits on a regular basis.

Plan de ahorros periódico Un plan de ahorros periódico es un método de guardar que implica depósitos que hace con regularidad.

Perpendicular lines Perpendicular lines intersect to form right angles.

Rectas perpendiculares Las rectas perpendiculares se intersecan para formar ángulos rectos.

English/Spanish Glossary

Pi Pi (π) is the ratio of a circle's circumference, C, to its diameter, d.

Pi Pi (π) es la razón de la circunferencia de un círculo, C, a su diámetro, d.

Place value Place value is the value given to an individual digit based on its position within a number.

Valor posicional El valor posicional es el valor asignado a determinado dígito según su posición en un número.

Plane A plane is a flat surface that extends indefinitely in all directions.

Plano Un plano es una superficie plana que se extiende indefinidamente en todas direcciones.

Polygon A polygon is a closed figure formed by three or more line segments that do not cross.

Polígono Un polígono es una figura cerrada compuesta por tres o más segmentos que no se cruzan.

Population A population is the complete set of items being studied.

Población Una población es todo el conjunto de elementos que se estudian.

Positive numbers Positive numbers are numbers greater than zero.

Números positivos Los números positivos son números mayores que cero.

Power A power is a number expressed using an exponent.

Potencia Una potencia es un número expresado con un exponente.

Predict To predict is to make an educated guess based on the analysis of real data.

Predecir Predecir es hacer una estimación informada según el análisis de datos reales.

Prime factorization The prime factorization of a composite number is the expression of the number as a product of its prime factors.

Descomposición en factores primos La descomposición en factores primos de un número compuesto es la expresión del número como un producto de sus factores primos.

English/Spanish Glossary

Prime number A prime number is a whole number greater than 1 with exactly two factors, 1 and the number itself.

Número primo Un número primo es un número entero mayor que 1 con exactamente dos factores, 1 y el número mismo.

Principal The original amount of money deposited or borrowed in an account.

Capital La cantidad original de dinero que se deposita o se pide prestada en una cuenta.

Prism A prism is a three-dimensional figure with two parallel polygonal faces that are the same size and shape.

Prisma Un prisma es una figura tridimensional con dos caras poligonales paralelas que tienen el mismo tamaño y la misma forma.

Probability model A probability model consists of an action, its sample space, and a list of events with their probabilities. The events and probabilities in the list have these characteristics: each outcome in the sample space is in exactly one event, and the sum of all of the probabilities must be 1.

Modelo de probabilidad Un modelo de probabilidad consiste en una acción, su espacio muestral y una lista de eventos con sus probabilidades. Los eventos y las probabilidades de la lista tienen estas características: cada resultado del espacio muestral está exactamente en un evento, y la suma de todas las probabilidades debe ser 1.

Probability of an event The probability of an event is a number from 0 to 1 that measures the likelihood that the event will occur. The closer the probability is to 0, the less likely it is that the event will happen. The closer the probability is to 1, the more likely it is that the event will happen. You can express probability as a fraction, decimal, or percent.

Probabilidad de un evento La probabilidad de un evento es un número de 0 a 1 que mide la probabilidad de que suceda el evento. Cuanto más se acerca la probabilidad a 0, menos probable es que suceda el evento. Cuanto más se acerca la probabilidad a 1, más probable es que suceda el evento. Puedes expresar la probabilidad como una fracción, un decimal o un porcentaje.

Product A product is the value of a multiplication or an expression showing multiplication.

Producto Un producto es el valor de una multiplicación o una expresión que representa la multiplicación.

English/Spanish Glossary

Profit When a business's expenses are less than the business's income, there is a profit.

Ganancia Cuando los gastos de un negocio son menos que los ingresos del negocio, hay una ganancia.

Proof A proof is a logical, deductive argument in which every statement of fact is supported by a reason.

Comprobación Una comprobación es un argumento lógico y deductivo en el que cada enunciado de un hecho está apoyado por una razón.

Proper fraction A proper fraction has a numerator that is less than its denominator.

Fracción propia Una fracción propia tiene un numerador que es menor que su denominador.

Proportion A proportion is an equation stating that two ratios are equal.

Proporción Una proporción es una ecuación que establece que dos razones son iguales.

Proportional relationship Two quantities x and y have a proportional relationship if y is always a constant multiple of x. A relationship is proportional if it can be described by equivalent ratios.

Relación de proporción Dos cantidades x y y tienen una relación de proporción si y es siempre un múltiplo constante de x. Una relación es de proporción si se puede describir con razones equivalentes.

Pyramid A pyramid is a three-dimensional figure with a base that is a polygon and triangular faces that meet at a vertex. A pyramid is named for the shape of its base.

Pirámide Una pirámide es una figura tridimensional con una base que es un polígono y caras triangulares que se unen en un vértice. El nombre de la pirámide depende de la forma de su base.

English/Spanish Glossary

Pythagorean Theorem In any right triangle, the sum of the squares of the lengths of the legs equals the square of the length of the hypotenuse. If a triangle is a right triangle, then $a^2 + b^2 = c^2$, where a and b represent the lengths of the legs, and c represents the length of the hypotenuse.

Teorema de Pitágoras En cualquier triángulo rectángulo, la suma del cuadrado de la longitud de los catetos es igual al cuadrado de la longitud de la hipotenusa. Si un triángulo es un triángulo rectángulo, entonces $a^2 + b^2 = c^2$, donde a y b representan la longitud de los catetos, y c representa la longitud de la hipotenusa.

Quadrant The x- and y-axes divide the coordinate plane into four regions called quadrants.

Cuadrante Los ejes de las x y de las y dividen el plano de coordenadas en cuatro regiones llamadas cuadrantes.

Quadrilateral A quadrilateral is a polygon with four sides.

Cuadrilátero Un cuadrilátero es un polígono de cuatro lados.

Quarter circle A quarter circle is one fourth of a circle.

Círculo cuarto Un círculo cuarto es la cuarta parte de un círculo.

Quartile The quartiles of a data set divide the data set into four parts with the same number of data values in each part.

Cuartil Los cuartiles de un conjunto de datos dividen el conjunto de datos en cuatro partes que tienen el mismo número de valores cada una.

Quotient The quotient is the answer to a division problem. When there is a remainder, "quotient" sometimes refers to the whole-number portion of the answer.

Cociente El cociente es el resultado de una división. Cuando queda un residuo, "cociente" a veces se refiere a la parte de la solución que es un número entero.

English/Spanish Glossary

R

Radius A radius of a circle is a segment that has one endpoint at the center and the other endpoint on the circle. The term radius can also mean the length of this segment.

Radio Un radio de un círculo es un segmento que tiene un extremo en el centro y el otro extremo en el círculo. El término radio también puede referirse a la longitud de este segmento.

Radius of a sphere The radius of a sphere, r, is a segment that has one endpoint at the center and the other endpoint on the sphere.

Radio de una esfera El radio de una esfera, r, es un segmento que tiene un extremo en el centro y el otro extremo en la esfera.

Random sample In a random sample, each member in the population has an equal chance of being selected.

Muestra aleatoria En una muestra aleatoria, cada miembro en la población tiene una oportunidad igual de ser seleccionado.

Range The range is a measure of variability of a numerical data set. The range of a data set is the difference between the greatest and least values in a data set.

Rango El rango es una medida de la variabilidad de un conjunto de datos numéricos. El rango de un conjunto de datos es la diferencia que existe entre el mayor y el menor valor del conjunto.

Rate A rate is a ratio involving two quantities measured in different units.

Tasa Una tasa es una razón que relaciona dos cantidades medidas con unidades diferentes.

Rate of change The rate of change of a linear function is the ratio vertical change horizontal change between any two points on the graph of the function.

Tasa de cambio La tasa de cambio de una función lineal es la razón del cambio vertical cambio horizontal que existe entre dos puntos cualesquiera de la gráfica de la función.

Ratio A ratio is a relationship in which for every x units of one quantity there are y units of another quantity.

Razón Una razón es una relación en la cual por cada x unidades de una cantidad hay y unidades de otra cantidad.

English/Spanish Glossary

Rational numbers A rational number is a number that can be written in the form $\frac{a}{b}$ or $-\frac{a}{b}$, where a is a whole number and b is a positive whole number. The rational numbers include the integers.

Números racionales Un número racional es un número que se puede escribir como $\frac{a}{b}$ or $-\frac{a}{b}$, donde a es un número entero no negativo y b es un número entero positivo. Los números racionales incluyen los enteros.

Real numbers The real numbers are the set of rational and irrational numbers.

Números reales Los números reales son el conjunto de los números racionales e irracionales.

Reason To reason is to think through a problem using facts and information.

Razonar Razonar es usar hechos e información para estudiar detenidamente un problema.

Rebate A rebate returns part of the purchase price of an item after the buyer provides proof of purchase through a mail-in or online form.

Reembolso Un reembolso regresa la parte del precio de compra de un artículo después de que el comprador proporcione comprobante de compra por un correo-en o forma en línea.

Recall To recall is to remember a fact quickly.

Recordar Recordar es traer a la memoria un hecho rápidamente.

Reciprocals Two numbers are reciprocals if their product is 1. If a nonzero number is named as a fraction,   , then its reciprocal is   .

Recíprocos Dos números son recíprocos si su producto es 1. Si un número distinto de cero se expresa como una fracción,   , entonces su recíproco es   .

Rectangle A rectangle is a quadrilateral with four right angles.

Rectángulo Un rectángulo es un cuadrilátero que tiene cuatro ángulos rectos.

Rectangular prism A rectangular prism is a prism with bases in the shape of a rectangle.

Prisma rectangular Un prisma rectangular es un prisma cuyas bases tienen la forma de un rectángulo.

English/Spanish Glossary

Reduction A reduction is a dilation with a scale factor less than 1. After a reduction, the image is smaller than the original figure.

Reducción Una reducción es una dilatación con un factor de escala menor que 1. Después de una reducción, la imagen es más pequeña que la figura original.

Reflection A reflection, or flip, is a transformation that flips a figure across a line of reflection.

Reflexión Una reflexión, o inversión, es una transformación que invierte una figura a través de un eje de reflexión.

Regular polygon A regular polygon is a polygon with all sides of equal length and all angles of equal measure.

Polígono regular Un polígono regular es un polígono que tiene todos los lados de la misma longitud y todos los ángulos de la misma medida.

Relate To relate two different things, find a connection between them.

Relacionar Para relacionar dos cosas diferentes, halla una conexión entre ellas.

Relation Any set of ordered pairs is called a relation.

Relación Todo conjunto de pares ordenados se llama relación.

Relative frequency relative frequency

of an event $= \dfrac{\text{number of times event occurs}}{\text{total number of trials}}$

Frecuencia relativa frecuencia relativa de un evento $=$

$\dfrac{\text{número de veces que sucede el evento}}{\text{número total de pruebas}}$

Relative frequency table A relative frequency table shows the ratio of the number of data in each category to the total number of data items. The ratio can be expressed as a fraction, decimal, or percent.

Mesa relativa de frecuencia Una mesa relativa de la frecuencia muestra la proporción del número de datos en cada categoría al número total de artículos de datos. La proporción puede ser expresada como una fracción, el decimal, o el por ciento.

Remainder In division, the remainder is the number that is left after the division is complete.

Residuo En una división, el residuo es el número que queda después de terminar la operación.

English/Spanish Glossary

Remote interior angles Remote interior angles are the two nonadjacent interior angles corresponding to each exterior angle of a triangle.

Ángulos internos no adyacentes Los ángulos internos no adyacentes son los dos ángulos internos de un triángulo que se corresponden con el ángulo externo que está más alejado de ellos.

Repeating decimal A repeating decimal has a decimal expansion that repeats the same digit, or block of digits, without end.

Decimal periódico Un decimal periódico tiene una expansión decimal que repite el mismo dígito, o grupo de dígitos, sin fin.

Represent To represent is to stand for or take the place of something else. Symbols, equations, charts, and tables are often used to represent particular situations.

Representar Representar es sustituir u ocupar el lugar de otra cosa. A menudo se usan símbolos, ecuaciones y tablas para representar determinadas situaciones.

Representative sample A representative sample is a sample of a population in which the number of subjects in the sample with the trait that you are studying is proportional to the number of members in the population with that trait. A representative sample accurately represents the population and does not have bias.

Muestra representativa Una muestra representativa es una muestra de una población en la que el número de sujetos de la muestra que tiene la característica que se estudia es proporcional al número de miembros de la población que tienen esa característica. Una muestra representativa representa la población con exactitud y no está sesgada.

Rhombus A rhombus is a parallelogram whose sides are all the same length.

Rombo Un rombo es un paralelogramo que tiene todos sus lados de la misma longitud.

Right angle A right angle is an angle with a measure of 90°.

Ángulo recto Un ángulo recto es un ángulo que mide 90°.

Right cone A right cone is a cone in which the segment representing the height connects the vertex and the center of the base.

Cono recto Un cono recto es un cono en el que el segmento que representa la altura une el vértice y el centro de la base.

English/Spanish Glossary

Right cylinder A right cylinder is a cylinder in which the height joins the centers of the bases.

Cilindro recto Un cilindro recto es un cilindro en el que la altura une los centros de las bases.

Right prism In a right prism, all lateral faces are rectangles.

Prisma recto En un prisma recto, todas las caras laterales son rectángulos.

Right pyramid In a right pyramid, the segment that represents the height intersects the base at its center.

Pirámide recta En una pirámide recta, el segmento que representa la altura interseca la base en el centro.

Right triangle A right triangle is a triangle with one right angle.

Triángulo rectángulo Un triángulo rectángulo es un triángulo que tiene un ángulo recto.

Rigid motion A rigid motion is a transformation that changes only the position of a figure.

Movimiento rígido Un movimiento rígido es una transformación que sólo cambia la posición de una figura.

Rotation A rotation is a rigid motion that turns a figure around a fixed point, called the center of rotation.

Rotación Una rotación es un movimiento rígido que hace girar una figura alrededor de un punto fijo, llamado centro de rotación.

Rounding Rounding a number means replacing the number with a number that tells about how much or how many.

Redondear Redondear un número significa reemplazar ese número por un número que indica más o menos cuánto o cuántos.

S

Sale A sale is a discount offered by a store. A sale does not require the customer to have a coupon.

Venta Una venta es un descuento ofreció por una tienda. Una venta no requiere al cliente a tener un cupón.

English/Spanish Glossary

Sales tax A tax added to the price of goods and services.

Las ventas tasan Un impuesto añadió al precio de bienes y servicios.

Sample of a population A sample of a population is part of the population. A sample is useful when you want to find out about a population but you do not have the resources to study every member of the population.

Muestra de una población Una muestra de una población es una parte de la población. Una muestra es útil cuando quieres saber algo acerca de una población, pero no tienes los recursos para estudiar a cada miembro de esa población.

Sample space The sample space for an action is the set of all possible outcomes of that action.

Espacio muestral El espacio muestral de una acción es el conjunto de todos los resultados posibles de esa acción.

Sampling method A sampling method is the method by which you choose members of a population to sample.

Método de muestreo Un método de muestreo es el método por el cual escoges miembros de una población para muestrear.

Savings Savings is money that a person puts away for use at a later date.

Ahorros Los ahorros son dinero que una persona guarda para el uso en una fecha posterior.

Scale A scale is a ratio that compares a length in a scale drawing to the corresponding length in the actual object.

Escala Una escala es una razón que compara una longitud en un dibujo a escala con la longitud correspondiente en el objeto real.

Scale drawing A scale drawing is an enlarged or reduced drawing of an object that is proportional to the actual object.

Dibujo a escala Un dibujo a escala es un dibujo ampliado o reducido de un objeto que es proporcional al objeto real.

English/Spanish Glossary

Scale factor The scale factor is the ratio of a length in the image to the corresponding length in the original figure.

Factor de escala El factor de escala es la razón de una longitud de la imagen a la longitud correspondiente en la figura original.

Scalene triangle A scalene triangle is a triangle in which no sides have the same length.

Triángulo escaleno Un triángulo escaleno es un triángulo que no tiene lados de la misma longitud.

Scatter plot A scatter plot is a graph that uses points to display the relationship between two different sets of data. Each point can be represented by an ordered pair.

Diagrama de dispersión Un diagrama de dispersión es una gráfica que usa puntos para mostrar la relación entre dos conjuntos de datos diferentes. Cada punto se puede representar con un par ordenado.

Scholarship A type of monetary award a student can use to pay for his or her education. The student does not need to repay this money.

Beca Un tipo de premio monetario que un estudiante puede utilizar para pagar por su educación. El estudiante no debe devolver este dinero.

Scientific notation A number in scientific notation is written as the product of two factors, one greater than or equal to 1 and less than 10, and the other a power of 10.

Notación científica Un número en notación científica está escrito como el producto de dos factores, uno mayor que o igual a 1 y menor que 10, y el otro una potencia de 10.

Segment A segment is part of a line. It consists of two endpoints and all of the points on the line between the endpoints.

Segmento Un segmento es una parte de una recta. Está formado por dos extremos y todos los puntos de la recta que están entre los extremos.

Semicircle A semicircle is one half of a circle.

Semicírculo Un semicírculo es la mitad de un círculo.

English/Spanish Glossary

Similar figures A two-dimensional figure is similar to another two-dimensional figure if you can map one figure to the other by a sequence of rotations, reflections, translations, and dilations.

Figuras semejantes Una figura bidimensional es semejante a otra figura bidimensional si puedes hacer corresponder una figura con otra mediante una secuencia de rotaciones, reflexiones, traslaciones y dilataciones.

Simple interest Simple interest is interest paid only on an original deposit. To calculate simple interest, use the formula where I is the simple interest, p is the principal, r is the annual interest rate, and t is the number of years that the account earns interest.

Interés simple El interés simple es el interés que se paga sobre un depósito original solamente. Para calcular el interés simple, usa la fórmula donde I es el interés simple, c es el capital, r es la tasa de interés anual y t es el número de años en que la cuenta obtiene un interés.

Simple random sampling Simple random sampling is a sampling method in which every member of the population has an equal chance of being chosen for the sample.

Muestreo aleatorio simple El muestreo aleatorio simple es un método de muestreo en el que cada miembro de la población tiene la misma probabilidad de ser seleccionado para la muestra.

Simpler form A fraction is in simpler form when it is equivalent to a given fraction and has smaller numbers in the numerator and denominator.

Forma simplificada Una fracción está en su forma simplificada cuando es equivalente a otra fracción dada, pero tiene números más pequeños en el numerador y el denominador.

Simplest form A fraction is in simplest form when the only common factor of the numerator and denominator is one.

Mínima expresión Una fracción está en su mínima expresión cuando el único factor común del numerador y el denominador es 1.

Simplify an algebraic expression To simplify an algebraic expression, combine the like terms of the expression.

Simplificar una expresión algebraica Para simplificar una expresión algebraica, combina los términos semejantes de la expresión.

English/Spanish Glossary

Simulation A simulation is a model of a real-world situation that is used to find probabilities.

Simulación Una simulación es un modelo de una situación de la vida diaria que se usa para hallar probabilidades.

Sketch To sketch a figure, draw a rough outline. When a sketch is asked for, it means that a drawing needs to be included in your response.

Bosquejo Para hacer un bosquejo, dibuja un esquema simple. Si se pide un bosquejo, tu respuesta debe incluir un dibujo.

Slant height of a cone The slant height of a cone, ℓ, is the length of its lateral surface from base to vertex.

Altura inclinada de un cono La altura inclinada de un cono, ℓ, es la longitud de su superficie lateral desde la base hasta el vértice.

Slant height of a pyramid The slant height of a pyramid is the height of a lateral face.

Altura inclinada de una pirámide La altura inclinada de una pirámide es la altura de una cara lateral.

Slope Slope is a ratio that describes steepness.

$$\text{slope} = \frac{\text{vertical change}}{\text{horizontal change}} = \frac{\text{rise}}{\text{run}}$$

Pendiente La pendiente es una razón que describe la inclinación.

$$\text{pendiente} = \frac{\text{cambio vertical}}{\text{cambio horizontal}}$$
$$= \frac{\text{distancia vertical}}{\text{distancia horizontal}}$$

Slope of a line slope =

$$\frac{\text{change in } y\text{-coordinates}}{\text{change in } x\text{-coordinates}} = \frac{\text{rise}}{\text{run}}$$

Pendiente de una recta pendiente =

$$\frac{\text{cambio en las coordenadas } y}{\text{cambio en las coordenadas } x}$$
$$= \frac{\text{distancia vertical}}{\text{distancia horizontal}}$$

Slope-intercept form An equation written in the form $y = mx + b$ is in slope-intercept form. The graph is a line with slope m and y-intercept b.

Forma pendiente-intercepto Una ecuación escrita en la forma $y = mx + b$ está en forma de pendiente-intercepto. La gráfica es una línea recta con pendiente m e intercepto en y b.

English/Spanish Glossary

Solution of a system of linear equations A solution of a system of linear equations is any ordered pair that makes all the equations of that system true.

Solución de un sistema de ecuaciones lineales Una solución de un sistema de ecuaciones lineales es cualquier par ordenado que hace que todas las ecuaciones de ese sistema sean verdaderas.

Solution of an equation A solution of an equation is a value of the variable that makes the equation true.

Solución de una ecuación Una solución de una ecuación es un valor de la variable que hace que la ecuación sea verdadera.

Solution of an inequality The solutions of an inequality are the values of the variable that make the inequality true.

Solución de una desigualdad Las soluciones de una desigualdad son los valores de la variable que hacen que la desigualdad sea verdadera.

Solution set A solution set contains all of the numbers that satisfy an equation or inequality.

Conjunto solución Un conjunto solución contiene todos los números que satisfacen una ecuación o desigualdad.

Solve To solve a given statement, determine the value or values that make the statement true. Several methods and strategies can be used to solve a problem, including estimating, isolating the variable, drawing a graph, or using a table of values.

Resolver Para resolver un enunciado dado, determina el valor o los valores que hacen que ese enunciado sea verdadero. Para resolver un problema se pueden usar varios métodos y estrategias, como estimar, aislar la variable, dibujar una gráfica o usar una tabla de valores.

Sphere A sphere is the set of all points in space that are the same distance from a center point.

Esfera Una esfera es el conjunto de todos los puntos en el espacio que están a la misma distancia de un punto central.

Square A square is a quadrilateral with four right angles and all sides the same length.

Cuadrado Un cuadrado es un cuadrilátero que tiene cuatro ángulos rectos y todos los lados de la misma longitud.

English/Spanish Glossary

Square root A square root of a number is a number that, when multiplied by itself, equals the original number.

Raíz cuadrada La raíz cuadrada de un número es un número que, cuando se multiplica por sí mismo, es igual al número original.

Square unit A square unit is the area of a square that has sides that are 1 unit long.

Unidad cuadrada Una unidad cuadrada es el área de un cuadrado en el que cada lado mide 1 unidad de longitud.

Standard form A number written using digits and place value is in standard form.

Forma estándar Un número escrito con dígitos y valor posicional está escrito en forma estándar.

Statistical question A statistical question is a question that investigates an aspect of the real world and can have variety in the responses.

Pregunta estadística Una pregunta estadística es una pregunta que investiga un aspecto de la vida diaria y puede tener varias respuestas.

Statistics Statistics is the study of collecting, organizing, graphing, and analyzing data to draw conclusions about the real world.

Estadística La estadística es el estudio de la recolección, organización, representación gráfica y análisis de datos para sacar conclusiones sobre la vida diaria.

Stem-and-leaf plot A stem-and-leaf plot is a graph that uses the digits of each number to show the data distribution. Each data item is broken into a stem and into a leaf. The leaf is the last digit of the data value. The stem is the other digit or digits of the data value.

Complot de tallo y hoja Un complot del tallo y la hoja es un gráfico que utiliza los dígitos de cada número para mostrar la distribución de datos. Cada artículo de datos es roto en un tallo y en una hoja. La hoja es el último dígito de los datos valora. El tallo es el otro dígito o los dígitos de los datos valoran.

Stored-value card A stored-value card is a prepaid card electronically coded to be worth a specified amount of money.

Tarjeta de almacenado-valor Una tarjeta del almacenado-valor es una tarjeta pagada por adelantado codificó electrónicamente valer una cantidad especificado de dinero.

English/Spanish Glossary

Straight angle A straight angle is an angle with a measure of 180°.

Ángulo llano Un ángulo llano es un ángulo que mide 180°.

Student Loan A student loan provides money to a student to pay for college. The student needs to repay the loan after leaving college. Often the student will need to pay interest on the amount of the loan.

Crédito personal para estudiantes Un crédito personal para estudiantes le proporciona dinero a un estudiante para pagar por el colegio. El estudiante debe devolver el préstamo después de dejar el colegio. A menudo el estudiante deberá pagar interés en la cantidad del préstamo.

Subject Each member in a sample is a subject.

Sujeto Cada miembro de una muestra es un sujeto.

Sum The sum is the answer to an addition problem.

Suma o total La suma o total es el resultado de una operación de suma.

Summarize To summarize an explanation or solution, go over or review the most important points.

Resumir Para resumir una explicación o solución, revisa o repasa los puntos más importantes.

Supplementary angles Two angles are supplementary angles if the sum of their measures is 180°. Supplementary angles that are adjacent form a straight angle.

Ángulos suplementarios Dos ángulos son suplementarios si la suma de sus medidas es 180°. Los ángulos suplementarios que son adyacentes forman un ángulo llano.

Surface area of a cone The surface area of a cone is the sum of the lateral area and the area of the base. The formula for the surface area of a cone is S.A. L.A. B.

Área total de un cono El área total de un cono es la suma del área lateral y el área de la base. La fórmula del área total de un cono es A.T. A.L. B.

English/Spanish Glossary

Surface area of a cube The surface area of a cube is the sum of the areas of the faces of the cube. The formula for the surface area, S.A., of a cube is S.A.   , where *s* represents the length of an edge of the cube.

Área total de un cubo El área total de un cubo es la suma de las áreas de las caras del cubo. La fórmula del área total, A.T., de un cubo es A.T.   , donde *s* representa la longitud de una arista del cubo.

Surface area of a cylinder The surface area of a cylinder is the sum of the lateral area and the areas of the two circular bases. The formula for the surface area of a cylinder is S.A.   L.A.   2*B*, where L.A. represents the lateral area of the cylinder and *B* represents the area of a base of the cylinder.

Área total de un cilindro El área total de un cilindro es la suma del área lateral y las áreas de las dos bases circulares. La fórmula del área total de un cilindro es A.T.   A.L.   2*B*, donde A.L. representa el área lateral del cilindro y *B* representa el área de una base del cilindro.

Surface area of a pyramid The surface area of a pyramid is the sum of the areas of the faces of the pyramid. The formula for the surface area, S.A., of a pyramid is S.A. = L.A. + *B*, where L.A. represents the lateral area of the pyramid and *B* represents the area of the base of the pyramid.

Área total de una pirámide El área total de una pirámide es la suma de las áreas de las caras de la pirámide. La fórmula del área total, A.T., de una pirámide es A.T. = A.L. + *B*, donde A.L. representa el área lateral de la pirámide y *B* representa el área de la base de la pirámide.

Surface area of a sphere The surface area of a sphere is equal to the lateral area of a cylinder that has the same radius, *r*, and height 2*r*. The formula for the surface area of a sphere is S.A. = $4\pi r^2$, where *r* represents the radius of the sphere.

Área total de una esfera El área total de una esfera es igual al área lateral de un cilindro que tiene el mismo radio, *r*, y una altura de 2*r*. La fórmula del área total de una esfera es A.T. = $4\pi r^2$, donde *r* representa el radio de la esfera.

Surface area of a three-dimensional figure The surface area of a three-dimensional figure is the sum of the areas of its faces. You can find the surface area by finding the area of the net of the three-dimensional figure.

Área total de una figura tridimensional El área total de una figura tridimensional es la suma de las áreas de sus caras. Puedes hallar el área total si hallas el área del modelo plano de la figura tridimensional.

English/Spanish Glossary

System of linear equations A system of linear equations is formed by two or more linear equations that use the same variables.

Sistema de ecuaciones lineales Un sistema de ecuaciones lineales está formado por dos o más ecuaciones lineales que usan las mismas variables.

Systematic sampling Systematic sampling is a sampling method in which you choose every nth member of the population, where n is a predetermined number. A systematic sample is useful when the researcher is able to approach the population in a systematic, or methodical, way.

Muestreo sistemático El muestreo sistemático es un método de muestreo en el que se escoge cada enésimo miembro de la población, donde n es un número predeterminado. Una muestra sistemática es útil cuando el investigador puede enfocarse en la población de manera sistemática o metódica.

T

Taxable wages For federal income tax purposes, your taxable wages are the difference between your earned wages and your withholding allowance. Your employer divides your withholding allowance equally among the pay periods of one year.

Sueldos imponibles Para propósitos federales de impuesto de renta, sus sueldos imponibles son la diferencia entre sus sueldos ganados y su concesión que retienen. Su empleador divide su concesión que retiene igualmente entre los períodos de paga de un año.

Tenths One tenth is one out of ten equal parts of a whole.

Décimas Una décima es 1 de 10 partes iguales de un todo.

Term A term is a number, a variable, or the product of a number and one or more variables.

Término Un término es un número, una variable o el producto de un número y una o más variables.

Terminating decimal A terminating decimal has a decimal expansion that terminates in 0.

Decimal finito Un decimal finito tiene una expansión decimal que termina en 0.

English/Spanish Glossary

Terms of a ratio The terms of a ratio are the quantities x and y in the ratio.

Términos de una razón Los términos de una razón son la cantidad x y la cantidad y de la razón.

Theorem A theorem is a conjecture that is proven.

Teorema Un teorema es una conjetura que se ha comprobado.

Theoretical probability When all outcomes of an action are equally likely, $P(\text{event}) = \dfrac{\text{number of favourable outcomes}}{\text{number of possible outcomes}}$.

Probabilidad teórica Cuando todos los resultados de una acción son igualmente probables, $P(\text{evento}) = \dfrac{\text{número de resultados favorables}}{\text{número de resultados posibles}}$.

Third quartile For an ordered set of data, the third quartile is the median of the upper half of the data set.

Tercer cuartil Para un conjunto de datos ordenados, el tercer cuartil es la mediana de la mitad superior del conjunto de datos.

Thousandths One thousandth is one part of 1,000 equal parts of a whole.

Milésimas Una milésima es 1 de 1,000 partes iguales de un todo.

Three-dimensional figure A three-dimensional (3-D) figure is a figure that does not lie in a plane.

Figura tridimensional Una figura tridimensional es una figura que no está en un plano.

Total cost of a loan The total cost of a loan is the total amount spent to repay the loan. Total cost includes the principal and all interest paid over the length of the loan. Total cost also includes any fees charged.

El coste total de un préstamo El coste total de un préstamo es el cantidad total que es gastado para devolver el préstamo. El coste total incluye al director y todo el interés pagó sobre la longitud del préstamo. El coste total también incluye cualquier honorario cargado.

Transaction A banking transaction moves money into or out of a bank account.

Transacción Una transacción bancaria mueve dinero en o fuera de una cuenta bancaria.

English/Spanish Glossary

Transfer A transaction that moves money from one bank account to another is a transfer. The balance of one account increases by the same amount the other account decreases.

Transferencia Una transacción que mueve dinero de una cuenta bancaria a otro es una transferencia. El equilibrio de un aumentos de cuenta por la misma cantidad que la otra cuenta disminuye.

Transformation A transformation is a change in position, shape, or size of a figure. Three types of transformations that change position only are translations, reflections, and rotations.

Transformación Una transformación es un cambio en la posición, la forma o el tamaño de una figura. Tres tipos de transformaciones que cambian sólo la posición son las traslaciones, las reflexiones y las rotaciones.

Translation A translation, or slide, is a rigid motion that moves every point of a figure the same distance and in the same direction.

Traslación Una traslación, o deslizamiento, es un movimiento rígido que mueve cada punto de una figura a la misma distancia y en la misma dirección.

Transversal A transversal is a line that intersects two or more lines at different points.

Transversal o secante Una transversal o secante es una línea que interseca dos o más líneas en distintos puntos.

Trapezoid A trapezoid is a quadrilateral with exactly one pair of parallel sides.

Trapecio Un trapecio es un cuadrilátero que tiene exactamente un par de lados paralelos.

Trend line A trend line is a line on a scatter plot, drawn near the points, that approximates the association between the data sets.

Línea de tendencia Una línea de tendencia es una línea en un diagrama de dispersión, trazada cerca de los puntos, que se aproxima a la relación entre los conjuntos de datos.

Trial In a probability experiment, you carry out or observe an action repeatedly. Each observation of the action is a trial.

Prueba En un experimento de probabilidad, realizas u observas una acción varias veces. Cada observación de la acción es una prueba.

Triangle A triangle is a polygon with three sides.

Triángulo Un triángulo es un polígono de tres lados.

English/Spanish Glossary

Triangular prism A triangular prism is a prism with bases in the shape of a triangle.

Prisma triangular Un prisma triangular es un prisma cuyas bases tienen la forma de un triángulo.

True equation A true equation has equal values on each side of the equals sign.

Ecuación verdadera En una ecuación verdadera, los valores a ambos lados del signo igual son iguales.

Two-way frequency table A two-way frequency table displays the counts of the data in each group.

Tabla de frecuencia con dos variables Una tabla de frecuencia con dos variables muestra el conteo de los datos de cada grupo.

Two-way relative frequency table A two-way relative frequency table shows the ratio of the number of data in each group to the size of the population. The relative frequencies can be calculated with respect to the entire population, the row populations, or the column populations. The relative frequencies can be expressed as fractions, decimals, or percents.

Tabla de frecuencias relativas con dos variables Una tabla de frecuencias relativas con dos variables muestra la razón del número de datos de cada grupo al tamaño de la población. Las frecuencias relativas se pueden calcular respecto de la población entera, las poblaciones de las filas o las poblaciones de las columnas. Las frecuencias relativas se pueden expresar como fracciones, decimales o porcentajes.

Two-way table A two-way table shows bivariate categorical data for a population.

Tabla con dos variables Una tabla con dos variables muestra datos bivariados por categorías de una población.

U

Uniform probability model A uniform probability model is a probability model based on using the theoretical probability of equally likely outcomes.

Modelo de probabilidad uniforme Un modelo de probabilidad uniforme es un modelo de probabilidad que se basa en el uso de la probabilidad teórica de resultados igualmente probables.

English/Spanish Glossary

Unit fraction A unit fraction is a fraction with a numerator of 1 and a denominator that is a whole number greater than 1.

Fracción unitaria Una fracción unitaria es una fracción con un numerador 1 y un denominador que es un número entero mayor que 1.

Unit price A unit price is a unit rate that gives the price of one item.

Precio por unidad El precio por unidad es una tasa por unidad que muestra el precio de un artículo.

Unit rate The rate for one unit of a given quantity is called the unit rate.

Tasa por unidad Se llama tasa por unidad a la tasa que corresponde a 1 unidad de una cantidad dada.

Use To use given information, draw on it to help you determine something else.

Usar Para usar una información dada, apóyate en ella para determinar otra cosa.

V

Valid inference A valid inference is an inference that is true about the population. Valid inferences can be made when they are based on data from a representative sample.

Inferencia válida Una inferencia válida es una inferencia verdadera acerca de una población. Se pueden hacer inferencias válidas si están basadas en los datos de una muestra representativa.

Variability Variability describes how much the items in a data set differ (or vary) from each other. On a data display, variability is shown by how much the data on the horizontal scale are spread out.

Variabilidad La variabilidad describe qué diferencia (o variación) existe entre los elementos de un conjunto de datos. Al exhibir datos, la variabilidad queda representada por la distancia que separa los datos en la escala horizontal.

Variable A variable is a letter that represents an unknown value.

Variable Una variable es una letra que representa un valor desconocido.

Variable expenses Variable expenses are expenses that change from one budget period to the next.

Gastos variables Los gastos variables son los gastos que cambian de un período económico al próximo.

English/Spanish Glossary

Vertex of a cone The vertex of a cone is the point farthest from the base.

Vértice de un cono El vértice de un cono es el punto más alejado de la base.

Vertex of a polygon The vertex of a polygon is any point where two sides of a polygon meet.

Vértice de un polígono El vértice de un polígono es cualquier punto donde se encuentran dos lados de un polígono.

Vertex of a three-dimensional figure A vertex of a three-dimensional figure is a point where three or more edges meet.

Vértice de una figura tridimensional El vértice de una figura tridimensional es un punto donde se unen tres o más aristas.

Vertex of an angle The vertex of an angle is the point of intersection of the rays that make up the sides of the angle.

Vértice de un ángulo El vértice de un ángulo es el punto de intersección de las semirrectas que forman los lados del ángulo.

Vertical angles Vertical angles are formed by two intersecting lines and are opposite each other. Vertical angles have equal measures.

Ángulos opuestos por el vértice Los ángulos opuestos por el vértice están formados por dos rectas secantes y están uno frente a otro. Los ángulos opuestos por el vértice tienen la misma medida.

Vertical-line test The vertical-line test is a method used to determine if a relation is a function or not. If a vertical line passes through a graph more than once, the graph is not the graph of a function.

Prueba de recta vertical La prueba de recta vertical es un método que se usa para determinar si una relación es una función o no. Si una recta vertical atraviesa la gráfica más de una vez, la gráfica no es la gráfica de una función.

Volume Volume is the number of cubic units needed to fill a solid figure.

Volumen El volumen es el número de unidades cúbicas que se necesitan para llenar un cuerpo geométrico.

English/Spanish Glossary

Volume of a cone The volume of a cone is the number of unit cubes, or cubic units, needed to fill the cone. The formula for the volume of a cone is $V = \frac{1}{3}Bh$, where B represents the area of the base and h represents the height of the cone.

Volumen de un cono El volumen de un cono es el número de bloques de unidades, o unidades cúbicas, que se necesitan para llenar el cono. La fórmula del volumen de un cono $V = \frac{1}{3}Bh$, donde B representa el área de la base y h representa la altura del cono.

Volume of a cube The volume of a cube is the number of unit cubes, or cubic units, needed to fill the cube. The formula for the volume V of a cube is $V = s^3$, where s represents the length of an edge of the cube.

Volumen de un cubo El volumen de un cubo es el número de bloques de unidades, o unidades cúbicas, que se necesitan para llenar el cubo. La fórmula del volumen, V, de un cubo es $V = s^3$, donde s representa la longitud de una arista del cubo.

Volume of a cylinder The volume of a cylinder is the number of unit cubes, or cubic units, needed to fill the cylinder. The formula for the volume of a cylinder is $V = \pi r^2 h$, where r represents the radius of a base and h represents the height of the cylinder.

Volumen de un cilindro El volumen de un cilindro es el número de bloques de unidades, o unidades cúbicas, que se necesitan para llenar el cilindro. La fórmula del volumen de un cilindro es $V = \pi r^2 h$, donde r representa el radio de una base y h representa la altura del cilindro.

Volume of a prism The volume of a prism is the number of unit cubes, or cubic units, needed to fill the prism. The formula for the volume V of a prism is $V = Bh$, where B represents the area of a base and h represents the height of the prism.

Volumen de un prisma El volumen de un prisma es el número de bloques de unidades, o unidades cúbicas, que se necesitan para llenar el prisma. La fórmula del volumen, V, de un prisma $V = Bh$, donde B representa el área de una base y h representa la altura del prisma.

Volume of a pyramid The volume of a pyramid is the number of unit cubes needed to fill the pyramid. The formula for the volume V of a pyramid is $V = \frac{1}{3}Bh$, where B represents the area of the base and h represents the height of the pyramid.

Volumen de una pirámide El volumen de una pirámide es el número de bloques de unidades, o unidades cúbicas, que se necesitan para llenar la pirámide. La fórmula del volumen, V, de una pirámide es $V = \frac{1}{3}Bh$, donde B representa el área de la base y h representa la altura de la pirámide.

English/Spanish Glossary

Volume of a sphere The volume of a sphere is the number of unit cubes, or cubic units, needed to fill the sphere. The formula for the volume of a sphere is $V = \frac{4}{3}\pi r^3$.

Volumen de una esfera El volumen de una esfera es el número de bloques de unidades, o unidades cúbicas, que se necesitan para llenar la esfera. La fórmula del volumen de una esfera es $V = \frac{4}{3}\pi r^3$.

W

Whole numbers The whole numbers consist of the number 0 and all of the natural numbers.

Números enteros no negativos Los números enteros no negativos son el número 0 y todos los números naturales.

Withdrawal A transaction that takes money out of a bank account is a withdrawal.

Retirada Una transacción que toma dinero fuera de una cuenta bancaria es una retirada.

Withholding allowance You can exclude a portion of your earned wages, called a withholding allowance, from federal income tax. You can claim one withholding allowance for yourself and one for each person dependent upon your income.

Retener concesión Puede excluir una porción de sus sueldos ganados, llamó una concesión que retiene, del impuesto de renta federal. Puede reclamar una concesión que retiene para usted mismo y para uno para cada dependiente de persona sobre sus ingresos.

Word form of a number The word form of a number is the number written in words.

Número en palabras Un número en palabras es un número escrito con palabras en lugar de dígitos.

Work-Study Work-study is a type of need-based aid that schools might offer to a student. A student must earn work-study money by working certain jobs.

Práctica estudiantil La práctica estudiantil es un tipo de ayuda necesidad-basado que escuelas quizás ofrezcan a un estudiante. Un estudiante debe ganar dinero de práctica estudiantil por ciertos trabajos de trabajo.

English/Spanish Glossary

X

x-axis The x-axis is the horizontal number line that, together with the y-axis, forms the coordinate plane.

Eje de las x El eje de las x es la recta numérica horizontal que, junto con el eje de las y, forma el plano de coordenadas.

x-coordinate The x-coordinate is the first number in an ordered pair. It tells the number of horizontal units a point is from 0.

Coordenada x La coordenada x (abscisa) es el primer número de un par ordenado. Indica cuántas unidades horizontales hay entre un punto y 0.

Y

y-axis The y-axis is the vertical number line that, together with the x-axis, forms the coordinate plane.

Eje de las y El eje de las y es la recta numérica vertical que, junto con el eje de las x, forma el plano de coordenadas.

y-coordinate The y-coordinate is the second number in an ordered pair. It tells the number of vertical units a point is from 0.

Coordenada y La coordenada y (ordenada) es el segundo número de un par ordenado. Indica cuántas unidades verticales hay entre un punto y 0.

y-intercept The y-intercept of a line is the y-coordinate of the point where the line crosses the y-axis.

Intercepto en y El intercepto en y de una recta es la coordenada y del punto por donde la recta cruza el eje de las y.

Z

Zero exponent property For any nonzero number a, $a^0 = 1$.

Propiedad del exponente cero Para cualquier número distinto de cero a, $a^0 = 1$.

Zero Property of Multiplication The product of 0 and any number is 0. For any number n, $n \cdot 0 = 0$ and $0 \cdot n = 0$.

Propiedad del cero en la multiplicación El producto de 0 y cualquier número es 0. Para cualquier número n, $n \cdot 0 = 0$ and $0 \cdot n = 0$.

Formulas

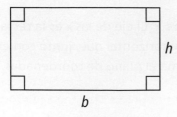

$P = 2b + 2h$
$A = bh$

Rectangle

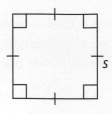

$P = 4s$
$A = s^2$

Square

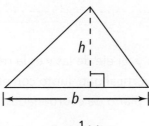

$A = \frac{1}{2}bh$

Triangle

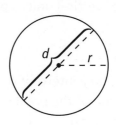

$A = bh$

Parallelogram

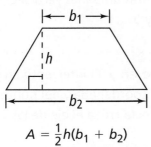

$A = \frac{1}{2}h(b_1 + b_2)$

Trapezoid

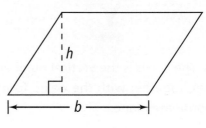

$C = 2\pi r$ or $C = \pi d$
$A = \pi r^2$

Circle

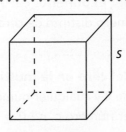

S.A. $= 6s^2$
$V = s^3$

Cube

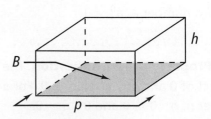

$V = Bh$

L.A. $= ph$

S.A. $=$ L.A. $+ 2B$

Rectangular Prism

Formulas

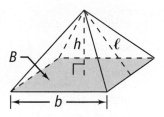

$V = \frac{1}{3}Bh$
L.A. $= 2b\ell$
S.A. $=$ L.A. $+ B$

Square Pyramid

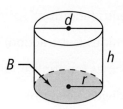

$V = Bh$
L.A. $= 2\pi rh$
S.A. $=$ L.A. $+ 2B$

Cylinder

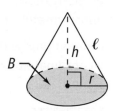

$V = \frac{1}{3}Bh$
L.A. $= \pi r\ell$
S.A. $=$ L.A. $+ B$

Cone

$V = \frac{4}{3}\pi r^3$
S.A. $= 4\pi r^2$

Sphere

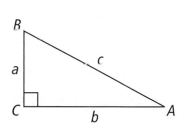

$a^2 + b^2 = c^2$

Pythagorean Theorem

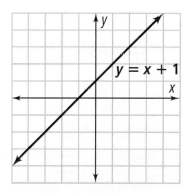

$y = mx + b$, where
$m =$ slope and
$b = y$-intercept

Equation of Line

Math Symbols

$+$	plus (addition)	r	radius
$-$	minus (subtraction)	S.A.	surface area
$\times$, $\cdot$	times (multiplication)	B	area of base
$\div$, $\overline{)}$, $\frac{a}{b}$	divide (division)	L.A.	lateral area
$=$	is equal to	ℓ	slant height
$<$	is less than	V	volume
$>$	is greater than	a^n	nth power of a
$\leq$	is less than or equal to	$\sqrt{x}$	nonnegative square root of x
$\geq$	is greater than or equal to	π	pi, an irrational number approximately equal to 3.14
$\neq$	is not equal to	(a, b)	ordered pair with x-coordinate a and y-coordinate b
$(\ )$	parentheses for grouping	$\overline{AB}$	segment AB
$[\ ]$	brackets for grouping	A'	image of A, A prime
$-a$	opposite of a	$\triangle ABC$	triangle with vertices A, B, and C
$\ldots$	and so on	$\rightarrow$	arrow notation
$\circ$	degrees	$a : b$, $\frac{a}{b}$	ratio of a to b
$\vert a \vert$	absolute value of a	$\cong$	is congruent to
$\overset{?}{=}$, $\overset{?}{<}$, $\overset{?}{>}$	Is the statement true?	$\sim$	is similar to
$\approx$	is approximately equal to	$\angle A$	angle with vertex A
$\frac{b}{a}$	reciprocal of $\frac{a}{b}$	AB	length of segment $\overline{AB}$
A	area	$\overrightarrow{AB}$	ray AB
ℓ	length	$\angle ABC$	angle formed by $\overrightarrow{BA}$ and $\overrightarrow{BC}$
w	width	$m\angle ABC$	measure of angle ABC
h	height	$\perp$	is perpendicular to
d	distance	$\overleftrightarrow{AB}$	line AB
r	rate	$\parallel$	is parallel to
t	time	%	percent
P	perimeter	P (event)	probability of an event
b	base length		
C	circumference		
d	diameter		

Measures

Customary	Metric
Length	**Length**
1 foot (ft) = 12 inches (in.) 1 yard (yd) = 36 in. 1 yd = 3 ft 1 mile (mi) = 5,280 ft 1 mi = 1,760 yd	1 centimeter (cm) = 10 millimeters (mm) 1 meter (m) = 100 cm 1 kilometer (km) = 1,000 m 1 mm = 0.001 m
Area	**Area**
1 square foot (ft^2) = 144 square inches (in.^{2}) 1 square yard (yd^2) = 9 ft^2 1 square mile (mi^2) = 640 acres	1 square centimeter (cm^2) = 100 square millimeters (mm^2) 1 square meter (m^2) = 10,000 cm^2
Volume	**Volume**
1 cubic foot (ft^3) = 1,728 cubic inches (in.^{3}) 1 cubic yard (yd^3) = 27 ft^3	1 cubic centimeter (cm^3) = 1,000 cubic millimeters (mm^3) 1 cubic meter (m^3) = 1,000,000 cm^3
Mass	**Mass**
1 pound (lb) = 16 ounces (oz) 1 ton (t) = 2,000 lb	1 gram (g) = 1,000 milligrams (mg) 1 kilogram (kg) = 1,000 g
Capacity	**Capacity**
1 cup (c) = 8 fluid ounces (fl oz) 1 pint (pt) = 2 c 1 quart (qt) = 2 pt 1 gallon (gal) = 4 qt	1 liter (L) = 1,000 milliliters (mL) 1000 liters = 1 kiloliter (kL)

Customary Units and Metric Units	
Length	1 in. = 2.54 cm 1 mi ≈ 1.61 km 1 ft ≈ 0.3 m
Capacity	1 qt ≈ 0.94 L
Weight and Mass	1 oz ≈ 28.3 g 1 lb ≈ 0.45 kg

Properties

Unless otherwise stated, the variables *a*, *b*, *c*, *m*, and *n* used in these properties can be replaced with any number represented on a number line.

Identity Properties
Addition $n + 0 = n$ and $0 + n = n$
Multiplication $n \cdot 1 = n$ and $1 \cdot n = n$

Commutative Properties
Addition $a + b = b + a$
Multiplication $a \cdot b = b \cdot a$

Associative Properties
Addition $(a + b) + c = a + (b + c)$
Multiplication $(a \cdot b) \cdot c = a \cdot (b \cdot c)$

Inverse Properties
Addition
$a + (-a) = 0$ and $-a + a = 0$
Multiplication
$a \cdot \frac{1}{a} = 1$ and $\frac{1}{a} \cdot a = 1, (a \neq 0)$

Distributive Properties
$a(b + c) = ab + ac$ $(b + c)a = ba + ca$
$a(b - c) = ab - ac$ $(b - c)a = ba - ca$

Properties of Equality
Addition If $a = b$,
then $a + c = b + c$.
Subtraction If $a = b$,
then $a - c = b - c$.
Multiplication If $a = b$,
then $a \cdot c = b \cdot c$.
Division If $a = b$, and $c \neq 0$,
then $\frac{a}{c} = \frac{b}{c}$.
Substitution If $a = b$, then b can
replace a in any
expression.

Zero Property
$a \cdot 0 = 0$ and $0 \cdot a = 0$.

Properties of Inequality
Addition If $a > b$,
then $a + c > b + c$.
If $a < b$,
then $a + c < b + c$.
Subtraction If $a > b$,
then $a - c > b - c$.
If $a < b$,
then $a - c < b - c$.
Multiplication
If $a > b$ and $c > 0$, then $ac > bc$.
If $a < b$ and $c > 0$, then $ac < bc$.
If $a > b$ and $c < 0$, then $ac < bc$.
If $a < b$ and $c < 0$, then $ac > bc$.
Division
If $a > b$ and $c > 0$, then $\frac{a}{c} > \frac{b}{c}$.
If $a < b$ and $c > 0$, then $\frac{a}{c} < \frac{b}{c}$.
If $a > b$ and $c < 0$, then $\frac{a}{c} < \frac{b}{c}$.
If $a < b$ and $c < 0$, then $\frac{a}{c} > \frac{b}{c}$.

Properties of Exponents
For any nonzero number *n* and any integers *m* and *n*:

Zero Exponent $a^0 = 1$
Negative Exponent $a^{-n} = \frac{1}{a^n}$
Product of Powers $a^m \cdot a^n = a^{m+n}$
Power of a Product $(ab)^n = a^n b^n$
Quotient of Powers $\frac{a^m}{a^n} = a^{m-n}$
Power of a Quotient $\left(\frac{a}{b}\right)^n = \frac{a^n}{b^n}$
Power of a Power $(a^m)^n = a^{mn}$